AF519664

Information Communication Technology for Teacher Education

INFORMATION COMMUNICATION TECHNOLOGY FOR TEACHER EDUCATION

SANTHOSH VALLIKKAD

KANISHKA PUBLISHERS, DISTRIBUTORS
NEW DELHI-110 002

KANISHKA PUBLISHERS, DISTRIBUTORS
4697/5-21 A, Ansari Road, Daryaganj
New Delhi-110 002
Phones : 2327 0497, 2328 8285
Fax : 011-2328 8285
E-mail: kanishka_publishing@yahoo.co.in

Information Communication Technology for Teacher Education

First Published 2009

ISBN 978-81-8457-114-1

PRINTED IN INDIA

Published by Madan Sachdeva for Kanishka Publishers, Distributors, 4697/5-21A, Ansari Road, Daryaganj, New Delhi-110 002, Typeset by Sunshine Graphics, Delhi, and Printed at Rajdhani Printers, Delhi.

PREFACE

Information and Communication Technologies (ICTs) have the potential to enhance access, quality, and effectiveness in education in general and to enable the development of more and better teachers. As computer hardware becomes available to an increasing number of schools, more attention needs to be given to the capacity building of the key transformers in this process, namely, teachers.

The objective of this book is to share some of the ideas aimed at the training of teacher educators in the integration of ICTs in the classroom. Based on this reflection, areas of attention in the promotion of the appropriate use of ICTs by teachers are identified.

ICTs are one of the major contemporary factors shaping the global economy and producing rapid changes in society. They have fundamentally changed the way people learn, communicate, and do business. They can transform the nature of education—where and how learning takes place and the roles of students and teachers in the learning process.

Education in the India faces a number of problems. These problems include the shortage of qualified teachers, very large student populations, high dropout rates of students and teachers, and weak curricula. All of these negative aspects result in poor delivery of education. The education crisis is based on the effects of the increasing poverty, a brain drain in the teaching community, budgetary constraints, poor communication, and inadequate infrastructure.

While societies in the nation undergo rapid changes as a result of increased access to information, the majority of the school-going youth continue to undergo traditional rote learning. Very little is done to take advantage of the wealth of information available on the Internet. Whereas the processing of information to build knowledge is one of the essential literacy skills vital for the workforce in the 21st century, it is often overlooked in current educational practices.

In order to function in the new world economy, students and their teachers have to learn to navigate large amounts of information, to analyse and make decisions, and to master new knowledge and to accomplish complex tasks collaboratively. Overloaded with information, one key outcome of any learning experience should be for learners to critically challenge the material collected in order to decide whether it can be considered useful input in any educational activity. This is the basis for the construction of knowledge. The use of ICTs as part of the learning process can be sub-divided into three different forms: as object, aspect, or medium.

- As object, one refers to learning about ICTs as specific courses such as 'computer education.' Learners familiarise themselves with hardware and software including packages such as Microsoft Word, Microsoft Excel, and others. The aim is computer literacy.
- As aspect, one refers to applications of ICTs in education similar to what obtains in industry. The use of ICTs in education, such as in computer-aided design and computer-aided manufacturing, are examples.
- ICTs are considered as a medium whenever they are used to support teaching and learning.

The use of ICT as a medium is rare where the availability of resources is a major obstacle to the widespread integration of ICTs in education. Technology is not new to education. However, contemporary computer technologies, such as the Internet, allow new types of teaching and learning experiences to flourish. Many new technologies are interactive, making it easier to create environments in which students can learn by doing, receive feedback, and continually refine their understanding and build new knowledge. Access to the Internet gives unprecedented opportunities in terms of the availability of research material and information in general. This availability of research material and information happens to both inspire and threaten teachers.

The computer equipment in the schools that have them tends to be underused and lacks appropriate education content. Commonly, the computer equipment is used as objects in computer lessons. A few other subject teachers undertake courses in software packages but are unable to integrate or meaningfully insert this knowledge in their daily teaching work. A worrying tendency is that boys are the targets rather than girls when investments in ICT hardware and training are made. If not taken seriously, this will increase gender disparities in education in the sub-region.

Respective governments in Indian states recognise that ICTs have a critical role to play in improving education and are engaged in drafting ICT policies or ICT chapters in a number of development plans across economic sectors. The policies tend to clearly link development to a forward-looking educational sector and increased investment in human resources and ICTs.

In the education sector, curriculum review efforts are geared towards modernisation, including the incorporation of important ICT components. However, even the reviewed curricula tend to treat ICT as a subject rather than as an application tool that can be used in all other subjects, in teaching and learning. Very recent discourse indicates that future curriculum reviews may consider a fully-fledged ICT mainstreaming process.

Teacher education institutions and programmes have the critical role to provide the necessary leadership in adapting pre-service and in-service teacher education to deal with the current demands of society and economy. They need to model the new pedagogies and tools for learning with the aim of enhancing the teaching-learning process. Moreover, teacher education institutions and programmes must also give guidance in determining how the new technologies can best be used in the context of the culture, needs, and economic conditions of their country.

Hoping that this book will helps the teachers and teacher educators as a handbook for ICT. I express my sincere gratitude to Kanishka Publishers for their cooperation for the publication.

SANTHOSH VALLIKKAD

Contents

1

Teacher Education

Teacher education is an integral component of the educational system. It is intimately connected with society and is conditioned by the ethos, culture and character of a nation. The constitutional goals, the directive principles of the state policy, the socio-economic problems and the growth of knowledge, the emerging expectations and the changes operating in education, etc. call for an appropriate response from a futuristic education system and provide the perspective within which teacher education programmes need to be viewed.

When India attained freedom, the then existing educational system was accepted as such because it was thought that an abrupt departure from the same would be disturbing and destabilising. Thus a predisposition to retain the system acquired preponderance and all that was envisaged by way of changes was its rearrangement. Consequently, education including teacher education largely remained isolated from the needs and aspirations of the people. During the last five decades certain efforts have been made to indigenize the system. The gaps, however, are still wide and visible. The imperatives for building the bridges may be as follows:

- To build a national system of teacher education based on India's cultural ethos, its unity and diversity synchronising with change and continuity.
- To facilitate the realization of the constitutional goals and emergence of the new social order.
- To prepare professionally competent teachers to perform their roles effectively as per needs of the society.
- To upgrade the standard of teacher education, enhance the professional and social status of teachers and develop amongst them a sense of commitment.

These are but a few of the major concerns, which call for an immediate action. A comprehensive, dynamic and responsive system of teacher education needs to be continually evolved keeping the overall scenario in view.

Scenario of Teacher Education

The need for improved levels of educational participation for overall progress is well recognised. The key role of educational institutions in realising it is reflected in a variety of initiatives taken to transform the nature and function of education both formal as well as non-formal. Universal accessibility to quality education is considered essential for development. This has necessitated improvement in the system of teacher education so as to prepare quality teachers.

Various Commissions and Committees appointed by the Central and the State Governments in recent decades have invariably emphasised the need for quality teacher education suited to the needs of the educational system. The Secondary Education Commission (1953) observed that a major factor responsible for the educational reconstruction at the secondary stage is teachers' professional training. The Education Commission (1964-66) stressed that 'in a world based on science and technology it is education that determines the level of prosperity, welfare and security of the people' and that 'a sound programme of professional education of teachers is essential for the qualitative improvement of education.'

India has a large system of education. There are nearly 5.98 lakh Primary Schools, 1.76 lakh Elementary Schools and 98 thousand High/Higher Secondary Schools in the country, about 1300 teacher education institutions for elementary teachers and nearly 700 colleges of education/university departments preparing teachers for secondary and higher secondary schools. Out of about 4.52 million teachers in the country nearly 3 million are teaching at the primary/elementary level.* A sizeable number of them are untrained or under-trained. In certain regions, like the North-East, there are even under-qualified teachers. As far as in-service education is concerned the situation is not very encouraging. It is estimated that on an average 40 per cent of the teachers are provided in-service teacher education once over a period of five years. Regarding non-formal education, though a number of models are in vogue in various states in the country, much more needs to be done to prepare teachers and other functionaries for the system.

The Programme of Action (POA 1992) has emphasised teacher education as a continuous process, its pre-service and in-service components being inseparable. The POA, among others, has pointed out the following in respect of teacher education:

**Source:* Selected Educational Statistics, 1996-97, MHRD, Government of India, New Delhi.

- Professional commitment and overall competencies of teachers leave much to be desired;
- The quality of pre-service education has not only not improved with recent developments in pedagogical science, but has actually shown signs of deterioration;
- Teacher education programmes consist mainly of pre-service teacher training, with practically no systematic programmes of in service training, facilities for which are lacking;
- There has been an increase in sub-standard institutions of teacher education and there are numerous reports of gross malpractices; and
- The support system provided by the State Councils of Educational Research and Training (SCERTs) and the University Departments of Education has been insufficient and there is no support system below the state level.

In pursuance of the NPE 1986 a major step was taken by the Central Government to enhance the professional capacity of a large number of teacher education institutions. Nearly 430 District Institutes of Education and Training (DIETs) have already been established by 1997-98. The DIETs are charged with the responsibility of organising pre-service and in-service programmes in addition to being the nodal resource centers for elementary education at district level. Likewise, Colleges of Teacher Education (CTEs) and Institutions of Advanced Study in Education (IASEs) have been given the responsibility of introducing innovations in teacher education programmes at the secondary and higher secondary stages and in vocational education.

The National Council for Teacher Education (NCTE) as a non-statutory body (1973-1993) took several steps as regards quality improvement in teacher education. Its major contribution was to prepare Teacher Education Curriculum Framework in 1978. Consequently, teacher education curricula witnessed changes in teacher preparation programmes in various universities and boards in the country. A similar effort was made in 1988.

During the last decade, new thrusts have been posed due to rapid changes in the educational, political, social and economic contexts at the national and international levels. Curriculum reconstruction has also become imperative in the light of some perceptible gaps in teacher education. Teacher education by and large, is conventional in its nature and purpose. The integration of theory and practice and consequent curricular response to the requirements of the school system still remains inadequate. Teachers are prepared in competencies and skills, which do not necessarily equip them for becoming professionally effective. Their familiarity with latest educational developments remains insufficient. Organised and stipulatory learning experiences whenever available, rarely contribute to enhancing teachers' capacities for self-directed life long learning. The system still prepares teachers who do not necessarily become professionally competent and committed at the completion of initial teacher preparation programmes. A large number of teacher training institutions do not practice what they preach. Several of the skills acquired and methodologies learnt are seldom practiced in actual school system. This highlights the need to bring realism and dynamism in the curriculum.

Constitutional Goals

The Constitution of India solemnly resolves "to constitute India into a sovereign, socialist, secular and democratic republic and secure to all its citizens: justice-social, economic and political; liberty of thought, expression, faith, belief and worship; equality of status and of opportunity; and to promote among them all fraternity assuring the dignity of the individual and the integrity of the nation." These are the main goals, which the nation expects to be realised through education. Teacher preparation must not lose sight of this basic thrust so as to empower teachers to inculcate the same among the students.

In order to reinforce faith in democratic socialism, secularism, justice, liberty, freedom etc. the role of education needs to be understood in its true perspective. Democracy is a process of building consensus among the citizens on matters of common concern. It expects high morality from them protects the interest and preserves their uniqueness, dignity and individuality. Quality of democracy depends on its citizens willing to discharge their responsibilities towards the self, the family, the community, the nation and humanity at large. Democracy is a way of life and its values need to be imbibed through education and practiced in the day-to-day life. Democratic socialism attempts to achieve a synthesis between individual freedom and social compulsion and combines liberty with responsibility and authority with accountability. The Indian situation demands citizens capable of making conscious and purposive efforts directed towards social cohesion and living together harmoniously.

Indian Society is plural and heterogeneous with an underlying current of unity. The imposition of a homogeneous and uniform curriculum of teacher education may prove counter productive under this situation. Except for identifying certain basics and essentials, regional autonomy must be exercised for developing region/culture specific curriculum of teacher education. Indian reality demands that plurality should be used for strengthening national solidarity and social cohesion.

The Indian state is secular. The Indian society, however, is religious. To resolve this dichotomy between the state and polity, the principle of equal respect for all the religions has been accepted. This is the essence of Indian secularism. The teachers themselves have to internalise the imperatives of secularism in national context and interpret the same effectively to the learners. That alone would develop the right attitudes among all citizens irrespective of their own backgrounds. In India religion is also the source of value and morality. The teachers have to develop values and morality in a different context. Teacher education has to respond to this reality.

Justice, liberty, equality of status and of opportunity and promoting fraternity constitute another set of inter-related goals. Justice protects the rights of the weak and ensures impartiality. To ensure justice and fulfill the constitutional commitments in this regard, certain positive and legal provisions have been made by the state. Special measures such as reservation in educational institutions, financial support, scholarships, hostel facilities, etc. have been extended to the under-privileged groups like Scheduled Castes, Scheduled Tribes, and other Backward Classes etc. It implies change in attitudes and values through education, in which the role of teachers needs to be stressed. Liberty of thought, expression, faith, belief and worship is another constitutional goal which education is expected to help realise. Indian Constitution ensures equality of status and opportunity to all its citizens. The objective is to minimise social and economic disparities, inequality of power and life chances by positive discrimination in favour of the weak. The education of teachers should equip them with the competencies needed to deal with discrimination, disparities and inequalities. Fraternity stands for acceptance of universal brotherhood, respect for human personality and feeling of oneness irrespective of linguistic, racial, cultural and religious diversities.

Teacher Education and Problems of the Nation

It is universally acknowledged that education is an effective means for social reconstruction and to a great extent it offers solutions to the problems a society is faced with. These problems may be economic, social, cultural, political, moral, ecological and educational. Since the teachers play a major role in education of children, their own education becomes a matter of vital concern. Teacher education must, therefore, create necessary awareness among teachers about their new roles and responsibilities.

Education of teachers needs to strengthen and stress upon the main attributes of a profession, such as, the systematic theory, rigorous training over a specified duration, authority, community sanction, ethical code and culture, generating knowledge through research and specialisation. It is acknowledged that formal professional training on continuous basis is necessary for becoming a good teacher as it caters to the development of one's personality and sharpening of communication skills and commitment to a code of conduct.

Economic Problems

Poverty, unemployment, and low rate of growth and productivity are some of the major economic problems of the country, which have led to the compulsions of the backward economy. These problems seek immediate solution and demand a realistic co-ordination between economic planning and manpower planning. Education can help find solutions if it is properly coordinated with manpower needs. Introduction of work education and vocationalisation of education in secondary schools will have to be given a modern and meaningful direction. The attitude towards the work culture needs a transformation. The Indian society needs education with special emphasis on science and technology, vocational inputs and realistic work experiences. Teacher education curriculum, therefore, has to promote such attitudes as are necessary for the emergence of a new economic order. Along with the vocational competencies and skills a new work culture will have to be created which necessarily involves the inculcation of dignity of work, the spirit of self-reliance and scientific temper among students. The courses of teacher education need to be enriched to enable teachers to understand the attributes of modernity and development.

Social Problems

Casteism, communalism and regionalism are some of the problems in the body politic of the society, which misguide the youth. Increasing delinquency, violence, terrorism and fissiparous tendencies and use of inappropriate means to get one's ends served are threats to the national integration and social cohesion. Democracy, violence and terrorism cannot coexist. Education has to develop a peace loving personality and the programme of teacher education has to contribute in this regard.

The explosion of population with all its allied disturbing trends is not only neutralising the economic gains but also creating many problems for the country. Indian society still suffers from evils like child labour, child marriage, untouchability, and discriminatory treatment to women, violation of human rights, etc. and most of the people are unaware of their legal rights.

Modern model of development, which puts man against nature by making it an object of exploitation, has disturbed the harmony and equilibrium between the two. Its consequences are visible in serious environmental degradation, pollution and ecological imbalances.

Strengthening national and social cohesion in a diverse and plural society, accelerating the process of economic growth, improving the life of the downtrodden and the people living below the poverty line, removing the widely prevalent ignorance, superstition and prejudices from the masses, inculcating scientific temper and developing a critical awareness about the social realities of Indian life are some of the issues which call for immediate attention. Teachers and the teacher educators have a special role to play in such efforts.

Problems of Cultural Reconstruction

Education is the process of transmission of dynamic and responsive components of cultural heritage and its continuous enrichment. There is a need to reinterpret the Indian culture in its distinct identity and composite strength. Its capacity to absorb the sublime from the other cultures needs to be highlighted. The teachers will have to play their role in cultural transmission and reconstruction.

Crises of Values and Morality

There has been a persistent erosion of values in the society. In the present day context certain values need to be redefined and reinstalled. There are situations when the values imparted and inculcated in schools are not generally practiced in society. Value education demands a planned and purposive approach. It is through education and as of necessity through teacher education programmes that the task of inculcating values can be substantially accomplished. Whereas values are emotive, the other related significant dimension is that of moral education which is essentially conative in character. Morals are situation-specific and demand immediate decision and action and yet there are morals, which are considered to be eternal and universal. Through committed teachers, the art of ensuring moral development in a secular, multi-religious and multi-ethnic society needs to be cultivated.

Problems Within Education System

The nation has yet to fulfill the constitutional commitment to provide free and compulsory education to all children till they attain 14 years of age. India is also a party to the global commitment for achieving the goal of Education for all by the year 2000. The education system however, has to respond to several major issues and problems, which have hindered the progress in this regard. Maintenance of educational standards against the pressure of increasing enrolment, relevance and quality of school education, efficacy of school functioning under the decentralized role of political power through the enactment of Panchayati Raj Act are some of the pertinent issues. In addition, specific requirements and need of social and economical groups of the society and of the minority communities, vocationalization of education, scientific and technological literacy, alienation of youth, rush for urbanisation, perceived urban orientation of educational system and its inflexibility to respond to rural, tribal and regional requirements are some of the dominant issues. These would determine the nature and shape of teacher education programmes and the efficacy and functioning of teachers in their new and emerging multifaceted roles.

Isolation of Teacher Education

Teacher education institutions, which were considered 'islands of isolation,' have gradually developed linkages with schools, peer institutions, universities and other institutions of higher learning as also the community. However, much remains to be done in this direction. The curriculum of the school, its actual transactional modalities, examination system, management processes and its ethos need to be the main thrust areas of teacher education programmes. To achieve these ends, teacher educators need to be made conversant with various aspects of school experiences. It is observed in day-to-day functioning that teacher educators often tend to lose contact with content areas relevant to their own disciplines resulting into gaps in communication and latest information. It is, therefore, a felt need in the present-day context that teacher education institutions keep in continuous touch with institutions of higher learning and peer institutions for effective transmission of knowledge and its upgradation.

The breaking of isolation from the community is essential for enabling teachers and teacher educators to reconstruct pedagogical and educational principles and practices in the light of experiences gained from mutually beneficial community interactions. Teacher as a professional and intellectual cannot remain indifferent to the events that are taking place in society. The academic and social issues are inter-related and inter-dependent. In contemporary context, the role of the teacher is no longer confined to teaching alone. The teachers are expected to play an active role in the developmental activities responding to progress of the community.

Expanding Scope of Teacher Education

Education of teachers is not an end in itself. Its target is the school. Any change in the nature, purpose, quality and character of the school demands a concomitant change in teacher education, especially in its curriculum. The implementation of the 10+2 scheme at the school level has transformed the complexion of education to a considerable extent from the pre-primary to the +2 stage. There has been an increase not only in the quantum of knowledge, but also in its nature and purpose. In addition, new transactional techniques and strategies have also been evolved. Certain new subjects have replaced the old ones whereas some others have changed their context, content, orientation, theme and philosophy. These changes at the school level, out of necessity, demand a new pedagogy and evaluation techniques. But the changes at the level of teacher education have not adequately responded to the emerging realities at the school level. All that the teachers are expected to do in their work places need to be reflected in the teacher education activities and programmes.

The teaching community has to face the challenges thrown by science and technology. There has been an explosion not only of scientific and technological knowledge but also in the means and techniques of acquiring knowledge. The scientific researches and developments related to theories of heredity, learning, mental health, neurology, attention, motivation etc. can no longer be treated alien to teacher education programmes.

Evolving a Culture-Specific Pedagogy

Every region and state has its typical cultural identity, and there is a need to utilise the same as a basis for developing meaningful, relevant pedagogies. Since there is no one universal way in which the children learn, there is a strong need for looking into the cultural context in which a child is placed. A child in a tribal society may process information in an altogether different manner as compared to the one from the urban area and high socio-economic stratum. Pedagogy, therefore, should be culture-specific. Cultural practices such as story-telling, dramatics, puppetry, folk-play, community living, etc. should become a strong basis of pedagogy instead of using one uniform, mechanistic way of student learning. Cultural specificity should get embedded in the pedagogical practices, which should be evolved for tribal, rural, urban communities and other ethnic groups.

Teacher Preparation for Alternative Systems/Approaches in Education

Global upsurge for universal education, explosion of knowledge, expectation and aspirations for better quality of life have led to the exploration of alternatives to formal system, which suffers from inherent inadequacies of rigidity and structural deficiencies. These alternatives include non-formal education, adult education, distance education, etc. While a good deal of work has been undertaken to spread and improve education through various alternatives, a major problem has been lack of trained functionaries. However, these functionaries cannot be prepared on the formal models of teacher preparation. Since they are required to perform functions of different nature, their training has essentially to be job-specific. Developing skills, competencies and commitments in the personnel involved in alternative strategies demand preparation and use of teaching and learning materials to be specifically designed for the programmes.

Non-formal Education

Non-formal education consists of an organised systematic and planned educational activity, essentially characterised by inbuilt flexibility and carried on outside the framework of the formal system. It provides learning experiences to children in the age group of 6-14 years who are not able to avail of the facilities of formal schooling. Children from the non-formal system are eligible to appear in the examinations leading to certification to join the formal stream.

In certain respects formal and non-formal education are similar as both are organised to augment, promote and facilitate learning. They differ in their institutional management and the organisation of the course content. The training of the functionaries at different levels including instructors, supervisors, material writers, project officers and managers is significant. The objectives of the training of the functionaries may be the following:

- To familiarise the functionaries with the latest developments in knowledge and technology specific to their job performance.
- To develop among them critical awareness about India's social reality.
- To acquaint them with special requirements of the groups they have to deal with.
- To provide them knowledge and skills as may help in the socio-cultural development of the clientele.
- To enable them to draw support from a wide variety of sources.
- To develop among them positive attitudes towards the under-privileged sections of society.
- To promote among them the desire to actively participate in the developmental activities.

Course Content

The curriculum for the functionaries of the non-formal education would be need-based and job-specific, depending on the nature of the task they have to perform. However, there are certain essentials, which need to be considered. These include:

- A sound background in India's composite culture, its unity and diversity.
- Science as an element of thought, its role in history and its impact on society.
- Indian national movement and Constitution of India.
- Economic planning in India and its impact on economy and society.
- National development problems and issues.
- Educational development and systems of contemporary Indian education.
- Environmental and population related issues.
- Basics of human psychology and behaviour.
- Communication skills, use of media and information communication technology and educational technology.
- Production of instructional materials.
- Identification of learners' needs and community interaction.
- Practical/field work.

Transactional Modalities

- Organisation of induction and recurrent orientation programme of suitable duration.
- Organisation of refresher courses and orientation programmes in the method and content.
- IT enabled education.
- Utilisation of community resources—human and material.
- Summer schools and short-term training programmes.
- Seminars, symposia and workshops.
- Interaction with local experts and skilled persons.
- Use of supplementary educational devices, media and educational technology.
- Evaluation.

Adult Education

To achieve its present status, adult education has undertaken a long journey. Literacy campaigns during the thirties led to strengthening of social education. In sixties, it took the shape of functional literacy programme, which was further reinforced to include functional literacy, numeracy and technocracy. It is now seen as an integral part of life-long learning. It duplicates certain functions of non-formal and continuing education. Adult education is expected to provide the skills needed to survive in the modern world for leading an effective and 'good life.' It includes adults of all ages. National literacy programmes focus specifically on those in the age group of 15-35 years in Indian context. It aims at developing the capacity of 'learning to learn' with or without the help of adult educator. Adult education concerns those who are not full time learners and have not been exposed to formal education. The knowledge gained and skills developed from it are utilised in a variety of situations. Thus, it has become need-based.

Objectives of Training of Adult Education Functionaries

The objectives of the training of the functionaries may include the following:

- To enable them to develop social awareness.
- To develop skills related to functional literacy programmes.
- To liberate adults from the bondage of prejudice, bias, ignorance, superstition etc.
- To prepare them for the participation in developmental activities.
- To develop among the learner the desire and potentialities of 'learning to learn.'
- To enhance their economic efficiency.
- To inspire the adult learner with the sense of patriotism, global consciousness and the will to live together.
- To promote among them a sense of national and social cohesion.
- To enable them to combine personal dignity with civic responsibility.
- To understand the learners and their needs.
- To develop awareness of human rights and legal literacy.
- To enable them to understand environmental and population concerns.
- To develop humanistic, moral and ethical values.

Training Programme and Content

The programme should be participatory, flexible, relevant, diversified and need-based. It might include, among other things, the following:

- Psychological and Sociological Principles of Adult Learning.
- Problems and Issues of Adult Education.
- Indian Heritage.
- Freedom Movement, Indian Constitution, Administrative System of India including Panchayat Raj.
- Contemporary India and the World.
- Information Communication Literacy.
- Planning and Developmental Activities.
- Economic and Social Problems.
- Problems of women, minorities and the under-privileged sections of the society.
- Acquaintance with approaches and methods of teaching adults.
- Right to information, social activism and legal literacy.

Distance Education

Distance education is emerging as an alternative to the formal education system. The emphasis on education for all, explosion of population along with the desire for education, limitation of the formal system in providing greater accessibility and the rising expectations from education are some of the factors for its increasing demand. The new communication technology has brought it within the reach of all. Originally designed to provide alternative educational avenues to the poor and the working people for higher education, it has now developed as a parallel system in India from the primary to tertiary levels and covers not only liberal but also scientific and professional studies as well.

Distance education implies the provision of educational opportunity at the place of learner from a distance by means of multiple media such as self-learning materials, audio-visual gadgets and short-term personal contact programmes. Information technology and cybernetics are simultaneously being utilised for upgrading the knowledge and skills.

In order that learning through distance education mode becomes effective, the following categories of functionaries need special inputs of training for persons involved in:

- Development and production of reading materials including assignments.
- Organisation and conduct of personal contact programmes.
- Production of radio, television and computer programmes.
- Use of teaching aids and technological gadgets and tele-conferencing.
- Academic counseling and resource persons manning regional/study centers.

Objectives

Objectives of the training programme for distance teacher educators are as follows:

- To enable the distance educators to understand the nature and purpose of distance education.
- To develop among them the technique to prepare self-learning and self-instructional materials.
- To facilitate learning at one's own pace.
- To promote the habit of self-appraisal.
- To organise personal contact programmes.
- To identify and utilise learning resources.
- To enable them to establish a healthy linkage with the formal system and make distance education an effective means for the national and social development.
- To train them to make use of various interactive techniques.
- To enable them to prepare, utilise and evaluate the assignments.

Courses, Modalities and Strategies

These will be need-based and have to be evolved depending upon the specific requirements of the target groups, nature and extent of resources and professional support available and the potentialities of the identified approach courses on distance education may be included at graduate and post-graduate levels. Considerable experience has been gained in the area by organisations like National Open School (NOS), Indira Gandhi National Open University (IGNOU), and others. Expertise exists to plan and design effective programmes in these sectors.

Education of Teacher Educators

The role of teacher educator is of prime importance for effective implementation of teacher education curriculum. Education and training of teacher educators is a pre-requisite for effective changes in the training and orientation of teachers. India has a large system of teacher education. There are more than 2000 elementary teacher education institutions, Colleges of Education and University Departments of

Education. Nearly 30,000 teacher educators are engaged in the preparation of school teachers. In addition, there are teacher educators working in pre-primary training schools as well as institutions concerned with the preparation of teachers for the education of children with special needs and alternative education such as non-formal education, distance education etc.

It is well recognised that the overall quality in education mainly depends on the quality of teachers and a sound programme of professional preparation of teachers is essential for imparting quality education. However, Teacher educators' own education leaves much to be desired. Teaching is an art, which can be inculcated through a series of well-designed activities in respect of education and training of teachers and is equally valid for professional preparation of teacher educators.

The teacher educators would not only be training pre-service and in-service trainees but would also be associating themselves with several other activities. New strategies and techniques of material development, the changing approach to evaluation, intensive interactions with the community, creating an activity-based environment in the training institutions, acquiring skills for resource mobilisation and several other such competencies at mastery level would be essential for professionals to function as teacher educators. Changes in the school curricula would be faster in the near future. Corresponding changes in training programmes and strategies shall have to be perceived and given a shape by the teacher educators.

In the context of universalisation of elementary education, teacher educators will be expected to display a deeper understanding of the issues pertaining to access, participation and attainment in their specific regions or areas. They need adequate professional competence to conduct such surveys and studies would reveal the region specific and area specific issues and problems which would help the functionaries of the education department and the community. They will prepare the trainees in responding to these issues during the training period and also in schools subsequently. The professional quality of teacher educator will determine the quality of the training of teachers, both pre-service as well as in-service. The professional level at which teachers are prepared would, in turn, determine the quality of school education. Again, teacher educators have to be fully familiar with the school realities, social environment and community expectations to realistically perform the challenging tasks before them. On the professional side, teacher educators need to be actively associated with policy formulations, implementation strategies and monitoring of programmes.

Existing System

At present, the only programme which is often treated as preparing teacher educators is that of M.Ed. Scrutiny of the curriculum of most of the M.Ed. programmes would reveal that these have not been specifically designed to prepare teacher educators. There are some M.Ed. programmes where provisions do not exist for writing a dissertation. The products of these programmes would certainly not be in a position to conduct research, initiate innovation on their own and induct teacher trainees in these areas, which are essential functions of teacher educators.

Prior to the establishment of the NCTE as a statutory body, NCERT acted as its secretariat and organised several professional development programmes for teacher educators in areas like micro-teaching and simulation, student teaching and evaluation, preparing research proposals, improvement of teacher education curricula and so on. The University Grants Commission (UGC) has been organising national and regional level workshops for improvement of the teacher education programmes. Through various schemes it offers financial support for seminars, workshops and research projects for teacher educators for such themes as higher education, educational technology, non-formal education, population education, environmental education, research methodology, etc. The National Institute of Educational Planning and Administration (NIEPA) organises programmes for Principals of Colleges of Education, Heads of University Departments of Education and other Administrators concerned with teacher education.

The SCERTs and State Boards of Teacher Education organise continuing education programmes for teacher educators on teaching methodologies for new subject areas and on innovations in education. Some University Departments of Education organise seminars, workshops, and orientation programmes for teacher educators on teaching, development of instructional skills, interaction analysis, teaching behaviour, educational technology, guidance and counselling and research methodology. Certain Colleges of Education and University Departments of Education have been upgraded as Colleges of Teacher Education (CTEs) and Institutions of Advanced Study in Education (IASEs) for taking up innovations in teacher education. NCTE after its establishment in 1995 as a statutory body has initiated several programmes aimed at enhancing professional competence of teacher educators.

In the absence of an appropriate policy of recruitment, especially at the pre-primary, primary and elementary stages of teacher preparation, the manpower in the institutions of teacher education does not necessarily possess the professionally required qualifications for the preliminary stages. At the pre-primary stage one comes across teacher educators who have passed high school or higher secondary examination and possess a certificate in teacher training, not necessarily meant for the pre-primary stage; graduates or those with higher qualification with absolutely no training background or with the background not appropriate for that stage or level. As regards the primary and elementary stages, the teacher educators, generally, possess graduate or higher qualification with teacher training mostly at the B.Ed. level. There are serious lacunae in the recruitment policies in as much as the professional qualifications prescribed are not stage-specific and mostly not suited to the education of teachers for the stage or level concerned. This situation calls for fresh thinking regarding recruitment policies for teacher educators and well-planned programmes of education for teacher educators.

Rationale and Objectives

IT enabled education and training of teacher educators has to focus its attention on the new role of teacher educators on the problems, which reflect the emerging global trends in education and the overall needs, and aspirations of the people in India. It has also to deal with specific problems confronting teacher education institutions and to make teacher education more responsible and responsive. It also has to encourage teacher educators' continuing professional growth. In addition, there are certain practical problems as well.

The rationale behind the IT enabled education and professional training of teacher educators lies in providing qualitative instruction through well-designed programmes of professional education. The following questions are relevant for designing a programme for education of teacher educators:

- What exactly should the education of teacher educators aim at?
- What are the significant issues and problems concerning the education of teacher educators?
- What are the roles of IT enabled education in teacher training programmes?
- What are the possible models of both pre-service as well as in service education of teacher educators?
- What patterns, contents and techniques are envisaged?
- What are the possible agencies and organisations, which could be profitably employed in providing continuing abd recurrent in service education to teacher educators?

Based upon the issues raised above, the following objectives can be comprehensively identified for the programmes of preparation of teacher educators:

- To develop competencies and skills needed for preparation of teachers and teacher educators.
- To enable them to organise competency-based and commitment oriented professional programmes.
- To enable them to develop pedagogy relevant to the education of teacher educators.
- To acquire an understanding of the needs and problems of teacher educators and teacher education institutions.
- To develop skills related to management of teacher education institutions.
- To develop competencies of curriculum development and preparation of learning and evaluation materials.
- To enable teacher educators to acquire capabilities to organise in-service continuing education programmes.
- To enable them to organise need-based and commitment oriented on the job training.
- To develop competencies for evaluating educational programmes and teaching learning materials.
- To develop the capacity of examination, analysis, interpretation, elaboration and communication of educational ideas.
- To relate education and the national needs and develop critical awareness about Indian realities.
- To enable them to understand the relationship between Indian ethos, modern technology and education.
- To promote the global perspective of educational development with special reference to the developing countries.

- To enable them to undertake meaningful educational research.
- To develop the capacities to reinterpret Indian heritage, culture and values to meet the requirements of the present-day Indian society.
- To develop the capabilities for self-directed and life-long learning.
- To enable them to appreciate and adopt emerging communication technology and innovative practices in Indian context.

Evolving Models of Pre-Service Education of Teacher Educators

The present system of pre-service education of teacher educators is characterised by lack of perspective in terms both of contents as well as qualifications. For instance, while it is well accepted that the B.Ed. qualification entitles a person to teach at secondary stage, it is doubtful if the M.Ed. programme adequately prepares a person to become teacher of secondary school teachers. The existing M.Ed. programme has little provision of training in and working out teaching and evaluation strategies suited to the needs of teacher trainees. And yet one finds M.Ed. degree holders entrusted with the responsibility of teacher preparation not only at secondary stage but also at the pre-primary, primary and elementary stages of teacher preparation. Likewise, while the B.Ed. qualification legitimately entitles a person to teach at the secondary stage, it cannot, at the same time, be accepted as a good enough qualification for being a teacher educator at the primary stage. The existing B.Ed. programme is designed mainly to teach high school students and not for preparing primary school teacher educators. Thus, it is imperative that the professional qualification of teacher educators is made stage-specific suited to the needs of teacher trainees of different categories.

It is time for seriously considering designing of definite programmes to prepare teacher educators rather than depend on the conventional B.Ed. or/and M.Ed. course. Education of teacher educators has necessarily to correspond to teacher preparation programmes. It is nonetheless necessary to consider alternatives and institute programmes like M.Ed. (Teacher Education) catering to the needs of stage-specific and category-specific preparation of teacher educators alongside general M.Ed. programmes.

Thrusts in In-service and Continuing Education

The present provision for continuing education of teacher educators is inadequate in respect of both quality and content. Planning in respect of in-service education of teacher educators needs to be evolved for different stages and levels. The major thrusts in respect of programmes for teacher educators among others may be as follows:

- Designing short-term programmes for those who are already placed in these institutions.
- Specific short-term induction programmes for those who do not have the experience in ICT for the stage they are supposed to be working at.
- Identification of certain university departments of education and Institutions of Advanced Study in Education as institutions, which may work mainly for teacher educators. They may focus on induction training, recurrent training,

orientation programmes, research studies and surveys, curriculum development, preparation of training materials, evaluation strategies and techniques, use of educational technology, media and others.

- Establishment of institutions for preparation of teacher educators for special education at different stages. These may be open to primary and secondary trained graduates willing to become teacher educators. Such programmes need to be designed with particular focus on the practicum that would familiarize the trainees with school situations in totality.
- Networking of various institutions and organisations for designing and carrying out collaborative programmes by pooling and sharing of resources.

The fact that our education system has inadequate facilities for preparation and orientation of teacher educators has been a major factor for not taking due care of the education and training of teacher educators in several respects. With the policy focus changing to quality and relevance of education; it is necessary that only those, who are professionally competent, committed and willing, be charged with the responsibility of preparing teachers for the nation. Teacher educators prepare teachers for various stages, levels and categories professionally. The quality and character of teachers therefore, would largely depend on the professional education of teacher educators. Towards this, it is necessary, therefore, that their education should be given a new orientation and improved qualitatively and adjusted properly with the demands of the new curriculum.

2

Information and Communication Technology and Teacher Education

Information and Communications Technologies are a diverse set of technological tools and resources used to communicate, and to create, disseminate, store, and manage information. In general we are talking about technologies and tools that people use to share, distribute, gather information, and to communicate with one another, one on one, or in groups, through the use of computers and interconnected computer networks.

ICT is emerging as major tool for learning and teaching and from one of the survey it is clear that the average rate of retention is high when learner learns through listening and even more by seeing. The learning Pyramid below clearly indicate this and hence, it is clear that how ICT is useful in teaching and learning. People retain only 20 per cent of what they see and 30 per cent of what they hear. But they remember 50 per cent of what they see and hear, and as much as 80 per cent of what they see, hear and do simultaneously.

ICT Tools and Resources for Supporting Curriculum and Teaching

There are various tools of ICT like white board video conferencing system, web-based resources electronic and digital libraries and many more, which supports learning and teaching. With the tools of ICT, students can dramatically raise knowledge levels, learn problem-solving techniques, develop the skills required to manage massive amounts of information, analyze concepts from several different perspectives, and develop the hard to-qualify higher-order analytic and critical thinking skills that are necessary for lifelong learning, not only student but teacher also benefited from it, as it help in reducing the duplication of effort when preparing lesson plans, worksheets and reports as well as it provide method for teaching like through Multimedia presentations of the content, by audio and through video conferencing and even they can share there view, resources and also get advices form other experienced person and many more. There are many tools of ICT some of them are given below:

- Web-based resources
- Electronic libraries and databases
- Multimedia resources
- White board

- Productivity and analysis tools
- Computer-based assessment
- Streaming video
- Discussion lists and newsgroups
- Student web publishing
- Conferencing systems

ICT in Teaching and Learning

By their very nature, ICT call for innovation. It is about exploiting the full capabilities of technology to open new perspectives for both teachers and students. At the same time, it is unwise to ignore traditional styles and models of learning as well as ideas from the past that were not implemented in the mass school but were precious exceptions. Therefore, we need to start with things that we are already doing, but consider them anew. Lots of possible areas are there for the use of ICT in teaching and learning like presentation, calculation, completing assignments, information sources, and some of the other possibilities are:

- Immediate oral communication
- Reading
- Writing
- Science experiments and observations
- School use of general and professional applications
- Virtual laboratory
- Organization of the learning process
- Information resources for education
- More Complex Educational Events
- Approaching the new literacy
- Foreign language learning
- Design and construction in learning
- Micro worlds
- Scientific research
- Research in social sciences and humanities
- Providing support to the school and community.

Information and Communication Technologies (ICTs) are a major factor in shaping the new global economy and producing rapid changes in society. Within the past decade, the new ICT tools have fundamentally changed the way people communicate and do business. They have produced significant transformations in industry, agriculture, medicine, business, engineering and other fields. They also have the potential to transform the nature of education-where and how learning takes place and the roles of students and teachers in the learning process.

Teacher education institutions may either assume a leadership role in the transformation of education or be left behind in the swirl of rapid technological change. For education to reap the full benefits of ICTs in learning, it is essential that pre-service and in-service teachers have basic ICT skills and competencies. Teacher education institutions and programmes must provide the leadership for pre-service and in-service teachers and model the new pedagogies and tools for learning. They must also provide leadership in determining how the new technologies can best be used in the context of the culture, needs, and economic conditions within their country.

To accomplish these goals, teacher education institutions must work closely and effectively with school teachers and administrators, national or state educational agencies, teacher unions, business and community organizations, politicians and other important stakeholders in the educational system. Teacher education institutions also need to develop strategies and plans to enhance the teaching-learning process within teacher education programmes and to assure that all future teachers are well prepared to use the new tools for learning.

The challenge confronting our educational systems is how to transform the curriculum and teaching-learning process to provide students with the skills to function effectively in this dynamic, information-rich, and continuously changing environment. Education is at the confluence of powerful and rapidly shifting educational, technological and political forces that will shape the structure of educational systems across the globe for the remainder of this century. Many countries are engaged in a number of efforts to effect changes in the teaching/learning process to prepare students for information and technology based society. The UNESCO World Education Report (1998) notes that the new technologies challenge traditional conceptions of both teaching and learning and, by reconfiguring how teachers and learners gain access to knowledge, have the potential to transform teaching and learning processes. ICTs provide an array of powerful tools that may help in transforming the present isolated, teacher-centered and text-bound classrooms into rich, student-focused, interactive knowledge environments. To meet these challenges, schools must embrace the new technologies and appropriate the new ICT tools for learning. They must also move toward the goal of transforming the traditional paradigm of learning.

To accomplish this goal requires both a change in the traditional view of the learning process and an understanding of how the new digital technologies can create new learning environments in which students are engaged learners, able to take greater responsibility for their own learning and constructing their own knowledge. There is widespread concern that the educational experiences provided in many schools will not prepare students well for the future. Many educators and government leaders believe that creating a paradigm shift in views of the learning process, coupled with applications of the new information technologies, and may play an important role in bringing educational systems into alignment with the knowledge-based, information-rich society.

The Learning Process

Learning is hard. Many view learning as a difficult and often tedious process. According to this view, if students are having fun or enjoying what they are doing in a learning activity, they probably are not learning.

The existing view of the learning process emerged out of the factory model of education at the turn of the 20th century and was highly effective in preparing large numbers of individuals with skills needed for low-skilled positions in industry and agriculture. As shown, the teacher is the expert and the dispenser of knowledge to the students. It is largely a 'broadcast' model of learning where the teacher serves as the repository and transmitter of knowledge to the students. The traditional educational paradigm is often characterized by the following views of learning:

Learning is Based on a Deficit Model of the Student

The system strives to identify deficiencies and weaknesses of the student. Based on noted deficiencies, students are tracked, categorized, remediated or failed. The impact of the deficit model of student learning is most obvious in compensatory education programmes. As implied by the term, compensatory education is designed to make up or remediate learning that some children, particularly poor minority children, do not have, but which the curriculum and structure of schooling assume are common to all children.

Bruer, in his book, Schools for Thought, notes that research overwhelmingly concentrates on the weaknesses of poor children. Very little research has been done on their strengths. In addition, the weaknesses identified are often deficiencies in terms of the traditional organization and content of schooling. Very little thought has been given to the idea of changing schooling to accommodate new kinds of students; all the effort has gone to changing the students so that they will fit into the schools. In addition, the underlying assumptions about poor students' motivation, language, and conceptual development have..."militated against offering them a literacy of thoughtfulness and have favoured a low-level, atomized, concrete, basic-skills curriculum. The language of that curriculum has been so simplified that it is both boring and artificial. It has been stripped of its richness and context and made fundamentally meaningless, which is to say unabsorbable by normal people, except through memorization, whose effects last only a few hours or days." (Bruer, 1993).

Learning is a Process of Information Transfer and Reception

Much of our present learning enterprise remains "information-oriented," emphasizing students reproducing knowledge rather than producing their own knowledge. It also remains teacher-centered. Many still see the role of the teacher as a dispenser of information and the role of the student as a passive receiver, storer and repeater of the transmitted information. The prevalence of this view is supported by observations that teachers continue to rely on old standbys such as lectures, textbook reading, and fill-in-the-worksheets practices that reduce students to passive recipients of information and fail to develop their thinking skills.

Learning is an Individual/Solitary Process

In a study of schools in the United States, the National Assessment of Educational Progress noted that most students spend long hours working alone at their desks completing worksheets or repetitive tasks. A London Times survey of English School children indicated that students almost unanimously rejected this daily ordeal of dull and ritualistically solitary classroom activity and called for a broader and more exciting curriculum. Above all, they wanted more work allowing them to think for themselves. They wanted to design and make things, to experiment and to engage in first-hand observation. The Times reported, however, that there was little evidence of changes in the curriculum that would respond to the students' wishes. (Resta, 1996).

Learning is Facilitated by Breaking Content

The educational system is often geared more to categorizing and analyzing patches of knowledge than to sewing them together. Bruer (1993) notes that the technology of mass education is quite adept at "breaking knowledge and skills into thousands of little standardized, decontextualized pieces, which could be taught and tested one at a time." Neil Postman in his book, teaching as a Subversive Activity, states that our educational systems break knowledge and experience into "subjects, relentlessly turning wholes into parts, history into events without restoring continuity." (Postman, 1969).

Learning is a Linear Process

Frequently, the textbook or teacher provides only one linear path through a narrowly bounded content area or sequence of standardized instructional units. For example, in a mathematics text only one correct problem solution trail may be offered for a specific subclass of problems. However, the problems encountered in daily life (or in mathematics) seldom have only one solution path or sequence.

Changes in Views of the Learning Process

In contrast to the traditional teaching-learning paradigm, a new paradigm of the teaching-learning process is emerging, based on three decades of research in human learning that encompasses the following views of the human learning process:

Learning is a Natural Process

The natural state of the brain is to learn, however, not everyone learns in the same way. There are different learning, perceptual and personality styles that must be considered in the design of learning experiences for the individual student. Given interesting and rich learning environments, and supportive and stimulating teachers, students will learn. Teachers have often noted that children who appear disruptive or to have short attention spans when confronted with typical classroom instruction, may spend long periods engaged in meaningful and interesting computer-related activities.

Learning is a Social Process

The communal context of knowledge and learning is beginning to be rediscovered, as evidenced by the rapid growth of quality circles and computer-supported collaborative work in business, government, medicine, and higher education. As Vygotsky (1978) noted long ago, students learn best in collaboration with peers, teachers, parents, and others when they are actively engaged in meaningful, interesting tasks. ICTs provide opportunities for teachers and students to collaborate with others across the country and across the globe. They also provide new tools to support this collaborative learning in the classroom and online.

Learning is an Active and not a Passive Process

In most fields, people are faced with the challenge of producing knowledge rather than simply reproducing knowledge. To allow students to move toward competence, they must be actively engaged in the learning process, in activities such as solving real problems, producing original writing, completing scientific research projects (rather than simply studying about science), dialoguing with others on important issues, providing artistic and musical performances, and constructing physical objects. The traditional curriculum asks students only to recall and describe what others have accomplished or produced. While all production of knowledge must be based on an understanding of prior knowledge, the mere reproduction of knowledge, without its connection to the production of knowledge, is largely a passive activity that neither fully engages nor challenges the student.

Learning May Either be Linear or Non-Linear

Much of what now happens in schools appears based on the notion that the mind works like a serial processor that is designed to process only one piece of information at a time in sequential order. But the mind is a wonderful parallel processor that may attend to and process many different types of information simultaneously. Cognitive theory and research sees learning as a reorganization of knowledge structures. The knowledge structures are stored in semantic memory as schema or cognitive maps. Students "learn" by augmenting, combining, and rearranging a collection of cognitive maps, many of which overlap or are interconnected through a complex network of associations. There are many ways that students may acquire and process information and assimilate it into their existing knowledge structures. Although some knowledge domains, such as mathematics, may perhaps lend themselves to a linear approach, not all learning can or should occur linearly.

Learning is Integrative and Contextualized

Pribram's holistic brain theory suggests that information presented globally is more easily assimilated than information presented only in a sequence of information elements (Pribram, 1991). It is also easier for students to see relations and to make connections. Jacob Bronowski (1990), in Science and Human Values, made the point that to discover the connection between what had seemed two isolated facts of existence is a creative act, whether the field is art or science. He calls it an act of unifying. This is not something that can be done for learners; these connections cannot be made in learners' minds. Information can be given; the connection can even be stated. But even if the information is repeated, it cannot be assumed it is really known. The learners must discover it for themselves. That is not to say that learners must discover everything unaided. The teacher's role is to help them in several ways to make connections and to integrate knowledge.

Learning is Based on a Strength Model of Student Abilities, Interest, and Culture

Based on the work of Howard Gardner and others, schools are beginning to consider the specific strengths and interests that students bring to the learning environment, and are designing learning activities that build on student strengths rather than focusing only upon remediating weaknesses. In addition, schools increasingly recognize diversity as a resource rather than a problem in the classroom. In contrast to the remedial and standardized concept of instruction, diversity and individual differences are valued and the learning process is designed to build on the strengths and assets brought by the learner to the classroom.

Learning is Assessed through Task Completion, Products, and Real Problem Solving of Both Individual and Group Efforts

Rather than simply evaluating students through paper and pencil tests, assessments are made using portfolios of actual performances and work in both collaborative and individual learning tasks. The traditional view of the learning process is typically teacher-centered, with teachers doing most of the talking and intellectual work, while students are passive receptacles of the information provided. This is not to indicate that the traditional lecture method is without value, as it allows the teacher to quickly convey lots of information to students and is a useful strategy for recall or rote learning. However, it is not the most effective way to help students develop and use higher order cognitive skills to solve complex real world problems. As noted by Driscoll (1994), we no longer can view learners as "empty vessels waiting to be filled, but rather as active organisms seeking meaning."

Don Tapscott, in his book Growing Up Digital: The Rise of the Next Generation (1998), notes that we are entering a new era of digital learning in which we are in the process of transitioning from "broadcast" learning to "interactive" learning. Today's students no longer want to be passive recipients in the information transfer model of learning. Rather they want to be active participants in the learning process. There is growing recognition that today's world requires that students be able to work collaboratively with others, think critically and creatively, and reflect on their own learning processes.

A Shift from Teaching to Learning

As technology has created change in all aspects of society, it is also changing our expectations of what students must learn in order to function in the new world economy. Students will have to learn to navigate through large amounts of information, to analyze and make decisions, and to master new knowledge domains in an increasingly technological society. They will need to be lifelong learners, collaborating with others in accomplishing complex tasks, and effectively using different systems for representing and communicating knowledge to others. A shift from teacher-centered instruction to learner-centered instruction is needed to enable students to acquire the new 21st century knowledge and skills. The following Table (Sandholtz, Ringstaff, and Dwyer, 1997) identifies the shift that will take place in changing from a focus on teaching to a focus on learning.

Shifting the emphasis from teaching to learning can create a more interactive and engaging learning environment for teachers and learners. This new environment also involves a change in the roles of both teachers and students. The role of the teacher will change from knowledge transmitter to that of learning facilitator, knowledge guide, knowledge navigator and co-learner with the student. The new role does not diminish the importance of the teacher but requires new knowledge and skills. Students will have greater responsibility for their own learning in this environment as they seek out, find, synthesize, and share their knowledge with others. ICTs provide powerful tools to support the shift to student-centred learning and the new roles of teachers and students.

The new view of the learning process is based on research that has emerged from theoretical frameworks related to human learning. Many reflect a constructivism view of the learning process. In this view, learners are active agents who engage in their own knowledge construction by integrating new information into their schema or mental structures. The learning process is seen as a process of "meaning-making" in socially, culturally, historically, and politically situated contexts. In a constructivism learning environment, students construct their own knowledge by testing ideas and approaches based on their prior knowledge and experience, applying these to new tasks, contexts and situations, and integrating the new knowledge gained with pre-existing intellectual constructs.

A constructivist environment involves developing learning communities comprised of students, teachers and experts who are engaged in authentic tasks in authentic contexts closely related to work done in the real world. A constructivist-learning environment also provides opportunities for learners to experience multiple perspectives. Through discussion or debate, learners are able to see issues and problems from different points of view, to negotiate meaning, and develop shared understandings with others. The constructivist-learning environment also emphasizes authentic assessment of learning rather than the traditional paper/pencil test. Some of the most influential theories that relate to new views of the learning process include:

Vygotsky's Socio Cultural Theory

Vygotsky's socio cultural theory of human learning describes learning as a social process and the origination of human intelligence in society or culture. The major theme of Vygotsky's theoretical framework is that social interaction plays a fundamental role in the development of cognition. Vygotsky believed everything is learned on two levels. First, through interaction with others, and then integrated into the individual's mental structure.

A second aspect of Vygotsky's theory is the idea that the potential for cognitive development is limited to a "Zone of Proximal Development" (ZPD). This "zone" is the area of exploration for which the student is cognitively prepared, but requires help and social interaction to fully develop (Briner, 1999). A teacher or more experienced peer is able to provide the learner with "scaffolding" to support the student's evolving understanding of knowledge domains or development of complex skills. Collaborative learning, discourse, modeling, and scaffolding are strategies for supporting the intellectual knowledge and skills of learners and facilitating intentional learning.

The implications of Vygotsky theory are that learners should be provided with socially rich environments in which to explore knowledge domains with their fellow students, teachers and outside experts. ICTs can be used to support the learning environment by providing tools for discourse, discussions, collaborative writing, and problem solving, and by providing online support systems to scaffold students' evolving understanding and cognitive growth.

Jean Piaget

Based on his research on the development of children's cognitive functions, Piaget's work is regarded by many as the founding principles of constructivist theory. He observed that learning occurs through adaptation to interactions with the environment. Disequilibrium (mental conflict which demands resolution) gives rise to Assimilation of a new experience, which is added to the existing knowledge of the learner, or to Accommodation, which is modification of existing understanding to provide for the new experience.

Specifically, Piaget posited that the existing cognitive structures of the learner determine how new information is perceived and processed. If the new information makes sense to the existing mental structure of the learner, then the new information item is incorporated into the structure (i.e., Assimilation). If, however, the data are very different from the existing mental structure of the learner, they are either rejected or transformed in ways so that it fits into the structure (i.e., Accommodation). The learner has an active role in constructing his or her own knowledge in both of these ideas. He observed that, as children assimilated new information into their existing mental structures, their ideas gained complexity and power, and their understanding of the world grew in richness and depth. These ideas are core concepts of the constructivism view of the learning process. (Jean Piaget Society, 2001).

Jerome Bruner

Similar to Piaget, Bruner emphasized that learning is an active process in which learners construct new ideas or concepts based upon their prior knowledge and experience. He identified three principles to guide the development of instruction. These include:

- Instruction must be concerned with the experiences and contexts that make the student willing and able to learn (readiness);
- Instruction must be structured so that the student can easily grasp it (spiral organization); and,
- Instruction should be designed to facilitate extrapolation and/or fill in the gaps (going beyond the information given).

Problem-Based Learning

The goals of Problem-Based Learning (PBL) are to develop higher order thinking skills by providing students with authentic and complex problems and cases.

This approach to learning provides a more authentic context for learning and engages students in authentic tasks. It is used frequently in fields such as engineering, medicine and architecture, and has been increasingly applied to K-12 settings. Through the process of working together, articulating theories, creating hypotheses, and critically discussing the ideas of others, students move to deeper levels of understanding of the problem. The self-directed learning strategies developed in PBL may help foster students' lifelong learning.

Anchored Instruction

Anchored instruction is an approach to designing instruction that is 'anchored' in a real world context, problem or situation. Technology has been used to help create 'real world' contexts and situations through the use of video. The video segments provide the context for the subsequent learning and instruction. (Bransford and Stein, 1993).

Distributed Cognition

Distributed cognition emphasizes that cognitive growth is fostered through interaction with others and involves dialogue and discourse, making private knowledge public and developing shared understandings. Tools for online collaboration have been designed to support collaborative knowledge construction and sharing in the classroom. (Oshima, Bereiter, and Scardamalia, 1995).

Cognitive Flexibility Theory

This theory asserts that people acquire knowledge in ill-structured domains by constructing multiple representations and linkages among knowledge units. It also notes that learners revisit the same concepts and principles in a variety of contexts. The theory is useful in understanding how knowledge is transferred in ill-structured knowledge domains. (Spiro *et al.*, 1988).

Cognitive Apprenticeship

Cognitive apprenticeship is a term for the instructional process in which teachers or more experienced or knowledgeable peers provide 'scaffolds' to support learners' cognitive growth and development. Cognitive apprenticeship permits students to learn through their interactions, construct knowledge, and share knowledge-building experiences with the other members of the learning community.

ICTs provide powerful new tools to support cognitive apprenticeships, enabling groups to share online workspaces to collaboratively develop artifacts and intellectual products. They also make possible tele-apprenticeships, in which an expert is able to work with or mentor a student who may be thousands of miles distant.

Situated Learning

Situated learning emphasizes the use of apprenticeship, coaching, collaboration, authentic contexts, tasks, activities and cognitive tools (Brown, Collins and Duguid, 1989). It occurs when students work on authentic tasks that take place in real-world settings (Winn, 1993). Learning is viewed as a function of the activity, context and culture in which it occurs, which contrasts with most classroom learning which is abstract and out of context (Lave, 1988). Situated cognition theory emphasizes providing an authentic context for the learner and encouraging social interaction and collaboration in the learning environment. Through collaborative problem solving, dialogue, and discussion students are able to develop deeper levels of understanding of a problem or knowledge domain.

Self-Regulated Learning

Self-regulated learners are those who are aware of their own knowledge and understandings, i.e., what they know and what they do not know or need to understand. It combines self-observation, self-judgment, and self-reaction. Self-regulation plays a crucial role in all phases of learning and has the potential to increase the meaningfulness of students' classroom learning (Schoenfeld, 1987). ICT tools can be used to make students' tacit knowledge public and to help them develop metacognitive skills and become more reflective and self-regulated learners (Hsiao, 1999).

ICTs AND TEACHER EDUCATION

The Society for Information Technology and Teacher Education has identified basic principles for development of effective ICT teacher education (SITE, 2002). These are:

Technology should be infused into the entire teacher education programme. Throughout their teacher education experience, students should learn about and with technology and how to incorporate it into their own teaching. Restricting technology experiences to a single course or to a single area of teacher education, such as methods courses, will not prepare students to be technology-using teachers. Pre-service teacher education students should learn about a wide range of educational technologies across their professional preparation, from introductory and foundations courses to student teaching and professional development experiences.

Technology should be introduced in context. Teaching pre-service students basic computer literacy-the traditional operating system, word processor, spreadsheet, database, and telecommunications topics is not enough. As with any profession, there is a level of literacy beyond general computer literacy. This more specific or professional literacy involves learning to use technology to foster the educational growth of students. Professional literacy is best learned in context. Pre-service students should learn many uses of technology because they are integrated into their coursework and field experiences. They should see their professors and mentor teachers model innovative uses of technology; they should use it in their own learning, and they should explore creative uses of technology in their teaching. Teacher educators, content specialists, and mentor teachers should expose pre-service teachers to regular and pervasive modeling of technology and provide opportunities for them to teach with technology in School classrooms.

Students should experience innovative technology-supported learning environments in their teacher education programme. Technology can be used to support traditional forms of learning as well as to transform learning. A PowerPoint presentation, for example, can enhance a traditional lecture, but it does not necessarily transform the learning experience. On the other hand, using multimedia cases to teach topics that have previously been addressed through lectures may well be an example of a learning experience transformed by technology. Students should experience both types of uses of technology in their programme; however, the brightest promise of technology in education is as a support for new, innovative, and creative forms of teaching and learning (SITE, 2002). While the proposed ICT in teacher education curriculum should aspire to no less, the trajectory of the development for countries, regions, and organizations should be appropriate to the level of resources, including expertise, leadership, and ICTs themselves. A widespread approach to reach a scattered population of teachers and organizations that are ready to move a small step forward with very limited resources may be helpful at an early stage. Creating centers of transferable excellent practice that encourages 'reference site' visits, and mentoring teachers in other locations, are also approaches that may be effective. This section will review the stages of teacher education and provide examples of approaches for teacher education in ICTs and through ICTs.

Teacher Education

Approaches to the professional development of teachers must be dependent on context and culture. Since there are a variety of approaches, an overview of the many stages in which teachers receive teacher education may prove helpful.

Professional development to incorporate ICTs into teaching and learning is an ongoing process and should not be thought of as one 'injection' of training. Teachers need to update their knowledge and skills as the school curriculum and technologies change. Individuals develop in stages and mature over time. Personal development must be accompanied by organizational development in schools, training centers, and universities.

In many regions, teachers engage in preparation before they start teaching in schools, a stage referred to in this document as pre-service teacher education.

When pre-service teachers begin to teach they may be given additional support to handle the complexity of their work for the first to third years of their career. This stage of professional development is called induction. The induction stage demands a great deal of effort and commitment, and research in developed countries reveals that around 30 per cent of teachers may drop out during this time. Some teachers do not have the benefit of a preparatory course and must learn while teaching in schools, a condition referred to as on-the-job training. Such training is probably carried out within the school, perhaps with the teacher receiving some release from normal duties. Teacher education is an ongoing process of lifelong learning. The final stage, consisting of additional professional development, is called in-service teacher education.

It is important to note that some very strong models of teacher education provide simultaneous professional development for more than one group. For example, pre-service preparation can be aligned with in-service teacher education. A practicing teacher may work with a pre-service teacher education student on an innovative educational project. This not only increases the research potential of the in-service teacher, but the pre-service teacher also experiences role modeling and, as a result, may have an easier transition into teaching.

Professional learning communities allow teachers to support the professional development of colleagues and receive support themselves. ICTs have increased the access to and reach of such professional associations. Mentorship can be fostered across geographic distances and supported by synchronous and asynchronous interaction. Professional development may also be enhanced by public or private partnerships with the community. Such partnerships may be particularly appropriate for professional development related to ICTs, with financial and technical support contributed by ICT companies, such as the Intel Teach to the Future Programme, or by local communities.

The professional development of teacher educators is also essential. Unless teacher educators model effective use of technology in their own classes, it will not be possible to prepare a new generation of teachers who effectively use the new tools for learning. It is also important to consider the question of who may teach. With ICTs, students often become teachers, using the processes of peer tutoring or reciprocal mentoring. Indeed, a teacher may facilitate learning by reversing the teaching-learning roles, with students acting as expert learners who model the learning process. ICTs provide extensive opportunities for this to occur in ways that can increase the self-esteem, motivation, and engagement of students. Teachers need encouragement to adopt such strategies rather than to feel ashamed to be taught by young learners. Members of the community also may become teachers, or at least invited experts. ICTs extend the range of such opportunities and provide access to extensive relevant supporting materials. The teacher's role changes to manager and facilitator in many of these situations as the teacher helps the expert communicate with the learners and scaffolds the learning process. The teacher also acquires professional development by learning from the expert.

The focus of professional development should also be expanded to those who work with teachers: the classroom assistants, school leaders, and members of regional and national organizations for curriculum and professional development. A common vision for the role of ICTs in education is important for its success. Teachers may find it impossible to incorporate ICTs into their work without support and encouragement from colleagues, parents, and leaders. To bring this about, these community members may also need professional development, along with the teachers.

Teacher Education in ICTs

The most obvious technique for professional development for teachers is to provide courses in basic ICTs knowledge and skills, delivered by experts in national and regional centers. These types of courses, taught at training centers or universities with a syllabus set by regional or national agencies, have been a common practice in many countries. However, this approach has had limited success without follow-on training and support, as compared to effective use of ICTs by trained teachers. Similarly, courses for teachers in particular software and hardware applications are difficult to implement in a way those results in use of these applications in classroom instruction or other professional practices without additional support. As noted in an earlier section, the development of ICTs does not improve education if the focus is on ICTs. The vision must focus on what ICTs can do to improve education.

ICTs in Teacher Education

In planning for the infusion of ICTs into teacher preparation programmes, several factors important to a programme's success must be considered. This section provides a holistic framework to assist in designing the integration of Information and Communication Technologies (ICTs) into teacher education. The framework is coherent with the context provided by today's society and reflects more recent understandings of the nature of learning, including aspects of learning communities during the school years and beyond into lifelong learning.

The holistic framework will help teacher educators and administrators consider the cultural and educational system context, technology resources, and other factors that are important in planning the integration of technology into the pre-service curriculum. Limited technology resources and conditions of rapid change in educational, economic and political systems challenge many contexts of this curriculum.

In some regions, the shortage of teachers, teacher educators, facilities and standards has been chronic for years and has reached crisis proportions. Access to ICT resources may also be quite limited. Within this document, ICTs should be broadly defined as including 'interactive radio' and multiple media including TV, as well as computers and hand-held electronic devices.

Integrating ICTs into Teaching

In an effort to implement ICT standards in a variety of coursework taken by pre-service teachers across all subject disciplines, a number of methods and strategies have been identified. Many of these strategies employ commonly used productivity tools such as word processing, database, spreadsheet, or browser applications. These software tools can be used in countless ways to support the subject area curricula.

Additional strategies, that are multipurpose in application, may also be used to help teacher candidates quickly develop technology-rich lessons for their fieldwork. An overview of proven effective models and strategies for web-based lessons, multimedia presentations, telecomputing projects, and online discussions is presented below.

Web-Based Lessons

Web Quests

A Web Quest is an inquiry-oriented activity in which most or all of the information used by learners is drawn from the Web. Web Quests are designed to use learners' time well, to focus on using information rather than looking for it, and to support learners' thinking at the levels of analysis, synthesis, and evaluation.

Cyber Guides

Cyber Guides include standards-based, web-delivered units of instruction centered on core works of literature. Cyber Guides provide a quick supplementary set of activities for students (and pre-service teachers) as they explore specific pieces of literature. Each Cyber Guide contains a student and teacher edition, targeted standards, a description of the task, a process by which the task may be completed, teacher-selected websites, and an assessment rubric. The teacher's guide includes an overview of the activities, suggestions from the author, and a library of links. The student guides include activity directions written in a format appropriate for the age and reading ability of the students. One example of a Cyber Guide Unit (for the intermediate grades) is "Dragonwings" by Laurence Yep (2001).

Multimedia Presentations

Multimedia combines media objects such as text, graphics, video, animation, and sound to represent and convey information. In this project-based method of teaching and learning, students acquire new knowledge and skills by designing, planning, and producing a multimedia product. Many teachers find that students are motivated to learn when they can use technology to present the results of a rich project or activity. The multimedia presentation contains content conveyed by the student's selection of media. The teachers in training can look at examples of projects and lessons, at Internet sites housing collections of student samples. Some examples of multimedia presentations include:

- Creating a web page or site.
- Developing a branching hypermedia stack.
- Using a multimedia slide show application to create a computer presentation.
- Shooting and editing video to create a computer-generated movie.

As new forms of multimedia are explored, the types of projects become more complex. Multimedia-authoring tools are used to link and branch screens, making them interactive and layered with information in photos, scanned images, movies, and text. Students and candidates can easily narrate their projects using a microphone.

Tele Computing Projects

Tele computing projects are Internet-enriched learning activities that often involve students in one location collaborating with students or adults in one or more other locations. They may share, among other things:

- Experiences
- Beliefs
- Data
- Information
- Problem-solving strategies
- Products they have developed or jointly developed.

Telecomputing tools include e-mail, electronic mailing lists, electronic bulletin boards, discussion groups, web browsers, real-time chatting, and audio-and video-conferencing. Online resources include websites, interactive environments, and remotely operated robotic devices. Judi Harris provides a variety of telecomputing project web pages. (Harris, 2001).

Online Discussions

A common type of telecomputing activity is online discussion. With the growth of infrastructure around the world comes the ability to access others through remote connections. Students and teacher candidates can connect to experts and peers through a variety of formats, such as chat rooms, electronic bulletin boards, and e-mail. Communicating online offers participants freedom to send and receive information efficiently across diverse geographic locations. Communication can occur asynchronously allowing time for reflection, or to compensate for varying time zones. In real-time online communication, as in chat groups, the communication is synchronous and provides immediate feedback for reinforcement and understanding.

Approaches to Quality Assurance

Quality assurance in teacher education is an ongoing process and is demonstrated in a number of different ways. The teacher education institution itself may be scrutinized along with individual programmes within the institution. The quality of the teacher education institution and its programmes is often judged by the performance of the teachers they produce and the success of their graduates in effecting improved student learning in their P-12 classrooms. Quality assurance is often determined through an accreditation process. Demonstrated competence of teacher candidates in use of ICTs in teacher education has become increasingly important in making accreditation, certification, and programme review decisions.

Student-Centered Teaching

Teaching in all settings should encompass student-centered approaches to learning. Technology should not be used only as a tool for demonstration, as an electronic overhead projector or blackboard; rather the use of technology by students should be an integral part of instruction. In student-centered approaches to learning, students become the source for problems investigated. Students and teacher candidates must have opportunities to identify problems, collect and analyze data, draw conclusions, and convey results using electronic tools to accomplish these tasks. Faculty should model the use of ICTs to demonstrate their usefulness and appropriateness for collaboration, acquisition of resources, analysis and synthesis, presentation, and publication.

Assessment

In addition to assessing teaching and student outcomes, institutions should continuously assess the effectiveness of technology for learning throughout the entire teacher preparation environment. The data obtained from this continuous assessment will:

- Inform the learning strategies used.
- Ensure that the vision for technology-use maintains the appropriate direction.
- Pinpoint potential problems.
- Provide data for altering policies and instructional strategies or for acquiring resources.

Changes made over time due to technology innovation will exemplify informed decision-making. The challenge confronting countries, regions and universities is to address the following basic principles for ICTs in teacher education (Society for Information Technology and Teacher Education, 2002):

- ICTs should be infused into the entire teacher education programme.
- Technology should be introduced in context.
- Students should experience innovative ICT-supported learning environments in their teacher education programme.

The most critical factor in the successful integration of ICTs into teacher education is the extent to which the teacher educators have the knowledge and skills for modeling the use of ICTs in their own teaching practices. To enable them to develop these skills requires a well-conceived and sustained programme of professional development. This section focuses on the professional development of teacher educators and the programmes for which they are responsible, such as pre-service programmes and certificates for practicing teachers. The section discusses teacher educator professional development in various contexts of infusing technology into the educational system and process. The discussion is underpinned by new approaches to teaching and learning and by the recognition of the stages of professional and organizational development. Eight case studies from around the world illustrate a range of approaches and models that may be used. The section closes with a brief discussion of the importance of robust evaluations and the role of all stakeholders in the evaluation process.

Basic Strategies

Countries that have initiated efforts to infuse ICTs into teacher education have found four professional development strategies helpful in successful technology integration. First, professional development needs to focus on teaching and learning rather than on hardware and software. It should be designed by first considering what student teachers are expected to know and be able to do in a specific discipline, and then infusing ICTs into the learning process so that acquiring the knowledge and skills is more efficient.

Second, professional development is practically useless unless leaders and teacher educators are provided with access to technology resources and have the time and support-when needed—to apply the new knowledge and skills that they have learned. A just-in-time approach to professional development is a model that works well. In this approach, professional development is provided to teacher educators when they have a need or opportunity to use a specific technology tool or application to enhance learning. Third, professional development in the use of ICTs is not a one-time activity. To keep current with new developments means that professional development in ICTs must be an ongoing process.

New Approaches to Teaching, Learning, and Assessment

An important aspect of professional development is not only enabling teacher educators to understand and use ICT tools in their teaching practices, but understanding how technology coupled with new approaches to teaching and learning, may enhance student learning. Many teacher educators recognize that approaches to education are changing and that new technology has the potential to improve education and student learning. They may also recognize the implications of increasing use of technology in society and employment, including employment directly related to their own disciplines and content areas. Less obvious are the implications for literacy and numeracy at the core of the educational process, and the need for teacher educators themselves to model good practice in their teaching so that their students can easily transfer these strategies into their own teaching practice. Teacher educators are experts in a domain, and it is important to respect this domain while helping them to revitalize and modernize their teaching with ICTs. The principles that this document espouses for the curriculum and professional development of teachers become even more relevant when applied to teacher educators. Similarly, the risk that established teacher educators must take to develop their practice needs to be recognized and mitigated as much as possible.

The Principles of Teacher Development Using ICTs

The integration of ICTs into the very idea of teaching and learning might be termed the 'informatization' of education. Informatization represents the necessary component, condition, and catalyst for the modernization of education, which will permit the move from the reproductive model of teaching and learning to an independent model that, promotes initiation and creativity with information. This new model of education reinforces the role of independent research. Learners are expected to collect, select, analyze, organize, and present knowledge. Teachers are expected to promote collective work and to facilitate individual and group activities. The implementation of this new model builds the information and communication competencies of students, including the habits of mastering the means of information and communication technologies.

The most important principle for the individual development of a teacher is active, project-based learning. Teaching must be carried out in such a way as to strongly reflect the general principles of education, such as the implementation of an informatization programme.

The Teacher as Learner

As preparation for understanding, it is essential to reconceptualize the roles of professor, teacher, and student in the teaching-learning process. In previous generations, and at least until the twentieth century, training teachers was a comprehensive task. Learners were organized in a pyramid, with each successive level representing a "better" learner. At the highest levels of the pyramid were the "best" learners, those who came through school with the best marks and could teach the others the content they had learned.

Today's school tries to establish a real-world environment and make possible an approach in which knowledge does not pass from educational designers and text authors to professors, from professors to teachers, and from teachers to pupils. Rather it comes from all directions, and the roles of student, teacher and professor are interchangeable. In a successful ICT project all are co-learners and students may very well support teachers, showing them how to use ICTs in their work. In any case, all participants should learn and practice educational design. We can create a learning school in which enthusiastic teachers, children, and teacher trainers (including designers) explore, design, discover, and invent together, and learn experientially along the way.

The Student as Both Child and Adult

The best path to learn how to use ICTs in teaching is to live, feel, think, and behave as if one were not only an adult teacher but also a pre-adolescent pupil. The child in us enjoys playful immersion in a flow of exciting events that can be eagerly explored. The adult professional is able to exploit previously accumulated wisdom, capacities for logical reasoning, and formal analysis to critically reflect on the very process of learning. To be able to assume both roles is quite an asset for an aspiring teacher.

Content and Pedagogy

How should we model for student teachers best instructional practices so that they may learn in the best way possible? Obviously, we want them to know how to help pupils to learn faster and feel better when using ICTs. We may begin by providing these student teachers with direct experience of ICT-assisted learning while they assume the role of pupil.

Generally speaking, anything that teachers consider necessary and want to teach their pupils is considered content. Often, when we say we want learners to "understand" content, we want students to acquire declarative knowledge, i.e., "knowing that" something is the case. In teaching declarative knowledge one may use the traditional teacher-centered approach of lecturing or telling the students the information or concepts to be learned. The learning of declarative knowledge may be enhanced by the use of ICT tutorial or drill and practice programmes [teacher-controlled ICTs], gradually advancing in complexity. At this stage ICTs are not taught to or learned by the pupils.

There is no need for them as long as the instruction remains entirely teacher controlled. Procedural knowledge, such as learning procedural rules may also be taught using ICTs in a totally teacher-controlled context. Noticeably better results, however, are achieved when control is given gradually to the pupil. In this case ICTs become subject matter to be taught and learned, if only partially and in subordinate status.

Hypermedia Composition

Compositions of this kind function as teachers' homework before their exposition of the lesson material in a classroom. After being deployed on the local network and then on the Internet, compositions can be used by other teachers and students in their own teaching and learning activities.

Multimedia Presentation

Pupils' presentations provide the opportunity to develop the communicative dimension of information competence. Instrumental support of textual theses, quotations, visual images, and sounds help organize more succinctly the thoughts and speech delivery of all students, even those who would, in other circumstances, need extensive scaffolding by the instructor in order to succeed.

Project and Process Design

Central to our model is the creation by the student of teaching objects and/or processes. It is important to remember the diverse ways in which these can be realized. For example, a design for classroom decoration, such as colouring and wall-painting, arrangement of plants, set-up of an aquarium, etc., or a playground design can remain at the programme-design stage on the computer screen, worked up as a model in cardboard or Lego-blocks, or given complete life-size implementation by the designers under the guidance of the art teacher or the teacher of materials technology. Any of these outcomes has a certain educational value, depending on the teaching objective. For other purposes, for example in assimilating new arithmetic content, simply designing the process and having it remain on the computer screen serves as a complete educational experience.

Demonstration of Technical Skills

In completing projects, students must demonstrate technical skills that may be applicable in a variety of professional environments. For example, today one of the most urgently needed skills is computer keyboarding. The achievement of typing speed which is higher than the speed of writing with a pen on paper typical of an average adult requires much less time and effort than is usually spent by children during the mastering of the basics of calligraphy. Hence, there exists the possibility to develop the child's communicative abilities not only after the development of psycho-motor writing habits is complete, but also in parallel, and even ahead of the latter. As for calligraphy, it can be mastered as an element of artistic culture in a step-by-step manner, and in organic conjunction with other forms of written communication. The student teacher will learn keyboarding and other professionally useful ICT skills in the first months of the education programme.

Immersion into Foreign Language

As a part of their project assignments, the students are required to experiment with computer-based (Internet) translators. They may also experiment with computer-based immersion programmes. The well-known method of immersion is based on the theory that language is best mastered if only native speakers surround the learner. The best of modern computer environments for learning a foreign language simulate an immersion environment by such elements as placing the student in situations which are interesting to the student, providing linguistic commentaries, checking and testing the student's progress, and providing automated recognition of the learner's speech. As part of their project activities, students may be encouraged to make use of such products to learn and appreciate other languages in the global learning environment.

Assessment

As a part of project-based programme, student teachers can experience, and learn to use computer-based testing. A computer can be downloaded with a great number and variety of exercises on arithmetic, grammar, completion tasks, etc. This makes it possible to assess in many ways, and to increase the efficiency of work of both teachers and students. When such testing is conducted in a computer lab, the teacher and students may receive the results immediately. Computer-based testing, however, has many limitations, and the teacher must understand the limitations. Including such instruction in the teacher education programme may be very beneficial.

Mitigation of Problems of Children with Disabilities

ICTs make it possible to compensate for even serious deficiencies of the sense organs and supporting-motor apparatus. In cases of deaf and hearing impaired, as well as blind and sight-impaired children, ICTs are used to enhance the functioning of a weakened organ, or to substitute for an inoperative one. For children with disrupted kinetic functions, even as serious as cerebral paralysis, ICTs provide the possibility of communicating and interacting by means of text input and manipulation of screen objects. During the teacher-training course such situations can be simulated by artificial restrictions of movement, low lighting, etc. An important emotional-motivational factor is offered by visiting a special educational institution, where ICTs are used to provide handicapped children access to learning and skills for future professional work in ICT environments.

Ongoing Support

The global network of the Internet makes possible individual contacts, communication, and interaction by student teachers with scientists and experts. There are thematic sites and specialized virtual conferences that facilitate intensive exchange and consultation on a wide range of topics. A search on the Internet, encouraged by the professor and stimulated by the overall environment, may become a constant and habitual activity for a teacher. During the course the student teachers often refer to their recent findings on the Internet, which they transform into new tasks for pupils, or themes for academic competitions.

Unified Information Space

Information on the Internet could be very important in a model of open education. For example, parents might gain better understanding of what and how their children are taught at school, their children's progress and attendance, agendas or results of meetings, etc. All proceedings of the courses for improving professional skills are supported in a unified information space, to which the students constantly refer while deploying their reports on completed projects, finding assignments and other information, work-planning, exchanging personal messages, making group announcements, and critiquing the development of the teaching and learning process. When a unified information space is used in this way for educator professional development, teachers are far more likely to use such virtual spaces in their classrooms.

Opportunities for Research

When ICTs are used extensively in the teacher education programme, there are extensive opportunities for research. Students may engage in recording, analyzing, and reflecting on teaching objects and projects. The student teachers thus become reflective practitioners, who understand both the value and the methods of educational research.

3

Data Information and Knowledge

DATA

Data (singular: datum) are collected of natural phenomena descriptors including the results of experience, observation or experiment, or a set of premises. This may consist of numbers, words, or images, particularly as measurements or observations of a set of variables.

The word data is the plural of Latin datum, neuter past participle of dare, "to give," hence "something given." The past participle of "to give" has been used for millennia, in the sense of a statement accepted at face value; one of the works of Euclid, circa 300 BC, was the Dedomena (in Latin, Data). In discussions of problems in geometry, mathematics, engineering, and so on, the terms givens and data are used interchangeably. Such usage is the origin of data as a concept in computer science: data are numbers, words, images, etc., accepted as they stand.

Definitions of DATA

- A collection of fact from which conclusions may be drawn; "statistical data."
- Data refers to a collection of organized information, usually the results of experience, observation or experiment, or a set of premises. This may consist of numbers, words, or images, particularly as measurements or observations of a set of variables.
- In computer science, data is any information in a form suitable for use with a computer. Data is often distinguished from programmes. A programme is a set of instructions that detail a task for the computer to perform. In this sense, data is thus everything that is not programme code. Information; A collection of object-units that are distinct from one another in computing, data is information that has been translated into a form that is more convenient to move or process. Relative to today's computers and transmission media, data is information converted into binary digital form. Factual information, especially information organized for analysis or used to reason or make decisions. Specifies that data coordinates are to be used in positioning the inset with the POSITION= option. The DATA option is available only when you specify POSITION= (x, y), and it must be placed immediately after the coordinates (x, y).
- Information, especially information in a form that can be used by a computer.

It can include text, numbers, sounds and pictures. A single piece of information is called a Datum. A representation of facts, concepts, or instructions in a manner suitable for communication, interpretation, or processing by humans.

- Data means any collection of raw hand figures facts. Data can be considered as the raw material of information. The data may be numerical such as payroll, employee Number, etc. or non-numerical like Student names, Product names, etc.
- Data: a collection of facts from which conclusions may be drawn; "statistical data" (communication theory) a numerical measure of the uncertainty of an outcome; "the signal contained thousands of bits of information."

Types of Data

The data types may be as follows:

- *Qualitative Data:* It denotes the characteristics of things such as Average, Fair etc.
- *Quantitative Data:* It is expressed in terms of measurable quantities such as 10 KG, 40 degree Celsius etc.
- *Numeric Types*: The data types may also be an integer (+, -) without any fractional part or real number, which includes integers and fractions.

Besides the above, the data types include alphabetic data and alphanumeric data.

Information

Many people speak about the Information Age as the advent of the Knowledge Age or knowledge society, the information society, the Information revolution, and information technologies, and even though informatics, information science and computer science are often in the spotlight, the word "information" is often used without careful consideration of the various meanings it has acquired.

Information as a concept has a diversity of meanings, from everyday usage to technical settings. Generally speaking, the concept of information is closely related to notions of constraint, communication, control, data, form, instruction, knowledge, meaning, mental stimulus, pattern, perception, and representation.

According to the Oxford English Dictionary, the earliest historical meaning of the word information in English was the act of informing, or giving form or shape to the mind, as in education, instruction, or training. A quote from 1387: "Five books come down from heaven for information of mankind." It was also used for an item of training, e.g. a particular instruction.

The English word was apparently derived by adding the common "noun of action" ending "-ation" (descended through Francais from Latin "-tio") to the earlier verb to inform, in the sense of to give form to the mind, to discipline, instruct, and teach: "Men so wise should go and inform their kings." (1330) Inform itself comes (via French) from the Latin verb informare, to give form to, to form an idea of. Furthermore, Latin itself already even contained the word information meaning concept or idea, but the extent to which this may have influenced the development of the word information in English is unclear.

As a final note, the ancient Greek word for form was [eidos], and this word was famously used in a technical philosophical sense by [Plato] (and later Aristotle) to denote the ideal identity or essence of something. "Eidos" can also be associated with [thought], [proposition] or even [concept].

Definitions of Information

- A message received and understood;
- Knowledge acquired through study or experience or instruction;
- Information as a concept bears a diversity of meanings, from everyday usage to technical settings. Generally speaking, the concept of information is closely related to notions of constraint, communication, control, data, form, instruction;
- A collection of related data; Knowledge about a topic; Data that have been processed into a format that is understandable by its intended audience;
- The result obtained by data processing is called information. That is, the processed data is known as information. However, information produced in one data processing step may be used as data in the next data processing step.

Data Vs Information

Data	*Information*
■ Raw records	■ Completed One
■ Un ordered	■ Ordered
■ Unrefined	■ Refined Data
■ What prevails	■ What is necessary
■ Meaningless message	■ Conveys significant meaning
■ Unprocessed or unevaluated message	■ Processed or organised data
■ Raw message or isolated items	■ Information is generated from data by transferring raw item into meaningful.
■ It is the result of observation or measurement done by the human brain in action	■ Information is the product of human brain in action. It may be concrete or abstract

Types of Information

1. *Conceptual Information*

Related to some concepts or the formation of concepts.

Being or characterized by concepts or their formation.

Relating to concepts or mental conception or relating to conceptualism.

2. *Empirical Information*

Derived from experiment and observation rather than theory; "an empirical basis for an ethical theory"; "empirical laws"; "empirical data"; "an empirical treatment of a disease about which little is known."

- A posteriori—requiring evidence for validation or support.
- Confirmable, verifiable, falsifiable—capable of being tested (verified or falsified) by experiment or observation.
- Experiential, existential—derived from experience or the experience of existence.
- Experimental, data-based, observational—relying on observation or experiment.

- Experimental, model (a), pilot (a), test (a), trial (a)—of the nature of or undergoing an experiment.
- Semi empirical—relying to some extent on observation or experiment.
- Trial-and-error—trying out various means or theories until error is satisfactorily reduced or eliminated.

3. *Procedural Information*

Procedural is a management term, which refers to an approach to programming in which the developer specifies exactly what has to be done, and in what order.

4. *Stimulatory Information*

Stimulatory information is that transmitted by direct communication resulting from the contagious enthusiasm of another individual.

5. *Policy Information*

Policy gives a clear insight into the task taken up, definition of the objectives, and purpose anticipated.

6. *Directive Information*

Directive information is to co-ordinate group activity and for giving directions.

Informatics

Informatics is the science of information, the practice of information processing, and the engineering of information systems. Informatics studies the structure, algorithms, behaviour, and interactions of natural and artificial systems that store, process, access and communicate information. It also develops its own conceptual and theoretical foundations and utilizes foundations developed in other fields. Since the advent of computers, individuals and organizations increasingly process information digitally. This has led to the study of informatics that has computational, cognitive and social aspects, including study of the social impact of information technologies.

Used as a compound, in conjunction with the name of a discipline, as in medical informatics, bioinformatics, etc., it denotes the specialization of informatics to the management and processing of data, information and knowledge in the named discipline, and the incorporation of informatics concepts and theories to enrich the other discipline; it has a similar relationship to library science.

Knowledge

The definition of knowledge is a matter of on-going debate among philosophers in the field of epistemology. Epistemology or theory of knowledge is a branch of philosophy concerned with the nature and scope of knowledge. The classical definition, described but not ultimately endorsed by, Plato, has it that in order for there to be knowledge at least three criteria must be fulfilled; that in order to count as knowledge, a statement must be justified, true, and believed.

Knowledge is defined (Oxford English Dictionary) variously as:

(i) Expertise, and skills acquired by a person through experience or education; the theoretical or practical understanding of a subject,

(ii) What is known in a particular field or in total; facts and information or

(iii) Awareness or familiarity gained by experience of a fact or situation. Philosophical debates in general start with Plato's formulation of knowledge as "justified true belief." There is however no single agreed definition of knowledge presently, or any prospect of one, and there remain numerous competing theories.

Knowledge acquisition involves complex cognitive processes: perception, learning, communication, association and reasoning. The term knowledge is also used to mean the confident understanding of a subject with the ability to use it for a specific purpose if appropriate.

Definitions of Knowledge

- Relevant information that one is able to recall from memory; The product of assumption; Recognition of cause and effect (which is NOT wisdom); All cognitive expectances that an individual or organisation factor uses to interpret situations and to generate activities; Awareness; Acquired.
- Organized body of information. The acquaintance with facts, truths or principles as from study or investigation or the familiarity with a particular subject, branch of learning, etc. see also information and wisdom.
- An integrated collection of facts and relationships which, when exercised, produces competent performance.
- Knowledge is part of the hierarchy made up of data, information and knowledge. Data are raw facts. Information is data with context and perspective. Knowledge is information with guidance for action based upon insight and experience.

Importance

- Knowledge derived from study, experience, or instruction.
- Cognition: the psychological result of perception and learning and reasoning.
- Knowledge of specific events or situations that has been gathered or received by communication; intelligence or news.
- A collection of facts or data: statistical information.
- The act of informing or the condition of being informed; communication of knowledge: Safety instructions are provided for the information of our passengers.
- Computer Science. Processed, stored, or transmitted data.
- Factual information, especially information organized for analysis or used to reason or make decisions.
- Computer Science. Numerical or other information represented in a form suitable for processing by computer.
- Values derived from scientific experiments.
- Plural of datum.
- The state or fact of knowing.
- Familiarity, awareness, or understanding gained through experience or study.
- The sum or range of what has been perceived, discovered, or learned.
- Learning; erudition: teachers of great knowledge.
- Specific information about something.

Communicating Knowledge

Symbolic representations can be used to indicate meaning and can be thought of as a dynamic process. Hence the transfer of the symbolic representation can be viewed as one ascription process whereby knowledge can be transferred. Other forms of communication include imitation, narrative exchange along with a range of other methods. There is no complete theory of knowledge transfer or communication.

Knowledge Management

Knowledge management is a management theory which emerged in the 1990s. It seeks to understand the way in which knowledge is created, used and shared within organizations. A significant part of Knowledge Management theory and practice aligns two models:

(i) The DIKW model, which places data, information, knowledge and wisdom into an increasingly useful pyramid.

(ii) Nonaka's reformulation of Polanyi's distinction between tacit and explicit knowledge.

An objective of mainstream knowledge management is to ensure that the right information is delivered to the right person just in time, in order to take the most appropriate decision. In that sense, knowledge management is not interested in managing knowledge per se, but to relate knowledge and its usage. This leads to Organizational Memory Systems. More recent developments have focused on managing networks (the flow of knowledge rather than knowledge itself) and narrative forms of knowledge exchange.

Document

The following are the definitions for document

- A document (noun) is a bounded physical representation of body of information designed with the capacity (and usually intent) to communicate. A document may manifest symbolic, diagrammatic or sensory-representational information.
- To document (verb) is to produce a document artifact by collecting and representing information. In prototypical usage, a document is understood as a paper artifact, containing information in the form of ink marks. Increasingly, documents are also understood as digital artifacts.
- Colloquial usage is revealed by the connotations and denotations that appear in a Web search for document. From these usages, one can infer the following typical connotations:
- Writing that provides information (especially information of an official nature).
- Anything serving as a representation of a person's thinking by means of symbolic marks.
- A written account of ownership or obligation.
- To record in detail; "The parents documented every step of their child's development."
- A digital file in a particular format.

- An artifact that meets a legal notion of document for purposes of discovery in litigation.
- The variety of usage reveals that the notion of document has rich social and cultural aspects besides the physical, functional and operational aspects.
- It's an object that provides information.
- Embodied thought.
- Stored work on a paper or any other material for easy physical handling.
- Most of the documents are created through direct human investigation.

Documents are classified into:

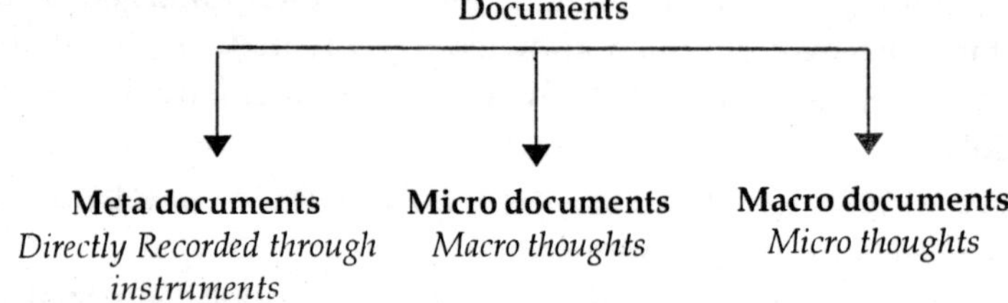

SR Ranganathan classified Documents

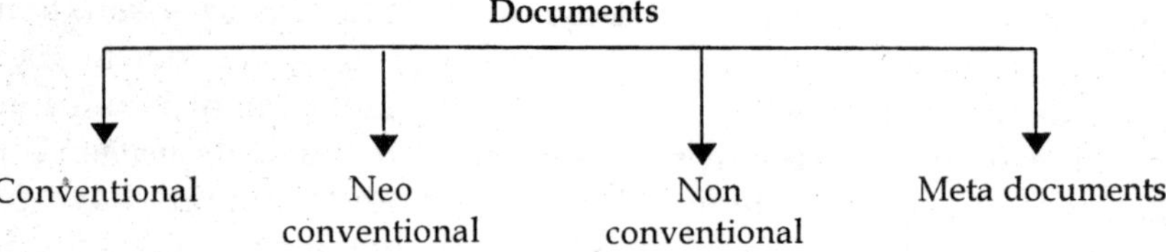

Conventional Documents

Recorded on a paper in a natural language by writing, typing, printing
Most popular in use
Books, periodicals, maps etc.

Neo Conventional Documents

Micro documents
e.g.—journals

Non Conventional Documents

Recorded in a non-conventional size
Audios, visuals, microforms etc.

Meta Documents

Records of phenomena made directly
A phenomena recorded by using instruments
Photography, Radars etc.

Books

Written informations
Monographic books
Collection of essays
Biographies

Periodicals

Written information that comes out periodically
Newspaper, magazines, journals

Journals

Scholarly in nature
Articles written by academicians and researchers

Newspaper

Factual accounts and events
Analysis of trends and events
Reporting of current events
Primary source

Magazines

Trade, news, opinion, literary

Reference

Only want to refer
Either to find a quick fact
Get a general overview of an issue

Encyclopedias

Dictionaries
Handbooks
Atlas

Electronic

e books
e journals
Database
Online encyclopedia

Document Production Technology

Document production technology has evolved significantly through history. While a great deal can be said about ancient production technologies including papyrus, palm leaves, stone tablets and marking devices ranging from quills to chisels, the modern form of the document has evolved largely under the influence of printing technologies. The Illuminated manuscript of Europe is a useful prototypical instance of the document at the end of its evolution before the widespread use of printing. The associated technology was largely a human one. Other cultures at this stage used other forms of pre-print era documents. The history of printing can be traced as follows:

Bronze Age civilizations made extensive use of seals for commercial and transactional purposes. The particular case of the signet ring was of particular importance, and is still in use in place of signatures in East Asian countries like Korea, where it is common for individuals to carry a seal.

Chinese Woodblock printing was the first widespread technology that automated important parts of the document production process.

The Gutenberg Printing Press enabled the mass production of faithful copies of documents, and hence the widespread dissemination of information. The widespread access to information enabled and necessitated fundamental changes to society in religion, government, law, business, and entertainment. Prior to the press the huge effort required to faithfully hand-copy severely limited the number of documents available, and hence access to the information contained therein. The effort to set type and prepare a document for reproduction was still high, but many high fidelity copies could be produced.

The development of Lithography constituted the next great advance in document production technology and continues today to dominate the economic landscape of document production. Lithography brought economies of scale and extremely high quality and low cost to documents.

The typewriter improved the accessibility of document production technologies and enabled it to enter mainstream workplaces. Carbon paper enabled a modest number of copies to be produced concurrently with the original. A brief era of photography-based technologies flourished (including photostat and cyclostyle processes) in parallel with the age of typewriters.

The Xerox Copier became a major milestone in document production by eliminating the typesetting effort required by a printing press. The Xerographic ("dry writing") technology (also referred to as electro photography) could produce durable and economical copies of a paper document easily and quickly. Modern digital printers from Xerox and other companies such as HP, Canon and Ricoh, can produce more than 240 black and white or 170 copies of a page each minute, and work with up to 6 colours and dry and wet inks.

Computers enabled information to be stored electronically in databases and electronic files on magnetic tapes, drums, and disks. This led to a radical disruption of all document production technologies. Initially most of this information was printed onto paper by teletypes (automated typewriters), but computer printers rapidly became faster and more sophisticated. Computers, by controlling lasers in xerography, micro-nozzles in inkjet systems, and tiny solenoids in mechanical systems, became capable of being serially embedded in the document production process. Computers are also critical to modern Lithography.

A whole interaction style with computers was developed around the metaphor of working with documents and folders on a desktop, to the point that the word document is now commonly associated with the information stored in a computer file according to the metaphor. Today, electronic paper is viewed as one potential future evolutionary physical form of the prototypical document, as it can present the electronic document with the readability of printed paper.

Document Life Cycle Management Technology

Technology to manage documents has evolved in parallel with documents themselves. Particular importances are practices concerning the preservation, archival, destruction and management of documents. These constitute what is known as the "document life cycle."

Physical Preservation: Documents in both traditional physical forms and in digital physical forms such as magnetic media must be physically preserved. This aspect of document management deals with such issues as the aging of paper (the innovation of acid-free paper is an advance in preservation) and obsolescence of magnetic media.

Storage: This aspect includes management of scarce resources such as shelf space and disk space, and associated technologies such as optimal space utilization. Modern libraries often use complex space-saving technologies such as robotic retrieval systems for stacks and moving bookshelves. In the digital realm, the entire discipline of compression technologies can be viewed as concerned with the storage of documents.

Cultural Preservation: This function, traditionally ascribed to librarians involves the selection, arrangement and storage of documents in safe places. The importance of this part of document life cycle management can be seen in the impact of historical events such as the destruction of books in ancient China and the burning of the library at Alexandria. Today, library and information science has evolved into an important academic discipline.

Bibliometrics: This aspect of document management involves functions of indexing, generating statistics and taxonomies, and improving the usability of large collections of documents. The modern history of this management technology dates back to Melvil Dewey and the Dewey Decimal System. Today, the science of bibliometrics is largely concerned with managing the impact of electronic technologies. This aspect must also deal with ISBN numbers, Library of Congress data and other standards.

Digital Content Management: The explosion of digital content has resulted in technologies to manage large collections of digital information generated by organizations. Such systems must manage access control and privileges, multiple electronic formats, interface with printing infrastructures and enable collaborative workflows around documents.

Digital-Physical Interaction Management: As long as both paper and digital documents continue to have value, the modern management technologies to manage their interaction will continue. Key to this management is the management of large scale and systematic scanning of physical documents (such as the Google book scanning project).

Destruction: With the increased cost of identity theft, corporate scandals and privacy concerns, the destruction of both paper and electronic documents has become increasingly important to manage. Technologies such as shredders play a role, as do verifiable processes of destruction of electronic documents to ensure compliance with privacy laws.

Security: Shannon's information theory has led to an entire discipline that concerns itself with the security of documents, and associated technologies such as encryption, as well as more physical security features such as watermarks and making currency documents safe from counterfeiting.

Transportation: The entire postal system, as well as modern courier systems, is largely built on the need to move documents physically from one location to the other.

The Document Economy

The economics of the production and management of documents indirectly impacts every economic sector. While the total economic value of the document economy is hard to estimate, the economic sectors with business models directly dependent on documents include:

Document Authoring Technology: This sector supports a huge variety of digital and physical production technologies, ranging from Microsoft Word to LaTeX to advanced layout software.

Education: The production and processing of documents is so critical that entire educational disciplines have evolved around writing, editing, layout and design of documents. The information sciences are also part of the document economy.

Electronic Document Management: Managing documents within organizations and in public and personal contexts supports a huge industry in content management systems, ranging from free public infrastructure such as wikipedia to proprietary enterprise applications such as Docushare and Documentum.

Physical Document Management: Large manufacturing sectors producing everything from 3-ring binders to filing cabinets and office desks exist largely due to the need to process documents.

Media: The paper industry exists to support the document economy.

Print Equipment: From lithography and xerography to pencils and crayons, an extra-ordinarily diverse set of equipment industries depend on documents.

Document Services: In large organizations, the life of documents in the work flows and processes of daily activity represent an enormous locus of value addition and cost reduction, which has led to a burgeoning industry in managed document services, ranging from specialized niches to managed office printing.

Retail Production: From large chains such as Kinko's in the United States to small copy shops and offset print shops, documents support a large production sector for the end user.

Publishing: All publishing, ranging from offset-based newspaper and magazine printing, to highly customized modern publishing using publish-on-demand digital print technology, is part of the document economy. The publishing industry includes major sub-areas such as the writer's market, small, medium and large publishing houses, small and large distributors and a vast network of independent and chain bookstores, online retailers, a large used-documents market and subscription-based markets.

Document Transportation: The international postal system, as well as the commercial package transportation systems represented by companies such as DHL and UPS has economic models based largely on the demand for document transportation.

Sources of Information

Sources of information are generally categorised as primary, secondary or tertiary depending on their originality and their proximity to the source or origin. For example, scientific information moves through a dissemination cycle. Initially, findings might be communicated informally by e-mail, and then presented at meetings before being formally published as a primary source. Once published, they will then be indexed in a bibliographic database, and repackaged and commented upon by others in secondary sources. The designations of primary, secondary and tertiary differ between disciplines or subjects, particularly between what can generally be defined as the sciences and the humanities. Primary sources for critic studying the literature of the Second World War are different from those for a research scientist investigating a new drug for arthritis. The critic's primary sources are the poems, stories, and films of the era. The research scientist's primary sources are the results of laboratory tests and the medical records of patients treated with the drug. You should always check with your lecturer or tutor if in doubt.

Primary Sources

There are a number of different definitions for primary, secondary and tertiary literature. These can vary according to academic discipline (i.e. science or humanities). These are original materials which have not been filtered through interpretation, condensation, or, often, even evaluation by a second party; for example journal articles, monographs, reports, patents, theses, diaries, letters, photographs, poems.

Some Definitions of Primary Sources

- Primary sources are original materials on which other research is based they are usually the first formal appearance of results in the print or electronic literature (for example, the first publication of the results of scientific investigations is a primary source).
- They present information in its original form, neither interpreted nor condensed nor evaluated by other writers.
- They are from the time period (for example, something written close to when what it is recording happened is likely to be a primary source).
- Primary sources present original thinking; report on discoveries, or share new information.

Some Examples of Primary Sources

- Scientific journal articles reporting experimental research results.
- Proceedings of Meetings, Conferences and Symposia.
- Technical reports.
- Dissertations or theses (may also be secondary).
- Patents.
- Sets of data, such as census statistics.
- Works of literature (such as poems and fiction).
- Diaries.
- Autobiographies.
- Interviews, surveys and fieldwork.
- Letters and correspondence.
- Speeches.
- Newspaper articles (may also be secondary).
- Government documents.
- Photographs and works of art.

- Original documents (such as birth certificate or trial transcripts).
- Internet communications on e-mail and newsgroups.

Secondary Sources

A secondary source is information about primary, or original, information, which usually has been modified, selected, or rearranged for a specific purpose or audience. It is not always easy to discern the difference between primary and secondary sources. Examples include biographies, histories, monographs, review articles, textbooks, and any index or bibliography used to locate primary sources.

Secondary sources are less easily defined than primary sources. What some define as a secondary source, others define as a tertiary source. Nor is it always easy to distinguish primary from secondary sources. A newspaper article is a primary source if it reports events, but a secondary source if it analyses and comments on those events. In science, secondary sources are those, which simplify the process of finding and evaluating the primary literature. They tend to be works, which repackage, reorganize, reinterpret, summarise, index or otherwise "add value" to the new information reported in the primary literature.

Some Definitions of Secondary Sources

- Describe, interpret, analyze and evaluate the primary sources
- Comment on and discuss the evidence provided by primary sources
- Secondary Sources are works, which are one or more steps, removed from the event or information they refer to, being written after the fact with the benefit of hindsight.

Some Examples of Secondary Sources

- Bibliographies (may also be tertiary)
- Biographical works
- Commentaries
- Dictionaries and encyclopedias (may also be tertiary)
- Dissertations or theses (more usually primary)
- Handbooks and data compilations (may also be tertiary)
- History
- Indexing and abstracting tools used to locate primary and secondary sources (may also be tertiary)
- Journal articles, particularly in disciplines other than science (may also be primary)
- Monographs (other than fiction and autobiography)
- Newspaper and popular magazine articles (may also be primary)
- Review articles and literature reviews
- Textbooks (may also be tertiary)
- Treatises works of criticism and interpretation

Tertiary Sources

These consist of information, which is a distillation and collection of primary and secondary sources. Twice removed from the original, they include encyclopedias, fact books and almanacs, guides and handbooks. Some secondary sources such as indexing and abstracting tools can also be considered tertiary sources. This is the most problematic category of all. Fortunately, you will rarely be expected to differentiate between secondary and tertiary sources.

Some Definitions of Tertiary Sources

- Works which list primary and secondary resources in a specific subject area.
- Works, which index, organize and compile citations to, and show you how to use, secondary (and sometimes primary) sources.
- Materials in which the information from secondary sources has been "digested" – reformatted and condensed, to put it into a convenient, easy-to-read form.
- Sources which are once removed in time from secondary sources.

Some Examples of Tertiary Sources

- Almanacs and fact books
- Bibliographies (may also be secondary)
- Chronologies
- Dictionaries and encyclopedias (may also be secondary)
- Directories
- Guidebooks, manuals etc.
- Handbooks and data compilations (may also be secondary)
- Indexing and abstracting tools used to locate primary and secondary sources (may also be secondary)
- Textbooks (may also be secondary).

Some examples of primary and secondary sources are:

Discipline	*Primary Source*	*Secondary Source*
Art	Original artwork	Article critiquing the piece of art
Engineering	Patent	Patents index
History	Explorer's diary	Book about exploration
Literature	Poem	Treatise on a particular genre of poetry
Science	Original journal article	Biological abstracts
Theatre	Videotape of a performance	Biography of a playwright

Evaluation

Once you have found Information Packages (Sources of Information) matching the topic and requirements of your teaching research, part of your Research Strategy should be to critically think about or evaluate these information sources. Just because a book, article, or Web document matches your search criteria and thus seems, at face value, to be relevant, does not mean that it is necessarily a reliable source of information.

It is important to remember that sources of information comprising the Library's print and electronic collections have already been evaluated for inclusion among the

Library's resources. This does not necessarily apply to sources of information on the Web for the general public. Many of us with Internet/Web accounts are potential publishers of Web documents, most of the content of which is published without editorial review.

Questions to Ask

What criteria should you use to judge information sources? The following questions should be asked when evaluating a source of information:

- Who is responsible for publishing the information provided by the source?
- What are the credentials and affiliation or sponsorship of any named individuals or organizations?
- How objective, reliable, and authoritative are they?
- Is the author or contact person listed with addresses (street, e-mail)?
- What can be said about the content, context, style, structure, completeness and accuracy of the information provided by the source? Are any conclusions offered?
- If so, based on what evidence and supported by what primary and secondary documentation? What is implied by the content?
- Are diverse perspectives represented? Is the content relevant to your information needs?
- When was the information provided by the source published?
- Is the information provided by the source in its original form or has it been revised?
- Is this information timely and is it updated regularly?
- Where else can the information provided by the source be found?
- Is this information authentic?
- Is this information unique or has it been copied?
- Why was the information provided by the source published?
- What are the perspectives, opinions, assumptions and biases of whoever is responsible for this information?
- Is anything being sold?
- Who is the intended audience?

Where to Look for Answers?

Books and Articles

An initial evaluation of books and articles can be done by examining their bibliographic citations provided in library catalogus or periodical indexes and databases, containing brief author, publisher and date of publication information. Once you have found the book or article, look for additional information about the author(s) or publisher. If little or no biographical information is provided about the author(s), ask a reference librarian for assistance.

Web Documents

Ideally, Web documents will include the following elements, which can be used in the evaluation process:

- Author or contact person with addresses (street, e-mail).
- Document Uniform Resource Locator (URL), including an institutional identifier (e.g., an edu with a URL identifies the sponsoring institution as an educational institution).
- Date of creation or revision.
- Link to sponsoring institution Website.

We live in an information age. The quantity of information available is so staggering that we cannot know everything about a subject. For example, it's estimated that anyone attempting to research and teaching what's known about depression would have to read over 100,000 studies on the subject. And there's the problem of trying to decide which studies have produced reliable results.

Similarly, for information on other topics, there's not only a huge quantity out there but also a very uneven level of quality. You don't want to rely on the news in the headlines of sensational tabloids near supermarket checkout counters, and it's just as hard to know how much to accept of what's in all the books, magazines, pamphlets, newspapers, journals, brochures, Websites, and various media reports that are available. People want to convince you to buy their products, agree with their opinions, rely on their data, vote for their candidate, consider their perspective, or accept them as experts. In short, you have to sift and make decisions all the time and you want to make responsible choices that you won't regret.

Evaluating sources is an important skill we need all the time. It's been called an art as well as work—much of which is detective work. You have to decide where to look, what clues to search for, and what to accept. You may be overwhelmed with too much information or too little. The temptation is to accept whatever you find. But don't be tempted. Learning how to evaluate effectively is a skill you need in our life.

Information and Communication Technology

What is IT?

Information Technology (IT) comprises the knowledge, skills and understanding needed to employ information and communications technologies appropriately, securely and fruitfully in learning, employment and everyday life. IT is to ICT as literacy is to books, journals or screen displays.

IT capability at school age includes:

- Understanding of how information is structured in a database;
- Skills in carrying out a search on the World Wide Web with sensitivity to meaning, accuracy of data and reliability of sources;
- Understanding of how computers can simulate real processes e.g. predator-prey relationships;
- Skills in using software e.g. word processing or e-mail to communicate effectively;
- Understanding that ICT can be used to control things;
- Knowledge of how to use ICT securely, with consideration of the feelings of other people, their rights to privacy and ownership of material.

Not all IT learning will involve the use of computers. For example, teachers might ask pupils to:

- Sort real objects into different categories as an introduction to databases;
- Read a piece of printed text in order to identify the key words that might characterise it and help to retrieve it electronically if necessary;
- Develop paper-based models and simulations of situations;
- Consider the use of font sizes and print effects in newspapers and magazines as part of their work with word processors;
- Give each other instructions as a way of teaching about precision and control;
- Compare the use of IT tools and software with other ways of undertaking a design, composition or analysis task."

Information Technology (IT), as defined by the Information Technology Association of America (ITAA), is "the study, design, development, implementation, support or management of computer-based information systems, particularly software applications and computer hardware." IT deals with the use of electronic computers and computer software to convert, store, protect, process, transmit, and securely retrieve information.

Today, the term information technology has ballooned to encompass many aspects of computing and technology, and the term is more recognizable than ever before. The information technology umbrella can be quite large, covering many fields. IT professionals perform a variety of duties that range from installing applications to designing complex computer networks and information databases. A few of the duties that IT professionals perform may include data management, networking, engineering computer hardware, database and software design, as well as the management and administration of entire systems.

When computer and communications technologies are combined, the result is information technology, or "InfoTech." Information Technology (IT) is a general term that describes any technology that helps to produce, manipulate, store, communicate, and/or disseminate information. Presumably, when speaking of Information Technology (IT) as a whole, it is noted that the use of computers and information are associated.

Definitions of Information Technology

- Includes all matters concerned with the furtherance of computer science and technology and with the design, development, installation, and...
- General term used to describe technologies that help produce, manipulate, store, communicate, or disseminate information.
- A term that encompasses all forms of technology used to create, store, exchange and use information in its various forms (data, voice conversations, still images, motion pictures, multimedia and other forms, including those not yet conceived).
- Includes all matters concerned with elctronic equipment that stores, sends, retrieves, or manages information. Includes computers, networks, electronic databases, CD-ROMs, laser discs, (IT) video cameras, tape-recorders, and fax machines.

What is ICT?

"Information and Communications Technologies (ICT) are the computing and communications facilities and features that variously support teaching, learning and a range of activities in education.

Such ICT-related activities include, for example, the use of:

- Broadcast material or CD-ROM as sources of information in history;
- Micro-computers with appropriate keyboards and other devices to teach literacy and writing;
- Keyboards, effects and sequencers in music teaching;
- Devices to facilitate communication for pupils with special needs;
- Electronic toys to develop spatial awareness and psycho-motor control;
- E-mail to support collaborative writing and sharing of resources;
- Video-conferencing to support the teaching of modern foreign languages;
- Internet-based research to support geographical enquiry;
- Integrated Learning Systems (ILS) to teach basic numeracy;
- Communications technology to exchange administrative and assessment data.

Information and Communications Technology—or technologies (ICT) is an umbrella term that includes all technologies for the manipulation and communication of information. The term is sometimes used in preference to Information Technology (IT), particularly in two communities: education and government.

Although, in the common usage it is often assumed that ICT is synonymous with IT; ICT in fact encompasses any medium to record information (magnetic disk/tape, optical disks (CD/DVD), flash memory etc. and arguably also paper records); technology for broadcasting information—radio, television; and technology for communicating through voice and sound or images—microphone, camera, loudspeaker, telephone to cellular phones. It includes the wide variety of computing hardware (PCs, servers, mainframes, networked storage); the rapidly developing personal hardware market comprising mobile phones, personal devices such as the Black Berry; MP3 players such as Apple's i Pod, and much more; the full gamut of application software from the smallest home-developed spreadsheet to the largest enterprise packages such as SAP and online software services such as salesforce.com; and the hardware and software needed to operate networks for transmission of information, again ranging from a home network to the largest global private networks operated by major commercial enterprises and, of course, the Internet. Thus, "ICT" makes more explicit that technologies such as broadcasting and wireless mobile telecommunications are included.

ICT capabilities vary widely from the sophistication of major western economies to lesser provision in the developing world. But the latter are catching up fast, often leapfrogging older generations of technology and developing new solutions that match their specific needs.

Concept of Information Communication Technology

Information science is "the science that investigates the properties and behaviours of information, the forces governing the flow of information, and the means of processing information for optimum accessibility and usability. The field is derived from those related to mathematics, logic, linguistic, psychology, computer technology, graphic arts, management and other fields." (R. Taylor in 1997 on libraries in post-industrial society, Oryx Press, Phoenix, AZ).

IT implies telecommunications involving a combination of computers, networks, satellites, telephones, radio, television and the like. IT resources involve not only hardware (equipment) but also software (programmes), people, education, government and association/collaboration resources. Application of IT to education involves many disciplines related to computers in handling, processing, management, automation and communication of information in the broader cultural and economic context of a society.

IT with reference to "technology in education" encompasses one or more of the following:

- Media and AV communication, e.g. Alternative instructional delivery systems such as Radio, ETV, etc.
- Vocational training tools, such as CBT (Computer Based Training), CAD (Computer-Aided Design), etc.;
- Computers and computer-based systems for instructional delivery and management, e.g. CAI (Computer Assisted Instruction) etc.
- Internet/web based education e.g. not only educational information with text, graphics, and video but also courses are offered by various websites.

While IT refers primarily to the components of media, computer tools and instructional uses of computer based systems, Instructional Technology lies at the core and in the starting point.

Besides education, there are a lot of subjects, which will be covered with adequate attention like Career Counselling, Employment News, Blind Friendly Programme, Adult Education, Women's Empowerment, Community Development, Rural Development, NGOs, Consumer Protection, Health Care, Sports and Mother & Child Care etc., which will help identify the Gyan Vani with the given area and the community. A good sample of folk song and music etc. will be given to make the programme format interesting and vivid in character.

Development

ICT can become a revolutionary vehicle in developing countries, provided technological innovations emerge on the following lines.

Local content in local languages the need of the hour is to enable the intelligentsia to develop information sources that are exclusively for fulfilling the needs of local communities. The content on the Internet that can fulfill these conditions is minuscule at present. Conditions have to emerge in which people are enthused to contribute towards the development of information databases that is exclusively disseminated through local networks, in languages/dialects that are popular in the region. The various modes of ICT may need to be integrated with one another, so that a meaningful volume of information can be generated in the minimum possible time.

Achievements

The Internet

The Internet has opened up many opportunities, from finding out information, conducting communications globally, e.g. through e-mail, voice mail, skype, e-commerce or generally just having fun through on line chats or instant messaging.

Teaching

PC—Internet based ICT is currently used within the English school curriculum. This kind of ICT (amongst others) is now seen as a core subject that is taught in some primary and secondary schools. The major advantage to this development is ICT has become a transferable subject. Computers or interactive whiteboards are now used across most school subjects as well as innovative schools using more technology like PDA's, Mobile (cell) phones and some games consoles. The interaction created by the use of this ICT makes lessons much more effective and allow children to learn in a way that they enjoy. Recent initiatives such as the One Laptop per Child programme are contributing to this development.

Communications

Apart from Internet a PC allows communication of information through Compact Discs, pen drives, printers, whether laser or inkjet, flash memory cards and exchange of information within a local network through LAN.

As communications scholars Gasher and Lorimer articulated "We depend on technology for our communications with others-whether they are just a house or two away or halfway around the world. In the second half of the twentieth century it became almost impossible to live without a television in our homes, much less without a telephone, and now we can hardly live without personal computers through which we gain Internet access and send and receive e-mail. The realty of new communications technology is that anyone is able to get in touch with anyone else, anywhere, at any time, for very little money-at least in the developed world." (Gasher and Lorimer, Communications Technology and Society: Theory and Practice).

Work Related Aspects

As well as benefiting school students to gather information for assignments, PC based ICT is often used in other jobs such as in the police, within libraries, in offices or even shops. It has also emerged as a source of employment in many emerging economies through Business process outsourcing or knowledge process outsourcing from companies in the developed world. People now have the chance to conduct remote logon, in which they can access their work computers (For example in an office) from home. This has opened up many more opportunities for those that struggle to find time to leave their house to go to work, so they can now just work from home.

Limitations

Previous information communication technologies have penetrated deep into the society and hence are often very cost effective; teachers in developing countries often use no more than a blackboard and chalk to pass on information about any subject to the students. Printed papers in the form of books, magazines or newspapers have become a part of daily routine of any educated citizen, as are broadcast media such as radio and television. The photocopy machine is widely used by students to access information from books they cannot afford to buy. The cost of a PC connected to the Internet is often prohibitive in developing countries. Power needs, physical space and connectivity issues are also factors that add to the challenge of getting these technologies to take root in developing countries.

Limitations of PC-Internet based ICT

Bandwidth

The time taken to access a particular piece of information on the Internet depends on the bandwidth available to the user at that time. Often, it takes several minutes, using an economical connection, to download a piece of information. Thus a user may have to spend substantial time before s/he finds the information s/he seeks.

Language

At present most of the information available on the Internet is in English, a limiting factor at the very least.

Text/Voice

Most information on the Internet requires action by the user as opposed to the passive nature of television and radio. As most of the Internet's information is textual, the user must be able to read it. Even more passive forms of Internet information such as video-sharing Websites require action (and reading) by the viewer for navigation.

Disruptive Software

Internet users are often susceptible to computer viruses. Commercial anti-virus software is often prohibitively priced. Thin client technology is a small, but growing alternative.

Participation

Social networks and increased user-managed information stores have emerged in the early part of this century. Increased interaction between the content (whether it be delivered via Internet, television or radio) is leading to an information revolution.

Security

Internet safety is an issue that impacts every online user from small children to International corporations. When ABC went into public service broadcasting online in the early 1990's, the safety of their users was its top priority. As ABC representatives state, "[the] relationship between liberty and security was crucial to the implementation of ABC Online interactive sites"<references*/*>. The Internet is an equalizer in that every user is vulnerable and in a sense, all at the same level.

The emergence of web logs, Internet forums and wikis is often grouped under the new technology umbrella term Web 2.0, and has helped to usher in a greater level of global participation.

New ICT with Education

- ICT's have become a driving force of educational reform and they are an integrated part of national educational policies and plans.
- The introduction of ICTs in schools has brought about a more positive attitude to school among learners.
- Online classrooms tend to be more successful if ICT is combined with appropriate pedagogy. The interactive feature of learning resources enable learner to become increasingly engaged in the construction of content and thus contribute to a more authentic learning situation.
- ICTs open a whole world of lifelong upgrading through distance education, asynchronous learning and training on demand. (Distance education is now being delivered in two different ways, namely: Synchronous mode:—participants are using ICTs to communicate.
- Asynchronous mode:—participants are learning/communicating independently.)
- ICTs altering the functions of libraries and are intrinsically change the roles of libraries.
- ICTs help to break the professional isolation from which t\many teachers suffer. With ICT they can easily connect with other professionals, colleagues, and mentors, with universities and centers of expertise and with sources of teaching materials.
- ICTs are used at all stages of Problem Based Learning process to add value to student learning in ways that are not possible in a non-digital environment.
- The term ICT embraces a range of technologies broadly concerned with information and communication. The popular idea of ICT hardware in the classroom or computer suite includes one or more multimedia desktop computers or laptops and a combination of the following; digital camera, printer, scanner, CD writer, data projectors, interactive white board, robot and in science classrooms, data loggers and perhaps digital microscope.
- ICT can support both the investigative (skills and attitudes) and more knowledge based aspects (concepts).
- ICT use can greatly enhance the opportunities for children to engage in effective communication at several levels.
- ICT can improve training by providing access to better educational resources; breaking the traditional isolation of teachers; and enabling individualized training opportunities.
- E-Learning provides a way for teachers to gain new knowledge and skills.
- The ease of access of information source develops the research spirit.
- Broader co-operation among individual within and beyond school is enabled through technologies.
- The availability of simulation, virtual-manipulation, graphic representation and rapid merging of data contributes to linkage in knowledge and leads to more integrated and g\better assimilated learning.

- Teacher gain information o new instructional resources and availability of support for their use much more readily with ICT.
- Teacher co-operation with others both within and beyond the school when planning activities.
- The orientation of planning is more towards students performing real works in co-operation with other students.
- Relationship between teachers and students more interactive and guiding rather than transferring information from teacher to student.
- A different vision of teaching and learning; learning seen more as continuous research than body of facts.
- Empowering learners to engage in meaningful challenging and enlightening tasks is the aim of all educators and ICT has a powerful role to play in this in every school, classrooms and beyond.
- The anytime anywhere access to information sources enables students to engage directly with expert sources when they are needed and the sight, sound, touch experience becomes a powerful motivation in learning.
- Today's classrooms need Internet access for research-distributed multimedia, curriculum on-line, access to digital libraries, distance education courses and remote collaboration tools.
- Information on demand for students also includes video, live- video broadcast, desktop video conferencing and 3D modeling.

Let's focus on the three words behind ICT:

- Information.
- Communications.
- Technology.

A good way to think about ICT is to consider all the uses of digital technology that already exist to help individuals, businesses and organization's use information.

ICT covers any product that will store, retrieve, manipulate, transmits or receives information electronically in a digital form. For example personal computers, digital television, e-mail and robots.

So ICT is concerned with the storage, retrieval, manipulation, transmission or receipt of digital data. Importantly, it is also concerned with the way these different uses can work with each other.

In business, ICT is often categorized into two broad types of product:

1. The traditional computer-based technologies (things you can typically do on a personal computer or using computers at home or at work); and
2. The more recent and fast growing range of digital communication technologies (which allow people and organizations to communicate and share information digitally).

Let's take a brief look at these two categories to demonstrate the kinds of products and ideas that are covered by ICT:

Standard Office Applications—Main Examples

Application	*Use*
Word Processing	E.g. Microsoft Word: Write letters, reports etc.
Spreadsheets	E.g. Microsoft Excel; Analyse financial information; calculations; create forecasting models etc.
Database Software	E.g. Oracle, Microsoft SQL Server, Access; Managing data in many forms, from basic lists (e.g. customer contacts through to complex material (e.g. catalogue).
Presentation Software	E.g. Microsoft PowerPoint; make presentations, either directly using a computer screen or data projector. Publish in digital format via e-mail or over the Internet.
Desktop Publishing	E.g. Adobe In design, Quark Express, Microsoft Publisher; produce newsletters, magazines and other complex documents.
Graphics Software	E.g. Adobe Photoshop and Illustrator; Macromedia Freehand and Fireworks; create and edit images such as logos, drawings or pictures for use in DTP, websites or other publications.

Specialist Applications—Examples

Application	*Use*
Accounting Package	E.g. Sage, Oracle; Manage an organization's accounts including revenues/ sales, purchases, bank accounts etc. A wide range of systems is available ranging from basic packages suitable for small businesses through to sophisticated ones aimed at multinational companies.
Computer Aided Design	Computer Aided Design (CAD) is the use of computers to assist the design process. Specialized CAD programmes exist for many types of design: architectural, engineering, electronics, roadways.
Customer Relations Management (CRM)	Software that allows businesses to better understand their customers by collecting and analysing data on them such as their product preferences, buying habits etc. Often linked to software applications that run call centers and loyalty cards for example.

Traditional Computer Based Technologies

The C part of ICT refers to the communication of data by electronic means, usually over some distance. This is often achieved via networks of sending and receiving equipment, wires and satellite links.

The technologies involved in communication tend to be complex. You certainly don't need to understand them for your ICT course. However, there are aspects of digital communications that you need to be aware of. These relate primarily to the types of network and the ways of connecting to the Internet. Let's look at these two briefly (further revision notes provide much more detail to support your study).

Internal Networks

Usually referred to as a Local Area Network (LAN), this involves linking a number of hardware items (input and output devices plus computer processing) together within an office or building.

The aim of a LAN is to be able to share hardware facilities such as printers or scanners, software applications and data. This type of network is invaluable in the office environment where colleagues need to have access to common data or programmes.

External Networks

Often you need to communicate with someone outside your internal network; in this case you will need to be part of a Wide Area Network (WAN). The Internet is the ultimate WAN—it is a vast network of networks.

ICT in a Broader Context

Your ICT course will almost certainly cover the above examples of ICT in action, perhaps focusing on the use of key applications such as spreadsheets, databases, presentation, graphics and web design software. It will also consider the following important topics that deal with the way ICT is used and managed in an organization:

The nature of information (the "I" in ICT); this covers topics such as the meaning and value of information; how information is controlled; the limitations of ICT; legal considerations.

Management of information—this covers how data is captured, verified and stored for effective use; the manipulation, processing and distribution of information; keeping information secure; designing networks to share information.

Information systems strategy—this considers how ICT can be used within a business or organizationas part of achieving goals and objectives.

As you can see, ICT is a broad and fast-changing subject. We hope our free study materials (revision notes, quizzes, presentations etc.) will help you master IT. Most businesses have now moved from manual methods to the use of ICT for processing data.

Advantages of the New ICT

- Processing of data is much faster on a computer.
  Example: Calculating an annual budget on a spreadsheet is instantaneous; doing the calculations by hand would take some time.
- Repetitive processing can be better done using computerized machinery.
  Example: Humans get tired, lose concentration and generally fed up if they have to repeat the same task over and over again. Robotic machinery will perform the same task repeatedly with consistent quality and never need a break, or software programmes can be written to process all the records in a database.
- Searching for data is much faster.
  Example: Finding a patient's record in a doctor's surgery can be done in seconds on a computerized database system, whereas it would take a receptionist some minutes to locate a folder in a paper filing system.
- Data storage capacity is almost limitless in a computer system.
  Example: Large quantities of data can be stored on hard discs or media such as CDs or DVDs instead of needing enormous quantities of paper and many large filing cabinets.
- Data communications are fast and accurate. Data transmitted over a network

will arrive at its destination anywhere in the world in just a few seconds. *Example:* A computer user can place an order for an item on an Internet website and it will be received immediately—posting an order in the mail would take a day or two to arrive.

- Data can be output on a computer in a variety of different formats. *Example:* Annual sales figures for a retail business can be printed as a spreadsheet, displayed as a graph, or as a multimedia presentation involving text, sound, graphics and animations.

4

Communication

Communication is the process of conveying information from a sender to a receiver with the use of a *medium* in which the communicated information is understood by both sender and receiver. It is a process that allows organisms to exchange information by several methods. Communication requires that all parties understand a common *language* that is exchanged. There are *auditory* means, such as speaking, singing and sometimes tone of voice, and nonverbal, physical means, such as *body language, sign language, paralanguage, touch, eye contact,* or the use of *writing*. Communication is defined as a process by which we assign and *convey* meaning in an attempt to create shared understanding. This process requires a vast repertoire of skills in *intrapersonal* and *interpersonal* processing, listening, observing, speaking, questioning, analyzing, and evaluating. Use of these processes is developmental and transfers to all areas of life: home, school, community, work, and beyond. It is through communication that *collaboration* and *cooperation* occur. Communication is the articulation of sending a message, through different media whether it be verbal or nonverbal, so long as a being *transmits* a thought provoking idea, gesture, action, etc.

Definitions

Communication is defined as:

- The exchange of thoughts, messages, or information, as by speech, signals, writing, or behaviour.
- Interpersonal rapport.
- The art and technique of using words effectively to impart information or ideas.
- The field of study concerned with the transmission of information by various means, such as print or broadcasting.
- Any of various professions involved with the transmission of information, such as advertising, broadcasting, or journalism.
- Something communicated; a message.

Communication happens at many levels (even for one single action), in many different ways, and for most beings, as well as certain machines. Several, if not all, fields of study dedicate a portion of attention to communication, so when speaking about communication it is very important to be sure about what aspects of communication one is speaking about. Definitions of communication range widely, some recognizing that animals can communicate with each other as well as human beings, and some are narrower, only including human beings within the parameters of human symbolic interaction.

Nonetheless, communication is usually described along a few major dimensions: Content (what type of things are communicated), source, emission, sender or *encoder* (by whom), form (in which form), channel (through which medium), destination, receiver, target or *decoder* (to whom), and the purpose or pragmatic aspect. Between parties, communication includes acts that confer knowledge and experiences, give advice and commands, and ask questions. These acts may take many forms, in one of the various manners of communication. The form depends on the abilities of the group communicating. Together, communication content and form make *messages* that are sent towards a *destination.* The target can be oneself, another *person* or being, another entity (such as a corporation or group of beings).

Communication can be seen as processes of *information transmission* governed by three levels of *semiotic* rules:

- Syntactic (formal properties of signs and symbols),
- Pragmatic (concerned with the relations between signs/expressions and their users) and
- Semantic (study of relationships between signs and symbols and what they represent).

Therefore, communication is social interaction where at least two interacting agents share a common set of signs and a common set of *semiotic* rules. This commonly held rule in some sense ignores autocommunication, including intrapersonal communication via diaries or self-talks.

Types of Communication

Interpersonal Communication

Communication between a minimum of two parties in which meaningful exchange is intended with the sender trying to effect a response from a person or group. People for whom it was not intended or both may receive by the person for whom it was intended or the message. The message may be distorted during transmission so that the recipient does not perceive the sender's intentions and the intended effect are not achieved. Effective interpersonal communication is essential for successful relationships between coach and athletes.

Intrapersonal Communication

Communication a person has with him or herself (e.g. self-talk). In coaching, it is generally less important than interpersonal communication.

Non-verbal Communication

Forms of communication, such as smiling and frowning, patting on the back and blowing on a whistle, which convey ideas, feelings, and attitudes without using words. Experimental evidence shows that non-verbal communication can be a very important source of motivation.

Communication Cycle

Communication is a fundamental part of all of our lives. There are many different methods of communication and we are gaining more and more all the time. Communication ranges from a note stuck on the fridge door, to video conferencing and phoning. The communication cycle is a structure that was thought up about how we communicate.

It suggests that we 'Aim' what we want to say, how we'll say it, what we want the other person to do with the information. This is the stage in which we think particularly about how we will communicate the information and to who we wish to communicate with. Once we have organized what we want to say, who to say it to and how to say it, we have to consider social influences and other things that may 'change' what we want to say. This is the 'Encoding' stage. We have to consider what language to say it in, what we assume of the receiver and are these assumptions correct? Their assumptions may hinder and change what we say. The next stage is vital in successful communication. This stage is the 'Transmission' stage. We need to be able to transmit the message that we wish to communicate in right format and at the correct time. We need to consider if there will be any distractions to hinder our communication attempt, if we need to summarize and if we can add anything to increase the clarity of what we are trying to say. When we receive the information from someone, if they are speaking, we must take into account that we think 3 times faster than we speak, and therefore, it is much easier for a speaker's words to get muddled up with other thcughts and distractions. Reactions and questions must not happen until after the speaker has finished with what they were saying. This stage is called 'Receiving.'

The next stage in the Communication Cycle is called 'Decoding'. This is the opposite of encoding. If the Sender has transmitted the information correctly and has given enough attention to what they are saying, including their body language and tone of voice, then you should be able to decode their message effectively. We may sometimes feel that some Senders are not approachable in certain circumstances, but we must

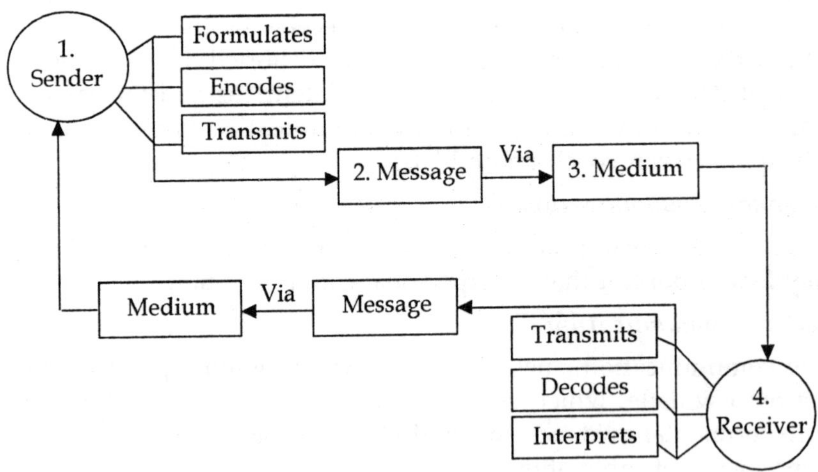

remember, the meaning of the message is the responsibility of the Sender and not the Receiver. The last stage in the Communication Cycle is 'Responding.' This gives the Receiver the chance to ask any questions and this also gives the Sender the chance to realize if they have missed out any stages in the Communication Cycle.

Communication Networks

Communication networks based on serial data transmission are the platform of up-to-date automation systems. Whether this is office automation or automation of manufacturing or process plants, the task remains always the same, exchanging data between different devices or participants within a system. Communication networks provide a number of advantages over systems in which a point-to-point line enables only two participants to communicate with each other.

Classification of Communication Networks

LANs are typically used to connect a set of hosts within the same building (e.g., an office environment) or a set of closely located buildings (e.g., a university campus). For larger distances, the network is said to be a Metropolitan Area Network (MAN) or a Wide Area Network (WAN). MANs cover distances of up to a few hundred kilometers and are used for interconnecting hosts spread across a city. WANs are used to connect hosts spread across a country, a continent, or the globe. LANs, MANs, and WANs usually coexist: closely located hosts are connected by LANs which can access hosts in other remote LANs via MANs and WANs.

Most networks are for the private use of the organizations to which they belong; these are called private networks. Networks maintained by banks, insurance companies, airlines, hospitals, and most other businesses are of this nature. Public networks, on the other hand, are generally accessible to the average user, but may require registration and payment of connection fees.

Internet is the most-widely known example of a public network. Technically, both private and public networks may be of LAN, MAN, or WAN type, although public networks, by their size and nature, tend to WANs. Point-to-point broadcast Depending on the application, i.e. manufacturing, process, office or building automation, the communication tasks to be performed vary in complexity and are sometimes even contradictory. The use of only one communication network would therefore not yield optimum results. So the market offers very different networks and bus systems that are more or less tailored to a specific application.

A quite general classification criterion is the distance over which communication takes place. There are local networks, LANs (Local Area Networks), as well as widely distributed networks, WANs (Wide Area Networks) with LAN, emphasis is put on fast and powerful data exchange within a locally restricted area, whereas WAN must be able to transmit data on very different data media and over several thousand kilometers.

The Internet is an example for a wide area network. This network is a world wide group of greatly varying communication networks which in turn can comprise many sub networks. Due to the increasing connection of LANs to the Internet, data, which was only locally available, is now available at any place in the world. Latest developments enable plants using field bus communication to be remotely monitored and operated via commercially available Internet browsers.

Demands on communication networks differ not only in the varying distance to be covered. Depending on the application, they also vary as to:

- Required data rate,
- Number of data bytes per communication cycle,
- Renewal rate of the data,
- Required real-time capability, and others.

To obtain a practice-oriented classification, the communication networks are assigned to different hierarchical or application levels, which form a communication pyramid with three, sometimes four, levels. At the bottom level, the number of participants, the required real-time capability as well as the message renewal rate is high. The higher the hierarchical level, the lower the number of participants. Requirements concerning real time and sampling rate are also lower. However, the complexity and the length of the message telegrams are increasing.

Network Topologies

The network topology describes the physical arrangement of the participants in relation to each other within a network. The term also describes the logical arrangement of the participants in relation to each other during communication, which is not necessarily the same as the physical arrangement. For the connection of more than two participants, very different networking structures are possible.

Mesh Topology

The most complex method is to create a mesh connecting all the participants with each other via separate communication lines. When it comes to network extensions, the flexibility is very low and the amount of hardware required is so high that this topology is rarely used in practice.

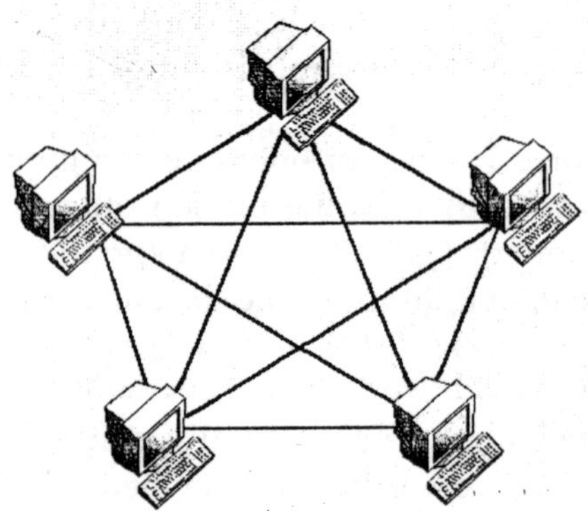

Line or Bus

A much clearer and simpler structure is the line or bus topology. In this case, all participants communicate over the same line and are connected via short stub lines so that each participant requires only one interface to the bus. Since all participants can see a transmitted message, broadcasting or multicasting of messages can be easily done. A special bus access control unit, which is usually able to maintain the functions of the bus-operated system even if one station happens to fail, controls the common transmission medium.

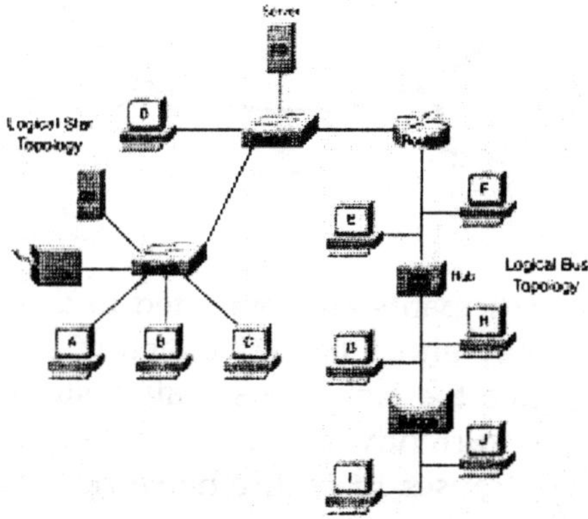

Tree Topology

The tree topology is in most respects similar to the bus topology, except that the tree structure enables several bus branches to be connected in so-called nodes. This topology makes it easier to network larger areas. As is the case for the bus structure, the maximum line lengths and the number of participants connected without line amplifiers (repeaters) are limited.

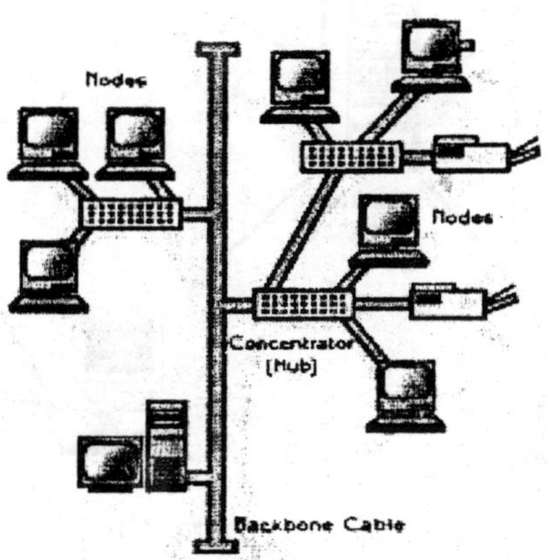

Ring Topology

When several two-point connections are used to create a physical ring, we speak of a ring topology. A transmitted message is forwarded from one participant to the next. As the signal can be amplified whenever it is forwarded, very long distances can be covered. Unfortunately, the transmission speed depends on the number and the processing speed of the participants. This means that the failure of a single participant can lead to network failure when no extra ring is provided.

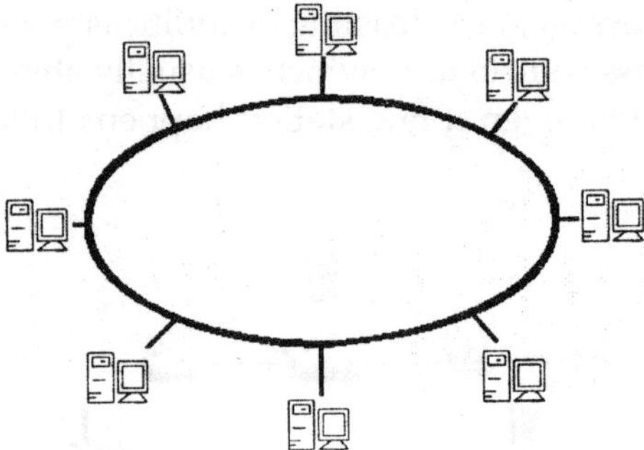

Star Topology

In the star topology, all participants are connected to a center station via two point lines. The center station may either be active, acting as a master for the network control, or passive or assume the task of a so-called star coupler, which establishes the connection between the currently active transmitter and recipient. In both cases, failure of the center station causes the entire network communication to fail.

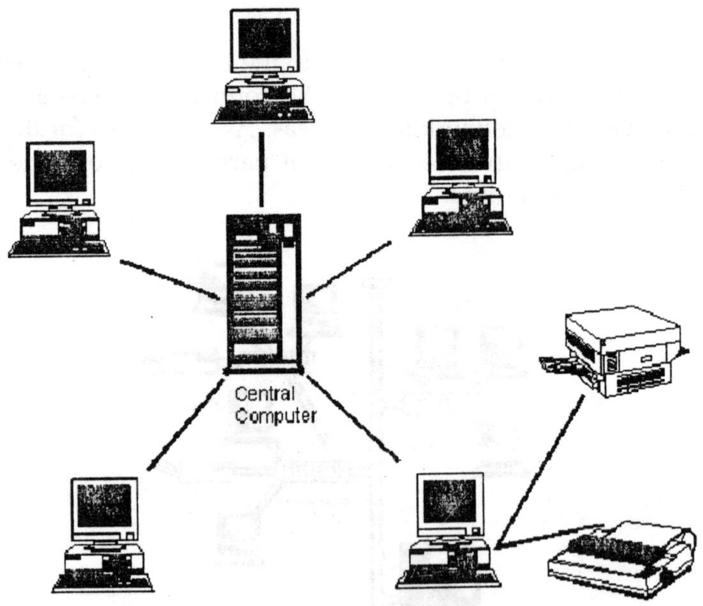

The topologies described above form the basis of almost every serial communication network. However, a lot of network specifications allow the use of free topologies or mixed structures so that line and tree topologies or tree and star topologies can be combined. To ensure compliance with the electrical specifications of the transmission medium, a coupler, amplifier or distributor (repeater, hub, etc.), as required, must be provided at the connection node.

Complex network structures often consist of several, partly autonomous, sub networks. Each sub network can be based on a different topology and a different communications protocol. In any case, each participant must be able to clearly identify any of his communication partners and address him directly. In addition to this, any of the communication participants must be able to access the transmission medium. The way in which the transmission lines are assigned to the various participants is determined by the protocol specification, which defines the access method.

Communication Channel

Charwat defines communication channel as follows:

"In general, a communication channel is a connection between one sending source and one receiving sink. In the human body the sense organs, the nerve tracts, the cerebrum, and the muscles form a communication channel. In case of competing sensations at different sense organs there is one channel preferred.

There is no total independence between the communication channels. For example: the capacity of received information coded with combined visual and auditive signals does not reach the sum of the single channels' capacities."

Channel, in communications (sometimes called communications channel), refers to the medium used to convey information from a sender (or transmitter) to a receiver.

A Channel can take many forms. Examples of communications channels are:

- A connection between initiating and terminating nodes of a *circuit.*
- A buffer from which messages can be put and gotten. See Actor model and process calculi for discussion on the use of channels.
- A single path provided by a transmission medium via either
  (a) physical separation, such as by multi pair cable or
  (b) Electrical separation, such as by frequency-or time-division multiplexing.
- A path for conveying electrical or electromagnetic signals, usually distinguished from other parallel paths.
- The portion of a storage medium, such as a track or a band, that is accessible to a given reading or writing station or head.
- In a communications system, the part that connects a data source to a data sinks.

Communication can be split into two parts—the message or content, and the channel it's transmitted on. For example, you may want to communicate something about your emotional state—let's say that you are angry. You can communicate that over a number of channels. You could write a letter. You could send e-mail. You could communicate it non-verbally or para-verbally. You could send a tape recording of your ranting about why you are angry. Those are all different channels.

Key Elements in Choosing the Channels of Communication

Three elements are essential in choosing which media is best for transmitting message.

Know Your Target Audience

Each country is culturally unique and often there are diverse cultures in a single country. Be aware of each culture's particular values and behavioural traits. Also, identify your target audience's age group, gender, socio-economic background, and literacy rate. Finally, find out which newspapers they read which TV and radio programmes are popular, and which religious groups, agencies, recreation centers, and businesses serve the community. Also determine the number of people you intend to reach.

Know Your Message

Choosing the right media also depends on what message you are trying to relay. Is the message intended to raise awareness about an issue or change attitudes and behaviour? If the message is intended to change behaviour, for example getting young children to wash their hands, perhaps interpersonal channels such as community workshops or posters in schools may be better than a television or newspaper campaign. Consider which channel best suits the message.

Know Your Country's Media

Find out how many television and radio stations there are, along with how many people are watching and listening. Find out how many newspapers there are and how many subscribers those newspapers have. These channels of communication are often the most effective method in getting a message out, so remember to consider all options when creating a health campaign. It is also helpful to keep in mind that mass media, such as television, radio, newspapers, magazines, billboards and the Internet, are good at reaching people quickly, but are less personal so may not be as effective in some campaigns as interpersonal communication. Sometimes peer counselling or group workshops are more effective because they provide an opportunity for clarification or feedback.

Studying your target audience, your message and your available media will help you decide which channels to choose.

Barriers of Communication

Many people think that communicating is easy. It is after all something we've done all our lives. There is some truth in this simplistic view. Communicating is straightforward. What makes it complex, difficult, and frustrating are the barriers we put in the way. Here are the 7 top barriers.

Physical Barriers

Physical barriers in the workplace include:

- Marked out territories, empires and fiefdoms into which strangers are not allowed.
- Closed office doors, barrier screens, separate areas for people of different status.
- Large working areas or working in one unit that is physically separates from others.

Research shows that one of the most important factors in building cohesive teams is proximity. As long as people still have a personal space that they can call their own, nearness to others aids communication because it helps us get to know one another.

Perceptual Barriers

The problem with communicating with others is that we all see the world differently. If we didn't, we would have no need to communicate: something like extrasensory perception would take its place.

Emotional Barriers

One of the chief barriers to open and free communications is the emotional barrier. It is comprised mainly of fear, mistrust and suspicion. The roots of our emotional mistrust of others lie in our childhood and infancy when we were taught to be careful what we said to others.

Some caution may be wise in certain relationships; excessive fear of what others might think of us can stunt our development as effective communicators and our ability to form meaningful relationships.

Cultural Barriers

When we join a group and wish to remain in it, sooner or later we need to adopt the behaviour patterns of the group. These are the behaviours that the group accepts as signs of belonging.

The group rewards such behaviour through acts of recognition, approval and inclusion. In groups, which are happy to accept you and where you are happy to conform, there is a mutuality of interest and a high level of win-win contact.

Where, however, there are barriers to your membership of a group, a high level of game playing replaces good communication.

Language Barriers

Language that describes what we want to say in our terms may present barriers to others who are not familiar with our expressions, buzzwords and jargon. When we couch our communication in such language, it is a way of excluding others. In a global market place the greatest compliment we can pay another person is to talk in their language.

Gender Barriers

There are distinct differences between the speech patterns in a man and those in a woman. A woman speaks between 22,000 and 25,000 words a day whereas a man speaks between 7,000 and 10,000. In childhood, girls speak earlier than boys and at the age of three, have a vocabulary twice that of boys.

The reason for this lies in the wiring of a man's and woman's brains. When a man talks, his speech is located in the left side of the brain but in no specific area. When a woman talks, the speech is located in both hemispheres and in two specific locations.

This means that a man talks in a linear, logical and compartmentalised way, features of left-brain thinking; whereas a woman talks more freely mixing logic and emotion, features of both sides of the brain. It also explains why women talk for much longer than men each day.

Interpersonal Barriers

There are six levels at which people can distance themselves from one another:

1. Withdrawal is an absence of interpersonal contact. It is both refusals to be in touch and time alone.
2. Rituals are meaningless, repetitive routines devoid of real contact.
3. Pastimes fill up time with others in social but superficial activities.

4. Working activities are those tasks, which follow the rules and procedures of contact but no more.
5. Games are subtle, manipulative interactions, which are about winning, and losing.
6. Closeness is the aim of interpersonal contact where there is a high level of honesty and acceptance of yourself and others.

Working on improving your communications is a broad-brush activity. You have to change your thoughts, your feelings, and your physical connections. That way, you can break down the barriers that get in your way and start building relationships that really work. No matter how good and effective a communicator one may be, yet the fact is that one does face certain barriers, from time to time, which forces them to work on becoming even more effective in their skills to communicate. Given here are the communication barriers that occur while listening, speaking and in the case of non-verbal communications.

Listening Barriers

Interrupting the speaker Not maintaining eye contact with the speaker Rushing the speaker to complete what he/she has to say Making the speaker feel as though he/she is wasting the listener's time Being distracted by something that is not part of the on going communication Getting ahead of the speaker and completing his /her thoughts Ignoring the speaker's requests Topping the speaker's story with one's own set of examples Forgetting what is being discussed Asking too many questions, for they sake of probing.

Barriers While Speaking

Unclear messages lack of consistency in the communication process incomplete sentences not understanding the receiver not seeking clarifications while communicating.

Other Common Barriers to Effective Communication

Use of Negative Words

An individual's subjective viewpoint towards the issues/people, which leads to some assumptions. An emotional block, which can lead to an attitude of indifference, suspicion or hostility towards the subject. An emotional block or bias that is based on a third party's viewpoint or on what you have read/heard. Words can have different meanings to different people, thus blocking communication. Use of negative words.

Muddled Messages

Effective communication starts with a clear message. Muddled messages are a barrier to communication because the sender leaves the receiver unclear about the intent of the sender. Muddled messages have many causes. The sender may be confused in his or her thinking. The message may be little more than a vague idea. The problem may be semantics. Feedback from the receiver is the best way for a sender to be sure that the message is clear rather than muddled. Clarifying muddled messages is the responsibility of the sender. The sender hoping the receiver will figure out the message does little to remove this barrier to communication.

Stereotyping

Stereotyping causes us to typify a person, a group, an event or a thing on oversimplified conceptions, beliefs, or opinions. Thus, basketball players can be stereotyped as tall, green equipment as better than red equipment, football linemen as dumb, Ford as better than Chevrolet, Vikings as handsome, and people raised on dairy farms as interested in animals. Stereotyping can substitute for thinking, analysis and open mindedness to a new situation. Stereotyping is a barrier to communication when it causes people to act as if they already know the message that is coming from the sender or worse, as if no message is necessary because "everybody already knows." Both senders and listeners should continuously look for and address thinking, conclusions and actions based on stereotypes.

Wrong Channel

A long conversation between a pork producer and a contractor about the farrowing house construction, with neither taking notes, surely will result in confusion and misunderstanding. Variation of channels helps the receiver understand the nature and importance of a message. Using a training video on cleaning practices helps new employees grasp the importance placed on herd health. A written disciplinary warning for tardiness emphasizes to the employee that the problem is serious. Simple rules for selection of a channel cause more problems than they solve. In choice of a channel, the sender needs to be sensitive to such things as the complexity of the message (good morning versus a construction contract); the consequences of a misunderstanding (medication for a sick animal versus a guess about tomorrow's weather); knowledge, skills and abilities of the receiver and immediacy of action to be taken from the message

Language

Words are not reality. Words as the sender understands them are combined with the perceptions of those words by the receiver. Language represents only part of the whole. We fill in the rest with perceptions. Trying to understand a foreign language easily demonstrates words not being reality.

Lack of Feedback

Feedback is the mirror of communication. Feedback mirrors what the sender has sent. Feedback is the receiver sending back to the sender the message as perceived. Without feedback, communication is one-way.

Feedback happens in a variety of ways. Asking a person to repeat what has been said, e.g., repeats instructions, is a very direct way of getting feedback. Both sender and receiver can play an active role in using feedback to make communication truly two-way.

Feedback should be helpful rather than hurtful. Prompt feedback is more effective that feedback saved up until the "right" moment. Feedback should deal in specifics rather than generalities. Approaches to feedback are as a problem in perception rather than a problem of discovering the facts.

Poor Listening Skills

Listening is difficult. A typical speaker says about 125 words per minute. The typical listener can receive 400-600 words per minute. Thus, about 75 per cent of listening time is free time. The free time often sidetracks the listener. The solution is to be an active rather than passive listener.

Interruptions

The interruptions may be due to something more pressing, rudeness, lack of privacy for discussion, a drop-in visitor, an emergency, or even the curiosity of someone else wanting to know what two other people are saying. Regardless of the cause, interruptions are a barrier to communication. In the extreme, there is a reluctance of employees and family members even to attempt discussion with a manager because of the near certainty that the conversation will be interrupted. Less extreme but serious is the problem of incomplete instructions because someone came by with a pressing question.

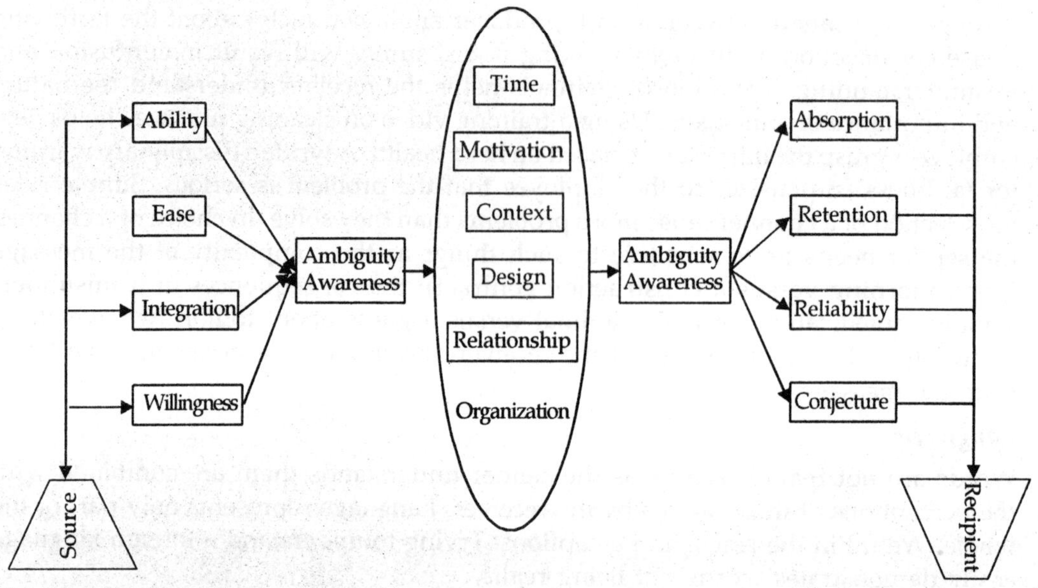

Physical Distractions

Physical distractions are the physical things that get in the way of communication. Examples of such things include the telephone, a pick-up truck door, a desk, an uncomfortable meeting place, and noise.

Noise is a physical distraction simply because it is hard to concentrate on a conversation if hearing is difficult. Facilitating Communication in addition to removal of specific barriers to communication, the following general guidelines may also facilitate communication.

- Have a positive attitude about communication. Defensiveness interferes with communication.
- Work at improving communication skills. It takes knowledge and work. The

communication model and discussion of barriers to communication provide the necessary knowledge. This increased awareness of the potential for improving communication is the first step to better communication.

- Include communication as a skill to be evaluated along with all the other skills in each person's job description. Help other people improve their communication skills by helping them understand their communication problems.
- Make communication goal oriented. Relational goals come first and pave the way for other goals. When the sender and receiver have a good relationship, they are much more likely to accomplish their communication goals.
- Approach communication as a creative process rather than simply part of the chore of working with people. Experiment with communication alternatives. What works with one person may not work well with another person. Vary channels, listening techniques, and feedback techniques.
- Accept the reality of miscommunication. The best communicators fail to have perfect communication. They accept miscommunication and work to minimize its negative impacts.

No matter how good the communication system in an organisation is, unfortunately barriers can and do often occur. This may be caused by a number of factors, which can usually be summarised as being due to physical barriers, system design faults or additional barriers.

Physical barriers are often due to the nature of the environment. For example, the natural barrier which exists, if staff are located in different buildings or on different sites. Likewise, poor or outdated equipment, particularly the failure of management to introduce new technology, may also cause problems. Staff shortages are another factor, which frequently causes communication difficulties for an organisation. Whilst distractions like background noise, poor lighting or an environment, which is too hot or cold, can all affect people's morale and concentration, which in turn interfere with effective communication. System design faults refer to problems with the structures or systems in place in an organisation. Examples might include an organisational structure, which is unclear and therefore makes it confusing to know who to communicate with.

Other examples could be inefficient or inappropriate information systems, a lack of supervision or training, and a lack of clarity in roles and responsibilities which can lead to staff being uncertain about what is expected of them. Attitudinal barriers come about as a result of problems with staff in an organisation. These may be brought about, for example, by such factors as poor management, lack of consultation with employees, personality conflicts which can result in people delaying or refusing to communicate, the personal attitudes of individual employees which may be due to lack of motivation or dissatisfaction at work, brought about by insufficient training to enable them to carry out particular tasks, or just resistance to change due to entrenched attitudes and ideas.

Different languages and cultures represent a national barrier, which is particularly important for organisations involved in overseas business.

Individual linguistic ability is also important. The use of difficult or inappropriate words in communication can prevent people from understanding the message. Poorly explained or misunderstood messages can also result in confusion. We can all think of situations where we have listened to something explained which we just could not grasp.

Psychological Factors

Psychological factors such as people's state of mind influence communication process. We all tend to feel happier and more receptive to information when the sun shines. Equally, if someone has personal problems like worries about their health or marriage, then this will probably affect them.

Physiological barriers may result from individuals' personal discomfort, caused, for example, by ill health, poor eyesight or hearing difficulties Presentation of information is also important to aid understanding.

Overcoming Barriers to Communication

Communication plays a major role in employer-employee relationships on farms. It also affects the relationships among family members on the management team. Although effective communication does not guarantee success of a farm business, its absence usually assures problems. A communication problem may soon become a crisis or it may linger on for years. More specifically, communication influences the effectiveness of the hiring and training of employees, motivation of employees, providing daily instructions, performance evaluations and the handling of discipline problems. These are the obvious roles of communication. Communication also affects the willingness of employees to provide useful suggestions. Removing barriers to communication is one of the easiest ways to improve communication. Removing these barriers starts with an understanding of a communication model. This chapter should help managers think about their own communication skills and the way they communicate day-to-day back home.

5

Educational Media

Media

In general, "media" refers to various means of communication. For example, television, radio, and the newspaper are different types of media. The term can also be used as a collective noun for the press or news reporting agencies. In the computer world, "media" is also used as a collective noun, but refers to different types of data storage options.

Computer media can be hard drives, removable drives (such as Zip disks), CD-ROM or CD-R discs, DVDs, flash memory, USB drives, and yes, floppy disks. For example, if you want to bring your pictures from your digital camera into a photo processing store, they might ask you what kind of media your pictures are stored on.

The Mass Media we use regularly use include radio, television, books, magazines, newspapers, movies, sound recordings and computer networks. The idea underlying each one is the same—a message that is transmitted to a large number of people at the same time. As you read the morning's newspapers you know that copies of the same newspaper is being read in at least half a million homes and offices at the same time. Or the popular soaps on television or the evening news bulletin.

Mass Media

Mass Media is those means of communication that reach and influence large numbers of people, especially newspapers, popular magazines, radio, and television. Mass Media goes along with Information and Communication Technology in this day and age so as to mold a new-fangled way of life to the majority living in this global generation.

Mass Media are those Medias that are created to be consumed by immense number of population worldwide and also a direct contemporary instrument of mass communication. Nonetheless, Mass Media is considered as the fourth estate of the society as well. It is the fourth branch of the government.

Then again, by and large when we speak about Mass Media, we immediately perceive that these are communications media that reach the mass of people. From Audio recording and reproduction like records, tapes, cassettes, cartridges, CDs, to Broadcasting Media such as Radio, Television, Cable, to Film or Motion Pictures whether in Cinema or in DVDs, and the Digital Media, the Internet, Mobile Phones, Satellite, and ultimately the Publishing or Print Media which includes Books, Newspapers, Magazines and the run-of-the-mill marvelous Video games.

Mass Media is a term used to denote a section of the media specifically envisioned and designed to reach a very large audience such as the population of a nation state. It was coined in the 1920s with the advent of nationwide radio networks, mass-circulation newspapers and magazines, although mass media (like books and manuscripts) were present centuries before the term became common. The term public media has a similar meaning: it is the sum of the public mass distributors of news and entertainment across media such as newspapers, television, radio, broadcasting, which may require union membership in some large markets such as Newspaper and Text Publishers. The concept of mass media is complicated in some Internet media as now individuals have a means of potential exposure on a scale comparable to what was previously restricted to select group of mass media producers. These Internet media can include:

- television,
- personal web pages,
- message boards,
- podcasts,
- blogs
- video hosting services.

The communications audience has been viewed by some commentators as forming a mass society with special characteristics, notably atomization or lack of social connections, which render it especially susceptible to the influence of modern mass-media techniques such as advertising and propaganda. The term "MSM" or "mainstream media" has been widely used in the blogosphere in discussion of the mass media and media bias.

History

Types of drama in numerous cultures were probably the first mass-media, going back into the Ancient World. The first dated printed book known is the "Diamond Sutra," printed in China in 868 AD, although it is clear that books were printed earlier. Movable clay type was invented in 1041 in China. However, due to the slow spread of literacy to the masses in China, and the relatively high cost of paper there, the earliest printed mass-medium was probably European popular prints from about 1400. Although these were produced in huge numbers, very few early examples survive, and even most known to be printed before about 1600 have not survived. Johannes Gutenberg printed the first book on a printing press with movable type in 1453. This invention transformed the way the world received printed materials, although books remained too expensive really to be called a mass-medium for at least a century after that.

Newspapers developed around from 1612, with the first example in English in 1620; but they took until the nineteenth century to reach a mass-audience directly. 20th century, the growth of mass media was driven by technology that allowed the massive duplication of material. Physical duplication technologies such as printing, record pressing and film duplication allowed the duplication of books, newspapers and movies at low prices to huge audiences. Radio and television allowed the electronic duplication of information for the first time.

Purposes

Mass media can be used for various purposes:

- Advocacy, both for business and social concerns. This can include advertising, marketing, propaganda, public relations, and political communication.
- Enrichment and education.
- Entertainment, traditionally through performances of acting, music, and sports, along with light reading; since the late 20th century also through video and computer games.
- Public service announcements.

Electronic media and print media include:

- Broadcasting, in the narrow sense, for radio and television.
- Various types of discs or tapes. In the 20th century, these were mainly used for music. Video and computer uses followed.
- Film, most often used for entertainment, but also for documentaries.
- Internet, which has many uses and presents both opportunities and challenges. Blogs and podcasts, such as news, music, pre-recorded speech and video.
- Publishing, in the narrow sense, meaning on paper, mainly via books, magazines, and newspapers.
- Video games, which have developed into a mass form of media since cutting-edge devices such as the PlayStation 3, XBox 360, and Wii broadened their use.
- Mobile phones, often called the 7th Mass Media, used for rapid breaking news, short clips of entertainment like jokes, horoscopes, alerts, games, music, and advertising.

Broadcasting

Broadcasting is the distribution of audio and/or video signals (programmes) to a number of recipients ("listeners" or "viewers") that belong to a large group. This group may be the public in general, or a relatively large audience within the public. Thus, an Internet channel may distribute text or music world-wide, while a public address system in (for example) a workplace may broadcast very limited ad hoc sound bites to a small population within its range.

The sequencing of content in a broadcast is called a schedule. With all technological endeavours a number of technical terms and slang are developed please see the list of broadcasting terms for a glossary of terms used.

Television and radio programmes are distributed through radio broadcasting over frequency bands that are highly regulated by the Federal Communications Commission. Such regulation includes determination of the width of the bands, range, licensing, types of receivers and transmitters used, and acceptable content.

Cable programmes are often broadcast simultaneously with radio and television programmes, but have a more limited audience. By coding signals and having decoding equipment in homes, cable also enables subscription-based channels and pay-per-view services.

A broadcasting organisation may broadcast several programmes at the same time, through several channels (frequencies), for example BBC One and Two. On the other hand, two or more organisations may share a channel and each use it during a fixed part of the day. Digital radio and digital television may also transmit multiplexed programming, with several channels compressed into one ensemble.

Computer

A computer is a machine especially designed for the manipulation of coded information, an automatic electronic machine for performing simple and complex operations. There are two types of computers, the digital and the analogy. The Digital computer, which is the most common, operates with numbers expressed directly as units in a decimal, binary, or other system. The Analogy computer operates with numbers represented by directly measurable quantities (as voltages, resistances, or rotations).

Advantages

- Because CAI is a computer-based system, it never sets tired, distracted, angry, or impatient, and it never forgets.
- CAI can use the storage facilities of the computer to assess individual progress and to initiate and monitor remedial work, as it is needed.
- Through the use of time-sharing, CAI can accommodate many students, each of whom appears to have exclusive use of the computer.
- Through the use of tele processing, one computer can service many terminals and many locations. Terminals and be separated by hundreds of miles.
- The control of the learning process is always vested in learning sequences created by instructional personnel. CAI permits the teaching staff to take on the co-ordinator's role in the teaching-learning process. The teacher can use his time more productively, etc. in individual counseling and in guidance of students who require additional assistance.
- CAI can perform its functions with less error and more speed than a human instructor.

Limitations

- Computers are very expensive educational instruments. While there have been some fantastic claims regarding very low cost per student hour, the fact remains that the initial investment in the equipment, the programmes, the training programme for the teachers, and the additional personnel required to handle the equipment adds substantially to the cost of instruction.
- The individual nature of the instruction provided by the computer confounds the arrangement of the student's daily programme.
- There are problems regarding physical location.
- Most of the programmes available today are quantitative in nature. There is a preponderance of programmes in the sciences and mathematics with very little in the social sciences and the humanities. If programmes are

developed and validated in all disciplines, the value of the computer will be enhanced.

There is a danger with any new instrument that it will be considered panaceas for educational life. With almost every new device that has been invented, a group of zealots has promoted the new invention as the solution to many educational problems. This type of media myopia prevents an honest assessment of possible alternatives to solving the problems. Some researchers have found, for example, that the computer had become an electronic page-turner. The reference point for the use of any new medium must still be the objectives, which have been defined prior to the determination of a strategy or the selection of instructional resources.

Internet

The Internet (also known simply as "the Net" or "the Web") can be briefly understood as "a network of networks." Specifically, it is the worldwide, publicly accessible network of interconnected computer networks that transmit data by packet switching using the standard Internet Protocol (IP). It consists of millions of smaller domestic, academic, business, and governmental networks, which together carry various information and services, such as electronic mail, online chat, file transfer, and the interlinked Web pages and other documents of the World Wide Web.

Contrary to some common usage, the Internet and the World Wide Web are not synonymous: the Internet is the system of interconnected computer networks, linked by copper wires, fiber-optic cables, wireless connections etc.; the Web is the contents, or the interconnected documents, linked by hyperlinks and URLs. The World Wide Web is accessible via the Internet, along with many other services including e-mail, file sharing and others described below.

Toward the end of the 20th century, the advent of the World Wide Web marked the first era in which any individual could have a means of exposure on a scale comparable to that of mass media. For the first time, anyone with a website can address a global audience, although serving to high levels of web traffic is still relatively expensive. It is possible that the rise of peer-to-peer technologies may have begun the process of making the cost of bandwidth manageable. Although a vast amount of information, imagery, and commentary (i.e. "content") has been made available, it is often difficult to determine the authenticity and reliability of information contained in web pages (in many cases, self-published). The invention of the Internet has also allowed breaking news stories to reach around the globe within minutes. This rapid growth of instantaneous, decentralized communication is often deemed likely to change mass media and its relationship to society.

Blogs (Web Logs)

Blogging has become a huge form of media, popular through the Internet. A blog is a website, usually maintained by an individual, with regular entries of commentary, descriptions of events, or other material such as graphics or video. Entries are commonly displayed in reverse chronological order. Many blogs provide commentary or news on a particular subject; others function as more personal online diaries. A typical blog combines text, images, and links to other blogs, web pages, and other media related to its topic. The ability for readers to leave comments in an interactive format is an important part of many blogs. Most blogs are primarily textual, although some focus on art (artlog), photographs (photoblog), sketchblog, videos (vlog), music (MP3 blog), audio (podcasting) are part of a wider network of social media. Micro-blogging is another type of blogging which consists of blogs with very short posts.

Podcast

A podcast is a series of digital-media files which are distributed over the Internet using syndication feeds for playback on portable media players and computers. The term podcast, like broadcast, can refer either to the series of content itself or to the method by which it is syndicated; the latter is also called podcasting. The host or author of a podcast is often called a podcaster.

Mobile

Mobile phones were introduced in Japan in 1997 but became a mass media only in 1998 when the first downloadable ringing tones were introduced in Finland. Soon most forms of media content were introduced on mobile phones, and today the total value of media consumed on mobile towers over that of Internet content, and was worth over 31 billion dollars in 2007. The mobile media content includes over 8 billion dollars worth of mobile music (ringing tones, ring back tones, true tones, MP3 files, karaoke, music videos, music streaming services etc); over 5 billion dollars worth of mobile gaming; and various news, entertainment and advertising services. In Japan mobile phone books are so popular that five of the ten best-selling printed books were originally released as mobile phone books.

Similar to the Internet, mobile is also an interactive media, but has far wider reach, with 3.3 billion mobile phone users at the end of 2007 to 1.3 billion Internet users (source ITU). Like e-mail on the Internet, the top application on mobile is also a personal messaging service, but SMS text messaging is used by over 2.4 billion people. Practically all Internet services and applications exist or have similar cousins on mobile, from search to multiplayer games to virtual worlds to blogs. Mobile has several unique benefits which many mobile media pundits claim make mobile a more powerful media than either TV or the Internet, starting with mobile being permanently carried and always connected. Mobile has the best audience accuracy and is the only mass media with a built-in payment channel available to every user without any credit cards or payable accounts or even an age limit. Mobile is often called the 7th Mass Medium and either the fourth screen (if counting cinema, TV and PC screens) or the third screen (counting only TV and PC).

Publishing

Publishing is the industry concerned with the production of literature or information—the activity of making information available for public view. In some cases, authors may be their own publishers.

Traditionally, the term refers to the distribution of printed works such as books and newspapers. With the advent of digital information systems and the Internet, the scope of publishing has expanded to include websites, blogs, and the like.

As a business, publishing includes the development, marketing, production, and distribution of newspapers, magazines, books, literary works, musical works, software, and other works dealing with information.

Publication is also important as a legal concept;

- As the process of giving formal notice to the world of a significant intention, for example, to marry or enter bankruptcy, and;
- As the essential precondition of being able to claim defamation; that is, the alleged libel must have been published.
- Certificate loss, change of name etc.

Book

A book is a collection of sheets of paper, parchment or other material with a piece of text written on them, bound together along one edge within covers. A book is also a literary work or a main division of such a work. A book produced in electronic format is known as an e-book. In library and information science, a book is called a monograph to distinguish it from serial publications such as magazines, journals or newspapers.

Publishers may produce low-cost, pre-proof editions known as galleys or 'bound proofs' for promotional purposes, such as generating reviews in advance of publication. Galleys are usually made as cheaply as possible, since they are not intended for sale.

Magazine

A magazine is a periodical publication containing a variety of articles, generally financed by advertising and/or purchase by readers. Magazines are typically published weekly, biweekly, monthly, bimonthly or quarterly, with a date on the cover that is in advance of the date it is actually published. They are often printed in colour on coated paper, and are bound with a soft cover.

Magazines fall into two broad categories: consumer magazines and business magazines. In practice, magazines are a subset of periodicals, distinct from those periodicals produced by scientific, artistic, academic or special interest publishers which are subscription-only, more expensive, narrowly limited in circulation, and often have little or no advertising. Magazines are usually published once a month or once a week.

Magazines can be classified as:

- General interest magazines (e.g., Frontline, India Today, The Week, etc.)
- Special interest magazines (Women's, Sports, Business, Scuba Diving, etc.)

Merits

- Selectivity of readers.
- Magazine reader is considerably younger and better educated than in the non-reader.
- Reader confidence is its asset.
- National coverage.
- Long life.
- Imaginative use of space adds to the flexibility and elasticity of display treatment.

Limitations

- Time consuming for planning and publishing a magazine.
- Only infrequent communication with the readers.
- Expensive.

Newspaper

A newspaper is a publication containing news and information and advertising, usually printed on low-cost paper called newsprint. It may be general or special interest, most often published daily or weekly. The first printed newspaper was published in 1605, and the form has thrived even in the face of competition from technologies such as radio and television. Recent developments on the Internet are posing major threats to its business model, however. Paid circulation is declining in most countries, and advertising revenue, which makes up the bulk of a newspaper's income, is shifting from print to online; some commentators, nevertheless, point out that historically new media such as radio and television did not entirely supplant existing.

Advantages

- The reader can choose which articles he wishes to read.
- A subject can be explored in more depth.
- The newspaper can go more specialised or technical information.
- Inexpensive.
- Can be kept and referred back to at a later date.
- Source of more accurate and authoritative information.
- Can be read in private, circulated among friends or read aloud publicity.
- It generally reaches the literate opinion leaders.
- Intensive and wide coverage of various items.
- Appeal is broad and diversified.
- In general a local medium, load, in origin, in coverage and in interest each is tailored to suit local needs.

Limitations

- They can not be read by illiterates without outside help and the group or individual to whom they are meant need not go through the same.
- It has a very short life, the time spends amounts to a few minutes, and few copies are filed for future reference. The reading is rushed and hurried.
- The quality of paper and the speed of printing make the medium less potential.
- Difficult to focus for a specific audience.

Kind of Newspapers

- *The Large Daily:* These papers have wide reading audiences, and yet they vary individually. Some serve different reading groups than others. They may serve different educational levels, different economic levels, or different religious preferences. Some papers or some editions may have greater coverage of rural areas. Study your newspapers to see where their special interests are and the kind of material they most like.

- *The Weekly or Semi Weekly Local Newspaper:* These papers are read rather thoroughly and they often have space. They may have urban rural coverage or both.
- *Foreign Language Newspapers:* These papers reach special groups. Their messages are favourably received.
- *Nature of News*: News is "the record of action." Something has just happened.

Software Publishing

A software publisher is a publishing company in the software industry between the developer and the distributor. In some companies, two or all three of these roles may be combined (and indeed, may reside in a single person, especially in the case of shareware).

Software publishers often license software from developers with specific limitations, such as a time limit or geographical region. The terms of licensing vary enormously, and are typically secret.

Developers may use publishers to reach larger or foreign markets, or to avoid focusing on marketing. Or publishers may use developers to create software to meet a market need that the publisher has identified.

Mass Wire Media

Mass wire media is a new frontier of news reporting in the high-tech age. A few decades ago news reporting was through newspapers and radio and television. The radio broadcasts that were made famous by Franklin D. Roosevelt during World War II changed the way radio was looked at. These fireside chats made the radio news and news radio. Things are different now as we are witnessing a revolution of people-oriented reporting in real time and other times. This element of intimate knowledge of the event or story being reported has dramatically changed the way we all view news stories.

This is called by some the Social Media Revolution. This revolution has intrinsically altered the way news is reported almost the way it happens. The trend of people-oriented reporting is only on the rise as reporting news becomes more personal and more accurate-although also more subjective.

Video Games

A video game is a computer-controlled game where a video display such as a monitor or television is the primary feedback device. The term "computer game" also includes games which display only text (and which can therefore theoretically be played on a teletypewriter) or which use other methods, such as sound or vibration, as their primary feedback device, but there are very few new games in these categories. There always must also be some sort of input device, usually in the form of button/ joystick combinations (on arcade games), a keyboard and mouse/trackball combination (computer games), or a controller (console games), or a combination of any of the above. Also, more esoteric devices have been used for input. Usually there are rules and goals, but in more open-ended games the player may be free to do whatever they like within the confines of the virtual universe.

In common usage, a "computer game" or a "PC game" refers to a game that is played on a personal computer. "Console game" refers to one that is played on a device specifically designed for the use of such, while interfacing with a standard television set. "Arcade game" refers to a game designed to be played in an establishment in which patrons pay to play on a per-use basis. "Video game" (or "videogame") has evolved into a catchall phrase that encompasses the aforementioned along with any game made for any other device, including, but not limited to, mobile phones, PDAs, advanced calculators, etc.

Motion Pictures

Film is a term that encompasses motion pictures as individual projects, as well as the field in general. The origin of the name comes from the fact that photographic film (also called film stock) has historically been the primary medium for recording and displaying motion pictures. Many other terms exist—motion pictures (or just pictures and "picture"), the silver screen, photoplays, the cinema, picture shows, flicks—and commonly movies.

Films are produced by recording people and objects with cameras, or by creating them using animation techniques and/or special effects. They comprise a series of individual frames, but when these images are shown rapidly in succession, the illusion of motion is given to the viewer. Flickering between frames is not seen due to an effect known as persistence of vision—whereby the eye retains a visual image for a fraction of a second after the source has been removed. Also of relevance is what causes the perception of motion; a psychological effect identified as beta movement.

Film is considered by many to be an important art form; films entertain, educate, enlighten and inspire audiences. Any film can become a worldwide attraction, especially with the addition of dubbing or subtitles that translate the film message. Films are also artifacts created by specific cultures, which reflect those cultures, and, in turn, affect them.

A motion picture (also called a movie or film) is a series of still pictures taken in rapid succession usually on 8mm or 16mm film stock, which, when projected through a motion picture projector, give the viewers an illusion of motion.

Advantages

- "Certain meanings involving motion can best be presented by motion pictures." This facilitates explanation of certain on-going process as viewing, growth of plants, functioning of a body system etc.
- "The motion picture compels attention." A darkened room creates an absorbing atmosphere in which you view the moving pictures.
- "The motion picture heightens realities."
- "The motion picture can control the time fact or in any operation or series of events." By the slow-down technique certain events like the analysis of muscular activities in dividing, various athletic performances, growth of any embryo, etc., can be shown.
- "The motion picture can bring distant past and the present into the class-room." All historical films capture the past form the present.
- "The motion picture can provide an easily reproduced record of an event or an operation."

- "The motion pictures can enlarge or reduce the actual size of objects."
- "The motion picture can be used to present a process that cannot be seen by the human eye." The technique of animated drawings can show us the working of a human heart, the physiological processes in an eye, the working of an engine, etc.
- "The motion picture builds a common denominator of experiences in the group. All receives the basic details of films; slight variations may exist in the clarity and quality of interpretation.
- "The motion picture can influence certain attitudes for the quality of emotionalisation.
- "The motion picture can promote an understanding of abstract relationship." Motion picture has a wide variety of visual and auditory devices like charts, diagrams, sound effect, back-ground music, etc. in analysing a point.
- "The motion picture is often a satisfying aesthetic experience." By utilising various film techniques of photography action, colour, or sound and harmony of intellectual and emotional experiences is generally created. Anything, that is aesthetic is personal and hence is easily learnt and permanently retained.
- Motion picture can record events as they happen and make the events available again.
- They combine sight and sound, thus acting on two senses sat one time.
- Films overcome the barrier of illiteracy.
- Through the process of. Photomicrography, motion pictures can extend the limits of human vision by combining the characteristic of the microscope with the motion picture camera.
- By using the one-frame-at-a-time concept an artist can prepare drawings, which are photographed by a motion picture camera to create an animated film. This procedure permits the conceptualization of ideas, which do not exist, in concrete form, such. As visual explanations of jet propulsion or the theory of flight.

Disadvantages

- Since motion pictures are somewhat expensive, it is necessary to purchase prints and place them in libraries, which serve a large number of teachers. Since copies are limited, teachers have to request them far in advance. This type of limited access has prevented optimal use of film. Lower costs have made 8mm films more available, thus helping to alleviate this problem.
- The cumbersome and confusing machine, which often faces teachers who try to use films, has been a major deterrent to extensive use of the film. The fact that one projector usually has to be shared by many teachers has also limited film use. Again, simpler projectors, such as the cartridge loading or self-threading unite help to over-some this limitation.
- We often complain that the available motion pictures are simply not suitable for their topic and audience. Educators have to depend upon the products of film producers. These materials are not usually made for highly specific purposes. As more films become available, this problem decreases.

- Films and projectors must be transported and maintained.
- Films are regarded as an entertainment device rather than an aid to teaching.
- The projector depends on a power source either mains or from a mobile generator.
- The audience has to be informed previously about the time and place of the film-show.

How to Use Films

- ***Selection Motion Pictures***
  Because Films are Expensive: to produce, they are intended for wide "Markets" as many different kinds of audiences as possible. You must therefore give special consideration to the quality and appropriateness of films you select. Educational films should be selected and used with specific purposes in mind. Films should not be used primarily from the point of view of entertainment. Obtain catalogue of film libraries Governmental and Non-Governmental and select the best film available for the topic.
- ***Using Motion Pictures***
  Good usage of educational films requires planning in preparation and follow-up activities.
- ***Preparation***
  After receiving the film, you should arrange to preview the film to preview the film to assure yourself that the film is suitable for the intended audience. Read the teaching guide, if any that comes with the film. You should note the main teaching points, important sequences and any difficult words that the audience might not understand. Compose three or four questions, which are answered in the film.
  Ensure proper physical environment and correct projection set up. Before the film is shown to the audience make sure that the projector is in good working order and that the room can be properly darkened if the film is to be shown during the day. The film should be threaded in the projector, read to go, before the audience arrives.
- ***Presentation***
  Your audience will learn a great deal more from the film if they are properly motivated and prepared. Hence the basic guiding principle should be the provision of motivation and maintenance of the intensity of interest. You should tell your audience the title of the film and generally what the film is about. You should explain why the material is important-relate the lesson to their own self-interest. Ask them to notice certain key scenes in the film. Define any difficult words. Pose questions and explain that these questions will be answered in the film. They should understand that they are seeing a teaching film, and that they will be expected to learn from it. As far as possible, the film should be shown without breaks—in a quiet area—without distractions.
- ***Follow-up Activities***
  Immediately after the film showing the instructor should encourage audience discussion. Questions should be asked of the audience. You can soon tell

whether the material in the film was fully understood. After a short discussion you may wish to show the film again. If appropriate, practice skills demonstrated in the film. Allow the audience to criticize freely in fact, encourage criticism of the film. If the film necessitates the use of other audio visual aids like models, mock-ups, charts, recordings, they may be incorporated. Follow-up can be through home-visits, small group meeting.

Remembers

- Motion pictures have special educational advantages.
- Three are many sources loaning films, free of charge.
- Motion pictures should be carefully selected and used for specific purpose.
- Using films properly requires planning and preparation.
- Choose the best teaching aid, not necessarily a film for specific points to be explained.
- Do not use film when other equally effective but less expensive teaching devices can be used.
- Be sure that audience doesn't get wrong time notion and wrong size notions.
- Films should not be a substitute for the teacher.
- A film should not be used in isolation. It should be a part of the total communication programme. It should be integrated with other activities and media.

Television

Television is an electronic system of transmitting still and moving images with accompanying sound over a wire or through space. The system employees equipment that converts light and sound into electrical waves and reconverts them into visible. Light rays and audible sound. The most common type of transmission is broadcast or open circuit television where programmes are radiated to any viewer within range of the station. This is the type of transmission used by commercial and some educational stations. The other type of system, frequently found in schools and colleges, is the closed circuit television system, which limits distribution of an image and sound to receivers directly connected to the origination point by coaxial cable or microwave link.

Characteristics

The simple closed circuit system is a good place to start. A video camera with lenses and a television receiver connected to the camera by a wire constitutes a basic system. To add sound, an audio-video mixer (a device which combines the video signal from a TV camera and the audio-single from a microphone and impresses them on a carrier signal for transmission in closed circuit system) is added. Sometimes a separate sound system consisting of a microphone, amplifier, and speaker can be used. The addition of a videotape recorder permits the recording and instant playback of audio and video images.

Videotape packages are now available as separate systems. These packages include a camera with lenses, a videotape recorder, a television receiver, a microphone, and associated electronic equipment and cables.

When closed circuit systems are extended from one or two locations to many locations on a college campus or in a school system, further modifications of the system must be made. If the closed circuit feature is to remain, the signals have to be carried by coaxial cable (often leased from the telephone company) to each location where TV receivers are installed. Another alternative is the use of low power (2500 megahertz band) transmission or microwave transmission. These wireless systems permit the distribution of four signals simultaneously from point to point on a direct light of slight.

When a broadcast station goes into operation, the entire system is multiplied many fold. There are cameras and film and tape sources for origination of the programmes; there are the audio and the video systems; and there is the transmitter, usually a separate installation with the transmitter tower adjacent. Signals are sent from the transmitter location. Any standard receivers in the broadcasting area are able to pick up the signals.

A further extension of the wireless space-to-space transmission of signals is the use of satellites, which pick up Signals from one location and send them to distant locations.

Advantages

Many of the advantages of other audio-visual media also apply to television:

- It offers a means for providing a common base of experience for all who see a given programme at the same time.
- It brings to the classroom people, places, and events, that could not otherwise be seen.
- Live television-the launching of a space vehicle, the address of the President, or the final game of the world saris-adds the dimension of immediacy to events.
- The preconditioned learner comes to school as a confirmed TV consumer. The use of TV in instruction can capitalize on this acceptance and help him to become a more critical viewer.
- The reality and concreteness of the visual images are as present in TV as in other audio-visual media.
- Specialized personnel are often available on TV or videotape, Schools that cannot locate or afford special teachers of elementary foreign languages, for example, can extend the talents of one teacher to many students by television. Very often the teacher who is using TV becomes part of a teaching team, which includes the TV teacher, the subject supervisor, and many of the classroom teachers. As teachers use television, many learn new techniques and ideas from the television teacher. This is a major fringe benefit, a type of in service training.
- The widespread use of videotape now permits programmes to be recorded and used when they are most appropriate. Portable videotape equipment can easily be brought to classrooms and laboratories for recording the performance of individuals or groups; these learners are able to analyze their efforts when the videotape is played back.

Limitations

- One of the primary problems of broadcast TV is scheduling. If a teacher does not use a programme when it is broadcast (or re-broad-cant), it is lost. Consequently, some teachers do not use TV because of timing, or some have used it at inappropriate times simply because it was available and they wanted their students to view the programme. The decreasing cost of videotape recorders now permits recording of pertinent programmes for playback at an appropriate time.
- Even on large classroom model TV receivers (21" and 24") students may have difficulty in seeing detailed images in large rooms.
- While there have been genuine attempts to use the visual aspect of the medium, too often instructional TV programmes are images of teachers talking. As more teachers gain more experience with the medium and as more is learned about what makes good TV instruction, the quality of programmes can be expected to improve.
- The very familiarity of TV sometimes contributes to habits of inattentiveness and passivity. Students do not know how to learn from TV. They often reject it, especially in the secondary schools and colleges, since it appears to be a further step toward depersonalization.
- Some teachers perceive TV as a threat, since another teacher is "taking over" when the TV set is on. Some teachers fear that they are being replaced.

Graphic Presentation

Graphic presentation enjoys numerous forms of expression ranging from the written word to the most abstract of drawings or statistical graphs. When expressed in other than the written word, it affords an important medium of expression, which, in health education helps to clarify literally, verbally, or statistically presented health information. The purpose of this medium is to enliven and delineate information by presenting it in concise manner and in such form or pattern as will be helpful to understanding. While this medium may be used alone in advanced study in many fields, it is, more often than not, used in support of, or in clarification of, data that are otherwise presented.

The purpose of the chart is to provide a concise summary or to compare, to contrast, to suggest relationships, or otherwise to explain. It is not a substitute for data; that is, it does not take the place. Thus it is a symbolic form, which, while representative, is explanatory. It may vary in pattern from the simple to the complex depending upon its type, colour arrangement, and the amount of detail that it presents. Its value in health education, as in general usage, is usually in direct proportion to its simplicity.

The graph is a chart form that is used to present statistical (quantitative) data and to present the relationships between variables. While the terms "chart form" and "graph" are at times used interchangeably, the fact that use of the graph is restricted to the presentation of numerical data sets this form apart from other graphic forms, which, though enjoying broader scope as to presentation, are limited in their possibilities for presenting quantitative data. It is this distinctive function of the graph that tends to set it apart from the chart, although it remains a chart form. With the graph as with the chart, the simplest form that serves the intended purpose is usually productive of best results. This most certainly is the case in school usage at both the elementary and secondary grade levels.

Definitions of Graphs and Charts

A graph or chart is an instrument to present statistical information in symbolic fashion. The chart is used to represent numerical data as well as material in abstract form. In addition a certain type of chart (e.g. map chart) may be considered a picture of a portion of the earth's surface.

Historically speaking, graphs probably had their origin in pictures. Many old paintings and engravings represent saints and royalty in large figures with halos surrounding them whereas persons of less importance are represented in smaller size. In other words, a person's social status was conveyed to the reader by means of a graphical technique.

Advantages

- Simplicity in reading the data: It is an efficient method of showing large numbers of observations.
- The results are more easily remembered. A visual impression is more permanent than sets of figures of words.
- Completeness in presentation. Complex relationships can be demonstrated easily and quickly so that the whole situation is presented simultaneously.
- Clarity and emphasis in presentation. By the use of colour and other devices, one can emphasize certain places. For example, a rising death rate might be pictured in red to bring out the aspect of danger involved.
- Popular appeal. One need not consult surveys or psychological test results to learn that the table of statistical data may be quickly skipped over but a lively chart will attract and a certain amount of learning.

Disadvantages

- A sacrifice in precision. A graph can be used only to show large or crude variations in the date.
- Lack of flexibility in the event new combination of the data seems appropriate. This follows as a result of the first disadvantage and is one of the reasons why it may be advisable to present the original data in a table or text accompanying the graph.
- Distortion of the situation may result from the desire to oversimplify the material. This may be intentional or otherwise.
- Construction of a graph or chart may be difficult or costly. This should only apply, however, to large-scale drawings, which are employed as posters to educate the lay public or similar groups.

Tape Recorder

Magnetic tape is an acetate or plastic ribbon coated on one surface with a layer of magnetizable iron oxide particles (see illustration). The ¼″ width tape is usually employed to record audio messages magnetically for subsequent reproduction. The tape recorder, with which the magnetic tape is used, can record a message and play it back or play back of pre-recorded tape. The unit contains recording and playback amplifiers and heads (see illustrations). The heads may be full track, half-track, dual track, or quarter track (see illustration).

Characteristics

There are a variety of controls on every tape recorder. Some of the most common controls and their functions are listed in the table below:

Recording Formats

Recording and playing times of tape are governed by reel size, tape thickness, number of tracks used in the tape, and speed selected for recording.

As a general rule, the faster the tape speeds, the better the quality of the recording. For example, a tape running at 1 7/8 inches per second (ips) or 3 ¾, ips is adequate for recording speech, but 7 ½ ips or, better still, 15 ips would be necessary to record music with a high degree of quality. If half-track is used, the amount of recording time on the chart can be doubled. With quarter track, it would be four times the time stated. This assumes that the equipment will record and playback on half track or quarter track. It is the machine, not the tape that determines recording time.

Tape can be used over and over much time. In addition, when a recording is no longer needed, the tape can be used for a new recording because each time a new recording is made, the old recording on the tape is automatically erased. It is difficult to estimate tape life; however, since the magnetic surface usually lasts a very long time, tape recordings rarely "wear our." Tape can break when the equipment, is faulty, when the tape is especially cry, or when the tape is suddenly stopped while running at fast forward or rewind speeds. The process for repairing the tapes is simple (see the illustration on the next page). Be sure to use spillicing tape especially designed for repairing magnetic tapes, and not ordinary cellophane tape, which could endanger the recording or the playback heads of the recorder.

Advantages

The tape recorder has become commonplace equipment in homes, cars and schools. The availability of tape recorders is the first major advantage. Other advantages include:

1. The opportunity to be in two places at one time is possible when a recording can substitute for an individual.
2. Recording people and events for later use-radio and TV programmes phonograph records and the work of the students themselves is possible.
3. The opportunity to hear one's self is a useful diagnostic tool for helping to improve speech or musical efforts.
4. The operation of tape recorders is relatively easy. Cartridge and cassette recorders require no threading.

Limitations

Some people become confused about the operation of equipment, which requires several distinct actions before it can be used. Difficulties with equipment operation cause tape to spill off the reel, to break, or to "jam" the machine. Other limitations are:

- It is difficult to locate specific recorded items on a magnetic tape: if a recorded message is in the middle of a reel of tape and there is no record of the number of revolutions or no marker on the reel, the search may take a long time.

The great variety of tape speeds and arrangement of tracks (half, quarter, stereo, etc.) may cause some difficulty if a recording is made on one machine and is played back on another which may not have the same features.

Learning and Teaching Medias

Three Dimensional Aids

All the AV materials, three-dimensional aids are nearest to living experiences. This side, such as models and Mock-ups are replies or reconstructions of the real thing. They are contrived experiences where reality is altered or simplified for teaching purposes. A simple classification of these aids is given below: -

Models

Recognizable three-dimensional representation of real things.

Objects

Real things which have been removed as units from their natural setting.

Specimens

Objects which are incomplete or which are representative of a group or class of similar objects.

Mock Ups

Devices, which are imitations of real things without involving similarity of appearance, the non-functioning parts that are unnecessary for understanding operational functions being omitted.

Dioramas

Three-dimensional scenes incorporating miniature objects and backgrounds in perspective.

Advantages

- To recreate things from the past or the future.
- To reduce the size of things.
- To make model of things too small to examine.
- To made model of things from faraway places.
- To explain difficult concepts.
- To show working parts.
- To attract interests attention.
- To promote increased learner participation.
- To show some selected aspect of the whole in a simple elemental way.
- To present an immediate sensation.

Limitations

- Time consuming.
- Requires extra talent.

Display Boards

This teaching tool is called by different names:

- Visual Board
- Frick Board
- Slap Board
- Felt Board
- Coherograph
- Videograph

The tool consists of only two Parts—a board covered with flannel and objects having fluzzy and napped backing. The principle involved is the interlooking of fibers of two rough or bairy surfaces, so that the pieces pressed on to a background, which is hard and vertical, will stay. It can be illustrated on a larger scale by pressing two tooth brushes or hair brushes together, so the bristle inter-look. In case of flannel graph similar principle of friction helps an object to cling to the surface of the board.

Advantages

- Permits numerous and varied arrangements of visual materials.
- Is appealing, because the audience is fascinated in watching the steps in the presentation.
- Permits the development of a complete story.
- Permits the use of either chart or small pieces of material.
- Promotes conscientious planning, which must precede the development of the material in the first place.
- Challenges one to develop symbols to portray such things as abstractions.
- Materials can be packed and transported.
- Permits use of various colours, which may be used for specific purposes.
- Materials can be left on board after meeting closes for those who wish more complete notes.
- Is effective because it permits two techniques for delivering a message, word of mouth-sound and symbols or pictures-sight.
- Easier to construct materials for flannel board than to make slides or movies.
- Speaker works in front of his audience in well-lighted surroundings.
- Chronological development of ideas on board promotes ease in note taking.
- After symbols are developed they can quite easily be used in constructing attractive designs.

Disadvantages

- Transportation and storing of boards and materials is a problem.
- Suitable tables to support boards must be available.
- Time and cost of making material for presentation present a problem.

- Cost of boards themselves can't be overlooked.
- Presentation is limited a new idea involves a lapse of time before the new material can be added.
- Might tend to deter one from using other more effective methods and techniques when it is evident that other methods might be more appropriate.
- To tell a complete story, it often takes either too much board space or smaller designs and materials some of which cannot be seen well.
- Requires considerable ingenuity and imagination to construct effective varied materials.

Great interest is aroused when colourful cutouts stay on the board without the use of any glue, tacks or staples to hold these symbols and pictures. If the flannel is good, the teacher can just flick the illustration on the board where it stays as if by magic. This medium provides ample opportunities to present properly the material without losing the sequence. It increases effectiveness and enables the teacher to remember more of the details. By the dramatic association of pictures and symbols supplemented by teacher commentary, learning interest is heightened and difficult concepts are made easy. It can be used by both the teachers as well the pupils, for teaching and learning various skills such as reading, telling stories, giving reports and demonstration etc.

Its appeal is in the action and suspense in a way, it is like a drama. It has a story or a plot. It has background or set. It has parts that move about like characters. Like a drama its characters unfold the story before our eyes. The action of moving characters attracts our attention and the suspense of the unfolding story holds our interest

Exposition is Based on Teaching

- *Simplification:* It shows the ability of the teacher to reach his pupils men.
- *Amplification:* It connotes the ingenuity of the teacher to reach his pupil physically. The power of observation is enlarged through amplification.
- *Dramatization:* Just as simplification of an idea helps to reach the learning mentally, amplification helps to reach them physically; dramatization helps the teacher to reach them emotionally. Emotions are powerful motors in human machinery.

Not only teachers but also even physiotherapists who are interested in simple equipment that can be changed frequently and easily have found flannel graph as an excellent tool. The patients need no drawing pins on glue or staples to hold the symbols and the pictures. Flannel graph can also find a place in the waiting rooms, reception halls and museums where a topical, current and attract display is wanted.

In teaching, the use of flannel graph can be made simple as well as elaborate. It may be used to illustrate a difficult point, which needs quite a build-up on the board, or to highlight a lecture or a speech. Teachers may use it as a means of demonstrating arrangement, to extend concepts and establish visual proof, to provide opportunities in building associations, to enhance dramatic story telling, to stimulate creative expression, to afford means of studying relationships, to provide simple presentation of complicated ideas, to summaries the lesson or the unit and to provide visual type of individual practices. Thus it is almost unrivalled in its use.

Some Characteristics of Flannel Board

- *Visual:* It visualizes theoretical ideas. It helps to recreate situations involving motions. It visualizes dimensions and colour. It helps to recreate part.
- *Audio:* It creates events through dramatization. It recreates environment.
- *Utilization:* It permits any sequence or arrangement. It permits restudy. It Permits discussion. It can be produced locally.

How to Use?

The technique of using an effective teaching tool is simply the technique of making an experience educationally significant. A pre-requisite of every teaching aid is the design of exposition. This design must have organisation and arrangement of ideas, facts and events in a purposeful order. Dewey said, "Essential experience has unity." So it is very essential to have proper layout prepared and then presented effectively keeping in a view the following simple principles of teaching.

1. Outline what you want to say.
2. Plan the layout keeping in view the principles of teaching.
3. Arrange the materials in such a way that they lend themselves best to illustrate what you want to say.
4. Try the layout to see that it fits the space on the flannel board.
5. Place the flannel board at eye level and at a slightly inclined angle. Lighting should also be checked.
6. Use a minimum number of objects to let the students focus their eyes on a few items at a time.

Talk to the class as much as possible but not to the board. Remove the cutouts from the board as soon as you have finished talking about them and place the next cutouts in position. It is better to have the interest focused on one or two cutouts than to have the attention wandering back to the illustrations already discussed. In case of story telling or developing a chart, however, the characters might be left on the board.

Different Types of Chart

The Data or Tabular Chart

The data chart is used to present data in summary or tabular fashion. It is, in fact, a table that brings together data that are arranged in such fashion as to simplify their interpretation or make possible their further delineation in chart or graph form. Indeed the preparation of a table or data chart is a necessary first step in the preparation of other more vivid and refined charts, which will further speed interpretation and enhance understanding of the basic data.

The Time Chart

The time chart is used to present data of chronological nature. Historical data are frequently presented in this manner as incidents occurring at different times are shown in sequential arrangement. While having something in common with the data or tabular chart, this form restricts itself to treatment of the time element. Thus, public health progress may be shown as administrative emphases are placed on different phases or areas of public health activity. The same story might well require several hundred words in the telling. Such a chart may accomplish the purpose in concise yet complete and interesting manner through a combination of words and symbols. The concept of time as a faster in public health progress is thus more readily appreciated than would be the case in the reading or hearing of words only. The time rate table and the time bar chart are other forms of the time chart. While commonly used to illustrate industrial and commercial operations, these forms find limited, though effective, application in health education.

The Tree or Stream Chart

This chart form is frequently used to illustrate biological studies and is readily adapted to use for depicting health programme growth and development. In its simplest form, this chart may consist of the outline of a tree with the trunk and branches appropriately marked to indicate source or origin and growth and development of any kind, e.g. the "family tree." As such, it is sometimes described as a pictorial growth chart. In compels form it may, through careful and detailed drawing, delineate the multiplicity of operations involved in the production and transportation of food, water, or medical supplies.

The Organization Chart

The purpose of the organization chart is to depict the structure of an organization. It may be used to indicate the administrative or functional relationships of component parts of the structure or both. The organization of a municipal, country, state or federal official health agency is usually shown in this form of chart. It is one of the simplest of the chart forms and is commonly used by health agencies in organizational planning.

The Flow Chart

The flow chart or flow diagram is used to depict the movement or flow of functions, materials, or services of an organization, or to illustrate the directions of flow of interagency responsibilities. For example, the directions of flow of personnel responsibilities within a health agency or the functional relationships of voluntary agencies to the official health department may be depicted in this manner. The concept of these agencies as ancillary or complementary agencies to the official community health agency is readily enhanced for the student as he is enabled to trace flows of responsibility visually.

The qualities of the organization chart and the flow chart are sometimes combined to produce an organization and flow chart. Such a chart may serve the dual purpose of showing the manner of agency organization and the flow of functions or services from its component parts.

The Bar Chart or Graph

The bar chart or graph is without doubt the most commonly seen of the many chart forms used in presenting the relationships between variables. Among its many, patterns are the simple bar and the compound, multiple, relative, and pictorial bars, all of which may be structured in either the vertical or horizontal planes. Vari-coloured and multi-coloured bars may be used depending upon the number of variables shown. In such usage, however, the careful selection and placement of colours in just a position is an important consideration in any case and particularly when these forms are used in conjunction with the teaching of elementary school children. Hatching may also be used to advantage in most bar chart forms; but in paper charts, this is time consuming activity which, if not carefully done, may result in optical illusions and resultant confusion rather than clarity. Both colouring and hatching are effective and are readily accomplished when the chalkboard is, used to present the bar chart or graph.

Bar chart or graph forms enjoy popular usage in health literature. Especially is this the case when birth, death, or morbidity rates are under consideration since comparisons of birth and death rates, case incidence and fatality rates, or specific morbidity and mortality rates are readily visualized with the help of these graphic presentations.

Histogram or Column Diagram

This is a graph on arithmetic paper for presenting data in frequency distributions. A column indicates the height of each interval. (The name is derived from its root, histo, meaning cell or frame.) There is no space between each column.

It should be used only when the data on the horizontal or x-axis are measured on an interval or ratio scale. If data have been grouped into intervals unequal in size (such as 0-4, 5-9, 10-14, 15-24 years of age), this type of graph is the one most suitable.

The percentage for the interval 25-34 years of age is actually 16.0 per cent, but since all the previous intervals were based upon units of five years, it was necessary to convert the percentage for the ten-year interval by dividing it in half. Similarly for the interval 35-44 years of age. Note that the width of the last two columns is twice that of the five-year columns. In other words, the total area represents relative differences in the frequency distribution.

If the graph is one involving rates, such mortality or morbidity, the occurrence of unequal intervals does not require a histogram. The conversation to a common base for comparison purposes has already been accomplished in the obtain rate because the denominator takes this factor into account.

In construction of the histogram, it is preferable to convert frequencies in each interval into percentages. Thus, comparisons of the height of a column in one distribution are not influenced by the total numbers of observations and enable comparisons between histograms. It also overcomes the objection of divining the frequency of larger intervals into fractions of a unit. Do not use a male-break in the histogram for it is the height of each column, which is being compared.

Component Band Chart

A variation of the bar chart is extremely useful when two or more sets of percentages are to be compared by graphical means. When only one set of percentages from nominal scale data is under study for comparisons within the set, earlier discussion indicated preference for the pie chart. When there is more than one set, however, the comparison, between two pie charts is not easily made. In its place, a convenient graph is the component band chart.

In interpreting this graph, it should be observed that the source of local funds increased greatly (over two times its proportional share five years previously) and that this increase came mostly from a reduction in the use of state funds.

Pictorial Statistics

This is popular variation of the bar chart. Instead of using a plain column, the length of the bar is composed of a series of small identifying symbols. Each symbol may be used to represent a fixed number of items. The number of items is determined by the variable being graphed and this in turn determines the length of the bar.

Some general rules in their construction are as follows:

- Use descriptive and suggestive symbols when possible. For public health work, some recommended symbols are figures of a man, woman, child, bed, wheel-chair, nurse, doctor, coffin, etc. (For a complete listing of all symbols see catalogue from pictograph corporation. No address is available; however, it may be out of business.
- There should be legend explaining the number of units for which each symbol stands. The number of units for which a symbol stands should be in round numbers, 5, 10, 25, 50, 100, etc. It is permissible to split a symbol into portions to show a number less than one unit.
- Represent differing amounts by varying the number of symbols instead of the size of the symbol, Distortion will result if the size of the symbol is changed.
- Each symbol should be the same size—called isotype. The space between symbols must also be constant.

The Line Graph

The line graph, like the bar graph, finds ready application to the needs of health education. This graph makes possible the presentation of data with a high degree of accuracy. In fact, careful work and use of the proper coordinate paper make possible the exact reproduction of numerical data, a quality not given to all forms of graphic presentation. Since different types of lines may be used in tracing the data, two or more illustrations, may be presented on the same graph. However, the graph is easily over-burdened. The compilation of more than two or three records on the same graph is not advised.

This is especially true if confusion is to be avoided when this graph form is used in the instruction of school children. The graph may be made attractive and distinctions made clearer when solid lines of different colours are used in place of solid and broken lines of the same colour. An accurately drawn grid and the careful placement of plotting points both on and between the scale divisions make possible the drawing of straight line segments or curves with accurate and artistic results that will prove attractive to pupils while contributing to the development of careful and precise work habits. Such a graph may be used to record the classroom temperature and humidity records; to illustrate annual food or milk production or consumption records;

to compare the changing costs of medical or other health services; or to record the data from health experiments conducted in the classroom or laboratory.

The Pictorial Graph

The pictorial graph, or pictograph, takes its name from the symbolic pictures or figures that it used in lieu of other forms of presentation.

Pictograph figure or picture symbols may be arranged in vertical or horizontal bar fashion, in circular or cluster fashion, or as single figures used to strengthen the concept of meaning or relationship of statistical data. As with other forms of graphic presentation, they are not intended to replace the written word, but to amplify or complement it. They range from simple stick figures to diagrams or full pictures of inanimate objects and, botanical, zoological, and anthropological forms. Thus diagrams or pictures of bicycles or automobiles may be used in instruction for safety and accident prevention; of battles of milk, or food items in the study of nutrition; and of plants, animals, or man in the study of heredity, communicable disease, community or public health, or health and medical economics. Such presentation is attractive and meaningful at all ages.

The Pie Chart or Graph

This circular presentation enjoys general usage and is probably familier to all educational workers. Its purpose is to present percentage or fractional differences within a single geometric pattern. Its use as a mnemonic device aids in the retention of information. This is particularly true with children. The use of this form is effective in presenting quantitative data in an interesting and colourful manner in elementary grades as well as in the secondary school. When a single circle is used it is called a simple pie chart or diagram. When two or more concentric circles are used, it is described as a concentric pie. In the latter case, its possibilities are further enhanced, although the degree of abstraction is increased as circles are added, as the number of pie slices or sections is increased, and as a variety of the hatching styles are used in the same pie.

It must be emphasized that the pie diagram should not be used haphazardly. Since fraction or percentage differences are to be distinguished, numerical values must be clearly shown and superfluous words should not be allowed to clutter up the pie. Colour may be used to advantage for identifying one or more of the pie slices. This is particularly effective with children.

The pie chart or diagram has ready application in the teaching of nutrition, safety, community and public health, and health economics. It is a versatile chart form, which adds interest to health studies and effectively supplements basic data.

Frequency Polygon

This is actually a type of graph, which comes under the classification of the arithmetic scale line graph (see II, 4 A.) It is used, to present data in the form of frequency distribution. Thus, the information from class observations on height would appear as follows:

For each height interval, a dot is centered in the interval a dot is centered in the interval and placed at level corresponding to the number of persons found in that height interval. These points are then connected by a series of straight lines. (This produces a many-sided figure with many angles. Hence, the graph derives its name).

This type of graph is the only one suitable if one wishes to compare two frequency distributions. Even thought the size of the intervals may be unequal, (indicating, the histogram) when two (or more) frequency distributions are to be compared the frequency polygon is needed. If the intervals are of unequal size, one must modify the level of the point, which is plotted in accordance with the rules for the histogram.

If more than one line is placed on a single graph, one can distinguish between the lines by colour, or making one of the lines broken, one solid, one dotted, etc. These different types of lines should be explained in a legend or key.

As in a histogram, the frequency polygon is best plotted when the data in the intervals of the frequency polygon is being employed is compare the shape of two frequency distributions, the use of percentages is mandatory. Since the two frequency distributions may have differing total numbers of observations, a valid comparison of the shapes of the frequency polygon can be made only when the vertical scale is in percentage form.

Some authors recommend that at each end the line be brought down to zero at the, middle of the adjoining intervals. This is to show that, the total area or percentages under the curve are equal to unity. In some cases where the frequency distribution has values starting at zero because of the scale of measurement, this creates a ridiculous situation and can be avoided by omitting these terminal lines.

Scatter Diagram

This is a special type of graph often useful to the research worker in pointing out relationships or associations. These relationships need not, always be causal in nature.

For each community a dot was placed to indicate the average amount of prenatal care as well as its maternal mortality rate for that year. The pattern of the points indicates that an association or relationship probably does exist between these two factors. The question whether this relationship is causal or not can not be answered by this procedure.

How to use the charts:

1. Construct or select charts that rate high on each at the following criteria:
   - Is the material closely related to the topic to be discussed?
   - Is the material interesting?
   - Is the material useful in attaining an objective of the programme?
   - Can the material be understood?
2. Make sure that the letters; figures, pictures and other material on the charts are large enough to be seen by all members of the group.
3. Place charts at a height where every members of the audience can see them.
4. Make sure that all charts are accounted for and arranged in the right sequence.
5. Check the lighting on the charts. Low foot lighting is often best.
6. Keep, the first page of the chart covered until readily to present it.

When presenting charts, the following suggestions should be kept in minds:

1. Present all of the material on the chart before discussing the information on the page. This will give the learners an over view of the material on the page before discussing the parts.
2. Use a pointer to indicate the item being presented.
3. Stand at one side of chart; never block its view.
4. Keep eyes on audience as much as possible. Glance at chart only briefly.
5. Avoid too much leader talk. Try to get learners to think and to discuss.

Picture

A picture is a two-dimensional visual representation of persons, places, or things. Most commonly it is a photograph, but it also may be a sketch, a cartoon, a mural, or even a chart, graph or map, Pictures may be used for individual study, for display on bulletin boards and in exhibits, and for projection when groups of students need to look at one picture at the same time.

Characteristics

Pictures are usually printed or photographically processes. They vary in size and colour. They may be highly representational or abstract. If a picture is desirable for use and it is in a book or pamphlet, which is available to an entire class, it probably would be most efficient to ask everyone to turn to the same page at the same time to look at the picture. If, however, only one copy of a picture is available, and group viewing is required, the picture could be projected on a screen:

The easiest method is to place the picture in the opaque projector. The room must be very dark and the screen must be large enough to accommodate the enlarged image. The picture will not be damaged.

The same picture could be copied on 35mm film, which would be processed into a 2″ × 2″ slide. Another option, if the picture is on clay-based paper (such as Life or Holiday), and the picture does not have to save, is to "lift" the picture from the paper by the picture transfer process using the rubber cement or a thermal process. The picture is transferred to clear acetate and is used on an overhead projector.

Pictures may be displayed on a bulletin board for individual or small group observation. Bulletin boards in the classroom and in school halls offer display opportunities.

Advantages

- Pictures are inexpensive and widely available.
- They provide common experiences for an entire group.
- The visual detail makes it possible to study subjects which would otherwise be impossible.
- Pictures can be help to prevent and correct misconceptions.
- Pictures offer a stimulus to further study, reading, and research, visual evidence is a powerful tool.
- They help to focus attention and to develop critical judgement.

Limitations

1. Sizes and distances are often distorted.
2. Lack of colour in some pictures limits proper interpretations.
3. Students do not always know how to "read" pictures.

Unless each student has a picture or the picture is properly projected, the medium should not be used.

Programmed Instruction

Definition

Programmed instruction is the use of programmed materials (or a programme) to achieve educational objectives. Some programmes are designed for devices which are commonly referred to as teaching machines. A teaching machine is a device that presents a programme. Most machines control the material to which the student has access at any moment, preventing him from looking ahead or reviewing old items. Many machines contain a response mechanism: a tape on which the student writes, a keyboard, or selection buttons, some provision is made for knowledge of results, either by revealing the correct answer after the individual responds or by advancing to the next item, thereby signaling correct completion of the previous item. However, most programmes are in the form of programmed texts. These texts do not different in outward appearance from conventional workbooks or texts; no equipment is required to use a programmed text.

Characteristics

In programmed instruction information is presented; the presentation is controlled, usually by small steps; The presentation stimulus demands and active response by the learner; the student is either told whether his response is correct, or he is permitted to judge whether his response is correct as he compares his with the one given in the programme; and there is no established pace at which the learner must move.

Advantages

Some of the advantages of programmed learning are inherent in the characteristics of the medium, i.e., the Individual can move at his own pace; the individual must respond to the stimulus (there is little opportunity for inactivity); and the individual knows immediately whether he is right or wrong. Other advantages include the following:

1. Student follows a logical sequence of thought.
2. By the time the programmed instruction reaches the learner, it has usually been fielded tested and verified, thus ensuring optimum learning and optimum use of student time.
3. Programmed instruction is especially well suited to many kinds of learning tasks.
4. A wide variety of media can be employed in presenting stimuli; audiotapes, films, slides, filmstrips, flat pictures, etc.

Limitations

- Programmed instruction usually works best with the cognitive learning objectives—those dealing with factual and skill learning. Many teachers question the success of programmed learning since it tends to emphasize content and does not permit feelings or emotions to be used.
- Some programmes, especially those that are organized in a linear fashion, tend to be somewhat dull, especially for brighter students.
- Programmes are difficult to prepare on a local basis. They are time-consuming to write and to field test. If commercial programmes are not available, and locally prepared programmes cannot be written, the use of PI is not possible.

Poster

Poster is a visual combination of bold design; colour and message, which is intended to catch and hold the attention of the passer by just, long enough to implant a significant idea in his mind. Good posters must have a dynamic, impelling quality. They must be essentially simple for there is not time to involve the viewer in detailed study. They must be striking enough to attract attention. Dramatic simplicity, appropriateness, limited test, attractiveness, design and colour are the good characteristics of the posters.

Advantages

- It can quickly put over one simple idea.
- It can represent a general concept in seeing terms.
- It can emotionalise an idea bringing surprise and shock.
- It is portable, can be used as often as needed.
- It needs no help to do its best work. It can stand-alone.
- It can serve as reminders.

Limitations

- The poster, which is seen too often, tends to become simply a part of environment. When it looses its freshness poster loses its principal value—the power to attract the eye and to impress the observer with an idea. Hence there is a need for frequent.
- The value of a poster is lost where not displayed in strategic places.

Characteristics of a Good Poster

It is very important that only a SINGLE idea or subject be presented in one poster. As the poster is generally seen from a distance and the person glancing at the poster seldom has time or inclination to stop and read the job of the poster is not at all simple.

- It has to STOP the hurriedly passing PERSON.
- It has to THRUST the MESSAGE upon him QUICKLY.
- It has to LEAD him to ACTION, immediately or eventually.

To incorporate successfully all these functions, there are 5 main principles of poster making:

- *Brevity:* Not more than 5 words is best.
- *Simplicity:* A good Poster is compact, has a minimum of individual units and bold illustration containing only essential details.
- *Idea:* The visualization of the idea must be clever and original so as to attract and impress the lesson of the Poster on the mind of the viewer.
- *Layout:* The arrangement of the elements of a Poster can make or break its effectiveness.

A Poster must be brief, so that:

1. It can be read in the shortest possible time.
2. The letters can be larger and bolder in the same amount of space and so can be read from a greater distance.

- A person glancing at a Poster, while passing, seldom has time to read long lines of wording, however interesting they may be. *Copy should be reduced to its shortest and clearest form.* There are no hard and fast rules as to the exact number of words a poster should contain. Usually there should be not more than 8 words; but 4 or 5 are better.
- What do we mean by "SIMPLICITY"? The fewer the units into which the given space is divided the more pleasing and legible it is to the eye. There should be no over crowding and confusion.
- It is better to have one bold illustration than a group of smaller ones competing with each for attention.
- The visualization of the IDEA to be depicted in a Poster is very important. Ideas count in all walks of life. The more original and clever the visualization the greater the appeal. Good symbolism helps in attracting attention, stimulating interest and has a lasting effect upon the memory. Try to show something UNUSUAL, DRAMATIC in presentation.
- The layout is the blue print for your Poster design. It decides the final appearance of the Poster. A good layout creates the right atmosphere for the Poster's message. A bad layout can make the Poster unattractive.
- Make several small scales, rough sketch layouts, arranging the material in various ways. You will be surprised at the number of arrangements you can make of the caption, illustration and subheading, if there is on.
- The use of COLOUR needs no recommendation. It has irresistible charm and universal appeal. Its proper use definitely helps in attracting attention and is the best method of emphasizing a particular point.
- Here again, the same trial method can be followed as in the case of layouts. Try different colour combination in small size and make a final selection.
- You can see the different effects when we change the colour of the background on this Poster.
- And the different effect with an all white background. Remember that WHITE IS ALSO AN IMPORTANT COLOUR, but is should be used as part of the design and within the design normally.
- In every poster some part is always lettering. A poster can be of lettering

only but it is seldom of illustration exclusively. Hence, due importance should be given to lettering.

- BOLD, SIMPLE LETTERS of easily readable style can be read from a distance and are easy to draw. These styles can be made medium oblong or bold according to your need. They can also be made slanting.
- Avoid fancy styles and letters of unequal thickness. They are not readable from a distance and are difficult to draw—not at all suitable for poster work.
- Space between letters is as important as the actual finishing of individual letters. Many beginners who can make fair alphabets have trouble with letter spacing. Using a foot rule to measure distance between letters seldom produces pleasing results and is generally detrimental to legibility.
- You must ADJUST SPACE BETWEEN LETTERS OPTICALLY.
- Expressive letters are letters, which instantly express from their very appearance what they mean. For example, VEGETABLES is written with letters in shapes of different vegetables.
- Drawing of detailed illustrations is very difficult. Start with easily recognized silhouettes, simple shapes and details.
- Symbolic type figures are easy to draw. Stick drawing is also very easy with a little practice.
- Photographs are easy to obtain and can be enlarged to the desired size at nominal cost. They can be used most affectively on posters.
- The simplest way to use a photograph is in square or rectangular shape. But you can add more interest by making it oval or round or by enclosing it in a silhouette out-out.
- You can create the figure itself with coloured or plain background. You can often find good pictures in magazines to cut out and paste into posters. When you have a picture you want to copy in a smaller or larger size, it is most easily done by marking off grid or graph lines on the original and making another graph the size you want your final picture to be.

Flash Cards

They are a set of pictured compact paper cards of varying sizes that are flashed one by one in a logical sequence before an audience to bring home an idea. The message on each card is brief and up to the point.

They are varying sizes depended upon the size of the audience:
5″ × 7″ – 3 or 4
15″ × 20″ – 20 or 25
22″ × 20″ – 30

Advantages

- Relatively inexpensive.
- Easy to carry.
- Can be used at any situation.
- Easy to make.
- It captures and holds the attention of the audience.

- It is flexible to meet the speaker's requirements.
- Overcomes the language barrier and even the illiterate can learn.
- We can depict anything we want, unlike the photograph.

Disadvantages

- The effectiveness of flashcard is purely influenced in the way it is used.
- As they are of paper they spoil soon.
- For storage they need more space.
- They cannot be used for a very big audience.
- The audience may loss their attention when more cards are used.

How to Use

Plan agenda and insert in suitable place the use of flashcard:

- Go through each card referring to the respective write up and be thorough with each card.
- Know the central idea and note down the important teaching points, which enhance that central idea.
- Develop three or four questions to be asked.

Rehearse

Arrange cards serially, stand before a mirror and present stressing only the important points just seeing the flashcard.

- Check yourself:
  1. Whether you are simple.
  2. Whether you are enthusiastic
  3. Whether you hold the cards against your chest.
  4. Whether your eyes forward.
  5. Whether you keep pace of your voice.
  6. Whether identify yourself in telling the story.
  7. Whether logical in adjusting the time dramatizes.

Prepare Your Audience

Don't let your audience to sit beyond 20' in front of you or not far off the side so the cards can be easily seen.

Presentation

- Brief introduction of the subject, which your flashcard deals.
- Greater the attention towards your aid.
- State the purpose. (Relate it to your audience's interest).
- Present materials:
  1. Stand erect.
  2. Hold the cards against your chest and high enough and turn towards all sides as to be easily seen by all.
  3. Stress important points.
  4. Don't wander from theme to theme.
  5. Keep the language simple and realistic.

6. Don't go in a breakneck speed or hand on a particular care.
7. Slip the cards behind the stock.

- Don't hesitate to repeat the card when doubt arises on that particular card.
- If necessary, present it again.
- Distribute cards among the audience one by one and lead the discussion.

Application

Discussion Practice i.e. demonstration question and answers.

Follow-up

Supply reading material.
Involve into action.
Fieldtrip.

Tips to Remember for Effective Use of Flashcards

- The story on each card must be familiar to you.
- You must use simple words and local expressions.
- The wording is as brief as possible.
- You must bring the local names of people and village.
- The Lettering is large enough for the audience to read.
- You must hold cards so people can see clearly.
- The class is prepared before flashing the cards.
- Hold the cards against body and not up in the air.
- The cards are the card is in time with the community.
- They are exposed long enough for comprehension.
- The first slow-paced flash-through is followed by a quick flash-through review.
- The cards can be circulated after the demonstration among the audience.
- This aid is used with other teaching tools.
- You glance down at card as you tell the story.
- You point to important objects without covering the card with your hand.
- You are enthusiastic and enjoy telling the story.

Pamphlet

A pamphlet has 8 to 80 pages paperbound. It is also called a brochure or booklet. Single sheet with one, two or more folds are often spoken of as pamphlets. They are folders or leaflets. An Unfolded sheet is a leaflet, flier or handbill.

The three classes of pamphlets are:

- Agitation aims to persuade the reader.
- Promotions–aims to build support for the organization.
- Education aims to teach something.

Advantages

- Can reach a large section of literate people simultaneously.
- Can be preserved and used for reference purposes.
- Comparatively cheap.
- Accurate information and minute details can be given.

- Can be made easy as well as enjoyable to read.
- Can be used to maintain or increase the tempo of work.
- Can be used to continue contacts.
- Can promote literacy.

Limitations

- It is of little use in areas of low literacy. But there is the possibility of diffusion from literate to the Illiterates.
- Cannot be used in exclusion of other methods.
- Will loss its significance if not carefully prepared and used. Suggestions for writing skillfully and for the effective use of the printing process apply here.

Some suggestions especially pertinent to the preparation of pamphlets and folders follow:

1. Make an attractive cover, which is meaningful and easy to understand.
2. Do not crowd the available space. Use more space or less copy.
3. Use two colours where possible. It will cost a little more because the pages have to be run through the press the second time, but it will increase the number of readers.
4. Write interesting copy. The six unwritten laws for writing the copy are:
   - Never publish anything that might be controversial.
   - Never call attention to negative developments. Be positive Smile.
   - Never risk offending any one.
   - Avoid specific and unqualified statements on major questions. The qualified general statement is always safe, though meaningless.
   - Shun simple, popular language. Be professional.
   - Never let a touch of humor brighten the text. It is undignified.
5. Make a dummy or layout to exact size on exact size sheets.
6. Don't write too much. Be brief. Be concise. The pamphlet is not a book.
7. Write your copy to fit the pamphlet length you think you should use. Fit the copy to a suitable space-not the space to carelessly written copy.
8. Use suitable type.
   - Use an appropriate size.
   - Look at the available typefaces and pet out the one that will look best. Use two compatible type faces if you want. They provide good contrast. Three or more different faces are usually undesirable.
   - Use few caps. They are hard to read.
   - Use italics rather than bold face for emphasis, in most cases. They blend better with most copy.
   - Use leading between the lines. Two-point leading is probably sufficient. It will make the copy much easier to read.
   - See that the type used in headings is compatible with the type in the body of the pamphlet.
   - Make captions under photographs one size smaller type than the body of the text.

9. Make captions brief and clear.
10. Reproduce photographs and pictures in large enough size to be attractive. Cut or "crop" the Picture and show the important part in larger size rather than trying to show the whole picture.
11. Have a provocative title.
12. Avoid putting the first line of a paragraph or a sub heading at the bottom of a page.
13. Stagger sub-heads on facing pages instead of putting them opposite each other.
14. Read your final proof carefully.
15. Use static's sparingly.
16. Estimate costs in advance. Plan to fit your copy to even pages. Saddle wire stitching is least expensive in a pamphlet. Have enough copies printed or hold type until you are sure of how may you want. Get prices on different quantities Additional copies are not very expensive once the presses are running.
17. After all, the most helpful thing you can do in getting out good pamphlets is to make a collection of the best pamphlets you can find and use the best of their ideas, along with your own.

Exhibitions

Almost every educator uses the exhibit to some extent. If you are not using exhibits, perhaps you should ask yourself whether you have opportunities to do so to advantage in libraries, in the department, health meetings, or schools, in store windows, public clinics, and in many other places.

An educational exhibit is a planned and systematic arrangement of graphic materials, models, specimens, dioramas, etc. correlated around a basic theme. It is designed to focus the attention of the observer on a topic of educational significance.

Advantages

- One of the best media for reaching illiterates.
- Publicity value.
- It has imaginative appeal.
- It caters to the mind, heterogeneous audience.
- It can fir into festive occasions and can serve recreational requirements.
- It can stimulate competitive spirit when several others put up exhibitions.
- By providing a wide variety of media, they create an atmosphere of learning and further widen the learning horizon.

Limitations

- Requires mush preparation and investment.
- Cannot be widely used (less frequent).
- Cannot be used repeatedly at the same plan without making substantial changes.
- It cannot represent all phases of work.
- A badly arranged exhibit will elicit damaging effects.

Planning and Preparing Displays

Begin planning well in advance. It takes time to get together a good exhibit. It is essential that the organization should be clear about the purposes or objectives before executing the displays. The purposes have got to be pinpointed and specific. The purposes, resulting in selection of location, contents and techniques of exhibits are related to the following questions:

- What is the central theme or important idea?
- What is to be communicated?
- What materials and contents will be most effective?
- Analyze and evaluate your audience.

The exhibit is for them, you know. You are not making it for yourself. It is to interest and educate a particular kind of audience and outlining preliminary plans. Finalize your plane for the display in a discussion session. It is essential and rewarding to involve as many workers as possible. Analyze the central theme into sub-topics for each individual display. Taking care that ultimately they have to be integrated into a coherent and meaningful exhibition. Make committee and keeping in view the individual abilities and interests, assign jobs and duties to execute and finalize the exhibits.

Type of Exhibit

In the order or decreasing interest, the three common types are:

- *Live Models:* people, demonstrations, animals, actual specimens, food to eat, babies being examined, laboratory Tests being made, an iron lung in operation.
- *Models:* a stage, set, working model of a sand filter, model of a street cleaning situation, models of insects which Carry diseases, diorama (three -dimensional display in which the model fades into a picture at the back), puppet shows.
- *Visualization*: pictures of people and activities (blown up all the way to life size), charts, diagrams, maps, Graphs, silhouettes, transparencies, slides, mirrors, motion pictures.
  1. Decide to what senses you will appeal.
  2. Sight (Of course).
  3. Hearing. (The voice direct or on film or record or by radio or telephone. Sound effects of various kinds. Of course you will not use more sound with your exhibit than you would be willing to have each of the other exhibitors use).
  4. Taste. (Food or beverages).
  5. Smell. (Flowers, smoke, leather).
  6. Touch. (Some apparatus or material can be handled).
- Visitors are interested in its hardness, its texture, its weight, etc. Prepare a more detailed visual plan or lay out of the Exhibit the "what" of your exhibit. Just what are you going to show? Write out your plan. Make a preliminary Sketch with dimensions, layout, and colour scheme indicated. Begin to fill in details.

Pay attention to the display fundamentals that involve:

- The size and shape of the materials.
- The space available.

- The use of colour.
- The provision for lighting.
- The lettering techniques.

Preparing the Exhibits

After the visualized plan has been properly analyzed, start collecting the materials, keeping in view the location and the space for the exhibits. Generally small exhibits can be developed on bulletin boards fixed at convenient sports. For bigger exhibitions, community halls, specially constructed pandals etc. can be used. Each of the exhibits has to be protested before putting into exhibition hall. While preparing and arranging the exhibits the following are some of the guiding principles:

Choose and Illustrate the Headline

- It should be brief, forceful, clear and direct.
- It should be hold, easy to read from any spot in the room, horizontal, colourful and contrasting.
- Use either script or block letters. The former can be made of string, wire, etc. and the latter, of cut paper cardboard, or wood.
- Clever wood combinations and phrases attract attention.
- Pose questions or create problems. They are motivating and involving.

Arrange and Illustrate the Contents

- Use illustrative materials that catch the eye. The choice can be made from a wide variety of graphic and three–Dimensional materials, such as photographs, drawings, charts, maps, graphs, posters, realias, objects, etc.
- Match the arrangement and materials against the background, shocking or intense backgrounds are hard to live with; colour must not dazzle or dance if it is to serve as background for acting and thinking.
- Compose the materials artistically, keeping in view the basis essentials of balance and continuity.
- Use arrows, colour and interesting shapes to draw attention to special areas.
- Highlight the main theme by a catchy device. It may be an illustration or it may be the brightest on the largest item on the board.

Use Colour in Pleasing Combinations

- Colours have functional aspects, which heighten the reconstruction of reality and provide strong emotional and psychological effects.
- A jumble of colourful splashes is worse than none. They divide rather than units. About three colours not counting the background are suggested.
- Create and accept with pure colour and use shades and tints in the larger areas. Use warns and cools colours together for contrast. Warm colours, such as red, appear closer to the observer than do cool colours such as blue.

Simulation

In popular usage, Simulation connotes an assumption of something without having its reality. A Dictionary of Scientific Terms defines simulation as the "Assumption of features or structures intended to deceive enemies, as forms of leaf and stick insects, and all varieties of protective Colour action. "In social sciences however, simulation is used as a method to study social or psychological phenomena and is devoid of the connotation of deception."

Method of Simulation

Many forms of simulation based on the principles of learning are utilized for training purposes in various enterprises. They all attempt to provide the trainees with such opportunities where in he would get a feel of what he would experience in a Real life situation and would gain some understanding of the likely outcome of various actions and responses that he would decide on.

Controlled Experience Sessions

The most comprehensive forms of simulation "Create" a vast field organization and the participants are required to Function in different key roles and deal with such situations, as they would encounter in real life.

Simulation by Games

Another very important form of simulation is the "game." Many people who use this tool for educational purposes prefer to call it simulations or simulation exercises rather than games because to those who are not familiar with gaming, it suggests entertainment rather than a serious educational approach. In simulations, which are described as games, the human participants act as decision makers within a simulated system, generally in a competitive system. Training Programme in management make wide use of these games to select and train their personnel. These games are not only effective in training their personnel in techniques of management and business operation, but they seem to have potential for research in economic systems, industrial relations and many other social sciences. Hence their use has spread to academic institutions also.

Other Types of Simulations

Besides these widely known simulation methods, a number of other simulation techniques have been developed and used in training programmers in recent years.

In Basket Problem

The In-Basket Problem is usually employed as an individual decision-making exercise. Each member of the training groups plays the role of an Administrative Officer in a hypothetical work situation and is required to take action on letters memos and papers that he finds in his incoming mail.

Incident Process

The Incident Process begins with each trainee being given a brief description of an incident of importance in a situation under review. The trainees study the situation either individually or in groups for about fifteen minutes and decide on what they need to know in order to clarify the issues involved in the situation.

Designing Situation

Before starting to construct a simulation game or exercise, its educational objective has to be defined and at every stage of the design attempts should be made to meet this objective. Next, information has to be gathered or data to be developed to provide the basis for the construction of the model. Then the basic structure of the game or simulation exercise has to be determined and its elements, rules and regulations have to be formulated. The components, variables and their relationships that have to be included in the model are to be identified or defined with good understanding and skill. Finally the mechanics of the game or the exercise must be devised in order the afford scope for decision-making and calculation of operating results as efficiently as possible during the play itself.

Simulation Methods

	(a) Controlled Experienced	*(b) Role Playing*	*(c) Games*
Participant's Role	Player	Player/Observer	Player/Colleague or Competitor
Data	Normal Working	Self-Generated	Normal Working Data
Trainer's Role	Organizer, Conductor or Review	Organizer, Conductor or Review	Organizer, Conductor or Review
Time Required	2 Sessions	1 to 15mts	2 Sessions
Trainer Requirements: Ratio	1 to 8	1 to 20	1 to 20
Time Preparation	High, Depending on Materials	1 to 2 hrs.	High Depending on Materials
Facilities Required	Real Setting Nothing e.g. Desks, Special Working Telephones etc.		One Room for 4 or 5 Participants

Advantages

There are several advantages of simulation, which make it highly suitable to meet needs of training. It permits the experimenters to study the process in ways that real life prohibits. It is essentially a technique for managing; Separating and observing related segments of the seamless. An experimenter can run the simulation several times by changing the in outs of the components; variables and their Inter-relationships and can study the outcome, which it is not possible to do real life. Simulation permits the trainer to compress or expand real time. He can simulate the operations of a system over a period of years in a matter of minutes, or he can slow down the process so that the can carefully analyze and study Phenomena.

Where practicing a new skill in full reality is dangerous or expensive or impractical, it is possible to design training opportunities by simulating those situations, which are one step, removed from real life. For instance the field area may be in such a stage of development that it may not provide on opportunity for trainees to learn certain specific types of skills. To meet such needs, the simulation exercise is a real aid to overcome the difficulty existing in real life.

At times a simulation exercise can be used to explain the general approach of the training programme. For instance if a training programme provides both for controlling and allowing the trainees to exercise their initiative, a simulation exercise including activities that control and allow freedom to exercise initiative could be administered more effectively than using the lecture method.

Another Purpose for which simulation can be used in a training programme is to "unfreeze" the students. That is in the early stage of the training programme, the training events should be such that they offer maximum stimulation to the participants and thus involve them by arousing their motivation. For instance describing an accident and asking the trainees to map the course of action they would take and to submit it writing could effectively employ an incident process. The trainer could later discuss this. This unfreezing will motivate them for learning during the next phases of the training programme.

Very often if training programmes divide the whole class of trainees into small groups for practical experience and are required to report back to the entire class about their achievements and failures; it is noticed that the groups evince such competitive behaviour that forbids them to learn from each other's experiences. In such Situations, methods of interview and counseling to provide interpretation are either impractical or too threatening but a simulation game which aims at driving home the futility of only provide the necessary insight but will also help the members to realize that they belong to a larger group whose aim is to learn more.

Role Playing

The role of playing technique is the spontaneous unrehearsed acting out of a situation by a group or by selected members of a group.

Advantages

- Clarifies points. The method is new and now.
- Gives additional insight of a problem.
- Useful for adult learning.
- Insures high degree of audience participation.
- Gives better understanding.
- To get a common focus on a problem, and in large meetings.
- To test for reality.
- To gain insight into feelings of another person.
- In the development of a skill.
- It introduces the situation to both sectors and observers a dramatic impact.
- To make meetings more interesting through involvement, and common focus.
- Pinpoints a problem and gets it outside of the group or individual.

Limitations

- Needs skillful leader.
- Needs friendly spontaneous atmosphere.

1. Role-playing is not always an appropriate method. The use of role playing can be worse than a waste of time when the situation is not suited to the use of the technique.
2. Role of playing takes time. It should not be tried unless there is sufficient time for the dramatic skit and adequate group discussion following the skit. A speaker, a role-playing demonstration and a discussion in one meeting is too much.

3. Role-playing can be very ineffective when it is considered as an end rather than a method of reaching a desired goal.
4. An effective role-playing scene is usually short. The method becomes ineffective if used too long. The scene must be cut at the proper time.
5. Sometimes the role-play is above or below the level of understanding and maturity of the group.
6. Groups should not attempt to deal with problems that are not their own or at their level.

Defining the Problem

Participation of the group in the selection and defining of the problem is desirable. The problem should be significant and close to the people playing the roles as well as to the observers. The problem must be valid and clear. It must be sufficiently simple in order for the participants to discuss it rationally. Care should be taken to avoid problems, which would uncover deep-seated issues, which would distract from the purposes of the role-playing process. The observers as well as the actors must understand the problem thoroughly.

Establishing a Situation

The design of the role-play or situation is dependent upon the outcomes desired. Care should be taken to avoid compels situations which might take the observers' attention away from the problem under consideration. The situation provide such content to make it real to the participants and group, and at the same time, give them the common orientation and insight desired.

Casting of Characters

The success of the role-playing process is often determined by the extent that proper roles and actors are selected. The roles to be acted out should be carefully selected. Only these that will contribute to the purpose of the meeting should be used. Ordinarily it is better to involve a few roles than a large number.

The best actor possible should be selected for each role. Roles should be given to those persons best qualified to portray them and most willing to do so. Persons should not to force to assume certain roles. Nor should persons be asked to assume roles, which might result in embarrassment following the presentation.

Briefing of Participants

Spontaneous role-playing necessitates no briefing. Planned and assigned role-playing may, however, demand considerable briefing and planning. It is important that the role players assume their roles at the appropriate times, and that they play their roles to the desired end. Briefing is necessary in order to acquaint the role players with their responsibilities. The briefing may be public or private as the situation demands. In no case should the briefing structure what rehearsed in advance.

Acting Out of Roles

It is usually best for the audience to be unaware of the roles that are being enacted. The action should be carefully timed and spontaneous. It is important when several role players are involved, that they move into the role-play at the same time, and that they keep their roles until it is time to cut the act.

Cutting

The effectiveness of role-play may be greatly reduced if the play is cut short, or if permitted to continue too long. The timing of the cutting is very important. Long role-playing scenes are usually ineffective. Only a few minutes may be required to enact the desired roles.

The scene should be cut as soon as there has been sufficient action for the group to analyse the situation and the direction it should take. In some cases the scene can be cut when the group can project what would happen if the roles were continued. The role-play should always end if the actors have reached an impasse due to improper casting or briefing.

Discussion and Analysis of Action

The final step in role-play is the discussion during which the action is analyzed. This step should be the "clincher." If the roles have been properly played, the observers will have developed the desired understanding of the problem under consideration. Discussion should be focused upon the facts and principles brought out rather than upon an evaluation of the role players. It is a good idea to permit those actors to express their viewpoints first. There will be fewer hesitances on the part of the observers after the actors have expressed themselves.

The Chairman or Director has the responsibility of pulling together the facts that have been presented during the role-play and in the discussion following, and formulating the conclusions concerning the solution to the problem.

Ground Rules for Role Play

- Do not have a person play his own role (exceptions to be noted).
- Audience and players must accept the role-play situation, just as it is (will sometimes try to escape by criticizing situation).
- Don't burlesque-introduces extraneous stimuli-can't see player as a real person.
- Role-playing needs warm-up period-players needs to get feelings about it.
- Role-playing demands that you have sufficient time for discussion afterwards. (One play planned by group- 2 hours).
- Better to ask people who are playing roles to express feelings first.
- To get audience participation, usually ask group to identify with players in some way.
- Except for very spontaneous role play-need a Director to see that ground rules are covered.
- Role-playing taken planning.

Questions to rise in use of role-play:

- Is this a skill that needs some insight?
- Is it a human relations problem?

Don't use it on compels problems, or problems needing knowledge, or data outside group. The best-known but less elaborate form of simulation is role-playing. The purpose of role-playing is to enable the Participants to experience what something "Feels like" taking action and actually starting action.

Type of role-playing:

- Simple Role-Playing.
- Multiple Role-Playing.

Electronic Media

Overhead Projector

An overhead projector typically consists of a large box containing a very bright lamp and a fan to cool it off, on top of which a large fresnel lens is that, collimates the light. Above the box, typically on a long arm, is a mirror and lens that focusses and redirects the light forward instead of up.

Transparencies are placed on top of the lens for display. The light from the lamp travels through the transparency and into the mirror where it is shone forward onto a screen for display. The mirror allows both the presenter and the audience to see the image at the same time, the presenter looking down at the transparency as if writing, the audience looking forward at the screen. The height of the mirror can be adjusted, to both focus the image and to make the image larger or smaller depending on how close the projector is to the screen.

Focal-Length Adjustment

Better-quality overhead projectors offer an adjustment wheel or screw on the body of the projector, to move the lamp towards or away from the Fresnel lens. When the mirror above the lens is moved too high or too low, it moves out of the best focal distance for an evenly white image, resulting in a projected image with either blue or brown colour fringing around the outside edge of the screen. Turning the adjustment wheel moves the lamp to correct the focal distance and restores the all-white projected image.

Illumination

The lamp technology of an overhead projector is typically very simple compared to a modern LCD or DLP video projector. Most overheads use an extremely high-power halogen lamp that may consume up to 750 watts yet produces a fairly dim, yellowed image. A high-flow blower is required to keep the bulb from melting itself due to the heat output. Further, the intense heat usually causes the halogen lamp to fail quickly, often lasting less than 100 hours before failing and requiring replacement. A modern LCD or DLP uses an arc lamp which has a higher luminous efficacy and lasts for thousands of hours. A negative to LCD/DLP technology is the warm up time required for arc lamps, but it is the instant turn-on of halogen lamps that may be the biggest factor in their rapid rate of failure.

Older overhead projectors used a tubular quartz lamp body containing the filament only, which mounted above a bowl-shaped polished reflector. However because the lamp was suspended above and outside the reflector, a large amount of light was cast to the sides inside the projector body that was wasted and required a very large lamp for sufficient screen illumination. More recent projectors use an integrated lamp and conical reflector assembly that allows the lamp to be located deep within the reflector so that more light is focused towards the Fresnel lens, allowing for a lower-power lamp.

The most recent innovation for overhead projectors with integrated lamps/ reflectors is the quick-swap dual-lamp control, allowing two lamps to be installed in the projector in movable sockets. If during a presentation one lamp were to fail, the presenter can merely move a lever to slide the spare into position and continue with the presentation, without needing to open the projection unit or waiting for the failed bulb to cool before replacing it.

History

The first overhead projector was used for police identification work. It used a cellophane roll over a 9-inch stage allowing facial characteristics to be rolled across the stage. The U.S. Army in 1945 was the first to use it in quantity for training as World War II wound down. It began to be widely used in schools and businesses in the late 1950s and early 1960s.

A major manufacturer of overhead projectors in this early period was the company 3M. As the demand for projectors grew, Buhl Industries was founded in 1953, and became the leading US contributor for several optical refinements for the overhead projector and its projection lens. In 1957 the United States' first Federal Aid to education programme stimulated overhead sales which remained high up to the late 1990s and into the 21st Century.

Uses in Education

The overhead projector facilitates an easy low-cost interactive environment for educators. Teaching materials can be pre-printed on plastic sheets, upon which the educator can directly write using a non-permanent, washable colour marking pen. This saves time, since the transparency can be pre-printed and used repetitively, rather than having materials written manually before each class.

The overhead is typically placed at a comfortable writing height for the educator and allows the educator to face the class, facilitating better communication between the students and teacher. The enlarging features of the projector allow the educator to write in a comfortable small script in a natural writing position rather than writing in an overly large script on a blackboard and having to constantly hold his arm out in midair to write on the blackboard.

When the transparency sheet is full of written or drawn material, it can simply be replaced with a new, fresh sheet with more pre-printed material, again saving class time vs. a blackboard that would need to be erased and teaching materials rewritten by the educator. Following the class period, the transparencies are easily restored to their original unused state by washing off with soap and water.

An overhead transparency is an image usually 8½"-11" on clear acetate or plastic which has been prepared for use on an overhead projector. An overhead projector is a device, which throws an image on a screen. It is placed In front of an audience and may be used in a completely lighted on semi-darkened room: it utilized 3¼" × 4", 7" × 7", 10" × 10", or most commonly, 8½" × 11" transparencies.

Characteristics

The lens system of the overhead projector is designed so that the projector can be placed in the front of a room. The projection angle often causes the image to appear in a trapezoid form sometimes called "key stoning." This is corrected by tilting the screen as shown in the accompanying figures. This distortion is not always bother some and does not measurably change the amount of light on the screen. The projector should be placed as low as possible, as illustrated, so that the body of the equipment does not interfere with the line of vision between the students and the screen.

Advantages

The overhead transparency and projector have become extremely popular since the early 1960's. The cost of the projector has decreased, and the potential for local production of transparencies has increased. In some instructional settings the overhead projector makes an excellent replacement for the chalkboard. There are many advantages to this simple projector and its associated materials.

- The equipment is used in the front of the room. The teacher can maintain eye contact with the class while using the equipment.
- A bright image can be projected in a fully room. This permits the teacher and learns to see each other.
- Materials to be used on the overhead projector are easily produced by the teacher in the local school. The teacher in the local school. The teacher may write on a piece of acetate during the class, as he would use the chalkboard. He may use transparencies which have been produced through heat or chemical processes. In either case the transparency is a highly accessible and easily used medium of instruction.
- The equipment is simple to operate and has no maintenance problems save the occasional replacement of the lamp.

Limitations

In their enthusiasm for use of the overhead projector, teacher often overlook some of the limitations.

- Unless the equipment is properly positioned the base and head of the projector may obstruct the student's line of sight. The projector should never be placed on the teacher's desk in the front of the room. A low projector stand or a table with a recessed out-out is essential.
- Since the overhead projector becomes such a vital part of the teaching—learning process, it cannot easily be scheduled for use in one classroom one hour and in another the next. Therefore it may be necessary to assign an overhead projector to each room if teachers have extensive needs for this piece of equipment. This may create an economic burden.

Slides

Slides are a flexible training aid. Each slide is an independent unit. A slide is a film transparency contained in either a 2″ × 2″ or 2i″ × 2t″ mounts. Lanternslides are 3(1/4)″ × 4″.

A slide projector is an instrument designed to project 2″ × 2″ or 2(1/4)″ × 2 or 3(1/4)″ × 4″ mounted transparencies; slides may be shown by individual handling or may be placed in a slide cartridge and operated by manual or remote control. Projectors which accept only 3(1/4)″ × 4″ slides are usually referred to as lanterns slide projectors. The most typical slide, the 2″ × 2″ transparency, is made form a strip of 35mm film with a width twice that of a filmstrip. After processing, the slides are mounted in cardboard or glass mounts for easy use and for protection.

Slide Projector

Slide projector is an opto-mechanical device to view photographic slides. It has four main elements: a fan-cooled electric light bulb or other light source, a reflector and "condensing" lens to direct the light to the slide, a holder for the slide and a focusing lens. A flat piece of heat absorbing glass is often placed in the light path between the condensing lens and the slide, to avoid damaging the latter. This glass transmits visible wavelengths but absorbs infrared. Light passes through the transparent slide and lens, and the resulting image is enlarged and projected onto a perpendicular flat screen so the audience can view its reflection. Alternatively the image may be projected onto a translucent "rear projection" screen, often used for continuous automatic display for close viewing. This form of projection also avoids the audience's interrupting the light stream or bumping into the projector.

Types of Projector

- Carousel slide projectors (includes tray-style projectors).
- Dual slide projectors.
- Large format slide projectors.
- Overhead projectors.
- Single slide projectors (manual form).
- Viewer slide projectors.
- Slide Cube projectors.

Stereo slide projectors (projects two slides simultaneously with different polarizations; slides appear as three-dimensional with polarizing glasses).

Advantages

- The sequence of slides can be altered to meet specific needs.
- One can control the length of time each one is shown to allow for explanation, questions from the audience, or discussion of the problem at hand. The audience will focus its attention on the one slide being shown.
- Slides are easily made with an inexpensive 35mm camera. Copying materials with the same camera is a relatively simple task. Local Photographic facilities can often be used in making slides, and even colour film can usually be processed at seas reproduction centers.
- One can easily learn to make satisfactory slides picturing the details and process of programmes for which they are responsible. Slides produced locally have the added advantage of showing new techniques in familiar settings. Exposed 35mm film usually comes back from the processor in 2 × 2 inch cardboard slide mounts ready for projection.

- Can be held on screen as long as needed.
- Can be arranged in any order to suit the specific need.
- Can be easily revised and updated.
- Easily handled, stored and rearranged for various uses.
- Increased usefulness with magazine storage and automatic projection.
- Can be combined with lapped, narration for greater effectiveness.
- May be adopted to group or to individual user.

Disadvantages

Can get out of sequence and be projected incorrectly if slides are handled individually use of the never automatic projectors will alleviate this problem as the sequence can be worked out and loaded into the special car bridge before presentation.

Filmstrips

Filmstrip is a length of 35mm film containing a series of still pictures intended fro projection in sequence one at a time. Some filmstrips come with a tape or disc recording that contains the narration. When the proper equipment is used, a low frequency signal activates a mechanism to advance the filmstrip one frame. (The filmstrip is sometimes called a stripfilm and a slide film).

A filmstrip projector is an instrument designed to accept 35mm filmstrips. It is often equipped with an adapter to accept 2″ × 2″ slides. Models are available with manual advance and remote control.

A filmstrip contains a series of still pictures in colour or black and white on film, which is 35mm wide. The film is perforated along both edges for movement through the projector. Each picture in a filmstrip is called a frame. Commercially prepared filmstrips vary in length some are as short as ten frames, while others may contain from 70 to 80 frames or more. The filmstrip format is less expensive than a set of individually mounted 35mm slides containing an equal number of pictures. It is far less expensive to print a series of pictures on a strip of film than it is to print, cut and mount the same pictures in a set of slides.

Advantages

The filmstrip is a widely used instructional medium because of the many advantages.

1. Provide a logical; pre-arranged order fro presentation.
2. The sequence of pictures is always the same. Careful planning has preceded the production of each filmstrip.
3. Present an idea or process not involving motion.
4. May be supplemented with captions or recordings.
5. Information can be presented either through photographs or through artwork depending on which tells the story better.
6. Individual pictures can be held on the screen for discussion for as long as desired and is therefore easy for group and individual study.
7. Pictorial or graphic materials can be used alone or in combination.
8. The small size of the filmstrip permits easy storage and handling.
9. Sound filmstrips insures the recording with suitable voice accept and dialect.

Speed of projection is governed by the recording so as to suit the purpose and target audience.

10. Filmstrip equipment is relatively inexpensive, lightweight, small, and easy to operate.
11. The room need not be extremely dark for projection.

Limitations

1. The fixed sequence does not permit easy flexibility.
2. Filmstrips lack the attention-compelling qualities of the motion picture and television, which are more familiar to student.
3. Filmstrips are relatively difficult to make in the local place and therefore selection is confined to materials made by outside sources.

How to Use the Filmstrip and the Projector

Most filmstrip and slide projectors are equipped with a blower fan to prevent scorching of the film. If yours does not have such a cooling fan, be careful not be hold the film in the aperture gate too long.

Clean your projector just before each use. Use a soft camels hairbrush or a soft lint-free cloth dampened in carbon tetrachloride, acetone or alcohol and clean water (hale and half). Clean the lenses and two glass plates through which the filmstrip passes. Dust particles and bits of film emulsion on the glass plates will scratch the film.

Always handle the film only by its edges. Finger marks will show up badly in projection. Clean your film, if it becomes dirty, with a soft cloth dampened in carbon tetrachloride or acetone.

35mm filmstrip projects are normally equipped with a 5" focal length lens. They should be placed slightly further back from your screen than your 16mm motion picture projector. When using the projector for slides, since the slide film is larger, your projector should be moved closer to the screen:

- Feed the film upside down between the glass sandwiches. See that the words read backwards when you look at the film while threading. Be sure that film perforations are properly engaged by transport mechanism.
- Frame this picture correctly by moving the framing handle up or down. Focus sharply by turning the lens.
- Advance the strip, frame by frame, by turning the film advance knob. If your are projecting from some one else who is doing the talking, arrange foolproof signals so that you advance each frame at the proper moment.
- Rewind the film so that the beginning is outside after each showing. Wrap carefully and place it in its proper storage box or cane.
- To change from filmstrip head to slide head, loosen thumbnut, remove filmstrip head, insert slide head and tighten the nut.
- Have two slides in carrier at all times to prevent white glare on the screen. Turn the projector light off while last slide is in the machine. Have a colleague turn room lights on at the same time.

Selection of Filmstrips

Filmstrips should be selected and used with definite purposes in mind. Instructors should select filmstrips that are applicable to the subject being taught are accurate, truthful and up-to-date present materials at a level suitable for the audience encouraging audience participation.

Prepare Yourself

You must preview the filmstrip before showing it to an audience. During the preview you should not the sequence and content of the filmstrip and consult the accompanying teaching notes, if available. Determine the main teaching points. Develop a list of three or four key questions. Note several key frames that will require detailed explanation. As you preview the filmstrip, plan the activities that will follow the showing.

Prepare Your Audience

When filmstrips are "just shown" they seldom contribute much to learning. You can do a number of things to help the learning process. You might begin asking questions about the topic covered by the filmstrip. A filmstrip on the prevention of cholera might be preceded by such questions as: "Do any one of you know what caused cholera?" "How can cholera be prevented?" "What are the first symptoms of cholera?" The showing of the filmstrip then becomes a means of verifying audience discussions.

Another method of preparing your audience is to tell them the title of the filmstrip and summaries its contents. Make clear how the material relates to them, the audience. For example: ("Five causes of cholera have been reported in this district"). Then state the major points that the audience should pay particular attention to and indicate that there will be a follow-up discussion.

Audience Participation

Every effort should be made to encourage audience discussion during the showing. If the audience is literate, and capable of reading the captions, the instructor should not read them. Rather, you should enlarge upon the captions by presenting additional information. Asking pertinent questions and calling members of the audiences to comment on certain frames can stimulate thinking. If questions arise concerning frames already passed, don't hesitate to turn back and review them.

Follow-up Activities

The showing should always be followed by some kind if follow-up discussion or activity. Discussion will help to clear misunderstandings. It provides you with an evaluation of how much learning really took place. The audience must be questioned on material presented. They should also be given an opportunity of criticize the filmstrip. If you feel that certain points still need clarification the filmstrip should be shown again.

Bottom of Form

Audio Recording and Reproduction

Sound recording and reproduction is the electrical or mechanical re-creation and/or amplification of sound, often as music. This involves the use of audio equipment such as microphones, recording devices and loudspeakers. From early beginnings with the invention of the phonograph using purely mechanical techniques, the field has advanced with the invention of electrical recording, the mass production of the 78 record, the magnetic wire recorder followed by the tape recorder, the vinyl LP record. The invention of the compact cassette in the 1960s, followed by Sony's Walkman, gave a major boost to the mass distribution of music recordings, and the invention of digital recording and the compact disc in 1983 brought massive improvements in ruggedness and quality. The most recent developments have been in digital audio players.

A music video (also promo) is a short film or video that accompanies a complete piece of music, most commonly a song. Modern music videos were primarily made and used as a marketing device intended to promote the sale of music recordings. Although the origins of music videos go back much further, they came into their own in the 1980s, when Music Television's format was based around them. In the 1980s, the term "rock video" was often used to describe this form of entertainment, although the term has fallen into disuse. Music videos can accommodate all styles of filmmaking, including animation, live action films, documentaries, and non-narrative, abstract film.

Liquid Crystal Display

A Liquid Crystal Display (LCD) is an electro-optical amplitude modulator realized as a thin, flat display device made up of any number of colour or monochrome pixels arrayed in front of a light source or reflector. It is often utilized in battery-powered electronic devices because it uses very small amounts of electric power.

- Polarizing filter film with a vertical axis to polarize light as it enters.
- Glass substrate with ITO electrodes. The shapes of these electrodes will determine the shapes that will appear when the LCD is turned ON. Vertical ridges etched on the surface are smooth.
- Twisted nematic liquid crystal.
- Glass substrate with common electrode film (ITO) with horizontal ridges to line up with the horizontal filter.
- Polarizing filter film with a horizontal axis to block/pass light.
- Reflective surface to send light back to viewer. (In a backlit LCD, this layer is replaced with a light source).

Overview

Each pixel of an LCD typically consists of a layer of molecules aligned between two transparent electrodes, and two polarizing filters, the axes of transmission of which are (in most of the cases) perpendicular to each other. With no liquid crystal between the polarizing filters, light passing through the first filter would be blocked by the second (crossed) polarizer.

The surfaces of the electrodes that are in contact with the liquid crystal material are treated so as to align the liquid crystal molecules in a particular direction. This treatment typically consists of a thin polymer layer that is unidirectionally rubbed using, for example, a cloth. The direction of the liquid crystal alignment is then defined by the direction of rubbing. Electrodes are made of a transparent conductor called Indium Tin Oxide (ITO).

Before applying an electric field, the orientation of the liquid crystal molecules is determined by the alignment at the surfaces. In a twisted nematic device (still the most common liquid crystal device), the surface alignment directions at the two electrodes are perpendicular to each other, and so the molecules arrange themselves in a helical structure, or twist. Because the liquid crystal material is birefringent, light passing through one polarizing filter is rotated by the liquid crystal helix as it passes through the liquid crystal layer, allowing it to pass through the second polarized filter. Half of the incident light is absorbed by the first polarizing filter, but otherwise the entire assembly is reasonably transparent.

When a voltage is applied across the electrodes, a torque acts to align the liquid crystal molecules parallel to the electric field, distorting the helical structure (this is resisted by elastic forces since the molecules are constrained at the surfaces). This reduces the rotation of the polarization of the incident light, and the device appears grey. If the applied voltage is large enough, the liquid crystal molecules in the center of the layer are almost completely untwisted and the polarization of the incident light is not rotated as it passes through the liquid crystal layer. This light will then be mainly polarized perpendicular to the second filter, and thus be blocked and the pixel will appear black. By controlling the voltage applied across the liquid crystal layer in each pixel, light can be allowed to pass through in varying amounts thus constituting different levels of gray.

The optical effect of a twisted nematic device in the voltage-on state is far less dependent on variations in the device thickness than that in the voltage-off state. Because of this, these devices are usually operated between crossed polarizers such that they appear bright with no voltage (the eye is much more sensitive to variations in the dark state than the bright state). These devices can also be operated between parallel polarizers, in which case the bright and dark states are reversed. The voltage-off dark state in this configuration appears blotchy, however, because of small variations of thickness across the device.

Both the liquid crystal material and the alignment layer material contain ionic compounds. If an electric field of one particular polarity is applied for a long period of time, this ionic material is attracted to the surfaces and degrades the device performance. This is avoided either by applying an alternating current or by reversing the polarity of the electric field as the device is addressed (the response of the liquid crystal layer is identical, regardless of the polarity of the applied field).

When a large number of pixels are needed in a display, it is not technically possible to drive each directly since then each pixel would require independent electrodes. Instead, the display is multiplexed. In a multiplexed display, electrodes on one side of the display are grouped and wired together (typically in columns), and each group gets its own voltage source. On the other side, the electrodes are also grouped (typically in rows); with each group getting a voltage sink. The groups are designed so each pixel has a unique, unshared combination of source and sink. The electronics or the software driving the electronics then turns on sinks in sequence, and drives sources for the pixels of each sink.

Specifications

Important factors to consider when evaluating an LCD monitor:

- *Resolution:* The horizontal and vertical size expressed in pixels (e.g., 1024 × 768). Unlike monochrome CRT monitors, LCD monitors have a native-supported resolution for best display effect.
- *Dot Pitch:* The distance between the centers of two adjacent pixels. The smaller the dot pitches size, the fewer granularities are present, resulting in a sharper image. Dot pitch may be the same both vertically and horizontally, or different (less common).
- *Viewable Size:* The size of an LCD panel measured on the diagonal (more specifically known as active display area).
- *Response Time:* The minimum time necessary to change a pixel's colour or brightness. Response time is also divided into rise and fall time. For LCD Monitors, this is measured in btb (black to black) or gtg (gray to gray). These different types of measurements make comparison difficult.
- *Refresh Rate:* The number of times per second in which the monitor draws the data it is being given. A refresh rate that is too low can cause flickering and will be more noticeable on larger monitors. Many high-end LCD televisions now have a 120 Hz refresh rate (current and former NTSC countries only). This allows for less distortion when movies filmed at 24 frames per second (fps) are viewed due to the elimination of telecine (3:2 pulldown). The rate of 120 was chosen as the least common multiple of 24 fps (cinema) and 30 fps (TV).
- *Matrix Type:* Active TFT or Passive.
- *Viewing Angle*: (coll., more specifically known as viewing direction).
- *Color Support:* How many types of colours are supported.
- *Brightness:* The amount of light emitted from the display (coll., more specifically known as luminance).
- *Contrast Ratio:* The ratio of the intensity of the brightest bright to the darkest dark.
- *Aspect Ratio:* The ratio of the width to the height (for example, 4:3, 16:9 or 16:10).
- *Input Ports* (e.g., DVI, VGA, LVDS, DisplayPort, or even S-Video and HDMI).

Opaque Projector

The opaque projector, epidioscope, epidiascope or episcope is a device which displays opaque materials by shining a bright lamp onto the object from above. A system of mirrors, prisms and/or imaging lenses is used to focus an image of the material onto a viewing screen. Because they must project the reflected light, opaque projectors require brighter bulbs and larger lenses than overhead projectors. Care must be taken that the materials are not damaged by the heat generated by the light source. Opaque projectors are not as common as the Opaque projectors are typically used to project images of book pages, drawings, mineral specimens, leaves, etc. They have been produced and marketed as artists' enlargement tools to allow images to be transferred to surfaces such as prepared canvas, or for lectures and discourses.

Types

At the beginning of the 20th century, projection was split into two classes: "If the light traverses the object, the projection is said to be diascopic, if by reflected light, episcopic."

Two main classes of opaque projectors thus existed:

1. the episcope, which solely projected images of opaque objects.
2. the epidiascope, which was capable of projecting images of both opaque and transparent images.

Movie Projector

A movie projector is an opto-mechanical device for displaying moving pictures by projecting them on a projection screen. Most of the optical and mechanical elements, except for the illumination and sound devices, are present in movie cameras.

Types of Projectors

Projectors are classified by the size of the film used, i.e. the film format. Typical film sizes:

8mm

Long used for home movies before the video camera, this uses double sprocketed 16mm film, which is run through the camera twice. The 16mm film is then split lengthwise into two 8mm pieces that are spliced to make a single projectable film with sprockets on one side.

Super 8

Developed by Kodak, this film stock uses very small sprocket holes close to the edge that allow more of the film stock to be used for the images. This increases the quality of the image. The film is premade in the 8mm width, not split during processing as is the earlier 8mm. Magnetic stripes could be added to carry encoded sound to be added after film development.

9.5mm

Film format introduced by Pathé Frères in 1922 as part of the Pathé Baby amateur film system. It was conceived initially as an inexpensive format to provide copies of commercially-made films to home users. The format uses a single, central perforation (sprocket hole) between each pair of frames, as opposed to 8mm film which has perforations along one edge, and most other film formats which have perforations on each side of the image. It became very popular in Europe over the next few decades and is still used by a small number of enthusiasts today. Over 300,000 projectors were produced and sold mainly in France and England, and many commercial features were available in the format. In the sixties the last projectors of this format were being produced. They are now collectors' items.

16mm

This was a popular format for audio-visual use in schools and as a high-end home entertainment system before the advent of broadcast television.

35mm

The most common film size for theatrical productions during the 20th century. In fact, the common 35mm camera, developed by Leica, was designed to use this film stock and was originally intended to be used for test shots by movie directors and cinematographers.

35mm film is typically run vertically through the camera and projector. In the mid 1950's the VistaVision system presented wide screen movies in which the film moved horizontally, allowing much more film to be used for the image as this avoided the anamorphic reduction of the image to fit the frame width. As this required specific projectors it was largely unsuccessful as a presentation method while remaining attractive as filming, intermediate, and source for production printing and as an intermediate step in special effects to avoid film granularity, although the latter is now supplanted by digital methods.

70mm

High end movie productions were often produced in this film gauge in the 1950s and 1960s and many very large screen theaters are still capable of projecting it in the 21st century. It is often referred to as 65/70, as the camera uses film 65mm wide, but the projection prints are 70mm wide. The extra five millimeters of film accommodated the soundtrack, usually a six track magnetic stripe. The most common theater installation would use dual gauge 35/70mm projectors.

70mm film is also used in both the flat and domed IMAX Projection System. In IMAX the film is transported horizontally in the film gate, similar to VistaVision. Some productions intended for 35mm anamorphic release were also released using 70mm film stock. A 70mm print made from a 35mm negative is significantly better in appearance than an all 35mm process, and allowed for a release with 6 track magnetic audio.

The advent of 35mm prints with digital soundtracks in the 1990s largely supplanted the widespread release of the more expensive 70mm prints.

Sound

Regardless of the sound format, any sound represented on the film image itself will not be the sound for the particular frame it occupies. All optical sound formats must be offset from the image because the image is projected with intermittent motion. If the sound head on the projector was adjacent to the gate, the sound would be a jerky start-stop-start-stop and so on. Therefore the sound head requires continuous motion and will be located a certain number of frames before or after the gate.

Optical

With 16mm and the larger sizes it is practical to add a narrow channel of optically encoded sound track. This is read using an illuminating light or laser and a photocell or photodiode. In 16mm, this is a single mono track, and the sound head is 26 frames after the gate. In 35mm, this can be mono or stereo, the latter including several different Dolby noise reduction systems (including Dolby A and Dolby SR). The sound head is located twenty frames after the gate for 35mm projectors. Originally optical sound was variable density, where the transparency/opacity level of the sound track was used to represent sound. This had disadvantages because the grain of the film caused a background hiss, and so was replaced with the now-universal standard variable area. In this system, a clear waveform on black background represents the sound, and the width of the waveform is equivalent to the amplitude. Variable area does have slightly less frequency response than variable density. In the 1970s and early 1980s, optical sound Super-8mm copies were produced mainly for airline in-flight movies. This technology was soon made obsolete by video equipment.

Digital

Modern theatrical systems use optical representations of digitally encoded multi-channel sound. An advantage of digital systems is that the offset between the sound and picture heads can be varied and then set with the digital processors. Digital sound heads are usually above the gate. All digital sound systems currently in use have the ability to instantly and gracefully fall back to the optical sound system should the digital data be corrupt or the whole system fail.

Dolby Digital

Also known as Spectral Recording Digital or "SR•D." Sound is printed between the perforations and is 26 frames before the picture (the offset can be varied based on processing presets). Dolby Digital Produces 6 discrete channels. In a variant called SR•D EX, the left and right surround channels can be dematrixed into left, right, and back surround, using Dolby Pro Logic. The audio data in a Dolby Digital Track is compressed in the 16-bit AC-3 compression scheme at a ratio of about 12:1. The images between each perforation are read by a CCD located either above the projector or in the regular analog sound head below the film gate. The information is then decoded, decompressed, and converted to analog; this can happen either in a separate SR-D processor that feeds signals to the cinema sound processor, or SR-D decoding can be built-in to the cinema processor.

Digital Theater Systems (DTS)

DTS actually stores the sound information on separate CD-ROMs supplied with the film. The CDs are fed into a special modified computer which syncs up with the film through the use of DTS time code, decompresses the sound, and passes it through to a standard cinema processor. The time code is placed between the optical sound tracks and the actual picture, and is read by an optical LED ahead of the gate. The time code is actually the only sound system which is not offset within the film from the picture, but still needs to be physically set offset ahead of the gate in order to maintain continuous motion. Each disc can hold slightly over 90 minutes of sound, so longer films will require a second disc. Three types of DTS sound exist: DTS-ES (Extended Surround), an 8 channel digital system; DTS-6, a 6 track digital system, and a now obsolete 4 channel system. DTS-ES derives a back surround channel from the left surround and right surround channels using Dolby Pro Logic. The audio data in a DTS track is compressed in the 20-bit APTX-100 compression scheme at a ratio of about 4.5:1. Of the three digital formats currently in use, DTS is the only one that has been used with 70mm presentations. DTS was premiered on Jurassic Park. A consumer version of DTS is available on some DVDs.

Radio

Radio is a medium, which reaches practically all the people.

Advantages

- It admits you to the homes of the people, providing a readymade audience, or, more exactly, innumerable separate audiences of one to six or more persons.
- You talk to people directly, and the voice is a very warn and friendly medium.
- Top-flight, big-name speaker, who could not be brought to local audiences, can be secured for radio.
- Interesting activities can be described to people while they are taking place through "on-the-spot" broadcasts.
- The voice is frequently the most revealing expression of human personality.
- Music is essentially a listening experience.
- Necessary scenery, properties, costumes, and weather conditions may be suggested by the imagination, stimulated by inexpensive sound effects, narration and dialogue.
- The metal pictures thus conceived may vary with the individual. This is especially convenient in dealing with Biblical themes, where many people have strong preconceptions.
- Unnecessary scenic details may be omitted, allowing the sound to concentrate on fundamental principles.

Limitations

- It is so easy for the listener to turn you off that you may lose your audience.
- You are in constant competition with other programmes on other stations.
- You cannot assemble a special group interested in a special problem. Your audience (at least at the beginning of your broadcast) is a rather general one.
- Your audience cannot review your statement by questions or discussion. To some extent you can provide repetition by skilfully restating ideas in different ways.
- Only in television is there visualization.
- With nothing to watch, listeners are more subject to distractions, thus limiting their attention span.
- Listeners are likely to imagine only those visual elements, which they have already seen; it is difficult to suggest new visual experiences through the cars alone.
- Some concepts may be portrayed more clearly in visual than in auditory terms, Maps, for example, make clear at a glance relationships which would be difficult, if not impossible, to describe orally.

Planning and Conducting Radio and Television Activities

- Have a friendly contact and understanding with the manager and programme.
- Check all material carefully for scientific accuracy.
- Use the best script writing skill available.
- Add interest to your programme through humour, the introduction of local incidents, and the use of music.

- Rehearsal enough to be sure that all of your programmes are accurately timed.
- Enough attention to audience building.
- Recognize the value of small local stations as well as big once.
- Make adequate use of spot announcements.
- Schedule programmes on your yearly calendar to meet season's needs and local happenings.
- Identify all speakers clearly on your programmes.
- Supply real health news to radio news editors when it is available.
- Get your acquaintances to report to you on the quality of your programmes.
- Offer to help school departments in their radio programmes which touch on health.
- Plan with school authorities for health programmes which will fit into school health instruction.
- Keep your programmes informal but on a high level.
- Test the extent of audience interest by offering free literature or through surveys by home visitors and other public health personnel.
- Express your appreciate adequately to the radio station and to the participants.

Folk Media

Folk is one of the Germanic roots that mean "(of) the people" or "our people" (as opposed to different clans, tribes, or nations). The Modern English word "folk," derives from Old English "folc" meaning "common people," "men," "tribe" or "multitude." The Old English noun itself came from Proto-Germanic "fulka" which perhaps originally referred to a "host of warriors." Compare Old Norse "folk" meaning "people" but more so "army" or "detachment."

Folklore

Folklore is the body of expressive culture, including tales, music, dance, legends, oral history, proverbs, jokes, popular beliefs, customs, and so forth within a particular population comprising the traditions (including oral traditions) of that culture, subculture, or group. It is also the set of practices through which those expressive genres are shared. The academic and usually ethnographic study of folklore is sometimes called folkloristic.

Reasons for Using Folk Media

No communication strategy would be complete unless it included the traditional media, which must rank alongside the more commonly accepted channels of communication.

Status and Function of Folk Media

- As an intrinsically valuable form of popular entertainment or artistic expression it is worth preserving and developing for its own sake.
- It is a means of changing values, attitudes and norms in order to provide a proper climate for social and economic progress.
- It is a method of promoting certain behaviour acts or patterns. The aim is to

get people to perform specific acts to achieve objectives of national policy (e.g. visiting clinics, investing in bonds, using fertilizer).

- It is a channel for conveying information about available techniques and facilities which people may use to solve problems.

The above purposes, it was noted, are not necessarily in compatible with each other. However, problems may arise in specific situations. Certain media may not be appropriate for certain purposes and certain purposes may not be achieved by employing particular folk media, or any folk medium. It is therefore important to evolve criteria both for selecting media and for selecting messages that pass through them.

Classification of Traditional Forms

Traditional forms of expression were identified. The classification covering the performing arts and the visual arts included music, song, drama, skits, puppet shows, poetry, speech, sounds, gesture, gossip, jokes, proverbs, painting, certain printed literature, sculpture, handicrafts, costuming, patterning and colouring of material and use of head-gear. Symbolic meanings may often be an important consideration in use of any one or combination of these forms of expression and therefore the thought-processes behind selection of forms assumed significance.

Advantages

Traditional media come from the people and antecede the mass media; their appeal has historically been both functional and aesthetic. Whether of roughly hewn folk origins or of classifiably rigid moulds, they have always served to entertain, educate to reinforce existing ideas or ideologies or to change existing values and attitudes.

Being close to people at the local level, these channels are potentially useful in the service of social concerns, as determined by local, provincial or national authorities themselves. They are, moreover, abundantly present in areas where mass media technology has not been fully or effectively developed to capture sustained interest at local, provincial or national levels. Folk media are personal forms of entertainment and communication. This is important because behavioural changes are most easily brought about by personal interaction. These forms of art are a part of the way of life of a community and provide acceptable means of bringing development issues into the community in its own-terms. They are capable of reaching intimate social groups, thus making use of already established communication networks in the audience.

These forms of entertainment evolved as grassroot expressions of the values and life styles of the people, dealing with values as well as information. These features are significant for development, planners in the field of population, since it is rapidly becoming apparent that something more than information is necessary to bring about the behavioural changes involved in the adoption and continued practice of health and Family Planning.

Another advantage of the traditional media is that they attract people who might not attend an educational meeting. With skill, new content might be added to the old forms, which are already familiar and dear to the people. Finally, unlike mass media programmes, produced for large and often diverse audience, the folk forms can use familiar dialects for the most intimate and local communication at the village level.

Folk media rather deal with values that relate to family life, such as the status of women, conjugal relationships, education and standard of living. Folk media can be seen as part of the social fabric of the community. While they could reinforce relevant social changes that are already occurring (or be used directly to introduce new ideas) folk forms should not be used for propaganda.

Limitations, on the other hand, included the dangers in "overloading" certain traditional channels with too many "messages" of an instrumental nature. Channels could only be loaded according, to their capacity and with respect, in particular to cultural, religious, or other sensitively integral elements. Sociologists and anthropologists could help planners define these sensitive factors affecting such limitations.

Some Criteria for Selection and Use

- Concern for plasticity of the medium, or capacity of a particular form to be "loaded" with specific innovative messages. Examination of religious or social functions attributed to the medium should be made so as not to distort its special role. In some, cases, examination may reveal such use to be unacceptable. However, it has been found that religious themes can be interpreted in modern context, providing impetus for social change.
- It would be determine whether the medium has an age or individuality (in which case positive identification of audience with actor can be the agent of change), or whether it is entirely non-individual. It has sometimes been found that certain messages can be best expressed without the personalities of, actors in evidence during performance, as in puppet show, mask presentations and giant figures.
- It should be noted, whether a particular medium or any aspect of its traditions and features could be used by or extended to, mass media presentation. If so, is this desirable in relation to both a medium and the message?
- Are the required resources, talent, materials, texts, available for extensive utilization of the medium?
- Does the selected medium have entertainment value and/or artistic appeal?
- Is it unique enough to prove a valuable communication channel?
- Is the form of the proposed medium flexible enough to incorporate a sufficiently broad range of content materials, such as family planning and other developmental messages?
- Is the medium sufficiently versatile to reach varied audiences? To properly assess this criterion, the country must be in a position to assess the range of traditional media and their suitability for audiences according to local and provincial make-up.
- Is the selected medium, relevant to the intended audience?

Puppet

Long years ages perhaps in our very village, men and women must have gathered time after time to watch puppet-shows. The puppets may have been different from those of today. Their costumes may have been more elegant, too, but the fun and the laughter must have been the same. There are many echoes from the past that make us sure that puppetry in India is one of the most ancient arts.

Some students of the art of puppetry think that this was the earliest kind of drama developed by man where and many think these artists were our Indian ancestors. However that may be, we at least have evidence of its existence hundreds of years ago. Still the most interesting fact for us is that even today puppetry is practiced in almost all the countries of the world. It has been weaving itself slowly and permanently into the cultures of all peoples both East and West.

Advantages

First, because the material for the puppets, the costumes and the stage can be found in even the poorest village.

Second, because the entire world loves to "play actor"; so the village people both old and young can find a place in some of the dramas.

Third, because rich and poor, scholar and illiterate, old and young, all love to see the best man wins in the play. They all alike laugh in the comedies, and weep in the tragedies and see that the problems of the play to all casters and creeds alike. It takes the edge off their prejudices, therefore.

Puppets, therefore, have unlimited possibilities in the village for:

- Entertainment.
- Education.
- Self-expression.
- Social Action.

Puppet Educate

- The persons who make the puppets and act out the plays are called puppeteers. They become more expert in acting writing the plays, the more plays they produce.
- By various means they get a keen insight into human nature and a deeper understanding of human emotions, Not only the puppeteer is being educated but the listeners are being educated as well and that quite painlessly.
- The audience is learning as it books and listern becomes a true audio-visual aid to teaching.
- Down through the years religious teachers have used puppets to make the stories from the sacred scriptures real to the people.
- Through this method and through the skill of story telling the sacred scriptures are now well known even to illiterates. However, today, in this era of science, teachers are using puppets as a medium for many scientific subjects.
- Health, agriculture, literacy, sanitation are dramatized on the puppet stage with startling effect. There is almost nothing that cannot be taught by the amazing little creatures called puppets. They dance, they sing, they turn a handspring but always in the interest of social action and inner change.
- Age-old traditions are being at critically as the puppets move about the stage, looking backward at the old and locking forward to the new.

- The illiterate stops, looks and listens:
- Since villagers are mostly illiterate the audience viewing the puppets are mostly so. Sometimes they are familiar with the play and sometimes not. If it is religious play they know it but if it is a new scientific idea, they do not.
- The audience comes for entertainment but usually goes away with a new idea. Both the literate and the illiterate see hope for a more wholesome community. The illiterate decides during the play that like the hero he will learn to read and write. The literate decides during the same play to begin teaching his illiterate neighbours. Both are being educated.

Puppets Help Self-Expression

You will notice that even shy people manipulate puppets and learn their parts. This is because the puppeteer is hidden from sight and he has no self-consciousness whatsoever. He lets himself go and finds his first chance at self-expression.

In the development of personality this is an important step, so use your shy villagers in the plays. You will help to make new leaders. He changes his voice, so that each puppet sounds different from the other puppet.

Types of Puppets

- The marionette or string puppet: The marionette or string puppet has a joined body and limbs. It can be made of wood, wire, paper, and string, cloth stuffed with paper, rag or sawdust. It is suspended by strings, which are attached to different places on the body and limbs and to a control in the puppeteer's hands. Movement of the puppet is produced by moving the control and by pulling or loosening the strings. This requires considerable practice.
- The rod puppet is controlled by rods or stiff wires from beneath. Its body consists of vertical rods. The middle rod is jointed, and on its upper end the head is fixed. The vertical rods are combined together by a horizontal rod or crossbar, where the shoulders should be and from this hand arms. It has no legs.
- Close or simple hand puppets.
- Shadow puppets.

Preparation

The Hand Puppet can be made in a short time and the materials used in making them can be easily obtained. The following are the materials required. Thin card board or used post card, old news paper, paper, glue two pieces of string, Indian Ink, both black and red colour box pens, brushes, coloured cloth, a pair of scissors, needle and thread. When the materials are ready for use the following procedure is to be followed step by step.

- A piece of cardboard or a used post card is rolled around the first finger and a tube is made to fit it. Glue is applied to make the tube firm. This tube will be neck of the puppet.
- A ball is prepared by crumpling a large sheet of old newspaper of rags and is pressed over and around the tube. The ball is shaped to form the stuffing of the head of the puppet.

- The head made of crumpled newspaper is covered with a sheet of plain paper or cloth. Care should be taken to see that one side of the ball is free from folds and creases. The paper or cloth is tied in place round the neck with a piece of string. The author has used cream coloured cloth and has got good results.
- The smooth side of the ball is painted with colours to be the face of the puppet. To look Impressive the face should have only a few broad features, for example, large black eyes and long sweeping eyebrows a distinct mouth and a few lines for the hair etc.
- A narrow tube of bright coloured cloth is made, long enough to cover the hand and forearm of the puppeteer.
- The head of the puppet is put upside down inside the cloth tube so that the seam is kept towards the back of the head.
- The cloth is tied on to the neck of the puppet firmly with a piece of string in such a way that the opening of the cardboard tube is not blocks.
- The cloth is turned right side out the puppet.
- Slits are cut for the thumb and the middle finger. Two small arms for the puppet can be made, so that the thumb and the middle finger can be inserted into them. By adopting this device the puppet can be made to clap or fold hands.
- The puppet is now ready. A name is given to it. If the puppet is to play the role of a man, a turban or cap is placed on his head and a moustache is painted on his face. If the puppet is a lady, well, a nice saree or gaghra could be made for her.
- Only by constant practices the puppeteer can make the puppet come to life. Before he gives any performance with the puppets it is advisable that he should practise moving them in front of a mirror until they look as if they are in life and blood. The puppeteer can work a puppet on each hand and can make each one to express by its gestures. He should change his voice as far as possible so that the left hand puppet and the right hand puppet will be able to speak in different voices. If one of them is a woman, the puppeteer is to produce a matching female voice, which often is difficult. The author has used the tape recorder in puppet shows and has got excellent results. In this case not only it is easier to match the quality of the voice with the role of the puppet but it is possible to produce background effect when occasions arise. The problem of synchronisation arises in such cases and so the puppeteer must try his best to move only the puppet who talks through the tape. The author has experienced no difficulty in maintaining perfect synchronisation between the gestures of the puppet and the dialogue of the puppet recorded on the tape. When a tape recorder is easily available this is worth experimenting.

Puppet Stage

A miniature stage with curtains and back drops can be made to produce dramatic effect. The professional puppeteers in India use few pieces of bamboo or wooden planks to construct the structure of the stage and then cover it with bright coloured curtains and drops. The back screen is usually of a light colour. The structure of the stage depends upon the type of puppets to be used. A stage for Marionettes has an altogether different structure. A shadow Puppet requires a simple stage as it is demonstrated behind an illuminated screen to produce silhouette effect. Rod Puppets and Hand Puppets are demonstrated in stages of simple structure. Very often hand Puppets are demonstrated in improvised stages. The space between the two pillars can be utilised as a stage for the hand puppets, if a saree or bed-sheet is stretched across the same. A saree or bed-sheet can be stretched across the space between two chairs placed face to face and a stage can be prepared in no time. The simplest method of improvising a stage is by using a charpoy, which is readily available in villages. The frame of the charpoy serves as the frame of the screen. A saree or a blanket or a bed-sheet can be draped over this frame and fastened tightly to form a screen. The three types of improved stages are shown earlier.

The puppeteers sit behind the screen and hold their arms up so that the audience can only see the puppets, which appear above the screen. The audience cannot see them. It is not necessary to use a dark background in such stages. Having a black screen behind the improvised can do this. Any carpenter can construct a portable and adjustable stage at a low cost. Such a stage can be elaborately decorated with curtains, wings and drops.

Hints to Writers of Puppet Plays

The puppet plays dramas and should, therefore, conform to the rules for writing drama. A drama is a play written to be acted on a stage. It must be full of action. A play is sometimes written to present a story for entertainment; sometimes a story that presents a problem and its solution.

One scene follows another in sequence so that the audience follows every detail clearly. The situation on the stage is continually changing. Periods of suspense during which emotions are aroused are followed by periods of emotional release. Laughter is one way of emotional release, and it is always good to introduce humour and wit into the play. Puppets can even give Songs and dancing. Early in the play the dramatic question should be introduced. This can be subtle but the audience must be aware of it and kept in suspense until the climax. Soon after the dramatic question is answered the play must end.

Although the bizarre and fantastic have their appeal, the play should not be too far removed from the experience of the audience. Otherwise they will fail to apply it to themselves. When teaching a lesson through a play teaches only one thing. This lesson revolves around the dramatic question and the idea must be clear when the play ends.

The characters in the play must be distinctive and may caricature. They should introduce themselves or be introduced by the other characters as they make their appearance. The characters should express in the dialogue their most outstanding characteristic. Speeches should be short. Remember that a puppet cannot change its facial expression nor can it perform too many gestures. It is extremely limited in action. Quick dialogue and short speeches are easy to present.

If necessary, each puppeteer can work two hand puppets at a time. Since the stage frequently permits space for only two puppeteers, this imposes a restriction on the number of characters that can appear together on the stage.

Time must be given to change the puppet on one's hand and yet there must be no long pauses. The plot should run on smoothly until the curtain drops at the end of a scene. If there are pauses the attention of the audience may wander and never be recaptured, changing of characters can take place between scenes or during the music. The writer must arrange for this when writing the play.

It is very confusing to the audience to have two puppets action one part, for the tendency is to think of each puppet as a person. Some people find it difficult to speak in two different voices. But change of voice must be attempted so the different puppets are not only different to look at but sound different. One person can present a man on one hand, and a woman or child on the other. He deepens his voice for the man and raises it for the woman or the child.

Repetition emphasizes a point and helps the listeners to remember the main idea. But repetition must not be dull. The same idea can be expressed in many different ways, particularly if the dialogue is amusing or the lesson music.

As you write your play keep your eye on "production." A play is written to be acted on the stage. Ask yourself questions as you review your play. Remember that each word should serve a purpose in the play. No phrase, however clever should be introduced, unless it contributes to building up the intended picture. Every world, gesture, action, in the play must contribute something to the whole production. Study the audience. Note its reactions. Never bore it. The audience wants to be entertained, to laugh and share in the fun. But the audience is willing to catch a new idea and if your story moves a listener deeply he may begin to better his own life and the life of his neighbours.

6

Media Effectiveness and Multi Sensory Approach

For decades, educators and instructional designers have struggled with the dilemma of choosing an appropriate media or medium to achieve desired learner outcomes. Such a process can be a very difficult and complex task. In other words, the educational community must embrace technology as a viable tool for learning and seek a better understanding of its characteristics in order to improve the instructional process. This process will improve as educators and software designers have a clearer understanding of the various media characteristics, learner related issues, problems associated with media selection, and determining the proper approach for media selection:

Various types of media (printed word, visuals, audio, video, simulators, multimedia, and interactive multimedia) have their own unique characteristics and qualities. Gagné and Reisner (1992) refer to these physical capabilities as "media attributes." For example, visuals or still graphics allow the learner to acquire and retain visual images. The printed word is most effective for good readers and necessary for most delivery methods. Sound, on the other hand, is most useful for poor readers or those with hearing impairments.

Video is more appropriate for mimicking human performance; whereas, simulators or real objects should be used to teach cognitive skills involving objects unfamiliar to the learner. With multimedia, a single instructional environment incorporates all types of media that can stimulate the learners various modalities. Interactive multimedia adds a further dimension to multimedia in that it gives the user the ability to create associational links within and across the various media in a linear or nonlinear way. Furthermore, the learner is often allowed to add his own information and construct his own relationships. Because these various media formats posses their own unique characteristics, they lend themselves more and less suitable for accomplishing certain kinds of learning tasks (Kozma, 1994).

Along with the media attributes, Najjar (2001) provides examples of proper media usage. For remembering small amounts of verbal information over a short period of time, auditory media should be chosen over text-based media. Conversely, verbal information that needs to be retained over a long period of time should be presented in a text format. Pictures allow for greater retention than text, but should not be used to communicate abstract concepts. When pictures and verbal information are used in concert, Najjar (2001) emphasizes that each must "...support, relate to, or extend the information presented in the other medium." This synchronized presentation allows the learner to make a better connection between prior knowledge and new information. Interactive multimedia, if cognitively engaging, encourages learners to process the learning material in more elaborate ways. Najjar (2001) further states that interactivity has a stronger effect on immediate learning than long-term retention. Therefore, one of the key components to media selection is acquiring a better understanding of the various media attributes and recognizing when to use it.

Other vital features to media selection are the various issues surrounding the learner or what many have labeled, "assessing the audience."Included in this assessment is the individual's learning style. The Gregorc Model of Learning Styles is "one of the most effective models for understanding learning style differences" (Tobias, 1994). Since no two individuals are the same, each person's ability to encode information is based upon his view of the world around him. This perception dictates a person's overall thought process. Furthermore, a person's perception determines the way he uses the information.

According to Gregorc's model, each person has two perceptual qualities: concrete and abstract. Concrete perception is one that involves the senses: sight, smell, touch, taste, and hearing. Abstract perception is the ability to conceive ideas, visualize, or believe what we cannot see. Though everyone uses both concrete and abstract perceptual abilities every day, each person is more comfortable using one over the other. Once the individual gathers the information presented, he begins to organize this information in a useful way. Gregorc's model provides two ordering abilities used by everyone: sequential and random. Sequential ordering is the ability to organize information in a linear, step-by-step manner. Random ordering is the ability to organize information by chunks in a non-linear fashion. Thus, Gregorc provides four learning style categories: concrete sequential, abstract sequential, abstract random, and concrete random. Keep in mind that no individual fits neatly into "one" category. However, each person, or learner, does posses a dominant style or styles that blend together to produce unique abilities and strengths. Therefore, those responsible for media selection must have a well-grounded understanding of how the target audience perceives and organizes information in order for media to have its greatest influence.

Other issues associated with the learner include his cultural and social backgrounds, age, and disabilities. Choosing media that is non-offensive to the learner's ethnic and social upbringing is more likely to deter any loss of motivation or concentration. Media that is void of slang or unfamiliar dialect will also reduce distractions. With regard to age, selecting media that is age-appropriate can increase motivation and concentration as well as influence the learner's overall attitude (Nowlan, 1999). Identifying individuals in the target audience with specific physical or learning disabilities should also be considered in the selection of instructional media.

After considering the media and learner characteristics, attention should be given to the instructional events or strategies. Gagné provides nine Instructional Events (Instructional Design, 2001):

- Gaining attention–give the learner a stimulus (a good problem, a new situation).
- Describe the goal; state what the learner will be able to accomplish after instruction.
- Stimulate recall of prior knowledge; remind learner of prior knowledge relevant to the current lesson (facts, rules, procedures or skills).
- Present the material to be learned; chunking of information is crucial.
- Provide guidance for learning; presentation of content is different from instructions on how to learn.
- Elicit performance; 'practice,' let the learner do something with the newly acquired behaviour.
- Provide information feedback; show correctness of the trainee's response.
- Assess performance; test if the lesson has been learned.
- Enhance retention and transfer; inform the learner about similar problem situations and provide additional practice.

Gagné, Briggs, and Wager (1992) provide five divisions of learner outcomes associated with general media selection.

- *Intellectual Skills*—Select media providing feedback to learner responses.
- *Cognitive Strategies*—Select media providing feedback to learner responses.
- *Verbal Information*—Select media able to present verbal messages and elaboration.
- *Attitudes*—Select media able to present realistic picture of human model and the model's message.
- *Motor Skills*—Select media making possible direct practice of skill, with informative feedback.

These learner outcomes are fundamental and should be one of the first considerations when approaching the instructional design process. Without such, media selection is of no importance. Furthermore, educators and the alike often let the media or medium determine the instructional method. Such an approach severely limits the ability to achieve the desired learner outcomes.

These concerns, as well as a few more, are also presented in Tony Bates' ACTIONS model (Freeman, 1998). ACTIONS is an acronym for access, costs, teaching and learning, interactivity and user-friendliness, organizational issues, novelty, and speed. In contrast to other models, Bates' model focuses on media selection in terms of current technology. Some of Bates questions to consider when selecting media include the following:

- A—How accessible is a particular technology for learners?
- C—What is the unit cost per student?
- T—What are the best technologies for supporting this teaching and learning?
- I—What kind of interaction does this technology enable?
- O—What changes in the organization need to be made?
- N—How new is this technology?
- S—How quickly can courses be mounted with this technology?

The instructional designer must determine the existing conditions (physical environment, current technology, administrative and financial constraints, and futuristic changes) and desired outcomes for all participants (learner outcomes, instructor/facilitator outcomes, possible administrative effects, validity of desired goals).

In summary, anyone involved in the media selection process should become acquainted with the various models and questions already established. One must also remember that media selection is not an exact science. Media selection for instructional purposes is a difficult, time-consuming, and seemingly an overwhelming task. If approached in a practical manner, the process seems less daunting. Such a task must begin with an assessment of the existing conditions and desired instructional goals. Furthermore, as the capabilities of the various media types continue to expand; hopefully, so will our understanding of media's influence on learning. Throughout these changes ahead, one critical point must be kept at the heart of media selection: the learner must be given priority over the medium. The method should dictate the media or medium. If this mindset is maintained, then learner outcomes will be achieved with the help of properly selected media.

Tasks Behind the Selection and Use of Educational Technology

- Analyze Learners.
- State Objectives.
- Select Media and Materials.
- Utilize Media and Materials.
- Require Learner Participation.
- Evaluate and Revise.

Analyze Learners

This first step is based on the recognition that some factors such as learning styles, prerequisite knowledge or skills, emotional, cultural or economic issues may interfere with how well students might learn.

- What are all the prerequisites?
- Which students are encountering this content for the first time?
- Do you know which students may have learning disabilities?
- Is your content designed to challenge firmly held beliefs?
- Have you included a rich array of instructional methods, including media; what are they; when do you plan to use them; WHY?

Stating Learning Outcomes

Do people perform consistently well when there is no standard set for which to strive? Do your students know what you expect from them? What is the goal for your learners to achieve? What new skill, knowledge or attitude should the learner have at the completion of the instruction? Outcomes can help you answer these and similar questions. An outcome is a measurable or observable result of instruction. It is a statement, not of what you are going to put in your lesson, but of what you expect the learner to get out of it. How can learning outcomes help you to determine what instructional techniques or methods to use? Some questions can help you focus what is really important and can help set clear standards for your students to aspire to.

- Is the usual learning environment suitable for the learning to take place? Could it be changed or modified to optimize learning possibilities?
- What is the most appropriate media to use or produce for your intended purpose. If, for instance, your students were learning subject material that had a motor skill component, you may elect to present the skill through the use of video. It is unlikely you would use an overhead transparency for such a task.
- How will you measure student performance? What are the acceptable standards? A clear learning outcome is your yardstick.

Attribute of Pictorial Representation

Attribute of Size and Colour

Usually, pictorial representation is more easily seen and understood when there is a minimum of ambiguity. In other words, bigger is usually better. Size is both absolute and proportional. Absolute size is the image seen on a projection screen or a textbook. The image as a whole has certain and measurable height and width. When certain parts or elements of a picture are either larger or smaller in relation to the picture as a whole and to the other parts of the picture then the size of the parts is said to be proportional. In proportional size, that which is larger is perceived to be closer to the viewer, more important than smaller elements or both.

- Colour also an important attribute about pictorial representation.
- Colour required to make meaning clear.
- It required ensuring that a given procedure be followed.
- Colour is necessary for emotional appeal.
- Colour to create a feeling of unity or continuity within a presentation.

Attribute of Movement

Learning procedures and motor skills requires the attribute of movement. Understanding processes such as capillary action in plants, patterns created by collisions between subatomic particles, the action of light waves traveling through gases of differing densities, and the coursing of blood through arteries and veins, are all enhanced through the use of the attribute of movement.

Attribute of Language

Critical is the ability to read at a given level of comprehension.

Basic vocabulary a prerequisite to the understanding of new material.

The content be learned entirely by someone with an adequate grasp of language, or is another medium required as well.

Attribute of Sound/Picture Relationship

The underlying theme or the harmonic structure of Bach's The Art of Fugue can be shown and demonstrated most effectively through the relationship of picture and sound. The picture shows the structure: the individual notes, the key, the pauses, and a particular refrain. The sound demonstrates how it works, it explains in certain terms why the composer made the choices that leave the listener mesmerized by the beautiful logic of this music.

Attribute of Arrangement

Different attributes are common to different technologies. (Joining computers into networks is a technology, which can potentially combine the most attributes in any location at any time thus overcoming restrictions of time and space). Understanding the attributes or characteristics of certain media or technologies is important for deciding which are most likely to enhance learning. Whether selecting material already produced or planning on producing your own learning materials, it is vitally important to match the requirements of your learning outcomes with the characteristics or attributes of any given technology. One way to proceed is to consider what you already know about the media available and then begin asking yourself a series of questions that eliminate what isn't feasible or possible. We have chosen some questions at random that might help you in your decision-making process.

- What are the most important tasks or requirements? What are my learning outcomes?
- Based on the learning outcomes, what are the most applicable media attributes?
- Are there any learning materials already available that I might be able to use?
- Should I consider using more than one technology or medium? Will they augment one another or detract from one another?
- Can student location, work schedule or other factors of access be addressed by the use of available technology?
- Where will I be teaching the material? What are the environmental factors?
- Do I have the skills needed to produce effective media? Do I have the resources to learn?
- Can the medium be produced by the time it is needed?
- Can the production, maintenance and operation costs be afforded?
- Does the medium fit the policies/programmes at the college?
- Is the medium a practical choice given its environment?
- Is the technology I want to use readily available? Is it easy to use?
- What is the main benefit to me of using the technology? What are the benefits for students?

Utilize Media and Materials

Once you have chosen your media or technology or have produced your learning materials, the important next step is preparation. One of the best things you can do is preview unfamiliar media or materials (videos, CD-ROMs, computer applications and the like). If you have the time, you should definitely practice integrating the technology or media into your instruction. If you do a lot of presenting you may decide to video tape your practice in order to detect any glaring omissions, mistakes or distractions. Next, prepare your learning environment. Make sure you have all the equipment, peripherals, aids for the disabled, support material, cables, and spare bulbs that you might need if something should go wrong, because sooner or later, something will go wrong. Get to your learning environment in plenty of time so that you can organize yourself and your material, set up your equipment and test it. This is very important next; you will need to prepare your students for the learning you expect from them. Use outlines, study questions, even a video tape or PowerPoint presentation to "set the stage."

Require Learner Participation

In the ASSURE model, if it could be said that one step was more important than another, then this might be it. All too often, media is used in a passive way. These results partly from one characteristic common to most media: they are channels for the delivery of some kind of (stored) information. Note that delivery implies travel in a single direction. Overhead transparencies, audio, even video are all essentially one way media. They do not depend on or encourage learner participation. This is certainly true for the home television set. It is a passive medium, with information traveling in one direction only. The viewer is rarely engaged, yet we know that people learn best when they're actively involved in the information being presented. (Being actively involved is not quite the same as being physically involved; your involvement might be strictly cognitive or emotional). How many studies have shown that for significant learning to take place the learner must be engaged in the information and the learning environment? How often do we reminisce about one of our old teachers, perhaps from high school, and think to ourselves that the only reason we passed Math/Physics/English that year was because some teacher made it interesting and relevant? But now we're in the era of computers and everything must be "interactive."

Evaluation and Revision

The following is a simple outline of nine steps for the evaluation of your use of technology. It begins with a consideration of your teaching goals, objectives or outcomes and proceeds to the revision stage.

- Devise an assessment method
    1. refer to your goals and outcomes.
    2. design an assessment method.
- Pre-test your students
- Evaluate performance/grade test
- Prepare students for mediated instruction
    1. create advance organizers.
    2. write study questions or other cues.
- Present material
- Require student performance
- Evaluate performance/grade post test
- Compare results with pre-test
- Revise as required

Rationale for Selection of Media

- Identification of a medium is appropriate to the content and objectives so as to have the appropriate stimulation.
- Permit the learner to involve in the teaching-learning process.
- Capable of transmitting all the desired information, stimulate the thinking and arouse responses.

Need of the Media

- To transmit the information/knowledge to the desired learners.
- To make the information transaction/communication more effective considering the attractiveness, clarity, motivational factors, feed backing factors.
- To attain the objectives at the desired level.
- To cater the needs of the individual differences.
- To make the education more individual.
- To make the education more accessible to a large group.
- To make education more productive.

Media Selection Factors

- Human consideration.
- Affordability.
- Practical constraints.

Specifically, They Include:

- Task factors.
- Learner factors.
- Instructional management factors.
- Economic factors.
- Technical factors.
- Administrative factors.

Task Factors

- Task identification.
- Task analysis.
    1. Sequencing the task.
    2. Compare with the objectives.

Learner Factors

- Age level of the learners.
- Performance level of the learner.
- Scope for learner participation/learner involvement.
- Scope for self pacing, immediate feed backing.

Institutional Management Fa.ctors

- The realization of the objectives.
- In time use of the media.
- Scope for meaningful instruction.
- Scope for management of time, discipline, space factor...

Economic Factors

- Affordability.
- Scope for improvisation.

Technical Factors

- Technically reachable for the teachers, such a way that the media selection, operation and feed backing will be free from technical jargons.

Administrative Factors

- Include the administration of the school in general and the class room in specific.
- Affordability of maintenance.
- On par with the normal set up of the class room.

There are a wide variety of items to consider before you decide which media to use in your teaching. Considering these items in your lesson-planning stage will insure that your choice of media enriches the learning experiences of your students and that your teaching will elicit the intended learning outcomes.

13 things to consider when selecting media:

1. Think pedagogy first, technology second.
2. Identify the characteristics of the learners.
3. Analyze your lessons to determine your needs.
4. Consider all your technology options.
5. Think about student's level of competency with regard to technology use.
6. Select media based on practical factors.
7. Consider time available.
8. Plan for alternate media where possible.
9. Provide a clear, well-organized structure and good directions.
10. Prepare yourself to teach with the desired media.
11. Count the direct and indirect costs to the student.
12. Arrange for copyright clearance if you use materials not your own.
13. Be sure to license any software you distribute.

1. Think Pedagogy First, Technology Second

Don't put the priority on technology. Always think first in terms of what is the intended learning outcome, in other words, what you want students to achieve or to do at the end of your lesson or activity (refer to your learning objectives), then select media that will support this. Think about what will best teach this topic. Also consider the tools that the student must work with and the prior experiences of the students. Do not spend the entire class time on teaching how to use a very sophisticated media unless that is your learning objective.

2. Identify the Characteristics of the Learners

Identify the characteristics of the learners in terms of their ability to read, to understand abstract symbols, and so on. Also, consider the learners' familiarity with the operation of the media.

3. Analyze your Course to Determine your Needs

Determine the instructional type of your learning activities. Will your activity be instructor-led, self-paced, or group learning?

Different learning tasks may require different media. For instance, when you want your students to be able to build their own concept maps, your class might be divided into four parts; introduction to concept mapping, demonstration of building a concept map with software (i.e., Inspiration), the student activity of building a concept map using the software, and assessment of the product.

For the demonstration part, you might want to use a smart board in order for all students to be able to see your demonstration. For the students' activities, you need to make sure that each computer that will be used has the software installed.

4. Consider all your Technology Options

Don't automatically assume that you always need higher-level technologies for students to achieve your learning objectives. Often, the objectives can be achieved with other types of media.

For instance, you can also demonstrate how to build a concept map in a whiteboard when you do not have access to a smart board. Also, students can build their own concept map on paper.

5. Think About Student's Level of Competency with Regard to Technology Use

Don't assume that students possess a certain level of competency in using technology, especially when you want them to manipulate media. Always consider students' prior knowledge and skills for the media use, and plan ahead how you will help them use technology for learning activities. Technology should not be an obstacle for learning.

If you plan to use a certain media in your teaching, don't assume that students will have access to the technologies you want to use; often they do not. For example, will they have access to a computer? What optional media selection will you have for those without access to the technology you've planned for?

6. Select Media Based on Practical Factors

Select media based on practical factors; cost, equipment availability, user expertise, and other general considerations. Certain types of media might not be a practical choice even though you are sure that your students will benefit from it. This may be for many reasons including budget, media availability, and so on. For example, it is not practical to wait a fourth of the available class time for stunning video clips to download from the web. The simpler and easier media that you can use and still meet your instructional objectives, the better. If you want to develop the media as your instructional activity, consider development timelines and budgets.

7. Consider Time Available

When you plan for media selection, consider the overall time needed such as preparation time of the media and the time needed for students to master the media, especially if students will use the media for learning. Also, consider given all the other tasks the student must carry out (textbook reading, studying lesson pages, doing homework, etc.), how much additional time are you asking them to spend in activities using technologies? You might want to supply some "givens" to get students on to the real learning you are interested in more quickly.

8. Plan for Alternate Media where Possible

Prepare for the potential that the technology you have chosen might fail. Also make a plan for an alternate way for students to submit lessons or complete assignments if the technology is not operational.

9. Provide a Clear, Well-Organized Structure and Good Directions

This is critical, especially for self-instruction activities. If the students cannot get immediate help from an instructor, the lessons should be designed well and provide good directions.

10. Prepare Yourself to Teach with this Media

There are two parts to this: the first part is becoming comfortable with using the media yourself, and the second is to plan how you will teach with it. How familiar are you with what you want to use? Will you require training? If so, how will you get it? Plan to practice prior to instruction.

11. Count the Direct and Indirect Costs to the Student

If you will ask your students to use a particular technology, count the direct and indirect costs to the student. For example, when developing a custom programme, is there commercially available software that would reduce/eliminate the need to custom build so much? Development costs are passed on to the student, at least in part. The learning gains for the student should be justifiable for the additional cost incurred.

There are also direct costs to the student for software purchases and Internet access, for example. Be careful not to drive up the cost of the learning activity by requiring too much technology.

12. Arrange for Copyright Clearance if you use Materials not your Own

Any media which you have obtained from others (images and text from the Web or a software programme are just two examples) may well be copyrighted, and using them without permission could be an infringement subject to legal action.

13. Be Sure to License any Software you Distribute

Some software (Netscape Navigator and SoftArc's First Class are two examples) requires no licensing and may be freely distributed. Most other software (Apple's QuickTime, Macromedia runtime files created in Authorware, Attain or Director, as examples) do require a standard license agreement in order to be legally distributed.

Criteria for Selection

Needs of the individual school based on knowledge of the curriculum and of the existing collection are given first consideration.

- Overall purpose.
- Timeliness of permanence.
- Importance of the subject matter.

- Quality of the writing/production.
- Readability and popular appeal.
- Authoritativeness.
- Reputation of the publisher/producer.
- Reputation and significance of the author/artist/composer/producer, etc.
- Format and price.

When choosing media for a distance education course, several questions should be considered:

- Which media are likely to appeal to the learners?
- Do the learning objectives suggest particular media?
- Is the technology needed to carry these media available?
- How should each of the preferred media be used, and how much should each be used (for example, for what share of the student's time)?
- What would it cost designers, instructors, and learners-in money, time, and flexibility-to use these media?
- Would less expensive media be sufficiently effective?
- Do the chosen media offer variety of stimulus and activity?
- How can the media be combined for maximum effect?

The Concept of Comparative Merits of Media

To make a start on criteria, the concept of comparative merits between media is offered as a more fruitful idea than the usual "advantages and disadvantages" of individual media. When media are being compared, it's common to appraise each medium for both its strengths and weaknesses, yet invariably, the evaluation can be expressed as a comparative merit. For example, print is rather impersonal, whereas audio-visual media can portray the teacher in person. This pair of evaluations can be expressed as a single comparison: personalising the teacher is a merit of audio-visual media compared to print.

Media and Functions of Teaching

Classroom-based teaching and training is still largely undertaken by means of the lecture or a similar form of presentation. It relies on the human voice to convey spoken language, although written words, diagrams and pictures can easily be provided to illustrate or reinforce the spoken word. If your teaching or training relies solely on printed materials, you can make full use of written language, symbols, diagrams, drawings, pictures and you can describe real events with words and illustrations. However, you cannot convey sounds or speech, animation or moving pictures. If you use computer-based materials, you can convey written language and symbols, still and animated pictures (possibly in colour) and, with some equipment, you may be able to include sounds or speech. Each medium you consider using can convey certain symbol systems, but not others.

An alternative approach is to consider your desired learning outcomes and then use this analysis to help in the selection of appropriate media. For example, any course seeking to develop skills in the use of a foreign language would need to include some means of conveying the sound of the spoken language; a demonstration of how a complex piece of equipment works would lose a great deal if moving pictures and sounds were not provided.

Most media are flexible, in that each can be used for a variety of teaching functions. However, while most media can present abstract knowledge and ideas, which are mainly conveyed through the use of spoken or written language, few media are able to present concrete examples of objects, processes, events, etc. Video material is a very rich and flexible medium capable of conveying both abstract knowledge and concrete examples, so it is particularly valuable for demonstrating procedures or events.

Consider the content or form of the teaching when trying to select which medium to use; the kind of learning skills to be developed must also is considered, e.g. motor skills, comprehension, problem-solving, interpersonal skills, etc. Certain media are better than others in terms of how they represent objects, facts, ideas, processes, etc., and their potential to develop learning skills. Text is particularly good for comprehension, abstract ideas, developing arguments, etc. Computers are good for rule-based knowledge, for which there are correct answers or procedures. Video material is particularly good for procedural and interpersonal skills and for conveying concrete examples. It is also good for presenting complex, real-life situations that require interpretation, where ambiguity may be advantageous and a variety of learner responses acceptable.

Media Attributes and Examples with Its Strengths and Limitations

Examples	*Strengths*	*Limitations*
TEXT		
Books Handouts Manuals Magazines Brochures Newsletters Catalogus	■ Relatively inexpensive to produce and duplicate ■ Can be produced quickly ■ Permanent record of instruction ■ Largely time-independent ■ Support individual student use ■ Require no equipment for use ■ Eminently portable ■ Highly accessible ■ Provide easy random access by page numbers and indexing ■ Can be annotated by learners to reflect their personal elaborations and emphases ■ Can add graphics to enrich contents	■ Requires the reading ability of the learner ■ Changing content can be difficult because of its unchangeable characteristics ■ When a very large, worldwide distribution is needed, distribution costs increase ■ Quality printing can be expensive ■ No interactions are built-in

Contd...

AUDIO		
Overall Characteristics	■ Ideal for extending voice and music ■ Costs are relatively inexpensive (compared to video) ■ Good for the less literate (or aural learners) ■ Good for stimulating listener's imagination ■ Good for evoking emotional responses	■ More linear structure ■ No visual element can be added ■ Requires playback device
Telephone Voicemail	■ Low cost (can be expensive based on distance) ■ Easy to use ■ Has feedback feature	■ Length may be limited ■ May involve toll charges
Audiotape Digital audio Compact disks	■ Inexpensive (costs are not related to distance) ■ Easily accessible ■ Easily duplicated	■ Require specific device ■ Hard to modify the recordings once produced and distributed
Audio conference (Teleconferencing)	■ Easy to set up ■ Has feedback feature ■ Remove distance constraint	■ Requires specific device ■ Challenging to schedule a time when everyone can participate
VISUAL AIDS		
Posters Film strips	■ Easy and inexpensive to make and update ■ Lower cost of producing multiple copies ■ Portable and transportable	■ Unsuitable for large groups ■ Anxiety might increase if an instructor has poor hand-writing or poor spelling ■ The sequence of visuals is fixed
Film slides	■ Don't need to re-shoot every film slide in order to make a change for one film ■ Teacher can decide which slides are to be shown ■ Professional in appearance ■ Slides stand up to wear and tear better than film strips ■ Good for large groups	■ Shown in the dark ■ Not good for simultaneous discussion and interaction ■ More difficult to update than other visual aids ■ Requires special equipment
Overhead Transparencies	■ Easy to create, update, and transport ■ Provides an informal atmosp-here	■ Impermanent; they yellow with age ■ Requires less common equipment

Contd...

	■ Open for interaction with groups ■ Good for large groups	
Photographic slides	■ Provide colour images that are realistic, intense, and bright ■ Can use superimposed attention-directing devices ■ Can show close-up, enlarged details of an image with unmatched clarity ■ Convenient, portable, and effective image medium ■ Economical to shoot (compared with motion media) ■ Good for large or small groups	■ No motion (still images) ■ Easy to scratch and bend ■ Not easy to duplicate in quantity ■ Requires projection equipment
Computer Projections (i.e., PowerPoint)	■ Easy to update ■ Professional in appearance ■ Easy to integrate with classroom discussion ■ Possibility for animation ■ Good for large or small group	■ Requires special equipment/ facilities ■ Requires initial training to create ■ Requires significant time to create ■ Requires basic graphics/ composition skills
Digital Photography	■ Can be downloaded directly to your computer and seen immediately ■ Ready for use on the computer immediately ■ Cheap (for lower quality)	■ Can be expensive (for higher quality) ■ Not tangible to hold in your hand ■ Requires a device to output or show its images
REAL OBJECTS		
Samples, Examples, and Mock-Ups	■ Authentic ■ Three dimensional ■ Sometimes inexpensive and readily available ■ Experience may be tactile/ auditory as well as visual	■ Sometimes difficult or impossible to acquire ■ Often difficult to handle or distribute ■ Requires storage space ■ Requires time to create
VIDEO (MOTION)		
Overall characteristics	■ Capable for display of images, motion and colour, along with sound ■ Zoom in for enlarged close-ups or zoom out for a telephoto view ■ Good when your message content is best communicated via sight, sound, and motion	■ More expensive than other visual aids ■ Requires special equipment ■ Not good for discussion and interaction ■ Production equipment is needed ■ Talent and technical knowledge

Contd...

	■ Helps learners visualize a process ■ Produces a change in affect (feelings) ■ Provides more motivation ■ Professional in appearance	are needed or require experts' help
DVDs Videotape Desktop video	■ Can compress time (i.e., time lapse) or expand time (i.e., slow motion) to attract learners' attention ■ Good for large or small groups	■ Expensive to produce ■ Requires time to produce ■ Requires playback equipment
Satellite Delivery Broadcast	■ Real time ■ Good for large and dispersed audience	■ Has time constraint ■ Cost of transmission ■ Limited bandwidth
Video Conferencing	■ Allow "real time" visual contact between students and the instructor or among students at different sites ■ Enables connection with experts in other geographical locations ■ Can provide access for at-risk or special needs students ■ Provides additional access for students at remote sites	■ Initial cost of the equipment and leasing the lines to transmit conferences may be prohibitive ■ Companies which produce codes have each developed unique methods of compression which are incompatible, although protocols have been established to allow communication among brand names. However, this "universal standard" compromises resolution and quality to a certain degree
TYPES	■ Small room videoconferencing this system is designed primarily for small groups (1-12 participants) at all sites seated around a conference table ■ Classroom videoconferencing this type of system usually uses high quality AV components, codes, and an interface that allows all participants to be seen on the monitors ■ Desktop videoconferencing this system utilizes a personal computer and videoconferencing software. These systems are less expensive, but offer limited resolution. They are most effective for individual and small group use	■ Unless a strong effort is made by the instructor, students not located with the instructor may remain uninvolved. ■ If visuals, like handwritten or copied materials, are not properly prepared, students may have a difficult time reading them ■ If the "pipe" that carries the transmission among sites is not large enough, the students may observe "ghost images" when rapid movement occurs in real time

Contd...

		■ If the system is not properly configured, class members may observe an audio "echo" effect. The result is audio interference that detracts from the learning environment
MULTIMEDIA		
Overall characteristics	■ Delivers dynamic graphics ■ Can foster a high level of interactivity ■ The ability of adaptation ■ Can control other media such as video-tape/disk players, slide projectors, and so on, and use these media and devices in an interactive way ■ Allows exact duplication of instruction at remote sites ■ Primary strength lies in its ability to display images, in motion and colour, along with sound ■ Good when individualized instruction and learning are desired	■ Can be impersonal ■ Can require expensive equipment ■ Might require some players
CD-ROM	■ Portable ■ Easy to handle ■ Can have interactive function ■ Good for individualized learning	■ Hard to make a change once produced and distributed
Computer	■ Holds a great deal of information in its memory ■ Manipulates information rapidly ■ Can adjust the type of feedback to the response of the learner ■ Can retain and analyze records of the progress of the learner and use this information to adapt future instruction sequences to the needs of the learner ■ Can maintain a high level of control over what the learner is allowed to attend to at one time, or it can put this control in the hands of the learner ■ When coupled with a CD-ROM drive, some limitations are overcome, such as lengthy segments of high-quality audio	■ The computer alone cannot efficiently present lengthy segments of high-quality audio, particularly voice ■ The computer alone, as of this writing, cannot efficiently present full-screen, smooth motion graphics of the same quality as a videotape

Contd...

World Wide Web	■ Ubiquitous multimedia container ■ Time and location independent (with Internet access) ■ Can access a seemingly limitless amount and range of information over networks, including local area networks, such as an organization's library and shared databases, and wider networks, including the Internet and World Wide Web ■ Good for inquiry learning	■ Requires development time and cost ■ Requires certain level of hardware, software, and browser ■ Transmission restrictions (bandwidth)
PEOPLE		
Expert(s) Instructor(s) Teacher(s)	■ Highly interactive (depending on the mood or wishes of the person) ■ Highly adaptable and flexible (depending on the skills and attitude of the person) ■ Possesses and reflects empathy ■ Simultaneously processes multiple sensory inputs from various sources and selects those that are most critical to the current situation	■ Can be expensive ■ Same content cannot be delivered every time ■ Highly Dependent on the person's ability to instruct ■ Unreliable for doing the same thing over and over in exactly the same way

Matching Instructional Media

The instructional media to teaching methods is a critical part of the design process. As we have worked through this step by step process, you can see that media is one of the final things to be considered in designing instruction. And yet, many of you are charged with using a particular medium for e-Learning. How do we match media to methods?

The matrix below lists learning outcomes matched to the teaching strategies we discussed in the previous page and now includes the media characteristics necessary to facilitate the intended learning outcomes. Notice that we define what kinds of characteristics the instructional medium (or media if you use more than one) must have in order to support your strategies.

Once you understand the media characteristics needed to support teaching strategies, you might ask yourself a series of questions to help determine exactly which instructional medium is right for your objectives. For example, you will note that intellectual skills and cognitive strategies have the same requirements for media characteristics: interactive feedback. As an e-Learning designer, you would want to consider using something that allows synchronous (or real time) chat, such as a phone or interactive chat room, or video conference; synchronous white board use (statistics cries out for this!), asynchronous interactive practice modules (that do not require real time connection to you) that allow learners to practice and get immediate feedback.

Learning Outcomes	*Sample Objectives*	*Sample Strategies*	*Media Characteristics*
Discrimination	Given a sample of a sonnet as a reference, the learner discriminates between sonnets and other poetic forms in a set of sample poems by indicating which poem is the sonnet.	Students are given a sonnet structure and asked to diagram the form. Focus on the distinctive features of the sonnet (such as the final couplet). The structure is presented as text and practice. Demonstration.	The medium must present verbal information (text/graphics and/or sound), and should provide interactive feedback. Real objects or simulations are helpful. Audio and graphic images (including video) may be needed for non-readers.
Concrete Concepts	Given a set of 8 recordings of blood pressure readings, the learner identifies when to write down the diastolic reading by correctly noting the pressure at the appropriate aural cue.	Students hear many different recordings of blood pressure readings and see the mercury rise to the point of no sound and drop to the final sounds for appropriate readings. Demonstration.	The medium must present verbal and auditory information (text/graphics and sound), and should provide interactive feedback. Real objects or simulations are helpful. Audio and graphic images (including video) may be needed for non-readers.
Defined Concepts	When asked to identify differences in tools, the learner classifies a random set of tools into ratchets, flat tools, and impact tools and labels them appropriately.	Students have several examples of tools. Distinctive features are identified for each type. Demonstration.	The medium must present verbal information (text/graphics and/or sound), and should provide interactive feedback. Real objects or simulations are helpful. Audio and graphic images (including video) may be needed for non-readers.
Rules	Given two types of t-test (one and two-tailed) and specific problems, the learner applies the correct test with 100 per cent accuracy.	Students must run t-tests on data in a variety of situations. Demonstration.	The medium must present verbal information (text/graphics and/or sound), and should provide interactive feedback. Real objects or simulations are helpful. Audio and graphic images (including video) may be needed for non-readers.

Contd...

Learning Outcomes	Sample Objectives	Sample Strategies	Media Characteristics
Higher Order Rules (problem solving)	Given the dimensions of a site, a limited budget, and building needs; the learner generates a design for a daycare center and explains his or her reasons for choosing the design.	Students must have an understanding of the correct calculations and measurements demonstrated by correctly practicing on smaller forms Demonstration.	The medium must present verbal information (text/graphics and/or sound), and should provide interactive feedback. Real objects or simulations are helpful. Audio and graphic images (including video) may be needed for non-readers.
Cognitive Strategies	When asked to recall the developmental theory of Jean Piaget, the learner adopts a key-word mnemonic technique for memorizing the major elements of Piaget's developmental theory.	Demonstrate the power of mnemonic memory strategies, rehearsal strategies, method of Loci, etc. Show examples of each.	The medium must present verbal information (text/graphics and/or sound), and should provide interactive feedback. Real objects or simulations are helpful. Audio and graphic images (including video) may be needed for non-readers.
Verbal Information	Given a verbal question, the learner can state at least two causes for World War II.	Present facts about the war from many perspectives.	The medium must present verbal information and elaborations. Audio and graphic images (including video) may be needed for non-readers.
Motor Skills	Using a standard keyboard and mouse, the learner designs a personal website that includes at least two graphics, a resume, and relevant examples of lesson plans.	Demonstrate website development using an html editor (software). Discuss layout, graphics and formats, copyright issues, linking, and content.	The medium must provide direct practice of skills with informative feedback.
Attitudes	When confronted with a "flame" during an e-mail discussion, the learner will choose to ignore the flame or will temper a response rather than continue to argue.	Propose several scenarios that allow students to compare reactions and motivations of speaker and listener. Demonstration.	The medium must present realistic examples of human behaviour models and the desired message.

Motor skills require direct practice with materials; however, you might consider creating realistic simulations. A great example that has been around a long time is flight and driving simulators. Web-based simulators (or CD-ROMs) might be a solution for your course.

This matrix is meant to be an aid to you as you design your e-Learning courses. Obviously, you will refine the design as you work with your students (consider learner characteristics) and update the learning objectives and assessments (goals and objectives and the assessment elements). Designing instruction, like good teaching, is an iterative process of re-evaluating and refining materials, strategies, and goals.

7

Factors in Media Selection

Instructional Media-Definitions

- Physical means to communicate instructional message (Gagne).
- Amalgam of stimulus modes-human interaction, realia, pictures, written symbols, sound (Rowntree).
- Software with the necessary hardware in a particular context of instructional communication (Heidt).

Media Types (Dale's Cone)

- Written text.
- Symbols, icons.
- Graphs, plots.
- Recorded audio.
- Pictures.
- Video film.
- Live audio.
- Live presentation.
- Performance.

Media Attributes

- Sensory modality (reading or listening; one or two channels).
- Symbolic modality (verbal or non-verbal).
- Design cues (typography, colour, texture, motion vs. still, intonation).
- Locus of control (pace, sequence).
- Interactive features (feedback, collaboration).

Media Selection Factors

- Type of learning task.
- Teacher's attitudes, skills etc.
- Characteristics of students.
- Methods selection.
- Practical constraints.
- Physical conditions.

- Target population.
- Subject matter and required student performance.

Some of the practical factors to be considered in media selection are:

- What size of group must be accommodated in one room on a single occasion?
- What is the range of viewing and hearing distance for the use of the media?
- How easily can the media be "interrupted" for pupil responding or other activity and for providing feedback to the learners?
- Is the presentation "adaptive" to the learners' responses?
- Does the desired instructional stimulus require motion, colour, still pictures, spoken words, or written words?
- Is sequence fixed or flexible in the medium? Is the instruction repeatable in every detail?
- Which media provide best for incorporating most of the conditions of learning appropriate for the objective?
- Which media provide more of the desired instructional events?
- Do the media under consideration vary in probable "affective impact: for the learners?
- Are the necessary hardware and software items obtainable, accessible, and storable?
- How much disruption is caused by using the media?
- Is a backup easily available in case of equipment failure, power failure, film breakage, and so on?
- Will instructors need additional training?
- Is a budget provided for spare parts, repairs, and replacement of items that become damaged?
- How do cost compare with probable effectiveness?

Media Feasibility

The instructional design characteristics identified in the following Table can be applied to each type of instructional technology to gauge the appropriateness of the various media. These characteristics can be applied to the use of technology to support resident courses as well as distance learning initiatives. The following criteria are used in this section to compare and contrast the media alternatives.

Development Effort	The time, effort, and/or resources required to plan, design, develop, implement, and evaluate the instruction.
Convenience of Instruction	The extent to which the participant is allowed to control or determine the time, place, pace, or duration of instruction, and/or accessibility of the instruction.
Student Motivation	The ability of the instructional system/media to motivate and/or involve the student when used as the primary vehicle for instruction.
Equipment and/or Support	The degree to which special equipment or other

Requirements	support systems are required for delivery of the instruction.
Instructor Requirements	The degree to which instructor involvement is required during delivery of the instruction to employ the medium effectively.
Level of Interactivity	The potential level of engaged response/ interaction between the student and the medium provided or supported by the medium.
Feedback Capability	The type and nature of student feedback supported by the instructional medium.
Ease of Revision	The complexity of revising or updating the medium to accommodate changes in course content.
Ease of Use	Comfort of the instructor and the student with the medium; degree to which time must be spent familiarizing users with the technology.
Versatility	The ability of the medium to support instruction and/or supplement other technologies.

Media Selection by Learning Outcome

Learning Outcome	*Exclusions*	*Selections*
Intellectual Skills	■ Exclude media having not interactive feature	■ Select media providing feedback to learner responses
Cognitive Strategies	■ Exclude media having not interactive feature	■ Select media providing feedback to learner responses
Verbal Information	■ Exclude only real equipment or simulator with no verbal accompaniments	■ Select media able to present verbal messages and elaboration
Attitudes	■ Exclude only real equipment or simulator with no verbal accompaniments	■ Select media able to present realistic picture of human model and the model's message
Motor Skills	■ Exclude media having no provision for learner response and feedback	■ Select media making possible direct practice of skill, with informative feedback

Instructional Handouts

Handouts can be a very useful instructional tool, but, like all instructional tools, they can only aid, not replace, a good lecture. Neither will handouts alone convert a poor lecture into a good one. For some students, handouts seem to improve learning, while for others they may merely make learning more efficient.

Some purposes of handouts:

- Provide an outline of the lecture and demonstrate that the lecturer has given careful thought to the lecture and to the instructional needs of that particular level of students.
- Emphasize what should be learned.
- Serve as an advanced organizer, putting the lecture into a meaningful whole.

- Provide "skeleton" notes, freeing students from the mechanics of note taking and allowing them to devote more attention to the lecture and the visuals being displayed by the lecturer.
- Illustrate lecture content, assuring that the illustration displayed on the slide is accurately conveyed to the students.
- Provide thought-provoking questions.
- Cite students to additional literature on the subject.

Some guidelines for preparing effective handouts to accompany lectures:

- Identify the course, lecture topic, date of lecture, and name of lecturer.
- Be sure that the handout is consistent with the lecture and visual illustrations in sequence, terminology, and points of emphasis.
- Begin with an advanced organizer that outlines what is to be covered in the handout itself.
- Demonstrate the relationship of components by written explanation and/or visual organization (indentation, listing, etc.).
- Place a reasonable limit on the number of main points to be covered in the lecture and the handout.
- Emphasize only those points worthy of emphasis. Effective use of headings, underlining, indentation, etc., is very important. Excessive use of these destroys the emphasis itself. Use a consistent means of providing emphasis (type size, all caps, bold, underline, Italics, etc.) so that the student is oriented immediately to how to recognize what you are emphasizing as most important.
- Define all terms with which students are likely to be unfamiliar, and identify terms that are being used interchangeably.
- Include an example (clinical example, etc.) that illustrates each major topic area.
- Guide students to carefully selected references. This is not a place to list a comprehensive bibliography on each subject. If the course textbook is appropriate, identify the pages where the topic is discussed.
- Use succinct phrasing that leaves space for the students to add points that help them to understand and remember.
- Include appropriate graphs, line drawings, and tables used in the lecture.
- Summarize the key points at the end of the handout with declarative statements or questions that the student should be able to answer.

Key questions that govern how an instructional handout should be constructed:

- How it is to be used?
  To duplicate all or part of the lecture.
  To illustrate part or all of the lecture.
  To explain a portion that is particularly difficult to quickly grasp.
  To resolve a controversy of perspectives—to explain your interpretation.
  To reinforce topic importance and what particular parts of the topic are most important.
  To provide important information not covered in other sources.

To provide questions the lecture content answers.
To provide a structure for note taking.

- How detailed should it be?
This depends on how it is to be used. Very detailed for some uses, and only sketchy for others.
- When to distribute it?

Before the lecture-a detailed handout given to students immediately before the lecture may cause them to read it instead of listening intently to the lecture or to decide not to attend the lecture at all. A detailed handout given to the students well before the day of the lecture allows the lecturer to expect the students to have familiarized themselves with the handout contents before the lecture. A sketchy outline may be the most effective tool for maximizing the impact of the lecture.
After the lecture-this approach prevents students from having divided attention during the lecture, but, not knowing the contents of the handout to be received later, it will not prevent them from copious note taking during the lecture.

Tips on Designing Visual Illustrations

Examples	*Learning Factual Information*	*Learning Visual Identifications*	*Learning Principles, Concepts, and Rules*	*Learning Procedures*	*Performing Skilled Perceptual-Motor Acts*	*Developing Desirable Attitudes, Opinions, and Motivations*
Still pictures	Medium	High	Medium	Medium	Low	Low
Motion pictures	Medium	High	High	High	Medium	Medium
Television	Medium	Medium	High	Medium	Low	Medium
3-D objects	Low	High	Low	Low	Low	Low
Audio recordings	Medium	Low	Low	Medium	Low	Medium
Programmed instruction	Medium	Medium	Medium	High	Low	Medium
Demonstration	Low	Medium	Low	High	Medium	Medium
Printed textbooks	Medium	Low	Medium	Medium	Low	Medium
Oral presentation	Medium	Low	Medium	Medium	Low	Medium

- Be sure they are legible. If images are not legible, they usually do more harm than good. Most projection set-ups, including those in the Volker Hall lecture halls, are designed so that the farthest viewer is no more than six image widths from the screen. You can simulate this condition by holding a horizontal slide or overhead transparency six image widths (9 inches for a slide; 54 inches for an overhead transparency) from your eyes. If you can read the information when doing this test, then the farthest viewer in the presentation room should be able to, also.
- Check original artwork. If the artwork is 1 foot wide, stand back 6 feet to view it.

- Use simple type style; avoid using all capital letters, and confine written material to a length and width that will enable adequate enlargement for projection. There is no way that a full page of typing will be legible on either a slide or an overhead transparency. Furthermore, lettering used in books and other printed materials designed for normal reading distance are seldom large enough for projection. Use the 6 image widths test and have them redone in larger type, if necessary.
- Use the horizontal format-so the image can be projected larger and placed higher on the screen for easier viewing; changing between verticals and horizontals is distracting.
- Make them as uncomplicated as possible. Subdivide complex information to make two or more simple visuals.
- Condense information into key words. Use your narration to expand on the concepts.
- Use "progressive disclosure" to present complex information and prevent confusion. For example, present the first part of a graph, discuss it, show a second visual which adds to the next part of the graph, discuss it, and so on.
- Disclose lists or organizational points progressively to keep the audience from reading ahead or becoming confused.
- Show only RELEVANT information via graphics and photographs. Use an overview shot and then close-ups if necessary. Show only trends, directions, etc. if numbers are not necessary.
- Include arrows, circles, labels, or other highlights to draw attention to important areas. Use of hand-held pointers is often awkward and distracting.
- Use colour appropriately to highlight or aid in discrimination. Too many colours in a visual can be distracting.
- Establish contrast between an image and the background. In situations where there may be stray light on the projection screen, yellow or white letters on a dark background are usually more effective than dark letters on a light background. Avoid red and green because of people's red/green colourblindness.

Slides vs. Overhead Transparencies

	Slides	*Overhead Transparencies*
Advantages	■ Excellent detail and colour ■ Easily controlled by presenter ■ Very compact and portable ■ Inexpensively produced ■ Easily up-dated ■ Freedom of movement by presenter ■ Many visual effects possible	■ Easy to manipulate, point to specific areas, add overlays, and progre-ssively uncover ■ Enables eye contact with the audience ■ Can be written on, erased, etc. ■ Inexpensive to prepare ■ Can be used with room lights on ■ Allows progressive build-up of visual
Disadvantages	■ Impractical for photographic images ■ Requires darkened room ■ Legibility can be a problem ■ Difficult to point to specific areas	■ Less freedom of movement by presenter ■ Must tilt screen to avoid picture distortion

ACTIONS Model (by T. Bates)

- Access.
- Cost.
- Teaching and learning.
- Interactivity and user-friendliness.
- Organisation.
- Speed.

Instructional Design

Instructional Design is the systematic development of course content, sequence, methods, and material using learning and instructional theory to ensure the quality of instruction. It is the entire process of analysis of learner needs and goals and the development of a delivery system to meet those needs. It includes both development of instructional materials and activities and evaluation of all instruction and learner activities.

Although learning may occur without instruction, instruction can greatly activate and support the processes of learning. If instruction is to bring about effective learning, it must somehow be designed to integrate events that will do the most effective job. Thus, the design of instruction must focus on creating the conditions under which learning best occurs with the given learner, subject content and instructional facilities/ setting.

Small Group Teaching

Small group teaching is not lecturing to a small group. It is facilitating the participation of the group in an inquiry or problem-solving activity. In small group teaching the instructor becomes a facilitator promoting collaborative learning. The facilitator concentrates on creating an environment in which all participants collaborate and become mutually supportive to enhance each individual's learning.

Small group teaching is optimal for active learning, which is becoming regarded as an essential element at all levels of education and which typically is not present in the traditional passive lecture. This is one technique for generating open communication among all the participants of the group and also between the group and the facilitator.

The most vital component of small group work is the group leader, who is ordinarily the instructor or a tutor. The leader's role in the group is not merely to listen to the different participant comments, but also to assist in identifying any biases, errors, or misconceptions among the members. An effective group leader provides only minimal intervention, but is always attentive and uses specific techniques that promote an intellectual experience for all the members.

Giving Feedback

Feedback is communication to another individual for the purpose of facilitating self-awareness and self-understanding. Because adults are essentially driven by internal motivators (i.e., satisfaction from successful task completion, recognition, or self-esteem), effective feedback is an integral part in helping adult students reach their maximum potential.

Effective feedback is non-judgmental and provides the student criteria by which to measure his/her skills, knowledge, and attitudes and also provides the student information to validate his/her own feelings or impressions about how well or poorly he/she performed. Without feedback, mistakes may go uncorrected, good performances may not be reinforced, and learners may develop an inaccurate perception of their performance. Therefore, feedback becomes an essential component in education simply because it provides information that the learner can use to make adjustments in completing one simple objective or in reaching a long-term goal.

Constructive Feedback

- Provided in terms of previously-outlined goals and expectations.
- Descriptive rather than judgmental/evaluative, directed toward remediable behaviour, and designed to elicit an appropriate remediative response.
- Specific rather than general (based on first-hand data, actions, and behaviour, not on the person or speculation about his or her intentions) and validated through agreement from other observers when possible.
- Presented as a method of improvement rather than as a punitive step and used as a method of building up the learner and strengthening the professional relationship between learner and mentor.
- Given at an appropriate time, in an amount the receiver can use, and checked for clarity of communication.

Giving Feedback Informally, Daily, and Publicly

- Give feedback constructively as issues arise, either privately or with colleagues.
- Demonstrate a correct procedure rather than letting students stumble along without guidance.
- Give feedback during a procedure but in a timely fashion and in a tension-decreasing rather than tension-increasing manner.

Giving Feedback Formally, Periodically, and Privately

- Schedule the feedback session at less stressful times, when both parties are least likely to be rushed or called away.
- Begin by asking for the learner's perspective on strengths, areas needing more work, etc.
- Be descriptive, focusing on behaviour and performance, and only rarely on personality traits.
- Be as specific as possible (including examples) and use non-judgmental language.
- Do not overload the learner with feedback; start with one or two high-priority issues.
- Be supportive when giving feedback; sandwich areas for improvement between positives at the beginning and end of the session.
- Be aware of some possible solutions to problems beforehand.
- Rely on personal observations rather than on other students' complaints; use such complaints to focus your observations.
- Help learners turn negative feedback into constructive challenges.

- Verify student understanding by asking the student for his or her summary of the session and add your own points of emphasis.

Web Course Design

Web-based instruction is simply using the World Wide Web (WWW) Internet utility to deliver interactive and non-interactive course material. With the web, the educational experience can be freed from the boundaries of the classroom and time restraints of class schedules. Learning resources of the world, through the Web, can supplement learning resources of the local institution.

The World Wide Web has the potential to be more than a source of information. When properly designed, web pages can provide learners an array of instructional activities that give information, allow an opportunity for practice, and then provide feedback to inform the learner of his/her strengths, weaknesses, and suggestions for enrichment or remediation.

Selecting Media for Distance Education

Distance education is usually carried out in one of the following three ways:

- *Through a single medium:* This was more commonly used in the past where the learning message was prepared in a single medium and the learner taught themselves through that medium;
- *Through a master medium and with other reinforcing medium:* Where all messages are delivered through one medium, with another medium used to reinforce complex or difficult messages delivered by the master medium; and
- *Through multi-media:* Where two or more media are used simultaneously to communicate the learning messages (Elliot 1989).

A number of different factors have been identified by researchers and practitioners for consideration when selecting media. A number of factors for consideration have been grouped as follows:

- learner factors
- circumstantial factors (of learners and educators)
- subject matter
- desired interaction pathways (learner-material and teacher-student interaction) and
- The inherent nature of media.

Prior to discussing these factors, a word about media biases. A "media bias" is an unjustified preference for one media over another for reasons unrelated to the above factors. A media bias may arise from a high level of familiarity with a particular media, lack of interest in utilising another media etc. When a bias for a particular media exists, instead of asking "what is the appropriate media for a particular distance learning situation," the question asked is "what course can be developed using this media" (Elliot 1989). Fedale's (1990) warning that in development, in many instances the needs of the potential target audience are subjugated to a particular technology, is equally applicable in distance education. To avoid a bias for a particular medium, the focus of the educator should be teaching and learning and the media should be considered merely a tool which is used in a given situation.

Learner Factors

Learner factors which could influence media selection include: the cost to students, for example a video cassette may be cheaper to purchase than a large printed text book. The cost of the equipment necessary to utilise the media must also be considered. Using the previous example, it may be cheaper to purchase a video tape than a large printed manual, but the cost to purchase/access a television set and video player to view the video cassette should be taken into account. The initial cost of purchasing the manual may be higher, but it is the only cost associated with using this medium.

The credibility of the media with the learner is an important consideration (FAO 1989). For example, some learners may consider information presented in books more credible than information on the radio which tends to be a more informal medium. The present and prior exposure to a medium will affect this perception (Ray 1987, Crowder 1990). Iams and Marion (1991) found television, radio, and newspapers are the preferred sources of educational information on energy conservation; and pamphlets, correspondence courses, and recorded telephone messages appear to be the preferred information sources for financial and health management education.

The medium should enhance, not compete with, the content for the learner's attention. Overestimation of the importance of the media and underestimation of the importance of media adaptation to local conditions and the relevancy of message content to local recipients is a common mistake in extension (Crowder 1990).

Some media assume certain skills in learners. For example, text materials assume literacy and computer tools assume computer competency. The level of familiarity of learners with the subject matter will affect the treatment of the information (in-depth/brief). A low level of familiarity with the subject will require more thorough treatment and students may need to refer back to the material a number of times to master it. A high level of familiarity will require a less detailed coverage, potentially favouring different media. Major characteristics which Evans (1984) considers for extension campaigns are age, sex, level of education, financial resources, facilities, occupation which are equally applicable to distance education programmes.

Circumstantial Factors (of Learners and Educators)

Circumstantial factors include those affecting both learners and educators; hence apply to both the production and use of media. Availability of technical assistance and funds. The social and economic systems in which media functions and how those systems influence media access, exposure and impact. These systems should be considered as well as simply how individuals respond to media and messages (Crowder 1991).

Certain infrastructure is required for some media, for example electricity, a radio station and Internet access. Access to some media will be affected by policies and regulations. In some places the use of certain media (e.g. radio and Internet) by groups other than the government is restricted or prohibited. When using communication technologies in rural areas, how access is controlled and who by;

who decides what information systems can be made available and to whom must be established (Norrish 1997).

Subject Matter

The nature of the subject matter will lend itself to different media (Gottschalk TH 1996). Further, different components of the subject may be distinguished, such as a theory and a practical component. Take a pesticide safety course as an example. Complex details, such as dosage rates and first aid instructions, are suited to a media which archives the information for easy reference, such as a booklet or manual. The practical component, of pest identification and spray application methods, lends itself to a visual media, such as diagrams, photos or video. A subject matter with and auditory component (e.g. language training for extension workers) lends itself to audiocassettes or radio.

The cost and ease of updating varies between media, so the frequency of change in subject matter may be a consideration. For example a Web page can be updated instantly with a minimal cost associated (generally time is the major investment and the cost is the same, regardless of the number of students). Conversely, reprinting course manuals involves layout, paper, printing and distribution costs and increases with the number of students.

Interaction Pathways

This refers to two types of interaction

- The interaction between the learner and the learning material and
- The interaction between learner and teacher. This heading attempts to simplify the concepts of "learning strategy," "teaching method" etc.

1. *The Interaction Between the Learner and the Learning Material*

Reading or observing is not enough; learners have to do something with the learning material because it is through interaction between learner and learning materials that promotes thinking and individual interpretation (Steinberg). Exposure to media alone does not create change but discussion is an essential element in the process (FAO 1989) as it encourages the student to actively engage with the course material.

The extent to which the student engages with the learning material depends largely on the nature of the learning materials (Steinberg) but there are a number of different ways media can be employed to increase interaction with the material. For example, a radio broadcast may be used to present a particular educational message. Simply listening to the programme (passive) may result in shallow knowledge of the topic. Incorporating questions into the radio broadcast can increase the depth of exploration of the topic by the learner (active) and result in a deeper level of understanding. The chief source of variance in learning results as much from differences within media as between media utilisation (Schramm 1977).

Examples of within media utilisation to increase interaction with learning materials are given in below. The examples in Table are usually pre-programmed (i.e. done in advance without the input of the students).

Ideas for Increasing Interaction with Subject Matter Using Different Media

Media	*Ways to Incredase Interaction with Subject Matter with Different Media*
Print	Include: - self-assessment activities - interactive exercises where learners are instructed to perform an activity and report it - questions about the content submitted to the teacher - feedback mechanisms between the student and teacher - possible examination questions
Tapes	- pose questions for individual consideration or for group discussions at the end of sections - build in exercises - ask student to repeat words, phrases, sounds etc. aloud
Radio	pre-recorded programme as above
Radio live broadcast	as above, but also request learners to send in comments (writing, recorded in audio-cassettes) which are announced/ discussed in following broadcast (like Farm Radio Forum in Canada) incorporate a phone-in session for questions, discussion
Video cassette	- self-a - include short segments with clear stopping points for discussion, thoughts, writing etc. - build in questions and activities for viewers
Television	Include: - short segments with clear stopping points for discussion, thoughts, writing etc. - build in questions and activities for viewers - use listening groups of just students or with tutors for discussion of interpretations, thoughts etc.
Video-conferencing	arrange segments with clear stopping points for discussion, thoughts, writing etc. which could involve student listening groups
Computer	include exercises with feedback mechanisms (message of encouragement)
Internet	- same as for print and audio and visual if these features are used - ask students to conduct research on Internet from sources other than course Web pages

Different approaches to the material (e.g. theoretical, practical, problem solving or memorisation approach) can favour particular media. Similarly, the evaluation method selected (multiple choice, essay, oral test, self evaluated) could also influence the choice of media.

2. The Interaction Between Learner and Teacher

A trend in distance education is, where possible, to increase the level of interactivity of the learning experience to reduce student's sense of isolation, increase exploration of subject matter and promote sharing of different perspectives and views.

There are many possible pathways of interaction between the "teacher" and the "learners." Examples of some interaction pathways are illustrated in Diagram

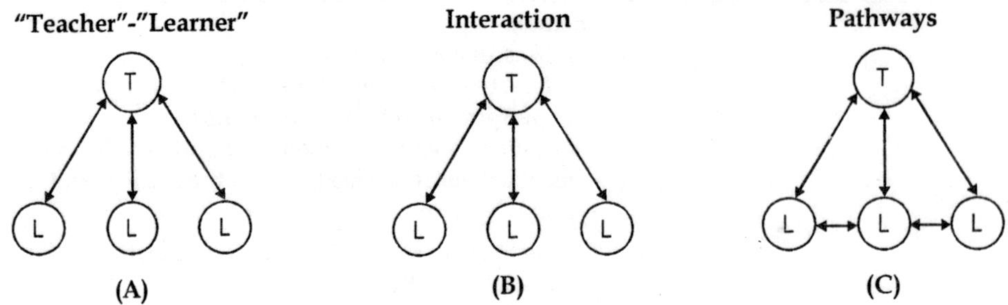

In Diagram figure (A) represents the simplest interaction, a one-way communication from the teacher to learners. Figure (B) represents a feedback loop between teacher and learners. Figure (C) shows multi-directional communication through teacher-learner and learner-learner pathways.

Where feedback is given (e.g. in B and C above), it can be differentiated by its nature (preprogrammed or personalised) and its speed (immediate as with preprogrammed responses in computer programmes, or delayed as in the case of feedback which is posted).

The desired interaction pathway and the way the medium is employed to accommodate the interaction may be a consideration for selecting a media.

Inherent Nature of Media

Naturally, each medium has inherent characteristics which define its strengths, limitations and capabilities for the delivery of distance education. For example television can transmit images whereas radio cannot. The inherent characteristics will influence the ability of the media to accommodate learner factors, circumstantial factors, and the subject matter and desired interaction pathways.

A grouping of media suggested by Gerard (1997), distinguishes media into the following four categories:

- print
- recorded instruction
- real time and
- Computer based.

This grouping is useful to highlight differences in utilisation within media because some media can fall into a number of categories. For example, radio could appear in both group 2 and 3, depending on the way it is utilised (pre-recorded programming versus live radio). Similarly, the Internet is both computer based and in the case of on-line chat sessions, real-time.

- printed materials-colour/black and white, text/diagrams/photos
- audio-cassettes
- radio including preprogrammed and live broadcasts
- video cassettes

- television prerecorded programmes
- video conferencing
- computer programmes
- Internet

Media can be described with respect to: forms of symbolic representation (text, diagrams, pictures, photographs, voice etc.), common pathways of communication between teacher and students how they are produced and updated, cost to produce, cost to student, mode of distribution/delivery, equipment and skills required to use, and dependence on place and time for delivery. Using these characteristics, it is hoped that differences between media (such as those presented by Gerard (1997)) are noted.

The media above are considered separately, however there are many overlaps. For example, with the Internet we see the "convergence" of a number of media that were previously considered quite separate as they involved specialised or dedicated equipment. The Internet has the capability to deliver text, audio and video (many of the strengths, weaknesses and comments for these other media apply to the Internet if these capabilities are utilised).

Relationship Between Factors

When selecting media, the priority given to each of the factors discussed above (learner, circumstantial, subject matter and desired interaction) differs in the literature. According to Schramm (1977), the rational choice of media should consider the task, learning effectiveness of different media for the task, and cost comparisons of the media. Elliot (1989) gives priority to the selection of the teaching message and the learning strategy over the nature of the media but recognises that this is not always possible. Gottschalk (1996 (1)) states that although "technology plays a key role in the delivery of distance education, educators must remain focused on instructional outcomes, not the technology of delivery. The key to effective distance education is focusing on the needs of the learners, the requirements of the content, and the constraints faced by the teacher, before selecting a delivery system." There is general agreement that the inherent nature of the media is not a primary consideration for its selection.

The following model, represented in Diagram is proposed for selecting media for distance education.

This Diagram attempts to show that the inherent nature of the medium will affect how it can accommodate learner factors, circumstantial factors, and the subject matter and desired interaction pathways. Each set of factors act as a "filter" which media must pass through in order to be considered for selection.

To help select which media to use a range of available media are considered for a given situation (e.g. a set of learner factors)? The media which match this situation are then tested against another situation (e.g. a set of circumstantial factors). Depending on the preferences of the distance educator, just some of the "filters" may be used to help select media, or all may be used. Similarly, the order of "filters" may be changed to aid selection. New "filters" or sets of factors may be added by the distance educator to describe the unique characteristics of their situation and to aid their decision.

Model for Selecting Media for Distance Education

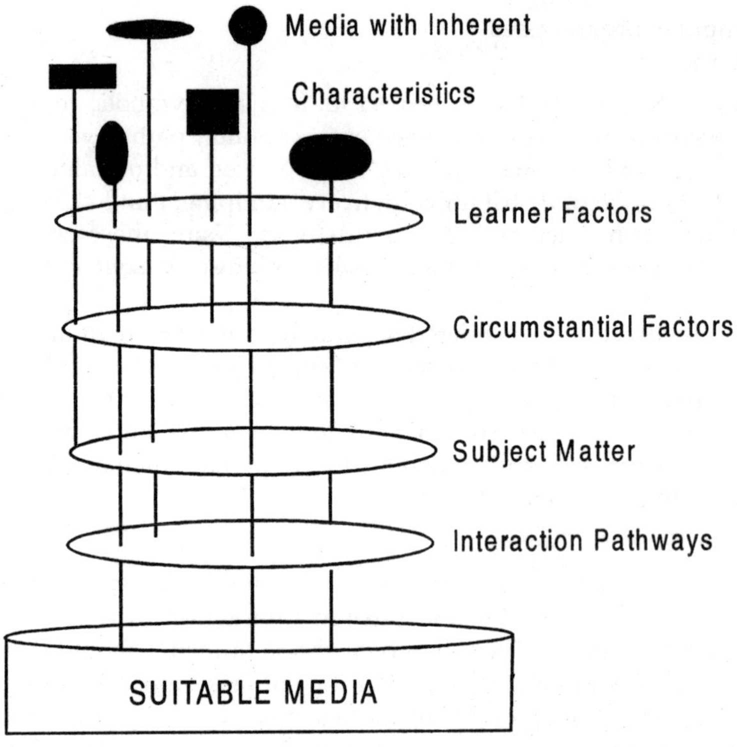

Using this model, in a situation where no media meets all the criteria, the points at which media do not match the situation can be identified and given extra consideration. To determine if the media meet the set of conditions for each of the factors, a series of questions are suggested as guidelines for reflection. These questions are presented as a starting point for the distance educator to develop their own set of questions/criteria specific to their situation.

Mapping Technologies to Intelligences

The unfolding Information Age media dictates the delivery of all the data we encounter. From the time we rise in the morning until we retire each night, the ways we consume information help to shape our knowledge base and our decisions. Yet people are not always conscious of each medium they encounter; mode of delivery seems to get lost in the mix as we are inundated by volumes of information in endless cycles. While it is easy to become desensitized as consumers of information, as educators we are in a unique position to maximize media selection and get a handle on this explosion of information for our students. As McLuhan suggested prophetically, the medium may not only be the messenger, it may be the message. When I am discussing the current state of technology with teachers around the country, it becomes clear that they feel bound by their access to technology, regardless of their situation. If a teacher has a television-computer setup, then that is what he or she will use in the classroom. On the other hand, if there is an LCD projector hooked up to a teacher demonstration station in a fully equipped lab, he or she will be more apt to use that set up. Teachers have always made the best of whatever they've got at hand. You can still easily find Apple IIe labs with filing cabinets full of 5" disks in use in school systems. Of course it's dated technology, but it's what we have to work with.

Gardner's multiple intelligences theory challenges us to look beyond our available technologies and stay focused on the fact that we are teaching children rather than teaching information. As we become ever more aware of the paths to learning, we are even more in need of vehicles to accommodate all these different modalities in the classroom. Half a century ago this would have been an even more daunting task. But in the Information Age, we have technologies evolving, even as we speak, that hold new promise to reach all learners. This is an incredible opportunity for educators, as the impact of brain research and technology together support our conviction that all children can be successful. The question we must ask ourselves is not about access but appropriate use of technology. Certainly we have more choices today, but how do we discern media that are most appropriate for a given learning task? When it comes to technology.

Multiple Intelligences and Instructional Technology

Media selection is a critical piece in the instructional design process. Unfortunately in this age of media saturation, media selection is often overlooked when implementing a lesson in the classroom. It is tempting to select the technology you want to use and then make it "fit" the intelligences. Rather, start with your knowledge of intelligences and consider which media will naturally support them.

Intelligence Technologies

Verbal/Linguistic

Let's take a closer look at each intelligence and the media that will offer appropriate support. Always well accommodated in the classroom, the verbal/linguistic intelligence can be even more effectively used through modern technologies. Set aside the traditional textbook, pencil, and paper and consider the ways word processing promotes not only composition but also editing and revising in ways that streamline the Writer's Workshop approach. Desktop publishing and web-based publishing take this idea to new levels of efficacy as students can see their work celebrated within the classroom and beyond in the "virtual" world. Electronic mail is a wonderful way to promote verbal/linguistic learning, as students are prompted to inquire of and respond to correspondents through written text.

- Textbook, pencil, worksheet,
- Newspaper, magazine, word processing,
- Electronic mail, desktop publishing, web based
- Publishing, keyboard, speech
- Recognition devices, text bridges.

Logical/Mathematical

The logical/mathematical intelligence is promoted through activities that stimulate reasoning. It can include a traditional lecture, analyzing data through a spreadsheet, conducting queries using a search engine or directory, participating in the problem solving process of a Web Quest, and even mastering a programming language or a networked system of computers.

- Lecture, Cuisenaire rods, Unifix cubes,
- Tan grams, measuring cups, measuring
- Scales, ruler/yardstick, slide rule, graphing
- Calculators, spreadsheet, search engine,
- Directory, FTP clients, gophers,
- Web quests, problem solving tasks,
- Programming languages
- Visual/Spatial
- Overhead projector, television, video,
- Picture books, art supplies, chalkboard,
- Dry erase board, slide shows, charting and graphing, monitor, digital camera
- Camcorder, scanner graphics editor, html
- Editor, digital animation/movies.

Bodily/Kinesthetic

The bodily/kinesthetic intelligence is stimulated by physical interaction with one's environment. When used in instruction, students who manipulate materials can develop a greater understanding of skills and concepts. Diagramming on the board, sorting manipulative materials by attributes, participating in a group simulation, or using an adaptive switch in order to input responses into a computer are all examples of how the bodily/kinesthetic intelligence can be accommodated.

- Construction tools, kitchen utensils,
- Screw, lever, wheel and axle, inclined
- Plane, pulley, wedge, physical education
- Equipment, manipulative materials,
- Mouse, joystick, simulations that require
- Eye-hand coordination, assistive
- Technologies
- Musical/Rhythmic
- Pattern blocks, puzzles, musical
- Instruments, phonograph, headphones,
- Tape player/recorder, digital sounds,
- Online pattern games, multimedia
- Presentations, speakers, CD ROM disks,
- CD ROM player.

Visual/Spatial Intelligence

The visual/spatial intelligence especially benefits from technology in modern education because there are so many new ways to stimulate this path to learning.

While the overhead projector, slide projector and TV/VCR have been around for thirty years or more, the use of digital slide shows is a newer way to create, manipulate and present learning in the classroom. Charting and graphing has been made so much easier from the days gone by through all kinds of applications (word processors, draw/paint programmes, spreadsheets, databases), and graphic editors allow us to manipulate any image to meet our needs. Throw in the possibilities for website design and construction and the recent advances in digital animation and movies and you can easily see why the visual/spatial intelligence is so aptly supported by technology.

Musical Intelligence

The musical/rhythmical intelligence is the intelligence of patterns. It is accommodated in a variety of ways via technology. For example, using the tape recorder in a listening center with books to follow along prompts the use of this intelligence. Incorporating digital sounds into a multimedia presentation also accommodates this path to learning. Playing online pattern games like Mastermind and Concentration can be very musical/ rhythmical. Even looking for visual patterns in the classroom or the schoolyard fosters musical/rhythmical thinking.

Intrapersonal

The intrapersonal intelligence is stimulated through activities that bring feelings, values and attitudes into play. For example, conducting a class debate on an environmental issue, following a real time expedition through uncharted islands, completing online surveys on an issue being studied in the classroom, completing an online form as a facilitating event for a unit of study, or evaluating one's own digital portfolio full of work from a semester or marking period are all ways to nurture the intrapersonal intelligence.

- Journals, diaries, surveys, voting
- Machines, learning centers, children's
- Literature, class debate, real time
- Projects, online surveys, online forms,
- Digital portfolios with self-assessments.

Interpersonal

The interpersonal intelligence can be accommodated through class discussion on relevant topics, collaborative projects that enrich and extend the curriculum, synchronous chat between groups of students or with experts, participation in newsgroups on an assigned topic, and even mailing lists that allow multiple classes to all share ideas and experiences asynchronously.

- Class discussion, post-it notes, greeting
- Cards, laboratory, telephone, walkie-talkie,
- Intercom, board games, costumes,
- Collaborative projects, chat, message
- Boards, instant messenger.

Naturalist

Organizing and making sense of information in categories and hierarchies stimulates the naturalist intelligence. Creating a database to sort and search through data is a wonderful naturalist exercise. Using a laserdisc on weather is an effective way to share scientific phenomena in the classroom. More than any other activity though, semantic mapping is decidedly the most naturalist.

- Magnifying glass, microscope, telescope,
- Bug box, scrap book, sandwich bag,
- Plastic container, database, laserdisc,
- Floppy drive, file manager, semantic
- Mapping tools.

Existentialist

Consider the use of the software application "Inspiration" in visually mapping out understandings of facts and concepts and how it allows the learner to manipulate ideas. The existential intelligence is stimulated through learning experiences that reinforce one's sense of the "big picture" of learning. Newspapers, magazines and virtual communities all help students feel like they belong to something larger than their family or classroom.

- Art replica, planetarium, stage drama,
- Classic literature, classic philosophy,
- Symbols of world religions, virtual
- communities, virtual art exhibits, virtual
- Field trips, MUDs, virtual reality, simulations.

Virtual art experiences and field trips help students to vicariously experience beauty and awe as it exists in the world far beyond the classroom. Even online interaction with significant people through interviews and archives can promote the use of the existential intelligence. The one caveat that has to be made here is that applications are not so neatly categorized by intelligences. Even though an HTML editing programme like Dream Weaver seems to be a visual tool at first glance, consider the intra-and interpersonal dynamics that come into play as a website is formed. Or then again, the listening center described above might actually be construed as a verbal/ linguistic activity rather than a musical/rhythmic task. In fact, it is both. The only way to determine the intelligences a technology stimulates is to look at the task the technology is being used to accomplish. The technology itself is not a goal for instruction; it is merely a tool to help you accomplish that goal. It is in the process of instruction identified by a learning objective that we see the true nature of any technology and its relationship to the intelligences. Dr. Sheryl Asen (1992) has identified ten criteria to guide incorporating technology into instruction. By using these criteria to plan for and evaluate the use of a technology, we can determine how well the technology supports educationally sound instruction.

- Students are involved in tasks that are broad in scope and challenging. Activities should span a range of related, intellectually demanding experiences that are not divided into fragmented tasks. (Existentialist)

- Students, rather than the teacher, have control over the learning. The teacher serves as more of a guide, coach, and resource rather than a supervisor or administrator. (Intrapersonal)
- Students work collaboratively and cooperatively. Learning tasks should not be accomplished in social isolation. (Interpersonal, kinesthetic)
- Students practice and apply communication skills during learning.
- Learning tasks should promote questioning, discussion, and interaction. (Verbal/linguistic)
- Students participate in varied learning tasks. This includes both variations in the format of the activities and in their objectives. (Musical/rhythmic, kinesthetic)
- Students have opportunities to address learning tasks in different ways. Different approaches to a presented activity can be explored. (Naturalist)
- Students learn and apply higher order thinking skills through problem solving tasks and reflection. Activities do more than ask students to recall rote facts, terms and definitions. (Logical/mathematical)
- Students are encouraged to offer varied solutions to a given problem. Reasoned answers and appropriate products are not limited to pre-set responses.
- All justifiable and fitting answers and products are accepted. (Visual/spatial)
- Students are encouraged to contribute personal ideas and experience to the learning task. Student input into the learning process is valid and valued. (Intrapersonal)
- Students are intrinsically motivated by the prescribed learning tasks. Accomplishing the task is rewarding on its own merits regardless of the technologies being used. (Existentialist)

From the objective to the assessment and every step in between, multiple intelligences can help teachers to expand their repertoire of instructional strategies and balance their selection of resources and materials, including technology.

By taking the intelligences into consideration, teachers can more effectively make use of the technologies they have at their disposal for instruction. The key is to place consideration of the intelligences into the media selection process after the learner and objective but before actually considering your technology options. In this way, teachers can avoid allowing technology to dictate their instructional choices and put it in its proper place in instruction: as a delivery vehicle for content, concepts and skills.

Media Effectiveness

	PRINT	*VIDEO*	*AUDIO*	*SIMULATION*	*ITV*
Developmental Effort	The effort required varies depending on the scope and content of the print materials. Professional authoring of complete instructional print documents, manuals, or textbooks requires significant time and effort to research, design, develop, edit, and publish effective instruction. Available desktop publishing software has made it much easier to develop professional-looking print materials in-house.	Professional quality, effective video instruction requires complex planning and a significant amount of time and effort to produce.	Requires less time and effort than most other instructional methods. Similar to print.	Requires significant advanced planning, lead-time, resources, and effort. Expertise is required to reduce the desired learning objectives to algorithms that capture real-world events. Software is complex and generally costly to develop and test-significant prototyping and testing of the instructional simulation programme are required.	Requires advanced production planning, coordination, and development efforts. Requires training for instructors.
Convenience of Instruction	Students can study at their own pace and review information as required.	Students can study and review information at their own pace.	Students can study and review information at their own pace.	Convenience of Instruction Simulation instruction may be developed for individual or group use. Group participation is less flexible since participants must start/ interact at the	Live lessons are scheduled only at specific times and because ITV broadcasts are accomplished in real-time, the student has little control of the timing, sequence, and pacing of the instruction.

				same time. Because simulation training is normally accomplished in real-time, the student has less control of the sequence and pacing of the presentation.	Success is also contingent on a host of technologies working without problems. Transmission/reception problems can interfere with flow of instruction. Has the advantage of distance learning in that the student does not have to travel to the training site at which the training is being conducted.
Student Motivation	Requires higher level of student motivation for effective learning to take place. Student learning is dependent on reading ability. Lack of reading skills significantly impacts effectiveness of instruction.	Requires a higher level of student motivation for effective learning to take place.	Requires a higher level of student self-motivation for effective learning to take place. Student learning is dependent on listening ability. Lack of auditory skills significantly impacts the effectiveness of the instruction.	A high level of learning normally takes place because of the realistic presentation and interaction provided.	Can provide a cost-effective means for conducting live, full motion quality training to large number of students at widely dispersed locations. Allows instructors to communicate visually and be seen by students at remote locations.
Equipment/ Support Requirements	Requires no special equipment or support.	Videotapes are highly transportable and can reach many students.	Audiotapes are highly transportable and can reach many students.	Requires access to the simulation computer/ equipment,	Requires special satellite uplink/ downlink and production equipment.

		A videocassette recorder is required and is readily accessible.	A cassette tape player is the only equipment required, and is widely available.	and availability of technical support. Development platforms required.	Requires the availability of studio facilities and student access to ITV classrooms. Facilitator training and technical support are required to ensure efficient and effective operations.
Instructor Requirements	Minimum supervision, participation, or communication required.	Little instructor supervision, participation, or communication.	Little instructor supervision, participation, or communication.	Simulations provide a real-world learning environment and allow active "hands on" participation and performance of tasks in a safe environment.	Requires active preproduction planning, coordination, rehearsals, and formal instructor training to ensure successful ITV instruction. But overall instructor requirements may be reduced if multiple iterations of the course are planned.
Level of Interactivity	Passive in nature—low level of student interactivity.	Passive in nature—low level of student interactivity.	Passive in nature—low level of student interactivity.	Requires instructor monitoring, supervision, management, and/or participation.	Provides verbal communication and interaction by the students; but there is little direct interaction with the medium.
Feedback Capability	Low level of feedback and reinforcement.	Low level of feedback and reinforcement.	Low level of feedback and reinforcement.	Participants and simulator provide immediate and realistic feedback to the student which can increase student motivation.	Allows for immediate verbal and visual feedback to the student. However, instructors cannot visually observe or receive visual feedback from the students.

Ease of Revision	While easier to revise than most other media, revisions will require sometime, resources, and effort to accomplish. Revised materials must also be reproduced and distributed to all applicable sites.	Course content needs to be stable since revisions normally require complete reproduction/ redevelopment of the taped instruction. Tapes must also be duplicated and distributed to all sites.	Course content needs to be stable. Revisions require re-taping, duplicating tapes, and distribution to all sites.	As with development, significant time, programming skills and expertise are required for changes and revisions.	Live broadcasts allow for immediate changes to the instruction.
Ease of Use	Print is the most familiar of media. Instructors and students are comfortable using it.	Videotape technology is familiar to instructors and students, and they are comfortable using it.	Audiotape technology is familiar to instructors and students, and they are comfortable using it.	Some degree of computer literacy and proficiency training will be required for students to ensure their effective use of the computer simulation instructional media.	Students and DL site facilitators will require training in the use of equipment.
Versatility	Handouts, outlines, booklets, brochures, ready reference guides can supplement other technologies/media.	Videotapes can provide effective instructional support for other types of instruction. Also, videotapes can be retained for future reference.	Audiotapes can provide effective instructional support for other types of instruction. Also, audiotapes can be retained for future reference.	Can be used in conjunction with, or to replace, training accomplished using actual equipment or other media. Can be used following formal training to permit transition between the laboratory and the real world–to permit students to practice what they have learned in a safe environment.	Can be used in conjunction with, or to replace, training accomplished using other media.

8

Multimedia and Online Teaching

Multimedia is more than one concurrent presentation medium (for example, on CD-ROM or a Website). Although still images are a different medium than text, multimedia is typically used to mean the combination of text, sound, and/or motion video. Some people might say that the addition of animated images (for example, animated GIF on the Web) produces multimedia, but it has typically meant one of the following:

- Text and sound
- Text, sound, and still or animated graphic images
- Text, sound, and video images
- Video and sound
- Multiple display areas, images, or presentations presented concurrently
- In live situations, the use of a speaker or actors and "props" together with sound, images, and motion video.

Multimedia can arguably be distinguished from traditional motion pictures or movies both by the scale of the production (multimedia is usually smaller and less expensive) and by the possibility of audience interactivity or involvement (in which case, it is usually called interactive multimedia). Interactive elements can include: voice command, mouse manipulation, text entry, touch screen, video capture of the user, or live participation (in live presentations).

Multimedia tends to imply sophistication (and relatively more expense) in both production and presentation than simple text-and-images. Multimedia presentations are possible in many contexts, including the Web, CD-ROMs, and live theater.

Definition of Multimedia

The term multimedia describes a number of diverse technologies that allow visual and audio media to be combined in new ways for the purpose of communicating. Applications include entertainment, education and advertising. Multimedia often refers to computer technologies. Nearly every PC built today is capable of multimedia because they include a CD-ROM or DVD drive, and a good sound and video card (often built into the motherboard). But the term multimedia also describes a number of dedicated media appliances, such as Digital Video Recorders (DVDs), interactive television, MP3 players, advanced wireless devices and public video displays.

History of Multimedia

The term Multi-Media, which was used during the 1970's to describe a particular theater-based film and slide-show collage experience, has now been shortened to just the word "multimedia." From the mid 80's through the late 90's, the prevalent meaning of multimedia was a category of "authoring" software that allowed designers to develop interactive computer programmes without having to have advanced programming skills. Examples include Apple's HyperCard, Icon Author Ware, Asymetrix Toolbox, and MultiMedia. This category of software still exists, and is sometimes referred to as multimedia, but the term is now is used to more generally describe nearly every hardware or software technology that displays images or plays sounds.

The Meaning of Multimedia has Expanded

In recent years, the term multimedia has taken on more and different meanings to an ever-increasing audience. Some of us are experiencing a form of multimedia "narrowcast" through digital cable. The term multimedia will continue to evolve and take on as many new meanings as the technologies and applications it is being used to describe.

- Generic description of the generation and transfer of voice/data/video traffic between users. A combination of multiple media types, including text, graphics, animation, audio and video. A form of communication combining text with graphics, page layout, video, audio, animation, and so forth. The use of several media, such as movies, slides, music, and lighting in combination normally for the purpose of education or entertainment. Computer-controlled presentations combining three or more of the following elements: text, graphics, animation, full-motion images, still video images, and sound. The combination of audio, video, animation, and graphics. Multimedia software presents information in all these contexts. Multimedia computers are required to run these types of programmes. Presenting data in more than one medium, such as combining text, graphics and sound.
- Software programmes that combine text and graphics with sound, video, and animation. A multimedia PC contains the hardware to support these capabilities.
- A term used to describe a range of products that have some audio and/or visual basis; for example, encyclopedia programmes are labelled as being "multimedia."
- This is software that combines graphics, audio and video to make us a media presentation.
- Systems that support the interactive use of text, audio, still images, video, and graphics. Each of these elements must be converted in some way from analog form to digital form before they can be used in a computer application.
- The Web's integration of audio, video, graphics and text.
- Multimedia is the integration of multiple forms of media. This includes text, graphics, audio, video, etc. For example, a presentation involving audio and video clips would be considered a multimedia presentation.
- This originally indicated a capability to work with and integrate various types

of things including audio, still graphics, and especially video. Now it is more of a marketing term and has little real meaning. Historically the Amiga was the first multimedia machine.

- A combination of various types of media, including sound, animation, video and graphics. Due to the generally large size of "multimedia" files, a CD-ROM is usually necessary to store files. As well, appropriate sound and video cards and speakers are also necessary.
- The use of a computer to display integrated text, graphics, animation and sound. As computers become more sophisticated and less expensive, the potential for use in multimedia presentations such as movies and interactive education increases.
- Applications combining the use of more than one media, i.e. data, voice and video.
- This is a method of presenting many forms of media, such as text, graphics and videos.
- French: multimedia a rapidly growing communications technology that allows people to communicate via computer using any combination of text, data, voice, graphics, photographs, video and audio simultaneously. Transmission that combine media of communication (text and graphics and sound etc.).
- Multimedia (Lat. Multum + Medium) is media that utilizes a combination of different content forms. The term can be used as a noun (a medium with multiple content forms) or as an adjective describing a medium as having multiple content forms.
- The use of different media to convey information; text together with audio, graphics and animation, often packaged on CD-ROM with links to the Internet; of, or relating to this combined use of media; of, or relating to an application that can combine such media into an integrated package.

Multimedia is media that utilizes a combination of different content forms. The term can be used as a noun (a medium with multiple content forms) or as an adjective describing a medium as having multiple content forms. The term is used in contrast to media which only utilize traditional forms of printed or hand-produced text and still graphics. In general, multimedia includes a combination of text, audio, still images, animation, video, and interactivity content forms.

Multimedia is usually recorded and played, displayed or accessed by information content processing devices, such as computerized and electronic devices, but can also be part of a live performance. Multimedia (as an adjective) also describes electronic media devices used to store and experience multimedia content. Multimedia is similar to traditional mixed media in fine art, but with a broader scope. The term "rich media" is synonymous for interactive multimedia. Hypermedia can be considered one particular multimedia application.

Major Characteristics of Multimedia

Multimedia presentations may be viewed in person on stage, projected, transmitted, or played locally with a media player. A broadcast may be a live or recorded multimedia presentation. Broadcasts and recordings can be either analog or digital electronic media technology. Digital online multimedia may be downloaded or streamed. Streaming multimedia may be live or on-demand.

Multimedia games and simulations may be used in a physical environment with special effects, with multiple users in an online network, or locally with an offline computer, game system, or simulator.

The various formats of technological or digital multimedia may be intended to enhance the users' experience, for example to make it easier and faster to convey information or in entertainment or art, to transcend everyday experience.

A laser show is a live multimedia performance. Enhanced levels of interactivity are made possible by combining multiple forms of media content. Online multimedia is increasingly becoming object-oriented and data-driven, enabling applications with collaborative end-user innovation and personalization on multiple forms of content over time. Examples of these range from multiple forms of content on Websites like photo galleries with both images (pictures) and title (text) user-updated, to simulations whose co-efficients, events, illustrations, animations or videos are modifiable, allowing the multimedia "experience" to be altered without reprogramming. In addition to seeing and hearing, emerging technology involving illusions of taste and smell may also enhance the multimedia experience.

Usage

Virtual reality uses multimedia content. Applications and delivery platforms of multimedia are virtually limitless. Multimedia finds its application in various areas including, but not limited to, advertisements, art, education, entertainment, engineering, medicine, mathematics, business, scientific research and spatial temporal applications. Several examples are as follows:

Creative Industries

Creative industries use multimedia for a variety of purposes ranging from fine arts, to entertainment, to commercial art, to journalism, to media and software services provided for any of the industries listed below. An individual multimedia designer may cover the spectrum throughout their career.

Commercial

Much of the electronic old and new media utilized by commercial artists is multimedia. Exciting presentations are used to grab and keep attention in advertising. Industrial, business to business, and interoffice communications are often developed by creative services firms for advanced multimedia presentations beyond simple slide shows to sell ideas or liven-up training. Commercial multimedia developers may be hired to design for governmental services and nonprofit services applications as well.

Entertainment and Fine Arts

In addition, multimedia is heavily used in the entertainment industry, especially to develop special effects in movies and animations. Multimedia games are a popular pastime and are software programmes available either as CD-ROMs or online. Some video games also use multimedia features. Multimedia applications that allow users to actively participate instead of just sitting by as passive recipients of information are called Interactive Multimedia. In the Arts there are multimedia artists, whose minds are able to blend techniques using different media that in some way incorporates interaction with the viewer. One of the most relevant could be Peter Greenaway who is melding Cinema with Opera and all sorts of digital media. Another approach entails the creation of multimedia that can be displayed in a traditional fine arts arena, such as an art gallery. Although multimedia display material may be volatile, the survivability of the content is as strong as any traditional media. Digital recording material may be just as durable and infinitely reproducible with perfect copies every time.

Education

In Education, multimedia is used to produce computer-based training courses (popularly called CBTs) and reference books like encyclopedia and almanacs. A CBT lets the user go through a series of presentations, text about a particular topic, and associated illustrations in various information formats. Edutainment is an informal term used to describe combining education with entertainment, especially multimedia entertainment.

Learning theory in the past decade has expanded dramatically because of the introduction of multimedia. Several lines of research have evolved (e.g. Cognitive load, Multimedia learning, and the list goes on). The possibilities for learning and instruction are nearly endless.

Engineering

Software engineers may use multimedia in Computer Simulations for anything from entertainment to training such as military or industrial training. Multimedia for software interfaces are often done as collaboration between creative professionals and software engineers.

Industry

In the Industrial sector, multimedia is used as a way to help present information to shareholders, superiors and coworkers. Multimedia is also helpful for providing employee training, advertising and selling products all over the world via virtually unlimited web-based technologies.

Mathematical and Scientific Research

In Mathematical and Scientific Research, multimedia is mainly used for modelling and simulation. For example, a scientist can look at a molecular model of a particular substance and manipulate it to arrive at a new substance. Representative research can be found in journals such as the Journal of Multimedia.

Medicine

In Medicine, doctors can get trained by looking at a virtual surgery or they can simulate how the human body is affected by diseases spread by viruses and bacteria and then develop techniques to prevent it.

Hypermedia

Hypermedia: a multimedia system in which related items of information are connected and can be presented together. Hypermedia is used as a logical extension of the term hypertext in which graphics, audio, video, plain text and hyperlinks intertwine to create a generally non-linear medium of information. This contrasts with the broader term multimedia, which may be used to describe non-interactive linear presentations as well as hypermedia. Hypermedia should not be confused with hyper graphics or super-writing which is not a related subject. It is also related to the field of Electronic literature. A term first used in a 1965 article by Ted Nelson.[1]

The World Wide Web is a classic example of hypermedia, whereas a non-interactive cinema presentation is an example of standard multimedia due to the absence of hyperlinks.

The first hypermedia work was, arguably, the Aspen Movie Map. Atkinson's Hypercard popularized hypermedia writing, while a variety of literary hypertext and hypertext works, fiction and nonfiction, demonstrated the promise of links. Most modern hypermedia is delivered via electronic pages from a variety of systems including Media players, web browsers, and stand-alone applications. Audio hypermedia is emerging with voice command devices and voice browsing.

Types of Multimedia Instructional Methodologies

Graphics

As a multimedia enhancement when the addition of colour improves the teaching value, e.g., a wiring diagram to show the different colours of wire. Always give a title or description. Be aware that it may be more economical to put a few colour graphics in the print-based CDC if that is the only multimedia element.

Video

When it presents a visual message that is clearer than text alone. When it demonstrates a procedure, process, or role-playing technique that is not well presented with text, we tend to be visual learners. Always give a title or description. Keep videos short. Instead of showing a long video all at once, split it up with text, audio, or questions in between. Make sure the video teaches something.

Animation

Animation is picture or diagram that shows a process or procedure using movement and colour. Some current animation technology choices are animated gifs, DHTML, and Macromedia Flash. Always give a title or description. Provide a button to replay; don't let the animation run continuously.

Simulation

A digitized approximation of real situations, tasks, or procedures, imitates real life. At the highest level, simulations allow students to practice making decisions without having the equipment available because it's too expensive or too dangerous. For example, this might be used to teach manipulation of dangerous chemicals or the transporting of missiles or bombs. This type of instruction can be time-consuming and therefore costly to design and develop. Interactive simulations are the highest level of MM enhancements.

Interactive Multimedia

When the multimedia user is allowed to control what elements are to be delivered and when they are to be delivered. Multimedia presentation where the end user can control what is being displayed by activating buttons and hyperlinks on a page.

Online Teaching and Learning

The most important factor-affecting student learning is the teacher. Everyone understands, on a personal level, the importance of teachers to their educational success. Teachers who know their subject, understand how to teach and can adjust their teaching to student needs will be successful in raising student achievement, research shows. Teacher expectations also are a significant factor in how much and how well students learn. Online learning provides the opportunity for every middle grades and high school student, regardless of where he or she lives or attends school, to have access to a quality teacher. Many of these students benefit by being challenged academically by an online teacher who, in some cases, possesses stronger academic credentials and essential teaching skills than traditional classroom staff, especially in certain geographic and subject shortage areas.

Access to quality online teaching can result in improved student academic performance and increased course completion rates. Quality online teaching reflects the attributes of any effective teaching, whether in the traditional classroom or online. Both traditional classroom teachers and online teachers need to know their subjects and how to teach them. They also must know their students, stay up to date in their subject areas, and manage and monitor students' academic progress to ensure success. But in the 10 years since Web-based courses were first made available to students, the understanding of what is required to be a successful online teacher has increased significantly. The technology used to access and provide Web-based courses effectively also has improved. Now it is important to re-examine what qualifications are needed to be an effective online teacher.

Equally important is an understanding of the attributes of today's students, who have access to and can use technology to pursue opportunities and information never before available to them. For many students, this access has changed the way they see the world and the way they work and play. Consideration of these student issues is critical for a teacher to be effective. Another often overlooked but important issue for online teachers: Delivery of Web-based courses are not restricted to a specific time or schedule. Because instruction does not start and stop at the same time for all students, time-management skills are extremely important, not only for the online teacher but also for students. The lack of these skills is a major reason why some students drop their online courses. Effective online teachers also must possess the ability to prepare quality written communications. Appropriate and effective writing not only conveys information—it encourages and supports students. Words and body language that traditional classroom teachers use must be translated to the online environment for online teachers to be successful.

The teacher should:

- Meets the state's professional teaching standards or has academic credentials in the field in which he or she is teaching;
- Provides evidence that he or she has credentials in the field of study to be taught;
- Knows the content of the subject to be taught and understands how to teach the content to students;
- Facilitates the construction of knowledge through an understanding of howstudents learn in specific subject areas; and
- Continues to update academic knowledge and skills;
- Demonstrates the ability to effectively use word-processing, spreadsheet and presentation software;
- Demonstrates effective use of Internet browsers, e-mail applications and appropriate online etiquette;
- Demonstrates the ability to modify and add content and assessment, using an online Learning Management System (LMS);
- Incorporates multimedia and visual resources into an online module;
- Utilizes synchronous and asynchronous tools (e.g., discussion boards, chat tools, electronic whiteboards) effectively;
- Troubleshoots typical software and hardware problems;
- Demonstrates the ability to effectively use and incorporate subject-specific and developmentally appropriate software in an online learning module; and
- Demonstrates growth in technology knowledge and skills in order to stay
- Current with emerging technologies;
- Demonstrates effective strategies and techniques that actively engage students in the learning process (e.g., team problem-solving, in-class writing, analysis, synthesis and evaluation instead of passive lectures);
- Facilitates and monitors appropriate interaction among students;
- Builds and maintains a community of learners by creating a relationship of trust, demonstrating effective facilitation skills, establishing consistent and reliable expectations, and supporting and encouraging independence and creativity;
- Promotes learning through group interaction;
- Leads online instruction groups that are goal-oriented, focused, project-based and inquiry-oriented;
- Demonstrates knowledge and responds appropriately to the cultural background and learning needs of non-native English speakers;
- Differentiates instruction based on students' learning styles and needs and assists
- Students in assimilating information to gain understanding and knowledge; and
- Demonstrates growth in teaching strategies in order to benefit from current research and practice;
- Consistently models effective communication skills and maintains records of applicable communications with students;

- Encourages interaction and cooperation among students, encourages active learning, provides prompt feedback, communicates high expectations, and respects diverse talents and learning styles; persists, in a consistent and reasonable manner, until students are successful;
- Establishes and maintains ongoing and frequent teacher-student interaction, student-student interaction and teacher-parent interaction;
- Provides an online syllabus that details the terms of class interaction for both
- Teacher and students, defines clear expectations for both teacher and students,
- Defines the grading criteria, establishes inappropriate behaviour criteria for both
- Teacher and students, and explains the course organization to students;
- Provides a syllabus with objectives, concepts and learning outcomes in a clearly written, concise format;
- Uses student data to inform instruction, guides and monitors students' management of their time, monitors learner progress with available tools and develops an intervention plan for unsuccessful learners;
- Provides timely, constructive feedback to students about assignments and questions; and gives students clear expectations about teacher response time;
- Gives students clear expectations about teacher response time;
- Facilitates student investigations of the legal and ethical issues related to technology and society;
- Establishes standards for student behaviour that are designed to ensure academic integrity and appropriate uses of the Internet and written communication;
- Identifies the risks of academic dishonesty for students;
- Demonstrates an awareness of how the use of technology may impact student testing performance;
- Uses course content that complies with intellectual property rights policies and fair use standards;
- Provides students with an understanding of the importance of Acceptable Use Policies (AUP);
- Demonstrates knowledge of resources and techniques for dealing with issues arising from inappropriate use of electronically accessed data or information;
- Informs students of their right to privacy and the conditions under which their names or online submissions may be shared with others;
- Applies experiences as an online student to develop and implement successful strategies for online teaching;
- Demonstrates the ability to anticipate challenges and problems in the online classroom;
- Demonstrates an understanding of the perspective of the online student through appropriate responsiveness and a supportive attitude toward students;
- Understands that students have varied talents and skills and uses appropriate strategies designed to include all students;

- Provides activities, modified as necessary, that are relevant to the needs of all students;
- Adapts and adjusts instruction to create multiple paths to learning objectives;
- Encourages collaboration and interaction among all students;
- Exhibits the ability to assess student knowledge and instruction in a variety of ways; and
- Provides student-centered lessons and activities that are based on concepts of active learning and that are connected to real-world applications;
- Creates or selects fair, adequate and appropriate assessment instruments to measure online learning that reflect sufficient content validity (i.e., that adequately cover the content they are designed to measure), reliability and consistency over time; and implements online assessment measures and materials in ways that ensure instrument validity and reliability;
- Continually reviews all materials and Web resources for their alignment with course objectives and state and local standards and for their appropriateness;
- Creates assignments, projects and assessments that are aligned with students' different visual, auditory and hands-on ways of learning; includes authentic assessment (i.e., the opportunity to demonstrate understanding of acquired knowledge and skills as opposed to testing isolated skills or retained facts) as part of the evaluation process;
- Provides continuous evaluation of students to include pre-and post-testing and student input throughout the course; and
- Demonstrates an understanding of the relationships between and among the assignments, assessments and standards-based learning goals;
- Assesses each student's background and content knowledge and uses these data to plan instruction;
- Reviews student responses to test items to identify issues related to test validity or instructional effectiveness;
- Uses observational data (e.g., tracking data in electronic courses, Web logs, e-mail) to monitor course progress and effectiveness; and
- Creates opportunities for self-reflection or assessment of teaching effectiveness within the online environment (e.g., classroom assessment techniques, teacher evaluations, teacher peer reviews);
- Employs ways to assess student readiness for course content and method of delivery;
- Employs ways for students to effectively evaluate and assess their own readiness for course content and method of delivery;
- Understands that student success (e.g., grade, level of participation, mastery of content, completion percentage) is an important measure of teaching and course success
- Provides opportunities for student self-assessment within courses.

Assessment

Assessment plays an important part in the learning process—both summative and formative assessments inform progress and guide learning; it is essential to the accreditation process; and, results are used in all sorts of ways to measure outcomes and success of the student, teacher, course, or institute.

Self-assessment encourages student independence, and helps students develop the necessary skills for autonomous (and lifelong) learning. Assessment, especially when embedded within and authentic' learning tasks or exercises, can also be an essential part of the learning experience.

Principal reasons why online assessment is of fundamental importance:

- Student learning and behaviour is affected by and often led by assessment requirements (Ramsden in McLoughlin and Luca 2001).
- When designing learning programmes, the assessment criteria and assessment constraints are usually key determinants of the teaching and learning strategies chosen. If teachers are to engage in new forms of teaching and take advantage of the greatly enhanced teaching options now possible through online and mixed-mode teaching then it stands to reason that we need to unpack assessment options and issues if online teaching and learning is to be maximised.
- Effective flexible learning regimes require assessment to be appropriately designed to match the new learning environments and diverse clientele (ANTAI in Clayton and Booth 2000; Booth, Hartcher and Hyde 2002).
- There is a new wave of pedagogy advocating 'alternative assessment' in which assessment is integrated with learning processes and real-life performance as opposed to display of 'inert knowledge'. Known as 'authentic assessment' it is very much based on the constructivist approach that enables students to demonstrate knowledge by working on authentic tasks, putting students in control of their own learning (McLoughlin and Luca 2001, p. 421).
- Constructivism is a theory of learning that advocates that students construct meaning through active participation with the environment and with others, incorporating new information with existing knowledge.
- The introduction of Training Packages and the Australian Quality Training Framework (AQTF) has focused attention in the VET sector on the quality of assessment. There is an increased emphasis now on the need for continuous improvement of assessment strategies and processes (Booth, Clayton, House and Roy 2002, p. 4).
- Developing expertise and capabilities in online assessment can provide market opportunities. Many industries, particularly larger ones, have a major challenge managing skill development of employees and a lot are now developing their own in-house training programmes. VET is expert in credentialing. Opportunities exist for VET to partner with industry to offer flexible assessment against industry standards, providing the sector can adapt to industry needs (Anderson 2001).

Providing Assessment Choices

- Negotiating assessment tasks to account for student's circumstances and needs.
- Providing flexibility in timelines or providing contingency options to cater for unreliability or differences in technology connections.

- Providing choice in location of assessment as students do assessment tasks in their place of study, which can be home, work or wherever they choose, providing supervision is not required.
- The extent to which these choices are available in online learning depends on many factors, including pragmatic issues of managing learning and learners, teaching strategies employed requirements to start and finish on given dates and so forth.

Key Issues

Key issues for the online learning context are:

- Identifying what assessment methods can effectively be transferred to or be done better or differently online.
- Identifying whether and how the medium and mode impacts upon the validity, reliability, fairness, and flexibility of assessment (including plagiarism concerns).
- Identifying the barriers to using online assessment.
- Understanding whether and how online changes how we select, monitors, and manages assessment activities.
- Authentication for summative assessments.

Online Assessment Options

Some of the online options listed in the literature include:

- Written assignments
- Participation in online discussions
- Essays
- Publication of student work/presentations
- Online quizzes and questions
- Experiential activities, such as role-play
- Collaborative assignment work
- Debates
- Portfolios
- Reviews
- Online Exams (open-book; structured; timed)
- Journals and reflection
- Practicals.

Assessment can be by: teacher, self, peer, or by an external person or group.

Online assessment, like online teaching, is still very much in an embryonic state (Hyde, Booth and Wilson forthcoming). The most common online assessment strategies used within VET currently are: using computer communications as a transfer medium to submit and comment upon assigned work such as essays; compiling and submitting portfolios; and for computer testing, i.e. short answer, multiple choice type questions and quizzes. There is growing interest in communication tools for learning interactions (Booth, Hartcher and Hyde 2002) and evidence that this can work well, but the use of conferencing and online group work as assessable activities is not yet wide-spread. Whilst numerous papers report innovative examples of online assessment such as group discussion, simulation tools, various types of case studies and project work, and peer and self assessment, and their use is not yet common place (McLoughlin and Luca 2001; Freeman and McKenzie 2000).

Online does not as yet lend itself easily to the testing of competencies that require the demonstration of a particular skill or work-based task (Booth, Hartcher and Hyde 2002). Both summative and formative assessments have very important roles to play in flexible learning. Currently online is used more for 'summative' assessment than for formative assessment (Anderson 2001; Booth, Hartcher and Hyde 2002). "Authentic" online assessment that is integrated with the learning experience, not separated from it, is considered to be one of the most effective ways of measuring student's learning. According to Anderson (2001) it promotes skills transfer and deeper level understandings—'learners are assessed within a relevant context and are required to collaborate extensively to produce a product that demonstrates the knowledge, understanding and skills they have learned and the ability to manage activities.'

Active Learning Strategies for Online Environment

Designing instructional strategies (traditional or online) to engage learners is challenging. Traditional strategies must be adapted and/or new strategies developed for the online learning environment. Widely used effective active learning strategies such as group work or role-play can even be successfully adapted for an online environment. When developing active learning strategies for an online environment, the instructor/designer should first consider sound design practices including, but not limited to: assessing the learners, knowing the context and environment in which learners will be operating, knowing instructional tools and techniques for delivery, developing supporting strategies in the form of directions and resources, incorporating assessment of learning outcomes and course design, and designing with active engagement in mind (Mantyla, 1999).

Starting from a basic instructional design model and continuing good teaching practices are important because according to Moore and Kearsley, "active learning is probably not going to happen in an online environment unless the interaction is deliberately planned and the instructor encourages it" (1999).

Components of good active learning activities are the same, whether presented in traditional or in online environments. Activities should

- have a definite beginning and ending;
- have a clear purpose or objective;
- contain complete and understandable directions;
- have a feedback mechanism; and
- and include a description of the technology or tool being used in the exercise.

Competencies for Online Teaching

Information technology is changing the way people live and learn. Not surprisingly, Information Technology (IT) is also transforming the nature of teaching. These remarks provide a framework for thinking about such changes and exploring work in progress that is relevant to the development of competencies specific to teaching online (i.e., teaching occurring outside a traditional classroom, typically in a virtual classroom facilitated by use of the Internet).

Competence, Competencies and Certification

Competence refers to a state of being well qualified to perform an activity, task or job function. When a person is competent to do something, he or she has achieved a state of competence that is recognizable and verifiable to a particular community of practitioners. A competency, then, refers to the way that a state of competence can be demonstrated to the relevant community. According to the International Board of Standards for Training, Performance and Instruction (IBSTPI), a competency involves a related set of knowledge, skills and attitudes that enable a person to effectively perform the activities of a given occupation or function in such a way that meets or exceeds the standards expected in a particular profession or work setting (Richey *et al.*, 2001). The structure and assessment of competencies may differ from one community of practice to another and even within a community. To facilitate a common understanding of competencies in the context of online and distributed learning some specifications have been elaborated (IMS, 2001). Typically, a competency is divided into specific indicators describing the requisite knowledge, skills, attitudes and context of performance.

The Worldwide Web: Its Uses as a Teaching Tool

The World-Wide Web (or the Web) is one of the most accessible tools available for academics to use. It allows an easy means of publishing material, it has a low learning curve, the majority of its browsers are graphical and user-friendly, and above all it is free to most people in Higher Education.

The Web works on a client-server principle. The user launches their browser (e.g. Netscape or Internet Explorer) on their machine, which in turn interrogates a server retrieving files. Files are located via their Uniform Resource Locator (URL)— a unique address detailing the protocol for transferring the data, the domain name of the Web server, and the pathname/filename of the actual document.

9

Computer

The term computer is derived from the Latin word compute, which means to calculate. A computer is an electronic machine, devised for performing calculations and controlling operations that can be expressed either in logical or numerical terms. In simple terms, a computer is an electronic device that performs diverse operations with the help of instructions to process the information in order to achieve the desired results. Computer application extends to cover huge area including education, industries, government, medicine, scientific research etc.

A computer is one of the most influential forces available in modern times. Due to its memory, high speed and perfection, its application can be extended to almost infinite levels. Millions of complex calculations can be done in mere fraction of time. Difficult decisions can be made with accuracy for comparatively little cost. Computers are widely seen as instruments for future progress and as tools to achieve substantiality by way of improved access to information by means of video conferencing and e-mail. Indeed computers have left such on impression on modern civilization that we call this era as the information age.

Characteristics of Computers

The main characteristics of computers are:

- Speed
- Storage
- Accuracy
- Versatility
- Automation
- Diligence
- Reliability

(a) Speed

Computers are capable of carrying out the task with enormous speed. Today's computers, according to their class, can perform from 4 MIPS (Millions of Instructions Per Second) to 100 MIPS. What may take days for manual calculations may take only a few hours for computers to perform. Inside the computer the information signal travels at incredible electronic speed.

(b) Storage

Computers can store enormous quantity of information. This is expressed in terms of Kilobytes (or) Mega Bytes (MB) or Gega Bytes (GB). It is achieved through its 'Main memory' or 'Primary storage' and through 'auxiliary storage' or 'Secondary storage.' The Hard disks Floppy disk, Compact Disc (CD) and Magnetic Tape storage are examples of secondary storages. These large volumes of storage occupy much lesser space compared to paper documents and this aspect of computers makes them more powerful.

(c) Accuracy

The accuracy of a Computer is consistently high. In fact, this quality of the computers make them indispensable in various fields such as Scientific Research, Space Research, Weather Predictions and many other areas where precision of a high order is required. The accuracy of the computer is best achieved by programming them in the most efficient manner. When it comes to very complex mathematical or scientific problem the computer's accuracy has no substitute.

(d) Versatility

Computers are versatile in that they can perform almost any task, provided they are given the appropriate logical steps. For example, they are capable of performing wide ranging tasks such as construction of a payroll, inventory management in a factory, hotel billing, hospital management, banking applications and any imaginable task in every walk of life.

(e) Automation

The biggest advantage of computers is that it is automatic in its operation. Once a programming logic is initiated the computer performs repeated operations without human interventions until programme completion.

(f) Diligence

Computers are machines and that do not get tired or 'lose concentration' like human beings. If a large number of calculations say million calculations are to be performed the resultant output will remain exactly the same even if operations are repeated any number of times. But when a human being is asked to do the same job this consistency cannot be achieved.

(g) Reliability

The computers give very accurate results with predetermined values. They correct and modify the parameters automatically, giving suitable signals. They give formatted results with high degree of precisions.

History of Computers

In the early days of mankind, man used to count the head of cattle by putting lines on trees. Slowly these lines changed to numbers. To do calculation on numbers he started inventing machines.

Abacus

Abacus was probably the earliest of counting devices. It consists of rectangular wooden frame with two compartments and beads sliding along the steel wires for counting. Multiplication and divisions are done using repeated additions and subtractions. Even today in which cross strings are fixed. Beads are inserted on to the strings. There are a number of rows of beads.

Napier's Logs and Bones

John Napier, a Scottish mathematician invented logarithms. The use of logarithms enabled him to transform multiplications and division problems of addition and subtractions. In the beginning he called logarithms as artificial numbers. But later he named them logarithms. Napier also invented a computing device consisting of sticks with numbers carved on them. These sticks are called bones as they were made of bones. These bones helped a lot in multiplication involving large numbers.

Slide Rule

As the name indicates, the slide rule has one scale sliding within the other. Suppose you want to add two numbers 3 and 5, set 3 on the fixed scale and slide the moving scale. So that its "0' coincides with"5" of sliding scale. This is the sum of 3 and 5. The process of reading could be quick if you are trained in the use of slide rule.

Calculating Machines and Pascal's Calculator

A French mathematician, Blaise Pascal invented a machine based on gear wheels. He was the son of tax collector who had to do lot of calculations as part of his job. Blaise Pascal wanted to make his job easier by inventing a calculator. You might be familiar with gear wheels in use in your bicycle which meshes with a driving chain. He used similar gear wheels with ten teeth for each digit position. He fixed them together so that one wheel drives the other. When the wheel corresponding to units position rotated by ten teeth, it drove the wheel corresponding to the next higher position by one tooth. Thus one could make calculations. Pascal provided dials, which indicated numbers stored on each wheel. He also used suitable "dialing system" to operate the gear wheels. Other people also made a number of such calculators. Computer scientists honoured Pascal by naming a programming language Pascal after him.

Babbage Difference and Analytical Engines

Babbage, a British National and the son of a wealthy banker wanted to correct the errors in the logarithm tables being used during his time. In 1822, he made a machine which calculated the successive difference of expressions (X2 + ax + b is an example of an expression) and prepared table which helped him in his calculations. The royal Astronomical society awarded a gold medal to him for his invention and granted a large sum of money to carry out further work. He wanted to make an accurate calculating machine called "Babbage's Analytical Engine." The analytical Engine was supposed to be very accurate. So it needed lot of parts made with precision. Babbage could not make such parts. He conceived that his machine would use input devices, would have a processing part called "mill" where you can perform calculations, would also incorporate.

It consists of rectangular frame in which cross strings are fixed. Beads are inserted on to the strings. There are a number of rows of beads. Since he was about 100 years ahead in his ideas, he could not get parts needed for his machine. This is because there were no tools to make such precision parts. He did lot of work related to making precision parts and spend all the grants (and lot of his money too) but failed in his attempt to make a machine. He ultimately died as a frustrated man.

Lady Ada Lovelace

Lovelace is the daughter of the famous English Poet Lord Byron. She was a mathematician. She studied the works of Babbage and wrote about them. From her account only, we can see the close resemblance of the modern day computers and Babbage's work. Lady Ada Lovelace's contributions are very important. Since she predicted that computers can be programmed, a language, Ada used widely in America's Department of Defence Computers was named after her.

Herman Hollerith's Machine

Governments all over the world collect details about the number of people living in their countries. This information helps the Government in planning for the future, Sometimes you find enumerators (people taking such details) coming to your house with forms to collect such details. This operation is called "census" which is normally done once in 10 years. In the United States a census was carried out in 1880 and the US Government was processing the census data. Even as this was going on, the next census was due in 1890. To process the census of 1890 fast, the Government announced a competition.

Dr. Herman Hollerith Produced cards out of special paper pulp designed punching machines to punch holes in the card to count census figures and invented sorting machines to read such punched card and collect data. He could complete the job within three years, achieving a speedup of about three times.

ABC Computer

In 1937, Dr. John Atanstoff with the help of his assistant Berry designed the Atanstoff Berry Computer (ABC). The machine laid the foundation for the development of electronic digital computer.

ENIAC—Electronic Numerical Integrator and Calculator

In 1947 John Mauchly and Eckart completed the first large scale Electronic Digital Computer, ENIAC. In this computer, each time a programme was changed, the wiring had to be completely rearranged. It weighed 30 tons, contained 18,000 vacuum tubes and occupied a space of 30-50 feet.

EDSAC—Electronic Delay Storage Automatic Calculator

Maurice V. Wilkes of Cambridge University completed EDSAC in 1949. EDSAC was the first computer to operate on the stored programme concept.

UNIVAC-I—Universal Automatic Computers

In 1947, after ENIAC became operational Mauchly and Eckart formed their own Company—"The Eckart-Mauchly Computer Corporation." Immediately after this they started the design of UNIVAC-I. This was purchased by US Bureau of Census.UNIVAC was the first computer dedicated to business applications.

Computer System

A computer system is a combination of various components. It performs the system functions such as input, processing, output, storage and control. A computer system consists of the following components:

- Hardware
- Software
- Human ware
- Firmware
- Bridge ware

Hardware

The physical components of the computer, such as electrical, electronics and mechanical unit are known as the hardware of the computer. That is, the input units, output units and CPU are called hardware. Thus hardware is the equipment involved in the function of a computer. It consists of the components that can be physically handled. The function of these components is typically divided into three main categories: input, output, and storage. Components in these categories connect to microprocessors, specifically, the computer's Central Processing Unit (CPU), the electronic circuitry that provides the computational ability and control of the computer, via wires or circuitry called a bus.

Software

The computer performs operations like addition, subtraction, multiplication and division only when the user instructs it to do so. The user issues instructions and the CPU acts in accordance with the instructions. The sets of instructions, which control the sequence of operations, are known as programmes, and collectively programmes are called software. The software can be broadly classified into two types. They are:

- System Software
- Application Software

Human Ware

The man-machine interface is called a human ware. The people who work with the computer are collectively called the human ware or livewire.

Firmware

The computer programmes permanently stored in ROM or PROM are called firmware. These programmes are provided by hardware manufacturer along with the computers. Generally these are booting programmes which help in the starting of a computer. Such programmes cannot be erased or overwritten.

Bridge Ware

The computer components and programmes used to translate instructions and information written for one type of computer into a format that another type of computer can understand is called bridge ware. This is necessary because different computers are made by different manufacturers.

Stores Large Amount of Date and Information

Business and commercial organizations need to store and maintain voluminous records and use them for various purposes such as inventory control, sales analysis, payroll accounting, resources scheduling and generation of management reports. Computers can store and maintain files and can sort, merge or update as and when necessary.

Improves Productivity

With the introduction of word processing software, Computers have recently been applied to the automation of office tasks and procedures. This is aimed at improving the productivity of both clerical and managerial staff.

Sharing of Data and Information

Due to networking of computers, where a number of computers are connected together to share the data and information, use of e-mail and Internet has changed the ways of business operations.

Competitiveness

Computers offer a reliable and cost-effective means of doing business electronically. Routine tasks can be automated. The customers can be provided support round the clock, which is 24 hours a day. With advancement in IT sector, corporates are spreading business around the world thus, increasing their presence and entering new markets.

Security

To provide security to data and important computer programmes, almost every organization has some security programmes to avoid the illegal access of the company's information by unauthorized persons. The three fundamental attributor of a security programme are confidentially, integrity and availability which allow access to only authorized persons in an organization.

Cost Benefits

The extensive availability of Internet based information means that companies have a wider choice of suppliers which leads to a more competitive pricing. Due to the presence of Internet the role of the middleman becomes less important as companies can sell their product or services directly to the customer.

Marketing

Corporates engaged in e-business can take help of their respective websites to create brand awareness of their products, thus, creating new avenues of promotion of their products. In addition, companies' websites can also provide better services such as after sales service to the customer.

Generations of Computers

The history of computer development is often discussed with reference to different generations of computing devices. In computer terminology, the word generation is described as a stage of technological development or innovation. A major technological development that fundamentally changed the way computers operate resulting in increasingly smaller, cheaper, more powerful and more efficient and reliable devices characterize each generation of computers.

First Generation (1940-1956): Vacuum Tubes

First generation computers were vacuum tube/thermionic valves-based machines. These computers used vacuum tubes for circuitry and magnetic drums for memory. A magnetic drum is a metal cylinder coated with magnetic iron-oxide material on which data and programmes can be stored. Input was based on punched cards and paper tape, and output was displayed on printouts. First generation computers relied on binary-coded language (language of 0s and 1s) to perform operations and were able to solve only one problem at a time. Each machine was fed with different binary codes and hence were difficult to programme. This resulted in lack of versatility and speed. In addition, to run on different types of computers, instructions must be rewritten or recompiled.

Examples: ENIAC, EDVAC, and UNIVAC.

Characteristics of First Generations Computers

- These computers were based on vacuum tube technology.
- These were the fastest computing devices of their times. (Computation time was in milliseconds).
- These computers were very large, and required a lot of space for installation. Since thousands of vacuum tubes were used, they generated a large amount of heat. Therefore, air conditioning was essential.
- These were non-portable and very slow equipments. The lacked in versatility and speed. They were very expensive to operate and used a large amount of electricity.
- These machines were unreliable and prone to frequent hardware failures. Hence, constant maintenance was required. Since machine language was used, these computers were difficult to programme and use. Each individual component had to be assembled manually. Hence, commercial appeal of these computers was poor.

Second Generation Computers (1956-1963): Transistors

In the sixties, there was lot of development in semiconductor field—a field of materials. In vacuum tubes, a filament is heated to emit electrons, (the basic component of an atom) that carry current. In 1946,Willam Shockley and a few of his colleagues invented transistors, which do not need any heating to liberate electrons in addition to being smaller in size, they saved power due to the absence of heating and hence the cooling needed. The smaller size resulted in smaller distances that the electrons have to travel to transmit information from one part of the computer to another. Hence calculations became faster. The reliability also increased. Today you cannot see any second generation computers. The smaller size of components saw mass production of computers which became cheaper. Many companies started buying and using them increasing the demand. Computer programming languages developed further to make programming easier and user friendly. Yet if you compare today's computers, they were a lot behind. The increased use of computers and them consequent mass production sent the prices crashing down. Computer scientists and electronic engineers were developing more sophisticated computers.

Characteristics of Second Generation Computers

- These machines were based on transistor technology.
- These were smaller as compared to the first generation computers.
- The computational time of these computers was reduced to microseconds form milliseconds.
- These were more reliable and less prone to hardware failure. Hence, such computers required less frequent maintenance.
- These were more portable and generated less amount of heat.
- Assemble language was used to programme computers. Hence, programming became more time efficient and less cumbersome.
- Second generation computers still required air conditioning.
- Manual assembly of individual components into a functioning unit was still required.

Third Generation Computers (1964-Early 1970s): Integrated Circuits

In second generation computers, one could recognize the circuit components such as transistors, resistors and capacitors distinctly. There were physically separate or "discreet." Slowly scientists started integrating these components together so that they are not separate. They were fused into the circuits. People called it Large Scale Integrated circuits (LSI). Computers using such components were called third generation computers. Since components were packed together more densely, the size of computers became smaller. Programmers also developed more sophisticated software. By 1970, engineers developed a device called microprocessor. Lot of circuits was packed into it. Intel 4004 was one such chip.

Characteristics of Third Generation Computers

- These computers were based on Integrated Circuit (IC) Technology.
- They were able to reduce computational time from microseconds to nanoseconds.
- They were easily portable and more reliable than the second generation.
- These devices consumed less power and generated less heat. In some cases, air conditioning was still required.
- The size of these computers was smaller as compared to previous computers.
- Since hardware rarely failed, the maintenance cost was quite low.
- Extensive use of high-level languages became possible.
- Manual assembling of individual components was not required, so it reduced the large requirement of labour and cost. However, highly sophisticated technologies were required for the manufacture of IC chips.
- Commercial production became easier and cheaper.

Fourth Generation Computers (Early 1970s—till date): Microprocessors

More and more circuits were packed in a microprocessor. The components were integrated further and Very Large Scale Integration (VLSI) Technology revolutionized computer field further. Intel Corporation made chips such as 8080 and 8086 to be followed by 80286, 80386, 80486 and now the Pentium processor. These chips perform calculations faster. They are not only used in computers, but also in measuring devices and even in house hold devices such as washing machines. Computers using such VLSI chips progressively shrunk in size. Computers using the microprocessors are termed as microcomputers. The software technology also developed further. Programmers developed more sophisticated and user friendly software. In course of time, the cost of these computers have come down so much that even individuals bought them so they came to be known as personal computers.

Characteristics of Fourth generation computers:

- Fourth generation computers are microprocessor-based systems.
- These computers are very small.
- Fourth generation computers are the cheapest among all the other generations.
- They are portable and quite reliable.
- These machines generate negligible amount of heat, hence they do not require air conditioning.
- Hardware failure is negligible so minimum maintenance is required.
- The production cost is very low.
- GUI and pointing devices enable users to learn to use the computer quickly.
- Interconnection of computers leads to better communication and resource sharing.

Fifth Generation Computers (Present and Beyond): Artificial Intelligence

Up to fourth generation, the classification was based purely on hardware. Fifth generation computers are classified based on software also. VLSI technology is used in fifth generation computers. They have large main memories. The speed is also high. In addition to all this, Fifth generation computers run software called 'expert systems.'

Characteristics of Fifth Generation Computers

Mega Chips

Fifth generation computers will use Super Large Scale Integrated (SLSI) chips, which will result in the production of microprocessor having millions of electronic components on a single chip. In order to store instructions and information, fifth generation computers require a great amount of storage capacity. Mega chips may enable the computer to approximate the memory capacity of the human mind.

Parallel Processing

Most computers today access and execute only one instruction at a time. This is called serial processing. However, a computer using parallel processing accesses several instructions at once and works on them at the same time through use of multiple central processing units.

Artificial Intelligence (AI)

It refers to a series of related technologies that tries to simulate and reproduce human behaviour, including thinking, speaking and reasoning. AI comprises a group of related technologies: Expert Systems (ES), Natural Language Processing (NLP), speech recognition, vision recognition, and robotics.

Types of Computer Systems

Our society is being reshaped by rapid advances in information technologies, Computer, Telecommunication networks and other digital systems that have vastly increased our capacity to know achieve and collaborate. These technologies allow people to transmit information quickly and widely, linking distance places and to create communities that just a decade ago were unimaginable. It is difficult to appreciate just how quickly information technology is evolving.

Five decades ago ENIAC, one of the earliest computers stood ten feet tall and stretched eighty feed wide; while today, one can buy a musical greeting card with a silicon chip that is 100 times faster than ENIAC. This extraordinary phase of information technology is bringing people and cultures together and creating new social dynamics in the process. It is leading to the formation of closely bonded and widely dispersed community of people united by their interest in doing business or in sharing experiences and intellectual pursuits. New forms of knowledge accumulation are developing, as are computer based learning system that opened the way to innovate modes of instruction and learning.

A computer is an electronic machine, operating under the control instructions stored inside its memory. As an aid in problem solving, it accepts data, both numeric and non numeric, processes and presents it in the desired form.

The following are the various types of computer systems:

Analog Computers

Analog is the Greek word, which means similar. So, in analog computers, the similarities between any two quantities are measure by electrical voltages or current. The analog computers operate by measuring instead of counting. The analog computer works on the supply of continuous electrical signals. The display is also continuous. Its output is in the form of graphs.

Analog Signal

An analog signal is a continuous variable electromagnetic wave. It can consume an infinite number of voltage or current values.

Characteristics of Analog Computer

The analog computer has the following important characteristics:

- It operates by measuring.
- It requires physical analog.
- It functions on continuously varying quantities.
- The output is usually represented in the form of graph.
- In analog, the calculations are first converted in equation and later converted into electrical signals.
- The accuracy of the output is poor.
- It has limited memory space.
- It is not versatile i.e., it has limited application.

- The speed of analog computer is low.
- Not suitable for business and industry.

Digital Computers

These computers work with quantities represented as digits. They operate on discrete quantities. In digital computer, both numeric and non-numeric information are represented as strings of digits. These computers use binary codes, 0's and 1's, to represent the information. The information is given to the computer in the form of discrete electrical signals. The basic operation performed by a digital computer is addition. Hence, the other operations such as multiplication, division, subtraction and exponentiation are first converted into "addition" and then computed. Characteristics of digital computer the digital computer have the following characteristics:

- It operates by counting.
- It functions on discrete numbers.
- The calculations are converted into binary numbers i.e., 1s and 0s.
- The output is represented in the form of discrete values.
- Its accuracy is good.
- It has large memory space.
- It is versatile in nature and is suitable for a number of applications.
- In digital computers, the numbers, words and symbols can be used.
- Its processing speed is high.
- It is highly suitable for business application.

Analog Computer	*Digital Computer*
It operates by measuring	It operates by counting
It requires physical analog	It functions on discrete numbers
The calculations are first converted to equations and later converted into electrical signal	The calculations are converted into binary numbers(1s and 0s)
The output is in the form of graph	The output is in the form of discrete value
Less accurate	More accurate
Less speed	High speed
Limited memory is available	More memory is available
Lacks flexibility	Highly flexible
Cannot process alpha-numeric information	Can process alpha number information
Limited application	More number of applications
Not suitable for business Applications	Highly Suitable for Business Applications

Hybrid Computers

The computer which possess the features of both analog and digital computers are called hybrid computers. That is, the hybrid computers have the good qualities of both analog and digital computer. With the hybrid computer the user can process both continuous and discrete data. This computer accepts either digital or analog or both types of input and gives the results as per requirements through special devices. In the hybrid computers a converter is fixed to convert the analog data into digital data and vice versa. These are special purpose devices and are not widely used.

General Purpose Computer

These are designed and constructed to cater almost all the needs of the society. They can perform various operations in the fields of engineering, science, commerce and industry. They are able to perform according to the programmes created to meet different needs. The general—purpose computer can be used to prepare stores reports, sales reports, payroll, etc. a general purpose computer can solve a much broader class problems specifically a general purpose digital computer is remarkably versatile.

Special Purpose Computers

These computers are designed to solve a particular problem or task, the computers are provided with limited memory and speed necessary for a particular job. The instructions needed to perform the particular task are incorporated into the internal memory of the computer. It does not posses unnecessary options, hence it is economical. e.g. Business purpose computers and scientific purpose computers.

Micro Computers

Because of its small size and the use of micro-processor, this computer is called micro computer. All the computers have three units namely input, output and Central Processing Unit, (CPU). The entire CPU is contained in a single or a few microchips. When equipped with memory and input/output control circuitry, it is called micro computer. Its storage capacity is low when compared to mini and main frame computers. It is able to accept most of the high level languages. However, it uses an interpreter or complier for running high level languages. Microchips contain micro electronic circuitries which are very tiny. Large numbers of these can be packed tightly on to a single tiny piece of silicon. Silicon is a material found in sand. The microchip is made by building up a series of very thin layers of silicon and of the tiny components which are held in it.

The Micro computers are small and portable. They are relatively inexpensive; the micro computers have excellent graphic capabilities. The maximum word length varies according to the configuration of the microcomputers. Kinds of Microchips The microchips can be classified as follows:

(a) *Micro Processors:* These are the most powerful kind. They are almost tiny computers in themselves. Each one has a processing Unit, a memory and a special area to handle input and output. Microprocessors are the most important part of the CPU of a modern computer.

(b) *Memory Chips:* These are the common form of computer memory. They are used to hold information either temporarily or permanently.

(c) *Input and Output Chips:* In these chip circuits the flow of information is the both directions.

Features of Micro Computers

Its storage capacity is low.

Its rate of acceptance and transfer of data is limited i.e., a maximum of 5 lack bytes/second.

It is able to accept most high level languages. However it uses an interpreter when running high level language because most micros do not have sufficiently large memory to support compliers.

The maximum word length it holds is 16-bits.

Advantages

They are small and portable.
They are relatively inexpensive.
They work as soon as they are switched on.
They have excellent graphic capabilities.
They do not occupy much space.
They do not consume much power.

Disadvantages

- Micros have a limited storage capacity.
- They are relatively slow.

Workstation

Workstation is a type of computer used for engineering applications (CAD/CAM), desk top publishing, software development, and other types of applications that required a moderate amount of computing power and relatively high quality graphics capabilities. Workstations generally come with a large, high-resolution graphics screen, at least 64MB (Mega Bytes) of RAM, built—in network support, and a graphical user interface. Most workstations also have a mass storage device such as a dish drive, but a special type of workstation, called a diskless workstation, comes without a disk drive. The most common operating systems for workstations are UNIX and Windows NT.

In terms of computing power, workstations lie between personal computers and mini-computers, although the line is fuzzy on both ends high-end personal computers are equivalent to low-end workstations. And high-end workstations are equivalent to minicomputers. Like personal computers, most workstations are single-user computers. However, workstations are typically liked together to form a local-area network, although they can also be used as stand-alone systems.

Mini Computers

The size of the mini-computer is in between the size of micro and main frame computers. It is more powerful than a micro computer. Mini computers are usually designed to serve multiple users. Today, mini-computers are the popular data processing systems in the field of business and industry. These computers accept all high level languages. Characteristics:

- It is a general purpose machine with a smaller CPU than a main frame.

- Its storage capacity is about 2 mega words.
- Its word lengths are usually 12, 16, 24, 32 bits.
- Its rate of acceptance and transfer of data is a maximum of 4 million bytes/seconds.
- It can support all high level languages.
- It can support many terminals i.e., more than 20 terminals.

Advantages

- It performs almost all the tasks that a mainframe computer does.
- It is relatively inexpensive and is within the purchasing power of the small and medium sized business firms.

Disadvantages

- They are very expensive.
- They required large room space.
- Their consumption of electricity is very high.
- Maintenance cost is also very high.

Super Computers

The super computers are very costly. Hence it is rarely used. Its capacity is abnormally high, it cannot be compared with any other computers in capacity, function, speed, accuracy, language etc., they have operations done in parallel, rather than sequential. They are employed for specialized applications that require immense amounts of mathematical calculations. The chief difference between a super computer and a main frame computer is that a super computer channels all its power into executing a few programmes as fast as possible. But main frame uses its power to execute many programmes concurrently. CRAY - 3, Cyber 205, and PARAM are some well known super computers.

Characteristics

- They use several processors working simultaneously.
- They process at a rapid speed.
- The main memory ranges form 8 to 64 megabytes.
- They have operations done in parallel, rather than sequentially. They are used in weather forecasting, supersonic aircrafts design and other works that require billions of calculations per second.
- They can be used for animated graphics-fluid dynamic calculations etc.

Laptop Computer

Laptop computer, simply laptop (notebook computer or notebook), is a small mobile computer, which usually weighs 2-18 pounds (1-6 kilograms), depending on size, materials, and other factors. Laptops usually run on a single main battery or from an external AC/DC adapter which can charge the battery while also supplying power to the computer itself. Many computers also have a 3 volt cell to run the clock and other processes in the event of a power failure.

As personal computers, laptops are capable of the same tasks as a desktop computer, although they are typically less powerful for the same price. They contain components that are similar to their desktop counterparts and perform the same functions, but are miniaturized and optimized for mobile use and efficient power consumption. Laptops usually have liquid crystal displays and most of them use different memory modules for their Random Access Memory (RAM), for instance, SO-DIMM in lieu of the larger DIMMs. In addition to a built-in keyboard, they may utilize a touchpad (also known as a track pad) or a pointing stick for input, though an external keyboard or mouse can usually be attached.

Basic Principles of Operation of Digital Computer

Today, the most commonly used computers in business are digital computers. Even though they may differ in constructional details, the basic principles of operation are almost the same.

A computer is basically a device used for processing of data; it performs the following three operations in sequence:

- Receives the data and instruction.
- Processes the data as per the instructions.
- Output the result i.e., information.

This cycle of operation of a computer is known as the input process—Output cycle. This can be explained in the following figure. IPO—Cycle Input Output Instructions.

The data are provided to the computer through the input devices. They are encoding such a way, which the computer can understand. The computer then processes the data with the help of instructions provided to it, and then it produces a meaningful and desired output known as information.

The above functions are collectively known as the basic principles of operation of a digital computer. These can be expanded as follows:

- Accepting inputs,
- Memory manipulation,
- Arithmetic operations,
- Decision making, and
- Giving output.

10

Components of Computer and their Functions

We generally refer to a computer as a system [Computer System) since computer is made up of integrated components: input and output devices, storage, Central Processing Unit etc. that work together.

The main components of a computer system are:

- Input Unit
- Output Unit
- Storage Unit (discussed in lesson 3.2)
- Central Processing Unit [CPU]

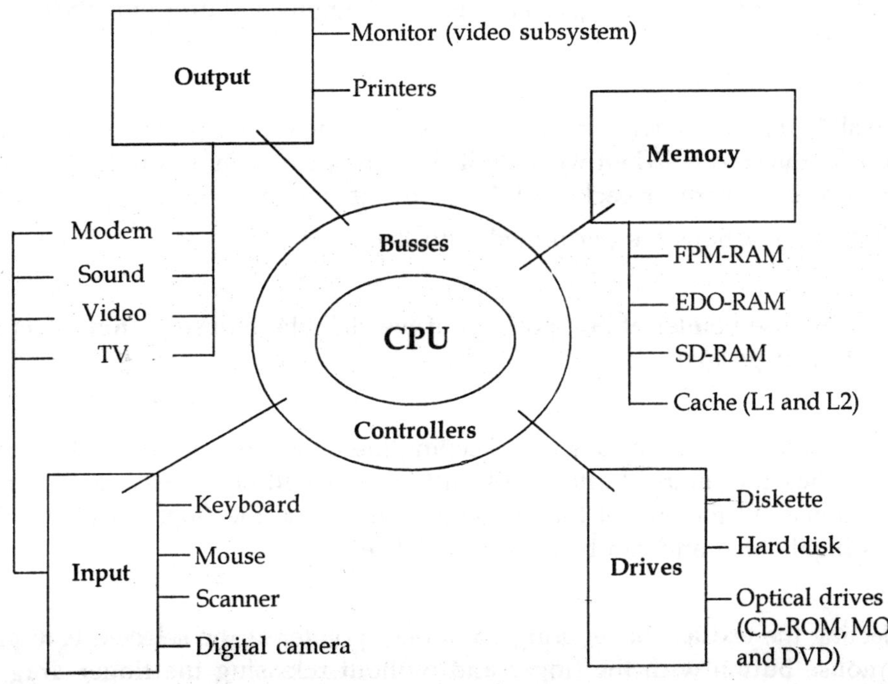

Input Unit

The input unit is used for entering the data and instruction into the computer for performing computation of the data. The input unit accepts or reads the list of instructions and data and converts these instructions and data in computer acceptable form. It supplies the converted instructions and data to the computer for further processing. The devices used for this purpose are called as Input Devices. Key Board and Mouse are the important input devices used in our offices. Light pen, Joy stick, tracker ball, Touch pad, Scanner and Pointing stick are some of the Input Devices.

(a) Key Board

The keys in Computer keyboards are almost similar to the keys in a typewriter but in addition there are some special operational keys carrying special symbols that help us in giving instructions to computer.

(b) Mouse

Mouse is an essential component in the modern computers which use Windows and other Graphical Use Interface [GUI] applications. Mouse is a small service in which a small ball is kept inside and the ball touches the pad through a hole at the bottom of the mouse. When the mouse is held in hand pushed along a flat surface [mouse pad], the ball inside the mouse rolls and this movement of the ball is converted into electronic signals and sent to the computer, now we get advanced versions of mouse like optical mouse, scroll mouse cordless mouse etc. using the mouse the cursor [the small blinking vertical line we see in the monitor] can be moved in any direction. The mouse is used for selecting part or full text or object, and also for dragging and dropping the selected text or object.

How to Handle the Mouse?

When we slide the mouse left across the mouse pad the mouse pointer of the screen moves left on the screen. When we slide it right the pointer moves right. When the mouse is moved forward or backward, it causes the pointer to move up and down.

The following actions are performed with the mouse:

Clicking

Keeping the mouse pointer at any position, if we click the mouse button the cursor will move to that position.

Selecting

To select a text for copying or deleting, keeping the mouse pointer at the beginning of the text, click the mouse button [left button] and without releasing the finger move the mouse till the end of the text and then release the finger. The text thus selected is highlighted and can be copied or deleted.

Dragging

After selecting the text as above, bring the mouse pointer at the selected text; press the left mouse button with the finger and without releasing the finger drag the selected text to any desired position.

Right Clicking

By pressing and releasing the right mouse button, the short cut menu is activated.

(c) Scanner

Scanner is an image acquisition device connected to the computer, which captures either an image of a text document or a picture and transfers it into bits of information, which a computer can understand and manipulate.

How does a scanner work?

The scanner uses a light source, typically a cold cathode lamp to illuminate the scanned object. The light is then reflected off the object and into Charged Coupled Device [CCD]. The Charged Coupled Device collects the information, and through a series of electronic devices converts the analog signal into as series of digital signals which can then be read and processed by a computer.

Uses of Scanners

Optical Character Recognition OCR—We can convert text based document images into text that can be edited by a word—processing software. Enrich our presentations and documents by adding images. Convert hard-copy images or documents into a fax format for faxing or for record purpose. Add scanned images to our e-mail to enrich the content.

Type of scanners: Flatbed Scanner, Sheet fed, Handheld, Card scan.

Flatbed Scanner

The flat bed scanner as shown in the illustration is one of the most commonly used and most recommended scanners. This scanner allows the user to place a full piece of paper, book, magazine, photo or any other object onto the bed of the scanner and have the capability to scan that object.

Flatbed Scanner

A sheet containing text can be scanned using the scanner and saved as an image file. There is software to convert the image file once again into a text file.

Sheet Fed Scanner

This scanner allows us to scan pieces of paper. The sheet fed scanner is a less expensive solution when compared to the flatbed scanner.

Sheet Fed Scanner Handheld Scanner

The handheld scanner allows the user to drag over select sections of pages, books, magazines, and other objects scanning only sections. However it can be tedious to drag the handheld correctly which can cause distortion in the image being scanned.

Card Scans Scanner

This scanner is mainly used to scan visiting cards for creating data base of the addresses.

(d) Punched Cards

Punched cards are still in use as medium for recording data and instructions in the format punched holes to denote and then they are sequentially read by the card

Reader. The card Reader sends the data and instructions to the CPU to process them. The punched cards used for data processing are made generally of 80 columns and 12 rows. Today 96 columns cards are available. In these cards a hole in punched to represent the binary l. The absence of a hole represents binary 0. If a card is punched wrongly, it cannot be corrected. Further, the punched cards are not reusable, i.e., cannot be used for any other data. Many numbers of cards are required for the computer programmes. Such a collection of cards is called a deck. Each card has the left top corner cut to identify the arrangement of the cards is correct or not. The cards are read by a Unit called a card Reader. The punched cards are placed in the Read Hopper after verification. On receiving the command from the control unit the device moves the cards one by one over two sub-devices. One of which, sense the punched holes (0s and 1s) and transcribes the pulses to the CPU. Then the output is given as per user specification.

Advantages

- It is very easy to read data on the cards.
- The cards are less expensive than other storage media.
- It is much simple to operate.
- After inserting a card, if an error is detected, the whole system stops functioning.

Disadvantages

- Punched cards are bulky when put together, so they require large space to store them.
- The cards are easily damaged and perishable.
- Transfer of data is relatively very slow.
- An incorrectly punched card cannot be corrected, it must be replaced.
- Unit Record machines require manual intervention at every stage.
- Data is not processed in ordinary language. It has to be translated into something we can understand.

(e) Paper Tapes

The punched paper tape is a continuous strip of a paper about one inch wide and up to 300 meters long. The characters are recorded on tape, which may be 5 or 8 as per the design of the tape. These punched positions are called as channels. It is the oldest media, of input and output media. Her also, a hole represent 1 and its absence represents 0. Data from the tape is read through a Tape Recorder per second. The tape comes in various forms viz., Oil paper, dry paper, metalized paper and laminated paper.

Advantages

- Compared to the punched card, it is more compact and economic on storage.
- It is less in weight and easy for mailing etc.

Disadvantages

- Since the roll is so long, correcting or inserting data can be very tedious process and time consuming.

- The life of the paper tape is short. This makes it inconvenient for storing over a long period. It is not durable.
- Moreover, it is sequential data processing medium.

(f) Magnetic Tape

Because of the problems faced in the paper media, magnetic substances have come. First among these was the magnetic tape. This is also a sequential media for normally between 1.25-2cms. Wide and up to 900 meters long. It is made of plastic with a metallic magnetic oxide coating on one side. Generally, data is recorded on either a 7 parallel-rack-tape or on a 9 parallel track-tape. Writing on and reading from the tape is done with the assistance of READ/WRITE head. The number of characters per inch length of tape stored is called the 'density' of the tape. This varies from 550 to 1600 or even 16K. The 9 Track tapes have the higher densities. Then comparing with the punched card and punched tape, the magnetic tape has certain advantages and disadvantages.

Advantages

- Data are stored very compactly.
- It is very easy to handle the Magnetic Tape than the Deck of Cards.
- The Magnetic tape costs less than the cards.
- It requires less storage space for data and therefore has a large capacity.
- It is reusable i.e., the old data can be wiped out and fresh information could be recorded on it.
- The speed of transferring the data is very high comparing to paper devices.

Disadvantages

- In magnetic tapes, the data has to be accessed sequentially. This makes the retrieval of data slow.
- The punched cards can be read visually, where as to read the magnetic tape an I machine is needed.
- The tape is subject to the usual wear and tear of time.
- Data will be erased if the tape is exposed or placed nearby any Magnetic field or high voltage circuits.

(g) Magnetic Disk

It is yet another step in the evolution of Input/Output devices. The Magnetic Disk has an advantage over the punched cards and Magnetic Tapes i.e., the data stored on a disk can be read randomly while in the magnetic tape, the data are read sequentially. Random access is that the particular record in the file can be detected directly and the access time is saved. In Magnetic disk the record is accessed in a fraction of second i.e., less than 0.01 sec. The disks varying in diameter are generally coated on both sides with magnetic oxide. Each surface of the disk is divided into a number of sectors, called storage segments. The storage segment is a specific portion of a specific side of the disk. A segment can store one or more record of a file, which will vary according to the size of the record. While searching, a particular record can randomly be selected and directly accessed, because, each storage segment is uniquely marked by an address with side number, track number, sector number etc.

(h) Joysticks and Trackballs

Joysticks provide an alternative method for feeding the computer visually interesting data. When you move the joystick, cursor on the screen moves in a corresponding way. A trackball is a plastic sphere mounted in a socket so that it is free to rotate in any direction.

(i) Touch Screens

Touch Screens are another favourite "user friendly" method for feeding data into computer. User can command the computer to perform various useful tasks simply by touching specific sectors of the screen with their forefingers. The computer senses the Location of the finger in various ways.

Output Unit

The results of the data processed by the computer are available in electronic signals. The output unit converts these signals into a form which could be easily understood by us. The output is usually given either on the screen by visual display unit/monitor or in a printed form by printers.

(a) Monitor (Visual Display Unit or Screen)

The monitor is made up of cathode-ray tube CRT due to which it also called C.R.T. terminal. The screen consists of horizontal and vertical sweep circuits similar to T.V. sets. The screen's inside is coated with dots of phosphor called pixel and can be used for games or graphics or displaying the results of a calculation done by computer. The more the number of pixel or dots in a screen, the better will be the capability of computer to display an information. This capability is known as resolution. The characters typed with the keyboard are displayed on the screen. We can thus verify whether the programmes we enter into computer is corrector not. Tips for avoiding computer vision syndrome:

Long hours of staring at a computer screen causes dryness and reduces the blinking rate of the eyes. Burning, itchiness and watering of eyes are the common visible syndromes of computer vision syndrome. Often headache is a direct consequence of the glare emitted by the screen.

- To avoid the syndrome the following measures are to be taken:
- Make sure that the computer screen is not too close to your face.
- Position the screen so that it is either at eye level, or slightly lower.
- Tilt the monitor slightly to eliminate reflection or glare.
- Make sure that primary light source [such as windows] is not shining into your face or directly on the monitor.
- Frequently look away from the screen and focus on far away objects.
- Reduce the contrast and brightness of the screen by adjusting the controls on the monitor.

(b) Printer

Printer is the most commonly used output device. It is used to prepare permanent documents in human—readable form [hard copy]. There are several types of printers that are designed for different types of applications.

Printers are of two types-impact and non impact. Impact printers use the familiar typewriter approach of hammering a typeface against paper and inked ribbon. Non-impact printers do not hit or impact a ribbon to print. They use thermal, electrostatic, chemical and inkjet technologies.

Depending on their speed and approach of printing, printers are also classified as character printers, and page printers.

Types of Printers

1. *Dot Matrix Printer*

In this printer characters to print are made up of a finite number of dots and so, the print head consists of an array of pins. Characters to be printed are made up of a finite number of dots and so, the printer. The character code is decoded by the printer electronics and activates the appropriate pins in the print head. Many dot matrix printers are bi-directional. i.e., they print from left to right as well as from right to left on return. This enhances the speed of printing. The printing speed is around 300 characters per second.

2. *Line Printer*

Unlike a dot matrix printer, line printer prints a complete line at a time. Two types of line printers are available.

3. *Drum Printer*

It consists of cylindrical drum. The characters to be printed are embossed on its surface.

4. *Chain Printer*

It has a steel band on which the character sets are embossed. Printing speed varies from 150 lines to 2500 lines per minute with 96 to 160 characters on a 15 inch line. Six to eight lines per vertical inch are printed. Usually 64 and 96 character sets are used with English letters.

5. *Inkjet Printer*

It consists of print heard, which has a number of small holes of nozzles. Individual holes are heated very rapidly by an integrated circuit resistor. When the resistor heats up, the ink near it vaporizes and is ejected through the nozzle and makes a dot on paper placed near the head. A high—resolution inkjet printer has around 50 nozzles within a height of 7mm and can print with a resolution of more than 300 dots per inch. Latest inkjet printers have multimedia heads, one per colour, which allow colour printing. The printing speed is around 120 characters per second.

6. *Laser Printers*

- In laser printer an electronically controlled laser beam traces out the desired character to be printed on a photo conductive drum.
- The drum attracts an ink toner on to the exposed areas.
- This image is transferred to the paper, which comes in contract with the drum.
- Very fast printers print 10,000 lines per minute. These printers give excellent outputs and can print a variety of fonts.

- Low speed laser printers, which can print 4 to 16 pages per minute, are now very popular.

Storage Unit and CPU

The purpose of the storage unit of the computer is to store the data entered before processing and also to store the results after processing. The Central Processing Unit [CPU] is the brain of any computer system. In a computer system all major calculations and comparisons are made inside the CPU. The CPU is also responsible for activating and controlling the operations of other units of a computer system.

Storage Unit

There are two types of storage devices.

- Primary Storage device.
- Secondary Storage device.

Primary Storage Device or Random Access Memory [RAM]

Primary storage is usually referred to as Random Access Memory [RAM] because it is possible to randomly select and use any location of this memory to directly store and retrieve data and instructions. It is also referred to as read/write memory because information can be 'read' from a RAM chip also be 'written' into it.

The Random Access Memory requires some times for accessing data and is considered to be the fastest memory. Each bit in a RAM stores RAM information by means of electric charge, where the presence of an electric charge indicates '1' and the absence of an '0'. RAM is called Temporary storage, because data persists until the machine is on.

ROM A Read Only Memory [ROM] is one in which information is permanently stored. The information from the memory can only be read and it is not possible to write fresh information into it. This is the reason why it is called ROM. When the power supply is switched off, the information stored inside ROM is not lost as it is in the case of a RAM chip. ROMs are mainly used by computer manufacturers for storing the micro programmes so that they cannot be modified by the users.

Secondary Storage Devices

This section of the memory is also referred to as backup storage because it is used to store large volume of data on a permanent basis which can be partially transferred to the primary storage as and when required for processing. The storage capacity of the primary storage of today's computers is not sufficient to store the large volume of time handled by most data processing centers. As a result, additional memory, called auxiliary memory or secondary storage, is used with most computer systems.

Hard Disk, Floppy Disk, Tape and Compact Disc are the main secondary storage devices.

(i) Hard Disk

The hard disk used in the PC is permanently fixed, hard disks with storage capacities of 8 GB, 10GB, 20GB, 40GB, are quite common, the CPU can use the hard disk to load programmes and data as well as to store data We should operate the PC within a dust-free and cool room (Preferably air-conditioned) to prevent hard disk crash.

(ii) Floppy Disk

Floppy disk is flexible circular disk of diameter 3 inches made of plastic coated with a magnetic material. This is housed in a square plastic jacket. The floppy disk can store 1.4Mbytes of data [also called 1.44Mnytes, since it holds 1440Kytes]. Data recorded on a floppy disk is read and stored in a computer's memory by a device called a floppy disk drive [FDD]. A floppy disk is inserted in a slot of the FDD. Some of the floppies have limited life time. The floppies have to be recycled periodically to keep them alive. A frequently recycled floppy [i.e. used] will have a life time of 3 to 4 years to do recycling take out old floppies occasionally and try to read them once, at least the directory.

(iii) Compact Disk

CD-ROM [Compact Read Only Memory] uses a laser beam to record and read data along spiral tracks on a 51/4" disk. A disk can store around 650/00MB of information. CD-ROMs are normally used to store data as back up. Using a CD Writer, lot of information can be written on CD-ROM and stored for future reference.

(iv) Tape Drives

Even though tape drives are one of the oldest of storage technologies, they can still hold the most data on a single cartridge. A computer tape drive works similar to a tape recorder or a VCR. A plastic tape ribbon is coated with magnetic particles which are polarized by a magnetic field generated by the read/write head. Since tape is a sequential, and not a random-access media, a tape drive has to wind through a tape to locate a specific bit of data. This makes accessing data slow so tape is mainly used for system backups and regular archiving of files and records. Tape dives allow users to backup large amounts of data. Tape drives are capable of backing up a couple hundred megabytes to several gigabytes of information without having to spend large sums of money on disks.

(v) DLT [Digital Linear Tape]

DLT drives are a robust and durable medium. The DLT segments the tape into parallel horizontal tracks and records data by streaming the tape across a single stationary head. Released in 1991 DLT drives are very reliable, high-speed, and high-capacity making the DLT drives an excellent use for Network backups.

(vi) DAT [Digital Audio Tape]

The popular choice for tape drives is DAT. This format is best known for digital audio recording although DAT drives can't play DAT audio. These drives use a recording technique called helical scanning which is used in VCRs. The 4mm tape is wrapped round a spinning read/write head that records data in overlapping diagonal tracks. These overlapping tracks allow for high data density and faster data transfer speeds. There are a few DAT standards but the most common is Digital Data Storage [DDS]. DAT tapes can hold 2GB [SSS] to 40GB [DDS-4] of compressed data. DAT.

(vii) Micro Vault USB Storage Media

Micro Vault media plugs directly into the computer's SB port—and acts just like another drive. It is small, light, Shock-proof and moisture—proof. This nifty flash memory storage device is compact and durable enough to carry in any pocket. The device is recognized automatically when we connect it to the computer. By connecting it via USB, the files can be transferred by dragging and dropping. There are no cables or adaptors needed no power cord and no driver software to install. It's compatible with both Macintosh and Windows operating systems, and even comes with software that password protects the contents of the device. They are perfect for sharing PowerPoint presentations, digital photos, MPEG video and MP3s, transporting files between work and home, or sharing files with friends and colleagues.

Central Processing Unit [CPU]

The Central Processing Unit [CPU] is the brain of any computer system. In a computer system all major calculations and comparisons are made inside the CPU. The CPU is also responsible for activating and controlling the operations of other units of a computer system. The control unit and the arithmetic logic unit of a computer system are jointly known as the Central Processing Unit. While the control unit takes care of the flow of data from input unit to storage unit and the flow of final results to the output unit, the arithmetic logic unit is the place where the actual execution of instructions taking place during the processing operation. The Central processing Unit consists of the following main components:

- Switched Mode Power Supply [SMPS]—for converting the current voltage,
- Mother Board [ROM],
- Arithmetic Logic Unit [ALU],
- Control Unit [Ram],
- Hard Disk—Storage Unit,
- Floppy Disk—Storage Unit,
- CD ROM—Storage Unit.

Hardware and Software

A computer system consists of hardware, the physical unit (parts) of the computer that are capable of computing and manipulating information and software (set of instructions or programmes) that carries out predefined tasks to complete a given job. The computer performs operations like addition, subtraction, multiplication and division only when the user instructs it to do so. The user issues instructions and the CPU acts in accordance with the instructions. The sets of instructions, which control the sequence of operations, are known as programmes, and collectively programmes are called software.

We can equate hardware and software with human body and human intelligence, respectively. All human physical actions such as walking and eating are based on the thoughts and feelings, which is raised by the brain. If the brain does not raise thoughts and feelings, we do not perform any physical activity. Similarly, the actions and functioning of every hardware equipment is driven by software. The combination of physical equipment (hardware) and logical instructions (software) gives modern computing system their power and versatility.

Components of Hardware

- *Input Unit:* This unit accepts instructions and data.
- *Output Unit:* This unit communicates the results to the user.
- *Storage Unit:* This unit stores temporary and final results.
- *Central Processing Unit (CPU):* This unit performs processing of instructions and data inside the computer.

The CPU has Three Components

- The Control Unit
- The Arithmetic Logic Unit (ALU) and
- The Memory Unit.

(a) Control Unit

It controls the overall operation of the computer system. It is considered as the heart of the computer system. It controls all the other units, directs them to operate in a proper way and co-ordinates various operations performed. It instructs the input device to transfer the data and instructions to the main memory and then to the Arithmetic and Logic Unit (ALU). Then, it sends the processed result from ALU to the memory unit for storage and transfers it to the visual display unit or to the printer. The control unit coordinates the various parts of the computer system—the arithmetic logic unit, the memory unit and the peripheral units. Besides, it controls the flow of data into, from and within the main storage as per the programme instructions. To perform its control operations effectively and quickly, the control unit has four basic components. They are:

- Instruction Register
- Decoder
- Address Register and
- Instruction Counter.

The instruction register receives one by one the instructions to be executed in the required sequence. Then, the operation code of the instructions is transferred to decoder, which decodes the operation code. And it activates the appropriate circuits of the arithmetic and logic unit to perform the operation. The address register enables the data in the location specified in the instruction to be transferred to a specified accumulator for the arithmetic and logic unit.

(b) Arithmetic Logic Unit (ALU)

This unit performs two kinds of operations, the arithmetic processing and logical processing. In arithmetic processing it performs all mathematical operations such as addition, subtraction, multiplication and division. In logical processing, it performs the relational and logical operations such as comparing larger or smaller values, true or false statements, etc.

(c) Memory Unit

This unit holds the intermediate results during the course of calculations and provides the data as and when required. This internal storage is also called primary memory or main memory. This memory takes the data from an input device and stores it until the computer is ready to process it. It also stores processed data and intermediate results. When the processing is finished, it transfers the results to an output device.

Software

Software is a generic term for organized collection of computer data and instructions. It is responsible for controlling, integrating, and managing the hardware components of a computer and to accomplish specific tasks. In other words, software tells the computer what to do and how to do it. For example, software instructs the hardware what to display on the user's screen, what kinds of input to take from the user, and what kinds of output to generate. Thus, software communicates with the hardware by organizing the control sequences, and the hardware carries out the instructions defined by the software.

A computer needs to be instructed to perform any task. These instructions are given in the form of computer programmes, which are written in computer programming languages. A programme controls the activity of the processor. The moment the hardware (processor, memory, etc.), acts as per the instructions of a programme, the programme is said to be in running or executing state. A set of programmes, which are specifically written to provide the user a precise functionality like solving a specific problem is termed as a software package. For example, word processing software package provides functionality to the computer so that it can be used to create text documents like letters and mailing lists. Similarly, an image processing software package assists a user in drawing and manipulating graphics.

Features of Software

1. *Ease of Use*

The software systems and applications are becoming more and more easy to use. In fact, software developers and system analysts go to great lengths to ensure that the products they develop are user-friendlier than their competitor's products.

2. *Graphical User Interface (GUI)*

GUI or graphical user interface has now become the default standard for most of the software applications. Gone are the days of the crude character based interfaces of UNIX and DOS application. Today's software applications and products provide the users with perceptive, graphical and easy-to-use interfaces. Now the users do not have to remember the cryptic system commands or shortcut keys that were a must in the character based era. Now almost any task can be accomplished by a mouse click.

3. *Multi-Platform Capability*

Today's software applications are not developed for just one platform. Most of the software applications supports multiple platforms-both hardware and software platforms. There are software applications that support hardware platforms ranging from mainframes to PCs and different software platforms like MVS, Solaris, AIX, UNIX, Windows and so on. For example IBM's DB2 Universal database is available for a variety or hardware and software platforms. Another important feature of today's software application is that they support multiple languages and multiple currencies. Many vendors are providing their applications in many languages like English, Arabic, Japanese, and Chinese and so on.

4. *Compatibility with Other Software*

Now the competition for each market segment in the software marketplace is rather fierce. We have many software vendors battling for the market share in the same segment. For example, Microsoft Word 2000 supports all previous versions of Work like Word 97, Word 6, and Word and so on. The two features—compatibility with earlier versions and compatibility with other products make it easier for the users, as they can choose the application they want and still use the old files they have created using other applications or using older versions of the same application.

5. *Mail Enabling*

Mail enabled applications are designed to take advantage of on e-mail. These are the familiar word processors, spreadsheets, and other individual desktop applications that have e-mail features built to them. There is another class of message-centered programmes that are built specifically around e-mail functions.

6. *Web Enabling*

With the ever-increasing popularity of Internet and the amount of information that is available on the net, most software applications are now web-enabled. Web enabling helps the user in many different ways. Its use starts while the user is installing the application. During installation, most of the applications will automatically connect to the Internet and to the vendor's website and will register their products (earlier one had to fill in a paper form and mail or fax it to the vendor).

Difference Between Hardware and Software

Hardware	*Software*
It is the physical unit of the computer	It is a collection of programmes to bring the hardware system into operation
It has permanent structure and cannot be altered	It has no permanent structure but can be altered and reused
It is normally affected by agent like dust, heat, humidity, etc.	It is not affected by these agents to some extent
Hardware understands only machine language, lower level language or binary	It is written by a well versed programmer and generally in higher level language which is readable by human being
It works with binary code, the presence or absence of Pulses as 1's or 0's.	It is represented by the Higher Level Languages such as BASIC, COBOL, etc.,

11

Networking

With standardized hardware and software, the microcomputers provide user-friendly environment. It meets the computing requirements of most users. But, the need for interaction with other computer users and with other computer systems for exchange of data etc. has increased over the years. Networks are increasingly meeting this need. From the users' point of view the networks may be of two types: Local area network and Wide area network. Computer networking is the process of inter connecting two or more computers so that the users can communicate with each other, share resources and overcome other limitations of stand-alone systems. The network can be established with a variety of combinations of computers such as a net of only microcomputers, microcomputers and one or more minicomputers and a set of microcomputers connected to a mainframe computer. The computers in typical network are autonomous in the sense that they have processing capability independent of the network.

Advantages of Networking

The main advantages of networking are:

(i) Hardware Resource Sharing

Network enables sharing of expensive resources such as processor, storage space and peripherals like modern, fax, and laser printer.

(ii) Sharing of Databases

The network permits concurrent access to the same data file by many users in the network. Thus, user in the sales department, production department, inventory department etc. share corporate databases.

(iii) Sharing of Software

Any user in a network can load and use the software installed on any of the computer of fileserver in the network.

(iv) Communication Between Users

The Network users can communicate between them. E-mail facility can also be used for communication.

(v) Decentralized Data Processing

In a network, the data processing can be decentralized by enabling local offices to capture and store data, and generate information to meet most of their requirements a local level itself.

(vi) Security of Data

In a networked environment the data is backed up with duplicate storage. Adequate security measures are also put in place to product the data.

Types of Network

The networks can be classified into three; Local Area Network (LAN), Metropolitan Area Network (MAN) and Wide Area Network (WAN). They are explained in the following sections:

Wide Area Network (WAN)

WAN is made up of number of autonomous computers distributed over a wide geographical area. WANs were originally developed in the late 1960s to enable communication between computer centers and sharing of hardware, software and other communication facilities. WAN can be implemented using private or public networks. In a private network an organization takes on lease telephone lines to connect such sites into a network. It is also possible to connect computers in different locations using microwave or satellite transmission. Public networks are installed by the Government owned telecommunication agencies.

WAN spans large geographic distances. It is also called long-haul network. WAN is usually operated at lower speeds then MAN and involves delay. Most organizations use private networks for communication. Society for Worldwide Inter bank Financial Transactions (SWIFT), a non-profit organization of banks, owns a private network. The network exchanges financial transactions between the participating financial institutions, about 3000 in number in over 60 countries. The terminals of these participating banks are hooked with SWIFT's access centers. The network offers data communication service 24 hours a day, 7 days a week. INDONET, NICNET, SBINET and WELCOMENET are some of the private network in India. CMC's INDONET offers e-mail service to customers for a fee. NICNET is a network of National Informatics Center that connects all the district headquarters in the country. SBINET is a private network of State Bank of India and connects its branches across the country. WELCOMNET connects the hotels of the Welcome Group.

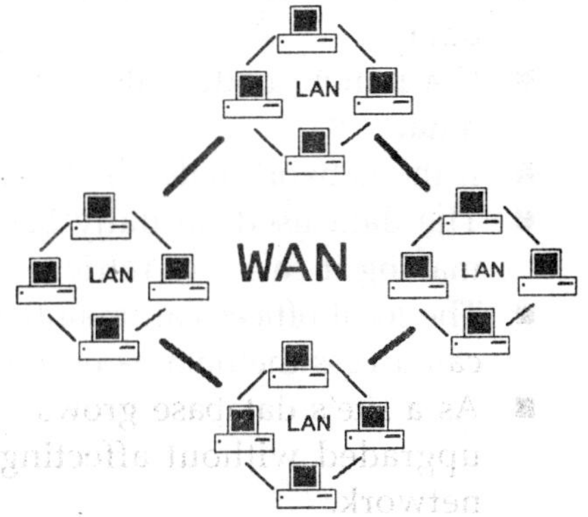

Features of Wide Area Network

A Wide Area Network (WAN) is used to connect LANs and nodes that are separated by great physical distance. Generally speaking it is larger version of LAN with several differences:

- It operates by means of the international telephone network.
- Unlike LANs which owned by their users, WANs operate on public and leased telephone lines provided by licensed common carriers, or by other means such satellite and microwave, which are regulated by government agencies.
- Data transmission is somewhere slower.
- The WAN compose any of the following system configurations:
- Single nodes.
- Clusters.
- LANs.

Suppose a company has its central headquarters in Coimbatore and the Coimbatore site contains all departments and equipment for product manufacturing prod distribution, accounting, and sales. The information pertaining to these operations is tracked by a single centralized database system. As the company becomes more profitable and expands, it established additional sales offices on Mumbai and Delhi. Each sales office maintains its own system to record and track customer orders for its region. At the same time the two sites are linked to the mode at corporate headquarters and relay each order shipment and inventory and invoice processing.

Advantages of WAN

The integration of the local nodes into the distributed database linked by the WAN provides the following advantages:

- The WAN allows access to database at remote sites, enabling exchange of data.
- If a remote node fails, remaining nodes on the network can still exchange data.
- If the network fails, the local mode can still access its own database.
- The data used on daily basis by the sales offices resides at the local site, making it easier to retrieve quickly.
- The local offices can maintain the data more effectively. The corporate office can access the data as needed.
- As a site's database grows larger, its system's storage capacity can be easily upgraded without affecting the transfer of data between other nodes on network.

One of the most significant aspects of a wide area network when comparing it with freedom of a local area network is the involvement of a public telecommunications authority. Regardless of whether the network is made up from system, the controlling authority is almost always the public authority. In order to protect their equipment and employees, the authority lays down rules, which must be observed by anyone connecting to their lines. In most countries stringent requirements are also imposed on the characteristics of the data transmissions.

Metropolitan Area Network (MAN)

Metropolitan area network covers a wider area than a local area network. Usually MAN covers a large metropolitan city and is a scaled down version of wide area network. It operates at high speeds over distances sufficient for a metropolitan area.

Local Area Network (LAN)

A LAN is a system of interconnected microcomputers, sharing common resources like disks, printers etc., and links a number of computers workstations together to allow many people to use the same software and data files. Each user in such a multi-user environment accesses the resources through his microcomputer workstation. The network operating system integrates all the network components and makes operation smooth and transparent. LAN works in restricted geographical area such as within a large building or offices within a few kilometers. The LAN is an interconnection of computers that need to communicate with each other in a limited geographical area. The network may have other sharable devices attached such as fax, laser printers and copiers. The network includes a central facility with huge storage capacity for the requirements of the organization. It also has a network operating system for managing the network.

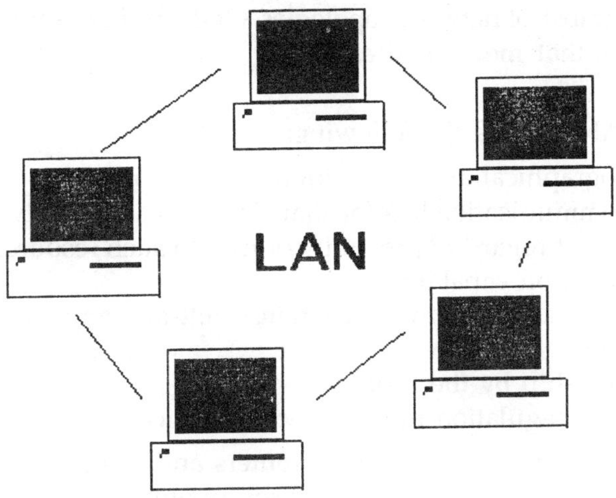

Types of LAN

Local area networks are mainly of two types: Client/Server LAN and Peer-to-Peer LAN.

(a) Client/Server LAN

Client Server LAN has servers and clients. The server is a computer that manages shared resources: hardware as well as software and data. It is usually a powerful computer with large RAM and secondary storage capacity. The LAN has a number of microcomputers, called clients, the request the server for services. The LAN may have many servers each specializing in one area of service such as file server, printer server, database server etc. A file server stores programme and data files and a database server stores data and a printer server controls printers on the local area network.

(b) Peer-to-Peer LAN

In a Peer-to-Peer LAN every computer is equal in status and functioning. All the computers on the network are capable of communicating independently with any other computer on the network without using a server. Thus, any computer on the network can access data and programmes stored on any other computer. The peer-to-peer LAN is less expensive than client/server LAN. But at the same time this LAN may be slower than a client/server LAN.

LAN Topology

The design of network requires selection of a particular topology and architecture for the interconnection of network component. Topology refers to the way the computers are physically connected into the network. The network architecture includes the specifications of the components that can be connected to the network. IBM's Systems Network Architecture (SNA) is an example of vendor developed network architecture. Such network architecture specifies network components such as terminals, workstations, printers, cluster controllers, host computer and communications controllers.

There area a number of network topologies. Of them ring, star and bus are popular network topologies that mentioned earlier.

Features of LAN

The features of LAN include the following:

- Limited geographical area say within a few kilometers.
- Common communication link for sharing information, software and peripheral devices without regard to proximity of user to such resources on the network.
- High transmission capability.
- Low error rate as the network contains built-in component for detecting for system errors.
- Private ownership by the user.
- Not subject to regulation by the telecom service.

LAN interconnects computers and computers and components within a limited geographical area. Such LANs are normally set up within a single site can have one or more business complex, a hospital, an office-building etc. The site can have one or more buildings but they should not be too for a way, say less then 5 kilometers. A LAN can also include a variety of computer systems and devices such as workstations, microcomputer, file servers, plotters, scanners, graphic terminals and printers.

A large personal computer or mini computer serves as the LAN's hub. A high capacity hand disk is attached to the hub as data files and software are stored on the network file server. The users can load the software on the file server and retrieve data files for processing. The output can be directed to the printer attached to the LAN.

Any the communication network that meets most or all of the following characteristics can be classified as LAN,

- All the devices on the network share a common transmission medium, that is, the cable and/or the controller.

- The devices connected to the network can operate independent of the network.
- Any device connected to it can communicate with any other device on the network, and
- The network is capable of supporting heavy data traffic over short distances compared to telecommunication network.
- The network covers a limited area usually a few kilometers in radius or a single site like a university campus, an office or a factory.

LAN Components

The components of LAN are File server, workstation, network operating system, LAN cable, Active and Passive hubs etc.

(a) Workstation

It is a single-user microcomputer with high power communication facilities. It can exchange message with other workstations or fileserver. Workstations can be of two types: user workstation and server workstation. User workstation is a microcomputer on the network, which is used to access the network. Service workstation performs service to process other workstations on the network. User workstation normally does not process requests from other workstations. Server workstation makes available all sharable network resources to other workstations. More than one server workstations may be added to the network such as printer server and fileserver. Normally the server workstation is the most powerful workstation. Server workstation may be dedicated or non-dedicated. In case of dedicated workstation, it is not available for other user applications. Non-dedicated server workstation doubles as an individual workstation and at the same time performs network-related functions.

(b) File Server

File server is actually a process running on a computer that provides the clients access to files on that computer. The term is loosely applied to mean computer that runs file server software. In this sense, it is a powerful computer with special software to serve files to other workstations on the network. The files, which may be programme files or data files, are simultaneously shared by a number of workstations. Novell Netware is a popular network operating system.

(c) Gateway

The gateway assists in communicating between LANs. A workstation may be dedicated to serve as gateway. This is required particularly when two networks with different technologies have to communicate with each other. Gateway may also be used to connect LAN with a mainframe computer.

(d) Network Interface Unit

The network interface is a printed circuit board installed in the microcomputer. It may be called network card, network adapter or network interface unit. It connects the workstations functionally and physically with the network.

(e) Active Hub

Hub is an electronic device to which multiple computers are attached usually using twisted pair cables. Active hub is a powered distribution point with active devices that drive distant nodes up to one kilometer away. It can connect up to eight nodes on the network. The maximum distance carried by an active hub is about 2000 ft.

(f) Passive Hub

This hub is a distribution point that does not use power or active devices in a network to connect up to four nodes within a short distance. The maximum distance covered by a passive hub is nearly 300 ft.

(g) LAN Cable

LAN requires superior cable capable of transferring data at high speed. Coaxial cables or Fibre optic cables may be used for networking computer.

(h) Network Operating System (NOS)

The NOS integrates all the network components. The NOS facilitates file and print serving along with other functions like communications and e-mail between workstations. In most LANs the NOS exists along with the computer's operating system. The computer's operating system processes the system requests first and processes them if they can be done with the workstation resources. If it is not a local request, meaning that the network resources have to be used, the request is transferred to NOS for carrying out. Thus, the NOS are responsible for controlling access to data, storage space and sharing of other peripheral resources.

(i) Applications Software

Another component of LAN is application software. It has to be ensured that the application software works in the multi-user environment.

(j) Protocols

Data transmission between devices requires protocol. Protocols are sets of rules and procedures to control the data transmission between computer and other devices. They are common technical guidelines for communication between devices. They specify the order in which signals will be transferred, the signal for completion of transfer etc. Only Devices using the same protocol can communicate directly. Both the sending and receiving devices must use the same protocol for effecting communication. For communication between devices using different protocols requires intermediate interpretation device or software. The protocol performs the following functions:

- Set up a link with the other device in the communication.
- Identify the component to other components in the communication (sending device's channel ID).
- Send and interpret the data.
- Provide a continuous feedback on data transmission like data is not being received and understood.
- Request for retransmission of garbled data.

- Engage recovery procedure when error occurs.
- Provide an acceptable way of terminating transmission so that all devices have completed the process.

The protocol is embedded in communication software designed to use a particular protocol. The user need not bother about the protocol as the components involved in the communication perform the protocol matching. The data communication protocols are of two main types: asynchronous and synchronous. The synchronous protocol permits continuous data transmission. The devices in communication must be synchronized with the other. The transmission is governed by a time interval and not by start-stop bits. For example, clock, in the modern, sets the time interval.

12

Software

The computer being a machine cannot perform on its own. It needs to be instructed to perform even a simple task like adding two numbers. Computers work on a set of instructions called computer software (programmes), which clearly specify the ways to carry out a task. Software can be categorized as system software and application software. System software is a generic term for referring to any computer programme whose purpose is to help the user to run the computer system, whereas application software employees the capabilities of a computer directly to a task that the user wishes to perform.

Categories of Software

System Software

System software consists of several programmes, which are directly responsible for controlling, integrating, and managing the individual hardware components of a computer system. You must have noticed that a new computer system is always accompanied by some software, either stored in a floppy or CD, which is supplied by the manufacturer. This software manages and supports the computer system and its information processing activities. System software is more transparent and less noticed by the users, they usually interact with the hardware or the applications this software provides a programming environment in which programmers can create applications to accommodate their needs. This environment provides functions that are not available at the hardware level and performs the tasks related to the execution of an application programme. Hence, system software acts as an interface between the hardware of the computer and the software application. In simple terms, system software makes the computer functional. They provide basic functionality like file management, visual display, and keyboard input are used by application software to accomplish these functions. Some examples of system software are:

- Operating system
- Device drivers
- Language translators
- System utilities.

1. Operating System

It is the first layer of software loaded into computer memory when it starts up. As the first software layer, all other software that gets loaded after it depends on it for various common core services. These common core services include disk access, memory management, takes scheduling, and user interfacing. In addition the operating system ensures that different programmes executing at the same time do not interfere with each other. It provides a software platform on top of which other programmes can run. In simple words, the operating system organizes and controls the hardware. Examples of operating systems are Windows XP, UNIX, and Linux. The basic functions of operating systems are:

(a) Process Management

It handles the creation, deletion, suspension, resumption, and synchronization of process.

(b) Memory Management

It handles allocation and de-allocation of memory space as required by various programmes.

(c) File Management

It is responsible for creation and deletion of files and directories. It also organizes, stores, retrieves, names, and protects all the files.

(d) Device Management

It manages all the devices of the computer system such as printers and modems. If any device fails, it detects the device failure and notifies the same to the user.

(e) Security Management

Protect system resources and information against destruction and unauthorized use.

User interface provides the interface between the user and the hardware.

2. Device Drivers

Device drivers are system programmes, which are responsible for proper functioning of devices. Every device, whether it is a printer, monitor, mouse or keyboard, has a driver programme associated with it for its proper functioning. Whenever a new device is added to the computer system, a new device driver must be installed before the device is used. A device driver is not an independent programme; it assists and is assisted by the operating system for the proper functioning of the device.

3. Language Translators

Computers only understand a language consisting of 0s and 1s called machine language.

To ease the burden of programming entirely in 0s and 1s, special programming languages called high-level programming languages were developed that resembled natural languages like English. Language translators help in converting programming languages into machine language. To be precise, they convert programming statements into the 0s and 1s that the computer is able to process. Depending on the programming language used, language translators are divided into three major categories: compilers, interpreter, and assembler.

(a) Compiler

The programmes written in any high-level programming language (C or Pascal) needs to be converted into machine language. This is achieved by using a complier.

(b) Interpreter

An interpreter analyses and executes the source code in line-by-line manner, without looking at the entire programme. In other words, an interpreter translates a statement in a programme and executes the statement immediately, before translating the next source language statement.

(c) Assembler

Compared to all the types of programming languages, assembly language is closest to the machine code. It is fundamentally a symbolic representation of machine code. The assembly language programme must be translated into machine code by a separate programme called an assembler. The assembler programme recognizes the character strings that make up the symbolic names of the various machine operations, and substitutes the required machine code for each instruction. In short, an assembler converts the assembly codes into machine codes, making the assembly programme ready for execution.

Typical software generally comprises millions of lines of programming statements or code. The code is divided into logical groups and stored in different independent modules so that the debugging and maintenance of the code becomes easier. Before execution, different object codes resulting from the independent modules have to be linked together to create and executable programme. A linker is a system programme that links together several objects modules and libraries to form a single, coherent, programme (executable programme). The part of the operating system that brings an executable file residing on disk into memory and executes it is known as loader. Being responsible for tasks like loading, linking and relocation, loader performs the function of a linked programme and then immediately schedules the executable for execution without creating an executable file as an output.

4. System Utility

System utility programmes perform day-to-day tasks related to the maintenance of the computer system. They are used to support, enhance, and secure existing programmes and data in the computer system. They are generally small programmes, having specific tasks to perform:

(a) File Management

These utilities make it easier to manage data files. Many programmes are written to help users to find the files, create and organize directions, copy, move, and remove files.

(b) Backup

It may happen that sometime data files are corrupted, or accidentally deleted. In such a case, data backups become very useful. A backup system utility is essential for those organizations, which want to keep their data intact.

(c) Data Recovery

It is the process of retrieving deleted or inaccessible data from failed electronic storage media such as computer hard disk drives, removable media, optical devices, and tape cartridges.

(d) Virus Protection

Anti-virus programmes are essential system utilities for a computer system functioning in a network. They provide the security to the system form viruses that can damage the computer system.

(e) Disk Management

Disk management programme includes various system softwares like disk defragmenter, data compressor and disk formatting tools. De-fragmentation implies putting fragments of files in a sequential order onto the disk which reduces the time to access the file.

(f) Firewall

It is commonly used to protect information such as e-mail and data files within a physical building or organization. Essentially, a firewall is designed to protect a computer from unauthorized access, especially via network.

(g) Disk Cleanup

To keep a computer running smoothly, regular maintenance is vital. Therefore, one should use the disk cleanup utility, which easily determines which files on hard drive are no longer needed, then delete those files.

Application Software

The most often seen software by a user is the application software. It used to accomplish specific tasks rather than just managing a computer system. For a user, the computer system has no specific use without application software. Application software may consist of a single programme, such as Microsoft's Note pad (for writing and editing simple text). It may also consist of a collection of programmes, often called a software package, which work together to accomplish a task, such as database management software. Application software may also include a larger collection of related but independent programmes and packages (a software suite), which have a common user interface or shared data format, such as Microsoft Office suite.

Applications softwares are dependent on system softwares. A system software (like operating system) acts as an interface between the user and the computer hardware, while application software performs specific tasks. Applications are pieces of software that perform tasks for the user besides helping the computer operate, which is the tasks of system software.

Applications softwares are controlled by system software, which manages hardware devices and performs background tasks for them. The distinction between the two is important. Without system software, the computer will not run, and without application software, the computer, no matter how powerful, will not be helpful in meeting user requirements. Think of it these way applications apply the computer's thinking power to business tasks such as tracking the general ledger or billing your customers. Application software ranges from games, calculators, and word processors (document creating programmes), to programmes that "paint" images on screen (image editors). Applications represent real world tasks. They can be easily divided by looking at exactly what function they serve. Some of the most commonly used application software is discussed below:

1. *Word Processor*

A word processor is software used to compose, format, edit, and print electronic documents. Word processing is one of the earliest applications for office productivity and the personal computer. It involves not only typing, but also checking the spelling and grammar of the text and arranging it correctly on the page. A variety of different typefaces is available for a verity of effects. It is possible to include pictures, graphs, charts and many other things within the text of the document. It also allows for changes in margins, fonts, and colour. Nowadays, virtually all personal computers are equipped with a word processing programme, which has the same function as a typewriter for writing letters, reports or other documents, and printing. Examples of some well-known word processors are Microsoft Word and Word Perfect.

2. *Spreadsheets*

One of the first commercial uses of computers was in processing payroll and other financial records, so the programmes were designed to generate reports in the standard "spreadsheet" format bookkeepers and accountants used. A spreadsheet application is a rectangular grid, which allows text, numbers, and complex functions to be entered into a matrix of thousands of individual cells. The spreadsheet provides sheets containing cells each of which may contain text and/or numbers. Cells may also contain equations that calculate results from data placed in other cells or series of cells. A simple example might be a column of numbers totaled in a single cell containing an equation relating to that column. Spreadsheet software are used predominantly for accounting a other numerically-based tasks, because financial and mathematical data and analysis are often managed in a tabular style, with columns of financial figures being manipulated and then influencing other data computations. Microsoft Excel and Lotus 1-2-3 are examples of spreadsheet applications.

3. *Image Editors*

Image editor programmes are designed specifically for capturing, creating, editing, and manipulating images. These graphics programmes provide a variety of special features for creating and altering images. In addition to offering a host of filters and image transformation algorithms, some image editors also enable the user to create and superimpose layers. Most graphic programmes have the ability to import and export one or more graphic file formats. These computer programmes enable the user to adjust an image to improve its appearance. With image editing software, one can darken or lighten an image, rotate it, adjust it contrast, crop out extraneous detail, and much more. Examples of these programmes are Adobe Photoshop, Adobe Illustrator and CorelDraw.

4. ***Database Management Systems***

Database management software is a collection of computer programmes that allow storage, modification, and extraction of information from a database in an efficient manner. It supports the structuring of the database in a standard format and provides tools for data input, verification, storage, retrieval, query, and manipulation. When such software is used, information systems can be changed much more easily as the organization's information requirements change. New categories of data can be added to the database without disrupting the existing system. It also controls the security and integrity of the database from unauthorized access. FoxPro and Oracle are database management systems.

5. ***Presentation Applications***

A presentation is a means of assessment, which requires presentation providers to present their work orally in the presence of an audience. It combines both visual and verbal elements. Presentation software allows the user to create presentations by producing slides or handouts for presentation of projects. Essentially, such computer programmes allow users to create a variety of visually appealing electronic slides for presentation. Microsoft PowerPoint is one of the most famous presentation applications.

6. ***Desktop Publishing Software***

The term desktop publishing is usually used to describe the creations of printed documents using a desktop computer. It is a technique of using a personal computer to design images and pages, and assemble type and graphics, then using a laser printer or image-setter to output the assembled pages onto paper, film, or printing plate. These softwares are used for creating magazines, books, newsletters, and so on. Such software assist in creating sophisticated documents including complicated page designs, detailed illustrations, and camera-ready types faces. Quark Express and Adobe PageMaker are desktop publishing software.

13

Programming Languages

Computers are machines. Unfortunately they cannot understand natural languages, such as Hindi, English, Malayalam, Tamil, etc. that human beings speak and understand. Therefore, to give instructions to computers, different languages have been developed. These languages are called computer languages. To get a particular work done by computers, programmers write instructions using these computer languages. Each computer language has its own vocabulary of a natural language that we speak. Each natural language has its rules and grammar. Similarly, each computer language too has its set of rules that are called as syntax. As computers are not intelligent, we have to use the exact syntax rules of the computer language whenever we write any computer programme. Otherwise, the computer will not be able to understand our instructions.

Over the last few decades, several computer languages have developed. Different computer languages are suitable for different applications. For example, COBOL (Common Business Oriented Language) may be more suitable for business applications, whereas FORTRAN may be more suitable for scientific or engineering applications. We can classify all computer languages into three categories.

Computer languages are classified into three categories:

- Machine language.
- Assembly language.
- High level languages.

Machine Language

The form in which information is denoted or represented by a combination of "1" and "0"s is called machine language. Programmes and data are ultimately represented in machine language in memory and other hardware of the computer. To start with computer programmers used machine language for programming. It was tedious since each operation that the computer has to perform is denoted by a particular combination of"1" s and"0"s. Also each computer had its own machine language code. One has to remember all these codes to write a programme.

While machine language had the drawbacks mentioned above, it was very efficient in using computer circuits. There was no necessity for software to convert since we can directly represent the machine language in the computer circuits without the necessity of conversion.

Advantages of Machine Language

Even though machine languages are not a human friendly language, it offers following advantages.

(a) Translation Free

Machine language is the only language that computers can directly execute without the need for conversion. Even an application using high-level languages, has to be converted into machine-readable form so that the computer can understand the instructions.

First Programmer Lady Lovelace Ada Augusta (officially the first programmer) suggested binary numbers for computer storage instead of decimals. A British mathematician, Alan Mathison Turing, was the first person to recognize that programming in machine language is less time consuming. In 1952, John Von Neuman proposed to have new programmes loaded from a magnetic tape to read. With differences in magnetic polarities, it can mean either ON of OFF states.

(b) High Speed

Since no conversion is needed, the applications developed using machine languages are extremely fast. It is usually used for complex applications such as space control system, nuclear reactors, and chemical processing.

Disadvantages of Machine Language

There are many disadvantages in using machine language to develop programmes. Some of these are:

(a) Machine Dependent

Every computer type differs from the other, based on its architecture. Hence, an application developed for a particular type of computer may not run on the other type of computer. This any prove costly as well as difficult for the organizations.

(b) Complex Language

Machine language is very difficult to read and write. Since all the data and instructions must be converted to binary code, it is almost impossible to remember the instructions. A programmer must specify each operation, and the specific locations for each piece of data and instructions to be stored. It means that a programmer practically needs to be hardware expert to have proper control over the machine language.

(c) Error Prone

Since the programmer has to remember all the opcodes and the memory locations, machine language is bound to be error prone. It requires a super human effort to keep track of the logic of a problem and, therefore, results in frequent programming errors.

(d) Tedious

Machine language poses real problems while modifying and correcting a programme.

Sometimes the programming becomes too complex to modify and the programmer has to rewrite the entire logic again. Therefore, it is very tedious and time-consuming, and since time is a precious commodity, programming using the machine language tends to be costly. Due to its overwhelming limitations, machine language is rarely used nowadays.

Assembly Language

As computer field advanced, computer scientists felt the necessity of making computer programming easier. They invented computer languages that are easy to remember and use. These languages called assembly language uses mnemonic codes. For Example:

For adding two quantities X and Y, You may code as follows.

ADD X Y ADD is called operation code that tells the computer what operation it has to perform. X and Y are called operation addresses.

These refer to the memory addresses where the quantities you want to add are stored. X refers to the location of first quantity and Y the second quantity. These are called symbolic address, since they do not refer to any fixed address. Software called assembler translates this assembly language programme into machine language programme which you can load into computer memory and execute. When the programme is loaded into memory for execution the symbolic addresses are automatically converted into actual physical addresses of operands involved in an instruction.

Assembly language offers the following advantages:

- The assembly language uses mnemonic codes, for programming. So it is easier for the programmer to use assembly language than machine language for programming.
- The assemblers, in addition to translating the assembler language programme into machine language, list the programme statements (called source code) and also the syntax errors that the programmer committed.

Assembly language has certain disadvantages too:

- One has to spend considerable time in writing the assembly language programme.
- An assembly language programme has to be converted into machine language programme using assembly.
- While it is easier to use than the machine language one still has to remember the operation codes for various operations.

High Level Languages

During 1960s computers started to gain popularity and it became necessary to develop languages that were more like natural languages such as English so that a common user could use the computer efficiently. Since assembly language required deep knowledge of computer architecture, it demanded programming as well as hardware skills to use computers. Due to computer's widespread usage, early 1960s saw the emergence of the third generations programming languages (3GL). Languages such as COBOL, FORTRAN, BASIC, and C are examples of 3GLs and are considered high-level languages.

High level languages are similar to English language. Programmes written using these languages can be machine independent. A single high-level statement can substitute several instructions in machine or assembly language. Unlike assembly and machine programmes, high level programmes may be used with different types of computers with little or no modification, thus reducing the re-programming time. In high-level language, programmes are written in a sequence of statements to solve a problem. For example, the following BASIC code snippet will calculate the sum of two numbers

```
LET X = 10
LET Y = 20
LET SUM = X + Y PRINT SUM
```

The first two statements store 10 in variable X (memory locations name) and 20 in variable, Y, respectively. The third statement again creates a variable named SUM, which will store the summation of X and Y value. Finally, the output is printed, that is, the value stored in SUM is printed on the screen.

Translating High-level Language to Machine Language

Since computers understand only machine language, it is necessary to convert the high level language programmes into machine language codes. This is achieved by using language translators or language processors, generally known as compliers, interpreters or other routines that accepts statements in one language and produces equivalent statements in another language.

(a) Compiler

A compiler is a kind of translator that translates a programme into another programme known as target language. Usually, the term compiler is used for language translator of high-level language into machine language. The complier replaces single high-level statement with a series of machine language instruction. A compiler usually resides on a disk or the storage media. When a programme is to be compiled, its compiler is loaded into main memory. The compiler stores the entire high-level programme, scans it and translates the whole programme into an equivalent machine language programme. During the translation process, the compiler reads the source programme and checks the syntax (grammatical) errors. If there is any error, the compiler generates an error message, which is usually displayed on the screen. In case of errors, the compiler will not create the object code until all the errors are rectified. Once the programme has been compiled, the resulting machine code is saved in an executable file, which can be run on its own at any time. To be precise, once the executable is generated, there is no need for the actual source code file. Anyway, it is worthwhile to keep the source file(s) because if the source code is modified, it is necessary to recompile the programme again to regenerate the executable file containing amendments.

(b) Interpreter

Unlike compilers, an interpreter translates a statement in a programme and executes the statement immediately, before translating the next source language statement. When an error is encountered in the programme, the execution of the programme is halted and an error message is displayed. Similar to compilers, every interpreted language such as BASIC and LISP has its own interpreters.

Advantages of High-Level Languages

High-Level Languages (HLL) are useful in developing complex software, as they support complex data structures. It increases the programmer's productivity (the number of lines of code generated per hour). Unlike assembly language, the programmer does not need to learn the instructions set of each computer being worked with. The various advantages of using high-level languages are discussed below:

Compilers

Compiler is a programme which translates source code written in a particular programming language into computer-readable machine code that can be directly loaded and executed. For each high-level language, a separate compiler is required. For example, a compiler for C language cannot translate a programme written in FORTRAN. Hence, to execute both language programmes, the host computer must have the compilers of both languages.

(a) Readability

Since high-level languages are closer to natural languages, they are easier to learn and understand. In addition, a programmer does not need to be aware of computer architecture; even a common man can use it without much difficulty. This is the main reason of HLL's popularity.

(b) Machine Independent

High-level language are machine independent in the sense that a programme created using HLL can be used on different platforms with very little or no change at all.

(c) Easy Debugging

High-level languages include the support for ideas of abstraction so that programmers can concentrate on finding the solution to the problem rapidly, rather than on low-level details of data representation, which results in fewer errors. Moreover, the compilers and interpreters are designed in such a way that they detect and point out the errors instantaneously.

(d) Easier to Maintain

As compared to low-level languages, the programmes written in HLL are easy to modify and maintain because HLL programmes are easier to understand.

(e) Low Development Cost

High-level languages permit faster development of programmes. Although a high-level programme may not be as efficient as an equivalent low-level programme, but the savings in programmer's time generally outweighs the inefficiencies of the application. This is because the cost of writing a programme is nearly constant for each line of code, regardless of the language. Thus, a high-level language, where each line of code translates to 10 machine instructions, costs only a fraction as compared to programme developed in a low-level language.

(f) Easy Documentation

Since the statements written in HLL are similar to natural languages they are easier to understand as compared to low-level languages.

Disadvantages of High-Level Languages

The main disadvantages of this language are:

(a) Poor Control on Hardware

High-level languages are developed to ease the pressure on programmers so that they do not have to know the intricacies of hardware. As a result, sometimes the applications written in high-level languages cannot completely harness the total power available at hardware level.

(b) Less Efficient

The HLL applications are less efficient as far as computation time is concerned. This is because, unlike low-level languages, high-level languages must be created and sent through another processing programme known as a compiler. This process of translation increases the execution time of an application. Programmes written in high-level languages take more time to execute, require more memory space. Hence, critical applications are generally written in low-level languages.

14

Operating System

It is the first layer of software loaded into computer memory when it starts up. As the first software layer, all other software that gets loaded after it depends on it for various common core services. These common core services include disk access, memory management, takes scheduling, and user interfacing. In addition the operating system ensures that different programmes executing at the same time do not interfere with each other. It provides a software platform on top of which other programmes can run. In simple words, the operating system organizes and controls the hardware. Examples of operating systems are Windows XP, UNIX, and Linux.

The operating system is a software programme that acts as an interface between the user and the computer. It is used to control and manage the hardware components such as keyboard, monitor, printer, scanner etc.

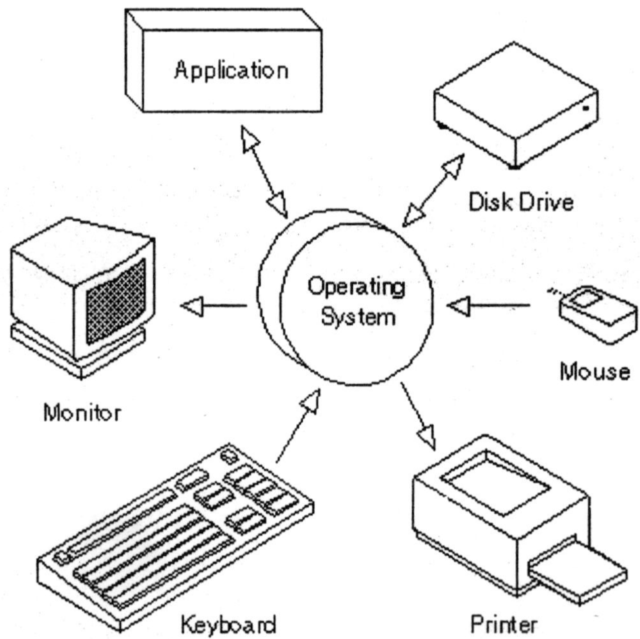

Functions of an Operating System

(a) Process Management

It handles the creation, deletion, suspension, resumption, and synchronization of process.

(b) Memory Management

It handles allocation and de-allocation of memory space as required by various programmes.

(c) File Management

It is responsible for creation and deletion of files and directories. It also organizes, stores, retrieves, names, and protects all the files.

(d) Device Management

It manages all the devices of the computer system such as printers and modems. If any device fails, it detects the device failure and notifies the same to the user.

(e) Security Management

Protect system resources and information against destruction and unauthorized use.

(f) User Interface

Provide the interface between the user and the hardware.

Types of Operating System

These are the different types of operating system: 15.3.1 DOS (Disk Operating System) MS-DOS was the widely used operating system before the introduction of the Windows operating system. Even now the MS-DOS commands are used for carrying out many jobs like copying the files, deleting the files etc. The DOS is a set of computer programmes. The main functions of DOS are to manage files, allocate system resources according to the requirement. It provides essential features to control hardware devices such a keyboard, screen, disk drives, printers, modems etc. Thus, DOS is a medium through which the user and external devices attached to the system communicate the command with the system. DOS translate communication issued by the computer in the format that is understandable by the computer and instruct computer to work accordingly. It is also translates the result and any error message in the format for the user to understand.

Features of DOS

- Single user system
- Machine independence
- Programme control
- Peripheral management
- Operating with Directories
- Managing files
- Processing commands
- Managing input and output
- Data securing

- Using Batch files
- Managing memory
- Setting up environment
- Command processing—DOS shell (a set of commands which is used to create the programmes)
- Operating with Assembler.

Advantages of DOS

The DOS provides the following advantages:

- Machine independence.
- More security.
- User friendly environment.
- More useful in commercial applications.
- Error finding and recovery is more efficient.
- Facilities more graphical user interfaces.
- Easy debugging.

Windows Operating System

Microsoft Windows is the most popular operating system around the world. Even those who are new to computers can use it with a little practice. With the help of Windows, we can operate the computer just by clicking the mouse buttons, Windows 95, Windows 98, Windows 2000 and Windows XP are the various versions of Windows. Windows is an operating system. It is the extension of the disk operating system. Windows is system software. It requires DOS to run the application programmes. The DOS should be loaded into the memory before the window is executed. After the windows is loaded into the memory the windows environment takes all the device controls. It also takes care of the memory management of the programmes run by the windows software."

Types of Windows

There are two types of windows. They are

- Application windows—displays the executable programme in graphical user interface mode.
- Document window—generated by executable or application programme.

1. Windows 98

Windows 98 is the upgraded version of Windows 95. It offers bug fixture and minor enhancements.

Features of Windows

The important features of Windows 98 are as follows:

(a) Graphical User Interface

Windows 98 provides user-friendlier interface to work on. Its improved graphical user interface makes learning and using Windows 98 more natural and easier for all types of users. It is more powerful, customizable and efficient.

(b) Type of Icons (Small Pictures)

There are three types of icons. They are

- Applications icons—the minimized version of the currently running application programmes. It appears at the bottom of the desktop and can be maximized.
- Document icons—the reduced document windows.
- Programme icons—appear with in programme manager and clicking on these icons activate the associated applications and also load the related documents or files.

(c) Start Button

Introduction of START button by Windows 98 made life much simpler while there is a need to access multiple programmes. It is the gateway of accessing most of the functionality available in the computer loaded with Windows 98. Just click on the start button anytime to start any programmes, open or find documents, change windows settings, get Help, manage Files, maintain System, much more.

(d) Taskbar

The Task bar provides information and access to the entire task that has been currently activated by Windows 98. Using this one can keep a track of what all programmes have been activated and switched between them.

(e) Windows Explorer

Windows Explorer more or less acts as File Manager for Windows 98, but with lots of new features. It is more efficient, faster and user friendly. Using Explorer one can easily browse through all the drives and network resources available and manage files.

(f) Right Mouse Button

Clicking on the right mouse button activates a pop-up menu in any programme so as to help in completing a task efficiently.

(g) Long File Names

As the MS-DOS convention follows, none-of the file used in DOS environment should be more than 8 characters of primary name and optimal secondary name (extension) of three characters. However Windows 98 has broken this barrier. Windows 98 supports long file names maximum of 225 characters. It also allowed space to be used in between file name. This helps to make files and folders (directory/subdirectory) easier to organize and find.

(h) Shortcuts

As the name suggests, SHORTCUTS are the shortest way to access programmes, files other resources in Windows 98. Instead of going through the structural process of accessing a programme, one can create "shortcuts" to access them. It creates links for easy access to file, programmes, folders and more.

(i) Multitasking

Multitasking allows the user to activate and accomplish more than one task at a time. For example, work on a document file WORD programmes, which copies file from other computer available in time on the network. With Windows 98, 32-bit computing environment, the user can do more than one task a time.

(j) Easy Internet Access

Integration of Internet Explorer 4.0 and Active Desktop, which coupled the Internet html hypertext links more tightly to the Windows 98 user interface.

(k) Software Compatibility

Windows 98 provides complete backward compatibility. It is easily compatible with other applications developed for MS-DOS and Windows 3.x environment. It also supports latest 32-bit technology. Most of the latest software packages are now built on Windows 98, operating environment.

(l) Great Gaming Platform

Windows 98 supports rich graphics, high quality audio and video. Software to take advantage of Intel's Multimedia Extensions (MMX) to the IA-32 instruction set, which are designed to improve the performance of multimedia applications and games developed for Windows 98 that uses MMX technology.

(m) Hardware Compatibility

Windows 98 provides greater Hardware compatibility as compared to any other operating environment. It has flexibility of supporting hardware from different vendors.

(n) Find Utility

Find Utility of Windows 98 allows the user to do searches by partial name, last modified date, or full text. In addition we can save, rename or view files from within the result pane.

(o) Help

Windows 98 provides online help to accomplish a task. If the user is not sure how to perform a task, Windows 98 Help will provide structured process how to accomplish the task. Simply right-click on any object in the user interface (icon) and he can get relevant description about that object.

(p) Manage More Numbers of PC's

Windows 98 can manage up to eight monitors on a- single PC. The user can drag and drop resize and move desktop items such as windows, folders, icons, and applications, from one monitor to the next.

(q) Additional Facilities

Windows 98 includes additional enhancement of Windows 95 that includes new backup utilities and disk defragmenter capabilities.

The UNIX Operating System

Like DOS and windows, there's another operating system called UNIX. It arrived earlier then the other two, and stayed back like enough to give us the internet. UNIX is a giant operating system and is way ahead of them in sheer power. It has practically everything an operating system should have, and several features which other operating systems never had. Its richness and elegance go beyond the commands and tolls that constitute it, while simplicity permeates the entire system. It runs on practically every hardware and provided motivation to the open source movement.

However, UNIX also makes many demands of the user. In requires a different type of commitment to understand the subject, even when the user is an experienced computer professional. It introduces certain concepts not known to the computing community before, and user numerous symbols whose meaning is anything but clear. It achieves unusual tasks with a few keystrokes, but it takes time to devices a sequence of them for a specific task. Often, it doesn't tell you whether you are right or wrong, and doesn't warn you of the consequences of your actions. That is probably the reason why many people still prefer to stay away from UNIX.

Features of UNIX

UNIX is an operating system, so it is has all the features an operating system is expected to have. However UNIX also looks at a few things differently and possesses features unique to it. The following section gives a clear idea of the major features of this operating system.

(a) UNIX: A Multi User System

From the fundamental point of view, UNIX is a multiprogramming system; it permits multiple programmes to run. This can happen in two ways

- Multiple users can run separate jobs.
- A single user can also run multiple jobs.

(b) UNIX: A Multi Tasking System Too

A single user can also run multiple tasks at the same time as UNIX is a multitasking system. It is usual for a user to edit a file, print another one on printer, send e-mail to a friend and browse the Word Wide Web—all without leaving any of the application. This kernel is designed to handle a user's multiple needs.

(c) The UNIX Toolkit

By one definition, UNIX represents the kernel, but the kernel by itself doesn't do much that can benefit the user. To properly exploit the power of UNIX, you need to use the host of applications that are shipped with every UNIX system. These applications are quite varied in scope. There are general—purpose tools, text manipulation utilities (called filters), compilers and interpreters, networked applications and system administration tools.

(d) Pattern Matching

UNIX features very sophisticated pattern matching features. UNIX features elaborate pattern matching schemes that use several characters from the Meta character set. The matching isn't confined to filenames only. Some of the most advanced and useful tools also use a special expression called a regular expression that is framed with characters from the set.

(e) Programming Facility

The UNIX shell is also a programming language; it was designed for a programmer, not a casual end user. It has all the necessary ingredients, like control structures, loops and variables, that establish it as a powerful programming language in its own right.

(f) Documentation

UNIX documentation is no longer the sore point it once was. Even though it is sometimes uneven at most times the treatment is quite. The principal online help facility available is the man command, which remains the most important reference for commands and their configuration files. Thanks to O'Reilly and Associates, one can safely say that there's no feature of UNIX on which a separate textbook is not available. Apart from the online documentation, there's a vast ocean of UNIX resources available on the internet. There are several newsgroups on UNIX where you can fire your queries in case you are stuck with a problem—be it a problem related to shell programming or a network configuration issue. The FAQ (Frequently Asked Questions) a document that addresses common problems is also widely available on the Net. Then there are numerous articles published in magazines and journals and lecture notes available by universities on their Websites. UNIX is easily tamed Operating System.

15

Internet

Internet is a communication network which bridges all the small computer networks worldwide as a whole. Internet is based upon Internet technology, in particular World Wide Web (WWW), to build Information System within organization or enterprise to accomplish standardization and automation. Fundamentally, it means network computing environments which let the users share the information through the Internet and Web browsers. Ultimately, it allows a certain organization to build a Groupware within Web environment at low cost on top of existing network infrastructure. By doing this, closed organization network would be interconnected with existing worldwide Internet, which results in diverse information that strengthens competitive advantages of the organization.

Basically, it runs on top TCP/IP and HTTP and filters out any illegal access through firewall. Where the Internet connects people and organizations and information sources by using common protocols to link computers on a public and open–to–all basis, an Internet uses the same common protocols for internal company or group purposes. Instead of adopting a common proprietary standard for its communications, information storage and presentation, etc., the company (or any group of people or companies) decides to use Internet standards and methods.

An Internet can be defined as a network connecting an affiliated set of clients using standard Internet protocols, esp. TCP/IP and HTTP or as an IP–based network of nodes behind a firewall, or behind several firewalls connected by secure, possibly virtual, networks. In general, a web is an unstructured client/server network that uses HTTP as its transaction protocol. The World Wide Web comprises all HTTP nodes on the public Internet. An internal web comprises all HTTP nodes on a private network, such as an organization's LAN or WAN. If the organization is a corporation, the internal web is also a corporate web. If a corporate web connects two or more trading partners, it is often referred to as a business-to-business web, or an extranet. Note that internal webs–also known as intranets–are only logically "internal "to an organization. Physically they can span the globe, as long as access is limited to a defined community of interest.

Core Features of the Internet

There are some characteristics of the internet that gave it the potential to deliver a special set of business benefits over and above existing IT technologies.

(a) Simplicity of Use

The software that is used access the Internet (the web browser software) is comparatively easy to learn and simple to use. It can operate on wide range of operating system platforms and can access any mainstream application like SAP and oracle. The flexibility of the web combined with the simplicity of the browser software has resulted in reduced staff training costs, lower development costs and an increase in the range of users who can have access to the organization.

(b) Breadth of Access

The internet is a global network like the telephone network. Its access is not conditioned by geographic boundaries. Unlike the telephone network the cost involved in global connection is not related to the distance involved. No other communication medium has had access to such a large audience and range of people which increases the ability to leverage the value of information to a scale that has never before been possible.

(c) Synergy with other Media

Apart from using the existing telecommunication technology, it supports or complements other media. Internet services have demonstrated a high degree of synergy with other media as can be seen from the following:

Example: Book, magazine and newspaper publishers have used the web to supplement and extend their written products. Publishers of CD-ROMs have used the web to maintain the currency of the information they can deliver. Microsoft's encyclopedias CD-ROM, Encarta, allows seamless interface to information accessed from the company's website.

Publishers of software and games now deliver their products directly over the internet. Entertainment companies regularly provide extracts of their films and music recordings to promote the real products.

(d) Low Relative Cost

The costs involved in conducting a process using internet technology are less than those involving other methods. The internet access requires telephone line for most individual users. The pricing of telephone service is one which is independent of distance. The charge for the usage of telecommunication line is based on local charge rate irrespective of what is sent over the line or how distant the recipient is.

(e) Extension of Existing IT Resources

Resource sharing was underlying rationale for the development of the internet. It allows the IT resources to be shared by multiple users in organizations and also with others related to the organization such as trading partners.

(f) Flexibility of Communication

The web browsers greatly extend the ways in which individuals can communicate. They support text, voice and multimedia formats and can provide immediate access to shared information. These facilities are available for intra-company communications as those between individuals in separate organizations.

(g) Security

Security has been a major issue in internet as any security breach can cause financial loss, leak of sensitive information, etc. standards for secure electronic transactions have been developed and reasonable security is in place now.

(h) Speed and Availability

The transmission speed is very low and it takes a bit too long for downloading files. However, compared to other means of communication, it is indeed fast. It also provides a wide range of communication services that are inexpensive and relatively easy to access for millions of users through a standard set of protocols. An internet can be as big as a community of interest. Scale is an important factor in web implementation, but it has no bearing on the logical association of clients that make up an intranet. For example, a workgroup with one web server, a company with several hundred web servers, and a professional organization with ten thousand web servers can be considered an intranet.

Internet Software

To connect to the Internet, a computer requires mainly three different kinds of software:

- *TCP/IP:* TCP/IP, or Transmission Control Protocol/Internet Protocol, is the basic communication protocol of the Internet. It allows programmes on user's computer to communicate properly over the internet. Usually, when you are set up with direct access to the Internet, your computer is provided with a copy of the TCP/IP programme. Similarly, every other computer that you may send messages to or get information from also has a copy of TCP/IP.
- *Dialer Software:* This software is provided by the ISP to instruct the modem to dial the phone number, and identify the user's machine to the access provider's system for access to the network.
- *Browser:* To use the Internet, a web browser is essential. This programme allows the user to view the information available on the World Wide Web.

Internet Applications

The Internet has grown from a small project to today's biggest network of computers. Due to this colossal growth, the Internet has become the biggest domain of information. Nowadays, an Internet user has access to a wide variety of services such as electronic mail, file transfer, vast information resources, interest group membership, interactive collaboration, multimedia displays, real-time broadcasting, shopping opportunities, and much more. Some of the important services provided by the Internet are briefed in the following few sections.

1. *World Wide Web: (WWW)*

The World Wide Web (abbreviated as the web or WWW) is one of the most popular services available on Internet. It is a subset of the Internet and it presents text, images, animation, video, sound and other multimedia in a single interface. This greatly enhances the experience of the Internet surfer. Although the World Wide Web is often referred to as the Internet, they are actually two different concepts. The Internet is the decentralized global network of computers that transfer information and the wring that makes all this possible whereas the web is a collection of documents or websites, that user can access using the Internet and a web browser.

The web is a part of the Internet and it refers to a system of Internet servers that supports hypertext using a specific Internet protocol called HTTP on a single interface (web browsers). In addition, almost every protocol type available on the Internet is accessible on the web. This includes e-mail, FTP, Telnet, and Usenet News. Since the WWW is a subset of the Internet, it stands to reason that the web could not exist without the Internet. However, the Internet would still be the Internet without the web. The operation of the web relies primarily on hypertext, as it is a means of information retrieval.

Hypertext is a document containing words that connect to other documents. These words are called links, which the user can select. A single hypertext document can contain links to documents and resources throughout the Internet. With the ability of the web to work with multimedia and advanced programming languages, the World Wide Web is the fastest growing and the most interesting part of the Internet. With video conferencing and wireless applications, the Internet is ready to take us to the new realm of communication and information exchange.

2. *Electronic Mail (e-mail)*

Electronic mail, or e-mail, is a fast, easy, and inexpensive way to communicate with other Internet users around the world. It is one of the basic and earliest services of the Internet and the most used application on the Internet too. E-mail overcomes most of the problems and delays of getting a physical document from one person to another. Rather, it has the dual advantage of not only being faster but cheaper to sue as well.

3. *File Transfer Protocol (FTP)*

FTP or File Transfer Protocol is a system of rules and a software programme that enables a user to long on to another computer and transfer information between it and his/her computer. It was the first service developed for the Internet so that government and educational institutions could easily exchange files. FTP allows the user to get access to the files stored in the directory of a remote computer that is connected to the Internet. Using FTP, one can upload and download files from the remote computer (known as FTP servers), if he/she has access permission on the remote machine.

4. *Telnet*

The word "telnet" is derived from telecommunications and network and is a protocol that allows a user to log on to a remote computer. Telnet is also known as remote login, which means connecting one machine to another in such a way that a person may interact with another machine as if it is being used locally.

5. *Internet Relay Chat (IRC)*

IRC or Internet Relay Chat is a service on the Internet that allows people to communicate in real time and carry on conversations via the computer with one or more people. It provides the user with the facility to engage in simultaneous (synchronous) online "conversation" with other user form anywhere in the world.

6. *Chatting and Instant Messaging*

Chart programmes allow users on the Internet to communicate with each other by typing in real time. They are sometimes included as a feature of a website, where users can log into chat rooms to exchange comments and information about the topics addressed on the site.

7. *Internet Telephony*

Internet telephone is the use of the Internet rather than the traditional telephone company infrastructure, to exchange spoken or other telephonic information. It consists of hardware and software that enable people to use the Internet as a transmission medium for telephone calls. There are many Internet telephony applications available. Some, such as Cool Talk and NetMeeting, come bundled with popular web browsers.

8. *Video Conferencing*

Video conferencing uses the same technology as IRC, but also provides sound and video pictures. It enables direct face-to-face communication across networks. A video conferencing system has to or more parties in different locations, which have the ability to communicate using a combination of video, audio, and data. A video conference can be person to person (referred to as "point-to-point") or can involve more than two people (referred to as "multipoint") and the video conferencing terminals are often referred to as "endpoints." The following five elements are common to all video conferencing endpoints:

- *Camera:* The camera captures live images to send across the network.
- *Visual Display:* It displays the images of the people taking part in the videoconference.
- *Audio System:* It includes both microphones to capture audio from the endpoint and loudspeakers to play back the audio received from other endpoints across the network connection.
- *Compression:* Videos are very bandwidth-intensive and they take a long time to load. Therefore, video systems include technologies, often referred to as codes, to compress and decompress video and audio data, allowing transmission across a network connection in near-real time.
- *User Interface and Control System:* The user interface allows the users to control interactions for example, placing calls, storing and locating numbers, and adjust environment settings such as volume. The control system handles the underlying communication that takes place between endpoints.

9. *Newsgroups (Usenet)*

Newsgroups are international discussion groups that focus on a particular topic and helps in gathering information about that topic. The topics discussed here cover all the fields such as politics, computers, technology, and many more. The information or articles that make up the "news" are written by people interested in a specific topic. These articles are posted to the newsgroup so that others can read, reply, and comment on them.

10. *Mailing Lists (List Server)*

The Internet is home to a large community of individuals who carry out active discussions, organized around topic-oriented forums that are distributed via e-mail. This method of Internet communications is known as mailing list and it enables people with similar interests from all over the world to communicate and share information with each other.

Extranet and E-mail

An Extranet is a private network that uses the internet protocol and the public telecommunication system to securely share part of business information or operations with-suppliers, vendors, partners, customers, or other businesses.

Through e-mail, documents are prepared and sent electronically. The recipients need not be present at the other end to send the message. The message gets stored in the electronic mailbox of the addressee. The recipient can open the mailbox whenever he is free and can read or print the message.

Extranet

An Extranet can be viewed a-part of a company's intranet that is extended to users outside the company. It has also been described as a "state of mind" in which the internet is perceived as a way to do business with other companies as well as to sell products to customers. Extranet extends the intranet from one location to another across the internet by securing data flow, to another intranet to a business partner. In these way intranets of business partners, suppliers, creditors, distributors, customers, and the like are connected to extranets by agreements. An Extranet requires security and privacy. These require firewall server management, issuances and use of digital certificate or similar means of user authentication, encryption of messages, and the use of virtual private networks that tunnel through the public network.

Characteristics of Extranet

The following are the important characteristics of the Extranet.

- It is an extended internet-private business networks located outside of the corporate firewall.
- It can be referred to an intranet that is partially accessible to authorized outsiders.
- It is a network that uses the internet to link businesses with others that share the common goals.

Uses of Extranet

Companies can use an Extranet to:

- Exchange large volumes of data using Electronic Data Interchange.
- Share product catalogus exclusively with wholesalers or those in the Trade.
- Collaborate with other companies on joint development efforts.
- Jointly develop and use training programmes with other companies.

- Provide or access services provided by one company to a group of other companies, such as an online banking application managed by one company on behalf or affiliated banks.
- Share news of common interest exclusively with partner companies.
- The manufacturing companies can coordinate the design manufacturing, scheduling and delivery across supply chain.
- With extranet the technology firms can support for their customers and partners and makes it.
- Possible for remote access for employees.
- The financial services firms by using extranet can reduce costs of proprietary networks.
- With extranet the publishing companies can increase the speed of design and production cycles.

Other Benefits

- Quicker turnaround time.
- Improved communication.
- Decreased paper flow.
- Traceable correspondence.
- Better service.
- Lower overhead and expenses.
- Improved employee morale.
- Increased Margins.
- Flexibility and scalability.
- Reduced transitional barriers.
- Versatility.

A Brief List of Examples of Extranet Could Include:

- Allowing suppliers access to relevant inventory levels.
- Allowing clients to review their account records.
- Allowing students to update address information in real time.

As with intranet, access is granted only where you establish that it is required. User access is controlled by the latest in security technologies, protecting sensitive material from intrusion.

E-mail

E-mail is an electronic message sent form one computer to another. We can send or receive personal and business-related messages with attachments, such as pictures or formatted documents. We can even send songs and computer programmes.

The e-mail communication is incredibly simple. A person with a PC and a modem to connect to the network can communicate with the other(s) so connected to the network. The message can be prepared and sent instantly. The other person finds the e-mail when he checks his mailbox and may replay to the message in the same way. The message sent is private and no other person can read it. Each user of e-mail service has a user ID or password serving as e-mail address.

First thing to do is to get online using modem and communication software. The system requires user id and password. Now the user can prepare his message in the form of a document using a word processor. The e-mail address of the recipient has to be typed in before the message is sent, with e-mail each person connected to the system is allotted a mailbox and the software required for sending and receiving e-mail. The mailbox is simply a file into which the e-mail system stores electronic documents. The user can check his mailbox for messages over the network. The sender specifies his identify and that of the recipient. The sender then prepares the document or retrieves the stored document and sends it. E-mail is a document communication facility. To ensure that the recipient also understands the emotions as well, a set of special symbols is used to convey some non-verbal signals.

E-mail is the transmission of information electronically from terminal to terminal. The document is prepared in a word processor and is mailed electronically. The basic facilities in e- mail include message creation, message transfer and post delivery service. The e-mail service may be traditional mainframe based or minicomputer based or LAN based system with PCS to access from.

How E-Mail Works?

The first thing to be done is to type the message and the e-mail address of the recipient. Once the 'send' button is clicked, this e-mail is sent through the telephone line after it's conversion into analog signal by the modem. The e-mail message arrives at our service provider's server. If the server recognizes the e-mail address as valid, the mail will be sent either through the network of the service provider or through internet gateway to the service provider of the recipient. To send e-mail, we need a connection to the internet and access to a mail server that forwards the mail. The standard protocol used for sending internet e-mail is called SMTP, short for Simple Mail Transfer Protocol. It works in conjunction with POP servers. POP stands for Post Office Protocol.

When we send an e-mail message, our computer routes it to an SMTP server. The server looks at the e-mail address (similar to the address on an envelope), then forwards it to the recipient's mail server. Once the message arrives at the destination mail server, it's stored until the addressee retrieves it. We can send e-mail anywhere in the world to anyone who has an e-mail address. E-mail route With the advent of MIME, which stands for multipurpose Internet Mail Extension, and other types of encoding schemes, we can not only send messages electronically, but we can also send formatted documents, photos, sound files, and video files.

Infrastructure Requirement for E-Mail

- Personal Computer
- Telephone Connection
- Modem
- Mailing software viz., Outlook Express or Netscape communicator or Internet Explorer etc.

Advantages of E-Mail

- Messages can be prepared and sent any time convenient for the sender.

- Message can be received at the convenience of the recipient.
- The transmission takes place instantly and the message gets stored in the mailbox of the recipient.
- The system can confirm delivery of message.
- Copies of message can be sent to multiple recipients.
- It reduces paper work.

Disadvantages

- Recipients must be having e-mail connectivity. They must have computer terminals, modem and telephone.
- They must be subscribing to the same e-mail service provider.
- Poor telecommunication affects the quality of message transmitted.
- Despite all the disadvantages e-mail is a cheap form of information transmission.

INDONET, NICNET, DARTMAIL and ICNET provide this service in India. A user can be a subscriber to such e-mail service providing agencies and use their facility. 18.3.3 E-Mail Addressing Pattern Internet e-mail addresses typically have two main parts: svallikkad@gmail.com First there is the user name (svallikkad) which refers to the recipient's mailbox. Then there's an axon sign (@). Next comes the host name (gmail), also called the domain name. This refers to the mail server, the computer where the recipient has an electronic mailbox. It's usually the name of a company or organization. The end of the domain name consists of a dot (".") followed by two or three letters (such as .com and .gov) that indicate the top-level domain. This part of the domain name indicates the type of organization or the country where the host server is located.

E-Mail Messages

E-mail messages are similar to letters, with two main parts. The header contains the name and address of the recipient, the name and address of anyone who is being copied, and the subject of the message. Some e-mail programmes also display your name and address and the date of the message. The body contains the message itself. Just like when sending letters, we need the correct address. If we use the wrong address or mistype it, our messages will bounce back with messages like—Return to Sender, Address Unknown routine. When we receive an e-mail, the header tells us where it came from, how it was sent, and when. It's like an electronic postmark. Unlike a letter, which is sealed in an envelope, e-mail is not as private. It's more like a post card. Messages can be intercepted and read by people who really shouldn't be looking at it. We should therefore avoid including any confidential information unless we have a way to encrypt it.

Usage of Mails

- Incoming mails can be checked on a daily basis at least 3 times a day.
- We can use the e-mail facility judiciously and extensively for communicating with
- Circle Office/Head Office/Service Branch/Customers.

- Communicate e-mail id to all domestic and overseas customers and use the facility for passing on information regarding new schemes launched by Bank and other important information to them.
- Encourage customers to contact branch through e-mail for information regarding their urgent banking requirements.
- Use the facility as a marketing tool to attract new customers, exchange greetings with existing customers and also inform them about recent happenings in the locality.

16

Information Systems

Information is data that has been processed and is meaningful to the user. It is a resource, produced by information systems and is important to the operation and management of organizations. It should be noted that information is neither a natural-resource, such as oil and coal nor a resource that is acquired from the external environment or the organization such as raw material or personnel. If it is designed suitably and properly managed, it can be the most effective resource of the organization.

Factors Influencing the Value of Information in Organizations

The following factors are to be considered while processing the information.

- Completeness.
- Accuracy.
- Timeliness—up to date.
- Consistency.
- Validity—unbiased, representative, verifiable.
- Suitability—meaningful and relevant, formatted to suit the user's needs.
- Distinctiveness.
- Relevance.
- Usability.
- Accessibility.

The Information Processing Cycle

The information processing cycle includes the following steps:

- Acquisition
- Input
- Validation
- Processing (manipulation)
- Storage
- Retrieval
- Output
- Communication
- Disposal/Archiving.

Let us see these steps one by one here under.

(a) ***Acquisition:*** It is the collection of raw data from the outside world so it can be put into an information system.

(b) ***Input:*** It is putting the acquired data into the information system.

(c) ***Validation:*** It is checking the quality of the data before it is processed. Processing invalid data gives waste information.

(d) ***Processing (manipulation):*** This is a key point. At this stage data is converted into information.

(e) ***Storage:*** Unless we want to input the data every time we process it, it is useful to store the data. We also may want to store information that we have produced so we need not have to keep repeating work.

(f) ***Retrieval:*** This involves the reverse process of storage. The stored data or processed information is taken back for further use. It is called as retrieval.

(g) ***Output:*** All the previous steps are used to produce the results. The important output devices include the following:
- CRT (Cathode Ray Tube) monitors and LCD displays
- Printers
- Sound cards/speakers

(h) ***Communication:*** This is nothing but sending data or information to another place. This usually involves LANs (Local Area Networks), WANS (Wide Area Networks—LANs joined together), and the internet.

(i) ***Disposal:*** This involves deleting data or archiving data. Issues involve the security, of so-called "deleted" data. When data is no longer needed it can be deleted. Very sensitive data-may needs more: when PCs delete data, they do not actually remove it from the disk. They just mark that part of the disk as "available for saving on." Thus data can stay on the disk and be easily restored by snoops. To really delete sensitive data it should be wiped out. That is overwritten with trash until it is no longer readable. Archiving means taking the data off the main storage and storing it offline usually on floppy or CDs. If in the future the data we needed again, it is still available and it is not taking up important hard disk space. Businesses tend to archive rather than delete data—just in case.

Need for Computer Based Information System

The computer based information system is required because of the following reasons:

Information is a valuable source to gain competitive advantage.

- Information helps line managers in taking effective control of operations.
- Information makes the planning more realistic.
- Information enhances customer relationship, maintenance of equipment, etc.
- Information helps in decision making process.
- Information helps in implementing business re-engineering.
- Improve the efficiency.
- Computer operations need information to process the data correctly and produce the desirable output.

- Individuals need information for managing and operating the organization.
- Organization needs information to improve the performance and growth.
- Banker needs information to provide loans or granting credit.
- Investors need information to know the financial status and the future prospects of the business units.
- Government agencies need information systems for calculating taxation and taking regulatory measures.

In this context we shall discuss about the following information systems:

- Management Information System
- Office Automation Systems
- Transaction Processing Systems
- Decision Support Systems
- Expert Systems

Management Information System

Management information system is a general term for the computer systems in an enterprise that provide information about its business operations. It's also used to refer to the people who manage these systems. Typically, in a large organization MIS refers to an entirely coordinated system of computer expertise and management, including mainframe system and the entire network of computer resources. In the beginning, business computers were used for the practical business of computing the payroll and keeping track of accounts payable and receivable. As application were developed that provided managers' with information about sales, inventories, and other data that would help in managing the enterprise, the term "MIS" arose to described these kinds of applications.

Today, the term is used broadly in a number of contexts and includes; decision support system, resource and people management applications, project management, and database retrieval applications. Thus, MIS can be defined as "MIS is a set of inter related elements which work together to render classified and interpreted data that are usable and used by managers in the process of planning, organizing staffing, directing and controlling the major activities of business."

Characteristics of MIS

MIS generally has the following characteristics.

(a) Management Oriented

Beyond any doubt is the fact that MIS is a management oriented system. This could be understood from the terminology itself. The information processing carried out by MIS if always attempting at helping the management.

(b) Management Directed

Similarly, all the activities of MIS are initiated by the management. It is the management's need that the MIS strives to satisfy. Hence, MIS is management directed.

(c) User-Machine System

The concept of user-machine system implies that some tasks of MIS are done by the users while others are best done by machines. There is co-existence of both men and machines in MIS.

(d) Integrated System

MIS hopes to provide the basis of integration of information processing. This leads to common data flows. Even tough applications in a system are implemented one at a time; their design is guided by an overall plan. In essence information system is designed as a federation of small systems.

(e) Involves Large Planning

The concept of MIS goes only with planning. There is a huge amount planning coupled with the installation and maintenance of MIS.

(f) Sub Systems

Naturally, a vast system like the MIS will be having plenty of sub systems which are mutually related with defined with definite relationships and properly ordered. It is based on subsystem concept.

(g) Use of Models

MIS uses scientific and mathematical models for planning, organizing, directing and controlling for its analysis.

(h) Data Base

One of the pre-requisites for installing, implementing and successful operating of MIS is data. Hence, there has to be a way to maintain data in data bases and there has to be a central database.

(i) Information as a Resource

MIS transforms data into information and the management is behind MIS. MIS provides procedure for measuring and matching cost of obtaining and using information.

(j) Flexibility in Use

MIS is so designed that it is flexible and adaptable to user requirements.

(k) Others

MIS is predictive and related to organizational levels.

DATABASE

A Computer Database is a structured collection of records or data that is stored in a computer system. The structure is achieved by organizing the data according to a database model. The model in most common use today is the relational model. Other models such as the hierarchical model and the network model use a more explicit representation of relationships (see below for explanation of the various database models).

A computer database relies upon software to organize the storage of data. This software is known as a Database Management System (DBMS). Database management systems are categorized according to the database model that they support. The model tends to determine the query languages that are available to access the database. A great deal of the internal engineering of a DBMS, however, is independent of the data model, and is concerned with managing factors such as performance, concurrency, integrity, and recovery from hardware failures. In these areas there are large differences between products.

History

The earliest known use of the term data base was in November 1963, when the System Development Corporation sponsored a symposium under the title Development and Management of a Computer-centered Data Base. Database as a single word became common in Europe in the early 1970s and by the end of the decade it was being used in major American newspapers. (The abbreviation DB, however, survives).

The first database management systems were developed in the 1960s. A pioneer in the field was Charles Bachman. Bachman's early papers show that his aim was to make more effective use of the new direct access storage devices becoming available: until then, data processing had been based on punched cards and magnetic tape, so that serial processing was the dominant activity. Two key data models arose at this time: CODASYL developed the network model based on Bachman's ideas, and (apparently independently) the hierarchical model was used in a system developed by North American Rockwell later adopted by IBM as the cornerstone of their IMS product. While IMS along with the CODASYL IDMS were the big, high visibility databases developed in the 1960s, several others were also born in that decade, some of which have a significant installed base today. Two worthy of mention are the PICK and MUMPS databases, with the former developed originally as an operating system with an embedded database and the latter as a programming language and database for the development of healthcare systems.

The relational model was proposed by E.F. Codd in 1970. He criticized existing models for confusing the abstract description of information structure with descriptions of physical access mechanisms. For a long while, however, the relational model remained of academic interest only. While CODASYL products (IDMS) and network model products (IMS) were conceived as practical engineering solutions taking account of the technology as it existed at the time, the relational model took a much more theoretical perspective, arguing (correctly) that hardware and software technology would catch up in time. Among the first implementations were Michael Stonebreaker's Ingress at Berkeley, and the System R project at IBM. Both of these were research prototypes, announced during 1976. The first commercial products, Oracle and DB2, did not appear until around 1980. The first successful database product for microcomputers was dBASE for the CP/M and PC-DOS/MS-DOS operating systems.

During the 1980s, research activity focused on distributed database systems and database machines. Another important theoretical idea was the Functional Data Model, but apart from some specialized applications in genetics, molecular biology, and fraud investigation, the world took little notice.

In the 1990s, attention shifted to object-oriented databases. These had some success in fields where it was necessary to handle more complex data than relational systems could easily cope with, such as spatial databases, engineering data (including software repositories), and multimedia data. Some of these ideas were adopted by the relational vendors, who integrated new features into their products as a result. The 1990s also saw the spread of Open Source databases, such as PostgreSQL and MySQL.

In the 2000s, the fashionable area for innovation is the XML database. As with object databases, this has spawned a new collection of start-up companies, but at the same time the key ideas are being integrated into the established relational products. XML databases aim to remove the traditional divide between documents and data, allowing all of an organization's information resources to be held in one place, whether they are highly structured or not.

Database Models

Various techniques are used to model data structure. Most database systems are built around one particular data model, although it is increasingly common for products to offer support for more than one model. For any one logical model various physical implementations may be possible, and most products will offer the user some level of control in tuning the physical implementation, since the choices that are made have a significant effect on performance. Here are three examples:

Hierarchical Model

In a hierarchical model, data is organized into an inverted tree-like structure, implying a multiple downward link in each node to describe the nesting, and a sort field to keep the records in a particular order in each same-level list. This structure arranges the various data elements in a hierarchy and helps to establish logical relationships among data elements of multiple files. Each unit in the model is a record which is also known as a node. In such a model, each record on one level can be related to multiple records on the next lower level. A record that has subsidiary records is called a parent and the subsidiary records are called children. Data elements in this model are well suited for one-to-many relationships with other data elements in the database.

This model is advantageous when the data elements are inherently hierarchical. The disadvantage is that in order to prepare the database it becomes necessary to identify the requisite groups of files that are to be logically integrated. Hence, a hierarchical data model may not always be flexible enough to accommodate the dynamic needs of an organization.

Network Model

In the network model, records can participate in any number of named relationships. Each relationship associates a record of one type (called the owner) with multiple records of another type (called the member). These relationships (somewhat confusingly) are called sets. For example a student might be a member of one set whose owner is the course they are studying, and a member of another set whose owner is the college they belong to. At the same time the student might be the owner of a set of e-mail addresses, and owner of another set containing phone numbers.

The main difference between the network model and hierarchical model is that in a network model, a child can have a number of parents whereas in a hierarchical model, a child can have only one parent. The hierarchical model is therefore a subset of the network model.

Programmatic access to network databases is traditionally by means of a navigational data manipulation language, in which programmers navigate from a current record to other related records using verbs such as find owner, find next, and find prior. The most common example of such an interface is the COBOL-based Data Manipulation Language defined by CODASYL.

Network databases are traditionally implemented by using chains of pointers between related records. These pointers can be node numbers or disk addresses.

The network model became popular because it provided considerable flexibility in modelling complex data relationships, and also offered high performance by virtue of the fact that the access verbs used by programmers mapped directly to pointer-following in the implementation.

However, the model had several disadvantages. Navigational programming proved error-prone as data models became more complex, and small changes to the data structure could require changes to many programmes. Also, because of the use of physical pointers, operations such as database loading and restructuring could be very time-consuming.

The network model tends to store records with links to other records. Each record in the database can have multiple parents, i.e., the relationships among data elements can have a many to many relationship. Associations are tracked via "pointers." These pointers can be node numbers or disk addresses. Most network databases tend to also include some form of hierarchical model. Databases can be translated from hierarchical model to network and vice versa. The main difference between the network model and hierarchical model is that in a network model, a child can have a number of parents whereas in a hierarchical model, a child can have only one parent.

The network model provides greater advantage than the hierarchical model in that promotes greater flexibility and data accessibility, since records at a lower level can be accessed without accessing the records above them. This model is more efficient than hierarchical model, easier to understand and can be applied to many real world problems that require routine transactions. The disadvantages are that: It is a complex process to design and develop a network database; it has to be refined frequently; it requires that the relationships among all the records be defined before development starts, and changes often demand major programming efforts; Operation and maintenance of the network model is expensive and time consuming.

Examples of database engines that have network model capabilities are RDM Embedded and RDM Server.

Relational Model

The basic data structure of the relational model is a table where information about a particular entity (say, employees) is represented in columns and rows. The columns enumerate the various attributes of an entity (e.g. employee name, address, phone number). Rows (also called records) represent instances of an entity (e.g. specific employees).

The "relation" in "relational database" comes from the mathematical notion of relations from the field of set theory. A relation is a set of tuples, so rows are sometimes called tuples. All tables in a relational database adhere to three basic rules.

- The ordering of columns is immaterial
- Identical rows are not allowed in a table
- Each row has a single (separate) value for each of its columns (each tuple has an atomic value).

If the same value occurs in two different records (from the same table or different tables) it can imply a relationship between those records. Relationships between records are often categorized by their cardinality (1:1, (0), 1: M, M: M).

Tables can have a designated column or set of columns that act as a "key" to select rows from that table with the same or similar key values. A "primary key" is a key that has a unique value for each row in the table. Keys are commonly used to join or combine data from two or more tables. For example, an employee table may contain a column named address which contains a value that matches the key of an address table. Keys are also critical in the creation of indexes, which facilitate fast retrieval of data from large tables. It is not necessary to define all the keys in advance; a column can be used as a key even if it was not originally intended to be one.

Relational Operations

Users (or programmes) request data from a relational database by sending it a query that is written in a special language, usually a dialect of SQL. Although SQL was originally intended for end-users, it is much more common for SQL queries to be embedded into software that provides an easier user interface. Many web applications, such as Wikipedia, perform SQL queries when generating pages.

In response to a query, the database returns a result set, which is the list of rows constituting the answer. The simplest query is just to return all the rows from a table, but more often, the rows are filtered in some way to return just the answer wanted. Often, data from multiple tables are combined into one, by doing a join. There are a number of relational operations in addition to join.

Normal Forms

Relations are classified based upon the types of anomalies to which they're vulnerable. A database that's in the first normal form is vulnerable to all types of anomalies, while a database that's in the Boyce-Codd Normal Form has no modification anomalies. Normal forms are hierarchical in nature. That is, the lowest level is the first normal form, and the database cannot meet the requirements for higher level normal forms without first having met all the requirements of the lesser normal form.

Database Management Systems

An RDBMS implements the features of the relational model outlined above. In this context, Date's Information Principle states: The entire information content of the database is represented in one and only one way. Namely as explicit values in column positions (attributes) and rows in relations (tuples). Therefore, there are no explicit pointers between related tables.

Applications of Databases

Databases are used in many applications, spanning virtually the entire range of computer software. Databases are the preferred method of storage for large multi-user applications, where coordination between many users is needed. Even individual users find them convenient, and many electronic mail programmes and personal organizers are based on standard database technology. Software database drivers are available for most database platforms so that application software can use a common Application Programming Interface to retrieve the information stored in a database. Two commonly used database APIs are JDBC and ODBC.

HTML

HTML, an initialism of Hyper Text Markup Language, is the predominant markup language for Web pages. It provides a means to describe the structure of text-based information in a document—by denoting certain text as links, headings, paragraphs, lists, and so on—and to supplement that text with interactive forms, embedded images, and other objects. HTML is written in the form of tags, surrounded by angle brackets. HTML can also describe, to some degree, the appearance and semantics of a document, and can include embedded scripting language code (such as JavaScript) which can affect the behaviour of Web browsers and other HTML processors.

Origins

In 1980, physicist Tim Berners-Lee, who was an independent contractor at CERN, proposed and prototyped ENQUIRE, a system for CERN researchers to use and share documents. In 1989, Berners-Lee and CERN data systems Engineer Robert Cailliau each submitted separate proposals for an Internet-based hypertext system providing similar functionality. The following year, they collaborated on a joint proposal, the Worldwide Web (W3) project, which was accepted by CERN.

First Specifications

The first publicly available description of HTML was a document called HTML Tags, first mentioned on the Internet by Berners-Lee in late 1991. It describes 22 elements comprising the initial, relatively simple design of HTML. Thirteen of these elements still exist in HTML 4.

Berners-Lee considered HTML to be, at the time, an application of SGML, but it was not formally defined as such until the mid-1993 publication, by the IETF, of the first proposal for an HTML specification: Berners-Lee and Dan Connolly's "Hypertext Markup Language (HTML)" Internet-Draft, which included an SGML Document Type Definition to define the grammar. The draft expired after six months, but was notable for its acknowledgement of the NCSA Mosaic browser's custom tag for embedding in-line images, reflecting the IETF's philosophy of basing standards on successful prototypes. Similarly, Dave Raggett's competing Internet-Draft, "HTML+ (Hypertext Markup Format)," from late 1993, suggested standardizing already-implemented features like tables and fill-out forms.

After the HTML and HTML+ drafts expired in early 1994, the IETF created an HTML Working Group, which in 1995 completed "HTML 2.0," the first HTML specification intended to be treated as a standard against which future implementations should be based. Published as Request for Comments 1996, HTML 2.0 included ideas from the HTML and HTML+ drafts. There was no "HTML 1.0"; the 2.0 designation was intended to distinguish the new edition from previous drafts.

Further development under the auspices of the IETF was stalled by competing interests. Since 1996, the HTML specifications have been maintained, with input from commercial software vendors, by the World Wide Web Consortium (W3C). However, in 2000, HTML also became an international standard (ISO/IEC 15445:2000). The last HTML specification published by the W3C is the HTML 4.01 Recommendation, published in late 1999. Its issues and errors were last acknowledged by errata published in 2001.

HTML Markup

HTML markup consists of several key components, including elements (and their attributes), character-based data types, and character references and entity references. Another important component is the document type declaration.

The Hello world programme, a common computer programme employed for comparing programming languages, scripting languages, and markup languages is made of 10 lines of code in HTML, albeit line breaks are optional:

```
<html>
<head>
<title>Hello HTML</ title>
</head>
<body>
<span>Hello World!</span>
</body>
</html>
```

Elements

Elements are the basic structure for HTML markup. Elements have two basic properties: attributes and content. Each attribute and each element's content has certain restrictions that must be followed for an HTML document to be considered valid. An element usually has a start tag (e.g. <element-name>) and an end tag (e.g. </element-name>). The element's attributes are contained in the start tag and content is located between the tags (e.g. <element-name attribute="value">Content</element-name>). Some elements, such as <br>, do not have any content and must not have a closing tag. Listed below are several types of markup elements used in HTML.

Structural markup describes the purpose of text. For example, <h2>Golf</h2> establishes "Golf" as a second-level heading, which would be rendered in a browser in a manner similar to the "HTML markup" title at the start of this section. Structural markup does not denote any specific rendering, but most Web browsers have standardized on how elements should be formatted. Text may be further styled with Cascading Style Sheets (CSS).

Presentational markup describes the appearance of the text, regardless of its function. For example <b>boldface</b> indicates that visual output devices should render "boldface" in bold text, but gives no indication what devices which are unable to do this (such as aural devices that read the text aloud) should do. In the case of both <b>bold</b> and <i>italic</i>, there are elements which usually have an equivalent visual rendering but are more semantic in nature, namely <strong>strong emphasis</strong> and <em>emphasis</em> respectively. It is easier to see how an aural user agent should interpret the latter two elements. However, they are not equivalent to their presentational counterparts: it would be undesirable for a screen-reader to emphasize the name of a book, for instance, but on a screen such a name would be italicized. Most presentational markup elements have become deprecated under the HTML 4.0 specification, in favour of CSS based style design.

Hypertext markup links parts of the document to other documents. HTML up through version XHTML 1.1 requires the use of an anchor element to create a hyperlink in the flow of text: <a>Wikipedia</a>. However, the href attribute must also be set to a valid URL so for example the HTML code, <a href="http://en.wikipedia.org/">Wikipedia</
a>, will render the word "Wikipedia" as a hyperlink. To link on an image, the anchor tag uses the following syntax: <a href="url"><img src="image.gif" /></a>

Attributes

Most of the attributes of an element are name-value pairs, separated by "=", and written within the start tag of an element, after the element's name. The value may be enclosed in single or double quotes, although values consisting of certain characters can be left unquoted in HTML (but not XHTML). Leaving attribute values unquoted is considered unsafe. In contrast with name-value pair attributes, there are some attributes that affect the element simply by their presence in the start tag of the element (like map attribute for the img element).

Most elements can take any of several common attributes:

- The id attribute provides a document-wide unique identifier for an element. This can be used by style sheets to provide presentational properties, by browsers to focus attention on the specific element, or by scripts to alter the contents or presentation of an element.
- The class attribute provides a way of classifying similar elements for presentation purposes. For example, an HTML document might use the designation class "notation" to indicate that all elements with this class value is subordinate to the main text of the document. Such elements might be gathered together and presented as footnotes on a page instead of appearing in the place where they occur in the HTML source.
- An author may use the style non-attributal codes presentational properties to a particular element. It is considered better practice to use an element's son-id page and select the element with a style sheet, though sometimes this can be too cumbersome for a simple ad hoc application of styled properties.

- The title attribute is used to attach sub textual explanation to an element. In most browsers this attribute is displayed as what is often referred to as a tool tip.

Character and Entity References

As of version 4.0, HTML defines a set of 252 character entity references and a set of 1,114,050 numeric character references, both of which allow individual characters to be written via simple markup, rather than literally. A literal character and its markup counterpart are considered equivalent and are rendered identically.

17

Reprography and Microforms in Communication

REPROGRAPHY

Photocopying, microfilming, photographing and digital scanning are including in the reprographic process. There are a number of skilled members of staff who are photographers and computer experts, working to produce these kinds of copies of material. Production and copying of information are very much important in the field of education.

Definitions of Reprography

- Reprography is a general term for the reproduction of documents or images especially those that are virtually indistinguishable from the original. Reprography can be by mechanical, electronic, or photographic means such as photocopying or xerography, scanning, digital printing, and photography.
- Also Known As: reprographics, photocopying, xerography, photographic reproduction.
- The process of copying and duplicating.
- Reprography is the reproduction of graphics through mechanical or electrical means, such as photography or xerography.
- The reproduction, reprinting and copying of graphics, especially using electromechanical or photographic methods.
- Reprography is the reproduction of graphics through mechanical or electrical means, such as photography or xerography. Reprography is commonly used in catalogus and archives, as well as in the architectural, engineering, and construction industries.

Large-format reproductions are produced with a variety of technologies dependent, in part, on the application of the final product and quantity needed. Examples of typical reproduction methods include: diazo (blue line), electrostatic (xerographic), photographic, laser, and ink jet.

Reproductions can be made from the same size or smaller/larger hard copy originals. Prints can also be computer generated from CADD (Computer Aided Design and Drafting) files or from a growing variety of desktop publishing and design software packages.

In addition to addressing the large-format reproduction needs of their customers, reprographers frequently sell reprographic equipment and consumable supplies. Other business services such as mounting and lamination, quick copying, microfilming, scanning and facility management are also provided.

Typical items produced by reprographers include architectural/engineering blueprints and renderings, indoor and outdoor signage, maps, billboards, backlit displays, trade show graphics, legal and medical exhibits, etc.

Why are All this Copying Needed?

- Reproductions for readers and users.
- Reproductions for the Library's own use, including exhibitions and promoting the Library.
- Reproductions to help preserve the Library's collection.
- Reproductions as part of projects involving other institutions.

Duplicating machines were the predecessors of modern document-reproduction technology. They have now been replaced by Digital Duplicators, scanners, laser printers and photocopiers, but for many years they were the primary means of reproducing documents for mass distribution.

Like the typewriter, these machines were children of the second phase of the industrial revolution which started near the end of the 19th century. The second phase of the industrial revolution is also called the Second Industrial Revolution. This second phase brought to mass markets things like the small electric motors and the products of industrial chemistry without which the duplicating machines would not have been economical. By bringing greatly increased quantities of paperwork to life the duplicating machine and the typewriter gradually changed the forms of the office desk and transformed the nature of office work.

They were much used in schools, where cheap copying was in demand for the production of newsletters and worksheets, and self-publishers used these machines to produce fanzines.

Mechanical Duplicators

The mimeo machine (mimeograph) used (heavy) waxed-paper "stencils" that the typewriter cut through. The stencil was wrapped around the drum of the (manual or electrical) machine, which forced ink out through the cut marks on the stencil. The paper had a surface texture (like bond paper), and the ink was black and odorless. You could use special knives to cut stencils by hand, but handwriting was impractical, because any loop would cut a hole and thus print a black blob. If you put the stencil on the drum wrong-side-out, your copies came out mirror-images.

The ditto machine (spirit duplicator) used two-ply "spirit masters" or "ditto masters." The first sheet could be typed, drawn, or written upon. The second sheet was coated with a layer of coloured wax. The pressure of writing or typing on the top sheet transferred coloured wax to its back side, producing a mirror image of the desired marks. (This acted like a reverse of carbon paper.) The two sheets were then separated, and the first sheet was fastened onto the drum of the (manual or electrical) machine, with the waxed side out.

The usual wax colour was aniline purple, a cheap, durable pigment that provided good contrast, but other colours were available. Unlike mimeo, ditto had the useful ability to print multiple colours in a single pass, which made it popular with cartoonists. One well-made ditto master could at most print about 500 copies—far less than a mimeo stencil could manage.

The hectograph was an earlier technology in which a dye-impregnated master copy, not unlike a ditto master, was laid on top of a cake pan full of firm unflavoured gelatin. After the dye soaked into the gelatin, sheets of paper could be laid on top of the gelatin to transfer the image. This was good for fifty copies at most. Hectography was slowing, clunky, and weird, but it could inspire great intrepidity in its users.

Ditto machines and mimeograph machines were always competing technologies. Mimeography was in general a more forgiving technology. Ditto machines required much finer operating tolerances and careful adjustments to operate correctly. Overall print quality was frequently poor, though a capable operator could overcome this with careful adjustment of feed rate, pressure, and solvent volume.

During their heyday, tabletop duplicators of both sorts were the inexpensive and convenient alternative to conventional typesetting and offset or letterpress printing. They were well suited for the short runs used for school worksheets, church newsletters, and apazines. Even the least technically-minded teachers, professors, and clergy could make use of them. They owed most of their popularity to this relative ease of use—and, in some cases, to their lack of a requirement for an external power source.

Mimeograph machines predated the spirit duplicator, had a lower cost per impression, superior print quality, finer resolution, and if properly adjusted could be used for multi-pass printing. Also, mimeographed pages didn't bleach white if exposed to sunlight, the way that dittoed pages did. As with ditto masters, mimeo stencils could be saved and reused for later print jobs. Mimeograph had a largely unwarranted reputation for being messier than spirit duplication. In truth, they weren't significantly messier; and if spilled mimeo ink was hard to get out of the operator's clothing, ditto's aniline purple dye was well-nigh impossible.

The perception may have been a side effect of their engineering. Mimeography, with its loose tolerances, absence of noxious solvents, and consequent open architecture (which put its inky pads and rollers on display), may simply have looked messier, and hence seemed more daunting. Spirit duplicators, whose demanding tolerances and constant fog of solvent fumes necessitated precisely machined metal parts and closed architecture, tended to have a deceptively clean and simple look. It should be noted that there are still diehard mimeography enthusiasts in the United States and Canada, and that mimeo technology is still in everyday use in the Third World.

Digital Duplicators

In 1986 the RISO Kagaku Corporation introduced the Digital duplicator. It uses the duplicator technology but improves on it. It improves upon the mimeo machine in that the operator does not have to create the stencil. The stencil, called a master is made by use of a scanner and thermal print head. Also the master is automatically removed as a new one is created and placed in a disposal box. This way the operator should not have to touch the used master material that is coated in ink.

There are also cost advantages over a copier the higher the volume. The main cost is in the master material. This ranges between .40–.80 cents per master depending on the manufacturer. When spread over 20 or more copies the cost per copy (2 to 4 cents) is close to photocopiers. But for every copy the costs decrease. At 1,000 prints the master cost per copy is only .0004–.0008 cents per copy.

How Digital Duplicators Work

Like the mimeo machine Digital duplicators have a stencil called a master, ink, and drum. But the process is all automated.

- The original is placed on a flat bed scanner or feed through a sheet feed scanner depending on the model.
- When the start button is pressed the image is scanned into memory by reflecting light off the original and into a CCD.
- The image is burned onto the master material that is coated on one side, in a series of small holes by the thermal print head.
- As the new master is burning it is stored while the old master is removed.
- There is a clamp plate on the drum that opens by motor. The drum turns and the old master material is feed into the disposal rollers and into the disposal box.
- The new master is fed into the clamp which closes, the drum is turned pulling the master onto the drum.
- The outside of the drum is covered in screens and the inside is coated in ink. The screens make sure the ink is regulated.
- The paper is fed to the drum and the ink only comes through the master material where there are holes.
- A pressure roller presses the paper to the drum and transfers the ink to the paper to form the image.
- The paper then exits the machine into an exit tray. The ink is still wet.

Duplicating Processes

This is a partial list of duplicating processes used in business and government from the Industrial Revolution forward. Some are mechanical and some are chemical. There is naturally some overlap with printing processes and photographic processes, but the challenge of precisely duplicating business letters, forms, contracts, and other paperwork prompted some unique solutions as well. There were many short-lived inventions along the way.

Within each type, the methods are arranged in very rough chronological order.

- **Methods of copying handwritten letters**
  - Manifold stylographic writer, using early "carbonic paper"
  - Letter copying book process
- **Mechanical processes**
  - Pantograph, manually operated, and can also enlarge or reduce the document

- **Printing/Applied ink methods**
  - Printing press
  - Gelatin methods (also indirect method)
- Hectograph
- Collography, autocopyist
- Chromograph, Copygraph, Polygraph
  - Flexography
  - Spirit duplicator (also Ditto machine, Banda machine)
- **Lithographic processes**
  - Transfer lithography
  - Anastatic lithography
  - Autographic process
  - Offset lithography
  - Photolithography
- **Stencil-based copying methods**
  - Papyrography
  - Electric pen, invented by Thomas Edison
  - Trypograph (also file plate process)
  - Cyclostyle, Neostyle
- **Stencil-based machines**
  - Mimeograph (also Roneo, Gestetner)
  - Digital Duplicators (also called CopyPrinters, e.g., Riso and Gestetner)
- **Typewriter-based copying methods**
  - Carbon paper
  - Blueprint typewriter ribbon
  - Carbonless copy paper
- **Photographic processes**
  - Reflex copying process (also reflectography, reflexion copying)
- Breyertype, Playertype, Manul Process, Typon Process, Dexigraph, Linagraph
  - Daguerreotype
  - Salt print
  - Calotype (the first photo process to use a negative, from which multiple prints could be made)
  - Cyanotype
  - Photostat machine
  - Rectigraph
  - Airgraph (also V-mail)
  - Kodagraph autopositive paper
  - Kodagraph repro-negative paper
  - Diffusion transfer
- Verifax, Copyproof
- Photomechanical transfer (also PMT')
  - Duostat, duoprint

- Retroflex (printing process)
- Dual spectrum process
- Light Jet
- Ozalid

- **Chemical processes**
  - Aniline process
  - Cyanotype (used for blueprints)
  - Diazotype (also whiteprint, ammonia print, or gas print)
- **Heat-sensitivity methods**
  - Thermofax (also thermography)
  - Eichner dry copy process
  - Adherography
- **Electrostatic methods**
  - Electro fax
  - Xerography, Photocopying
- **Ultraviolet-sensitivity methods**
  - APT process, for transferring drawings to animation cells
- **Image scanning and digital printing**

A photocopier (or copier) is a machine that makes paper copies of documents and other visual images quickly and cheaply. Most current photocopiers use a technology called xerography, a dry process using heat. (Copiers can also use other output technologies such as ink jet, but xerography is standard for office copying).

Xerographic office photocopying was introduced by Xerox in the 1960s, and over the following 20 years it gradually replaced copies made by Verifax, Photostat, carbon paper, mimeograph machines, and other duplicating machines. The prevalence of its use is one of the factors that prevented the development of the paperless office heralded early in the digital revolution.

Photocopying is widely used in business, education, and government. There have been many predictions that photocopiers will eventually become obsolete as information workers continue to increase their digital document creation and distribution, and rely less on distributing actual pieces of paper. However, photocopiers are undeniably more convenient than computers for the very common task of creating a copy of a piece of paper.

MICROFORMS

Microform is a generic term for any medium, transparent or opaque, bearing micro images. A micro image is a unit (e.g., a page) of textual, graphic, or computer-generated material that is contained on aperture cards, microfiche, microfilm, micro opaque, or other micro formats and that is too small to be read without magnification. Microforms may be reproductions of existing textual or graphic materials or they may be original publications.

Microforms are any form, either films or paper, containing micro reproductions of documents for transmission, storage, reading and printing. Microform images are commonly reduced about 25 times from the original document size. For special purposes, greater optical reductions may be used.

All microform images may be provided as positives or negatives, more often the second. Three formats are common: microfilm (reels), aperture cards and microfiche (flat sheets). Micro cards were similar to microfiche, but printed on paper cardboard rather than photographic films.

Microforms are images, which have been reduced in scale from that which is readable by the unaided eye, and transferred to either transparent or opaque materials.

Microfilm

Microfilm is produced in long strips, like motion picture film, and comes in 16 and 35-millimeter sizes. The microfilm strips are loaded on to reels, similar to motion picture film reels, although much smaller. The reels are placed in boxes, which are labeled with call numbers and (often) some bibliographic information. These boxes are placed in trays, each of which can hold up to ten microfilm reels, and shelved in call number order on the ranges of shelves that stand south of the microform readers in the Microforms Reading Room on the east side of the third floor of the Joseph Regenstein Library.

Microfiche

Microfiche are transparencies that come in either 3" × 5" or 4" × 6" sheets. The microfiche in the Library's collection are also marked with call numbers and stored in call number order in cabinets interspersed among the microfilm shelves.

Micro Cards and Microprint

Opaque microforms include micro cards, which are 3" × 5" and microprint, which are 6" × 9". Opaque (micro cards and microprint) can have images on both sides while microfilm and microfiche, as transparencies, can have images on only one side. The micro cards are also arranged in call number order, in a cabinet in Room 308. The microprint collection is shelved in boxes, arranged in call number order, along the west wall of the Microforms Reading Room, to the north of the video collection.

Ultra Fiche,

The standard reduction ratio (the factor by which the microform image must be multiplied to equal the size of the original image) for microforms ranges from 12 to 25. The microform readers, reader-printers, and scanner in the Microforms Reading Room possess lenses that easily accommodate microforms in the 12 to 25 magnification ratio. Our machines can also accommodate microforms with ratios up to 50 or 60, but those much smaller images may make it difficult to obtain clear paper copies. The Joseph Regenstein Library microforms collection contains several large microfiche collections with magnification ratios larger than 60. These, which are called ultra fiche, must be viewed on a special microfiche reader which the library obtained specifically for the purpose of reading ultra fiche.

Equipment for Viewing, Photocopying, and Scanning Microforms

The machines for viewing, photocopying, and digitally scanning microforms are located in the north end of the Microforms Reading Room, located on the east side of the third floor of the Joseph Regenstein Library.

The following microform machines are available for viewing, photocopying, and scanning digitally:

- Seven Canon machines that can accommodate and make copies from either microfilm or microfiche.
- One Canon machine that is linked to a computer terminal for saving digital images from either microfilm or microfiche on to a flash drive.
- Two Dukane microfilm readers.
- One Northwest 2020 reader.
- Two microfiche readers for reading standard microfiche.
- One microfiche reader—just outside of JRL 309—equipped with a special lens for reading ultra fiche. Photocopies can not be made from ultra fiche.
- One reader for opaque-micro print and micro cards. Photocopies can not be made from microprint or micro cards.

History

Using the Daguerreotype process, John Benjamin Dancer was one of the first to produce micro-photographs, in 1839. He achieved a reduction ratio of 160:1. Dancer perfected his reduction procedures with Frederick Scott Archer's wet collodion process, developed in 1850-51, but he dismissed his decades-long work on micro-photographs as a personal hobby, and did not document his procedures. That microphotography could be no more than a novelty was an opinion shared by the 1858 Dictionary of Photography, which called the process "somewhat trifling and childish."

Microphotography was first suggested as a document preservation method in the early 1850s—in 1851 by James Glaisher, an astronomer, and in 1853 by John Herschel. Both men attended the 1851 Great Exhibition in London, where the exhibition on photography greatly influenced Glaisher: he called it "the most remarkable discovery of modern times," and argued in his official report for using microphotography to preserve documents.

The developments in microphotography continued through the next decades, but it was not until the turn of the century that its potential for practical usage was seized by a wider audience. In 1896, Canadian Engineer Reginald A. Fessenden suggested microforms as a compact solution to engineers' unwieldy, but frequently consulted materials. He proposed that up to 150,000,000 words could be made to fit in a square inch, and that a one foot cube could contain 1.5 million volumes.

In 1906, Paul Otlet and Robert Goldschmidt proposed the liver micro photographique as a way to alleviate the cost and space limitations imposed by the codex format. Otlet's overarching goal was to create a World Center Library of Juridical, Social and Cultural Documentation, and he saw microfiche as way to offer a stable and durable format that was inexpensive, easy to use, easy to reproduce, and extremely compact. In 1925, the team spoke of a massive library where each volume existed as master negatives and positives, and where items were printed on demand for interested patrons.

At the annual meeting of 1936, the American Library Association endorsed microforms. Before this official acceptance, microforms were used in related fields: between 1927 and 1935, the Library of Congress microfilmed more than three million pages of books and manuscripts in the British Library; in 1929 the Social Science Research Council and the American Council of Learned Societies joined to create a Joint Committee on Materials Research, which looked closely at microform's potential to serve small print runs of academic or technical materials; in 1933, Charles C. Peters developed a method to micro format dissertations; in 1934 the United States National Agriculture Library implemented the first microform print-on-demand service, which was quickly followed by a similar commercial concern, Science Service, and in 1938 University Microfilms was established and the Harvard Foreign Newspapers Microform Project was implemented.

In 1940, the format most broadly used today–microfilm–was developed. Formats it bested include the Photo scope, the Film-O-Graph, the Fiske-O-Scope, film slides. Early cut sheet microforms and microfilms (to the 1930s) were printed on a nitrate film and pose high risks to their holding institutions, as nitrate film are explosive and flammable. From the late 1930s to the 1980s, microfilms were usually printed on a cellulose acetate base, which is prone to tears, vinegar syndrome and redox blemishes. Vinegar syndrome is the result of chemical decay and produces "buckling and shrinking, embitterment, and bubbling." Redox blemishes are yellow, orange, red, or spots 15-150 micrometers in diameter created by oxidative attacks on the film, and are largely due to poor storage conditions.

Uses

Systems that mount microfilm images in punched cards have been widely used for archival storage of engineering information.

For example, when airlines demand archival engineering drawings to support purchased equipment (in case the vendor goes out of business), (as of 1999) they normally specified punch-card-mounted microfilm with an industry-standard indexing system punched into the card. This permits automated reproduction, as well as permitting mechanical card-sorting equipment to sort and select microfilm drawings.

Aperture card mounted microfilm is roughly 3 per cent of the size and space of conventional paper or vellum engineering drawings. Some military contracts around 1980 began to specify digital storage of engineering and maintenance data because the expenses were even lower than microfilm, but these programmes are now finding it difficult to purchase new readers for the old formats.

Microfilm first saw military use during the Franco-Prussian War of 1870–71. During the Siege of Paris, the only way for the provincial government in Tours to communicate with Paris was by pigeon post, and, as the pigeons could not carry paper dispatches, the Tours government turned to microfilm. Using a microphotography unit evacuated from Paris before the siege, clerks in Tours photograped paper dispatches and compressed them to microfilm, which were carried by homing pigeons into Paris and projected by magic lantern while clerks copied the dispatches onto paper.

Libraries began using microfilm in the early 1900s as a preservation strategy for their deteriorating newspaper collections. Books and newspapers that were deemed in danger of decay could be preserved on film and thus access and use could be increased. Microfilming was also a space-saving measure. In his 1945 book, "The Scholar and the Future of the Research Library," Fremont Rider calculated that research libraries were doubling in space every sixteen years. His suggested solution was microfilming, specifically with his invention, the micro card. Once items were put onto film, they could be removed from circulation and additional shelf space would be made available for rapidly expanding collections. The micro card was superseded by microfiche. By the 1980s, microfilming had become standard policy in libraries as a means of reformatting both books and newspapers.

Advantages

The medium has numerous advantages:

- It is compact, with far smaller storage costs than paper documents. Normally 98 document size pages fit on one fiche, reducing to about 0.25 per cent original material. When compared to filing paper, microforms can reduce space storage requirements by up to 95 per cent.
- It is cheaper to distribute than paper copy. Most microfiche services get a bulk discount on reproduction rights, and have lower reproduction and carriage costs than a comparable amount of printed paper.
- It is a stable archival form when properly processed. Preservation standard microfilms use wet-processed silver halide dyes in hard gelatin emulsion on a polyester base. With appropriate storage conditions, this film has a life expectancy of 500 years. Unfortunately, in tropical climates with high humidity; fungus eats the gelatin used to bind the silver halide. Thus, diazo-based systems with lower archival lives (20 years) which have polyester or epoxy surfaces are used.
- Since it is analog (an actual image of the original data), it is easy to view. Unlike digital media, the format requires no software to decode the data stored thereon—it is instantly comprehensible to persons literate in the language; the only equipment that is needed is a simple magnifying glass. This reduces the possibility of obsolescence.

Disadvantages

- The principal disadvantage of microforms is that the image is too small to read with the naked eye. Libraries must use special readers that project full-size images on a ground-glass screen.
- Reader machines used to view microfilm are often difficult to use, requiring the user to carefully wind and rewind until they have arrived at the point where the data they are looking for is stored. Also, photographic illustrations reproduce poorly in microform format, with the image usually not being as sharp as the original. The last problem with the machines is that printers are not always available, limiting the user's ability to make copies for their own purposes.
- Colour microfilm is extremely expensive, thus discouraging most libraries wishing to use microfilm from having colour material available. This results in the loss of some information, as colour materials will be preserved using regular microfilm in order to save money. When stored in the highest-density drawers, it is easy to misfile a fiche, which is thereafter unavailable. Some

libraries therefore keep the microfiche cabinet in a restricted area, and retrieve fiches on demand. Some fiche services use lower-density drawers with labelled pockets for each card.

- A conventional photocopier cannot reproduce the images. Libraries using microfiche often have a few viewers that can produce a photocopy of an image, for a nominal fee.
- Like all analog media formats, microfiche is lacking in features taken for granted by users of digital media. Analog copies degrade with each generation, while digital copies have much higher copying fidelity. Digital data can also be indexed and searched easily.

Readers and Printers

Desktop readers are boxes with a translucent screen at the front on to which is projected an image from a microform. They have suitable fittings for whatever microform is in use. They may offer a choice of magnifications. They often have powered movement of roll film. When coding blips are recorded on the film a reader is used that can read the blips to find any required image. Portable readers are plastic devices that fold for carrying; when open they project an image from microfiche on to a reflective screen.

A microfilm printer contains a xerographic copying process, like a photocopier. The image to be printed is projected with synchronised movement on to the drum. These devices offer either small image preview for the operator or full size image preview, when it is called a reader printer. Microform printers usually accept positive or negative films, to give positive images on paper. Newer readers allow the user to scan a microform image and save it as a digital file.

Media

Flat Film

105 × 148mm flat film is used for micro images of very large engineering drawings. These may carry a title photographed or written along one edge. Typical reduction is about 20, representing a drawing that is 2.00 × 2.80 metres, that is 79 × 110 inches (2,800mm). These films are stored as microfiche.

Microfilm

16mm or 35mm film to motion picture standard is used, usually un perforated. Roll microfilm is stored on open reels or put into cassettes. The standard length for using roll film is 30.48m (100 ft). One roll of 35mm film may carry 600 images of large engineering drawings or 800 images of broadsheet newspaper pages. 16mm film may carry 2,400 images of letter sized images as a single stream of micro images along the film set so that lines of text are parallel to the sides of the film or 10,000 small documents, perhaps cheques or betting slips, with both sides of the originals set side by side on the film.

Aperture Cards

Aperture cards are Hollerith cards into which a hole has been cut. A 35mm microfilm chip is mounted in the hole inside of a clear plastic sleeve, or secured over the aperture by an adhesive tape. They are used for engineering drawings, for all engineering disciplines. There are libraries of these containing over 3 million cards. Aperture cards may be stored in drawers or in freestanding rotary units.

Microfiche

A microfiche is a flat film 105 × 148mm in size, that is ISO A6. It carries a matrix of micro images. All microfiche are read with text parallel to the long side of the fiche. Frames may be landscape or portrait. Along the top of the fiche a title may be recorded for visual identification. The most commonly used format is a portrait image of about 10 × 14mm. Office size papers or magazine pages require a reduction of 24 or 25. Microfiche are stored in open top envelopes which are put in drawers or boxes as file cards, or fitted into pockets in purpose made books.

Image Creation

To create microform media, a planetary camera is mounted with vertical axis above a copy that is stationary during exposure. A flow camera moves copy smoothly through the camera to expose film which moves with the reduced image. Alternatively, it may be produced by computers, i.e. COM (Computer Output Microfilm).

Film

Normally microfilming uses high resolution panchromatic high resolution monochrome stock. Positive colour film giving good reproduction and high resolution can also be used. Roll film is provided 16, 35 and 105mm wide in lengths of 30 metres (100 ft) and longer, and is usually UN perforated. Roll film is developed, fixed and washed by continuous processors.

Sheet film is supplied in ISO A6 size. This is either processed by hand or using a dental X-ray processor. Camera film is supplied ready mounted in aperture cards. Aperture cards are developed, fixed and washed immediately after exposure by equipment fitted to the camera.

Cameras

Flat Film

The simplest microfilm camera that is still in use is a rail mounted structure at the top of which is a bellows camera for 105 × 148mm film. A frame or copy board holds the original drawing vertical. The camera has a horizontal axis which passes through the centre of the copy. The structure may be moved horizontally on rails.

In a darkroom a single film may be inserted into a dark slide or the camera may be fitted with a roll film holder which after an exposure advances the film into a box and cuts the frame off the roll for processing as a single film.

Roll Film

For engineering drawings a freestanding open steel structure is often provided. A camera may be moved vertically on a track. Drawings are placed on a large table for filming, with centers under the lens. Fixed lights illuminate the copy. These cameras are often over 3 meters (10 feet) high. These cameras accept roll film stock of 35 or 16mm.

For office documents a similar design may be used but bench standing. This is a smaller version of the camera described above. These are provided either with the choice of 16 or 35mm film or accepting 16mm film only. Non adjustable versions of the office camera are provided. These have a rigid frame or an enveloping box that holds a camera at a fixed position over a copy board. If this is to work at more than one reduction ratio there is a choice of lenses.

Some cameras expose a pattern of light, referred to as blips, to digitally identify each adjacent frame. This pattern is copied whenever the film is copied for searching.

Flow Roll Film Cameras

A camera is built into a box. In some versions this is for bench top use, other versions are portable. The operator maintains a stack of material to be filmed in a tray, the camera automatically takes one document after another for advancement through the machine. The camera lens sees the documents as they pass a slot. Film behind the lens advances exactly with the image. Special purpose flow cameras film both sides of documents, putting both images side by side on 16mm film. These cameras are used to record cheques and betting slips.

Microfiche Camera

All microfiche cameras are planetary with a step and repeat mechanism to advance the film after each exposure. The simpler versions use a dark slide loaded by the operator in a dark room; after exposure the film is individually processed, which may be by hand or using a dental X-ray processor. Cameras for high output are loaded with a roll of 105mm film. The exposed film is developed as a roll; this is sometimes cut to individual fiche after processing or kept in roll form for duplication.

Computer Output Microfilm

Equipment is available that accepts a data stream from a mainframe computer. This exposes film to produce images as if the stream had been sent to a line printer and the listing had been microfilmed. Because of the source one run may represent many thousands of pages.

Within the equipment character images are made by a light source, this is the negative of text on paper. COM is sometimes processed normally. Other applications require that image appears as a conventional negative; the film is then reversal processed. This outputs either 16mm film or fiche pages on a 105mm roll.

Because listing characters are a simple design, a reduction ratio of 50 gives good quality and puts about 300 pages on a microfiche. A microfilm plotter, sometimes called an aperture card plotter, accepts a stream that might be sent to a computer pen plotter. It produces corresponding frames of microfilm. These produce microfilm as 35 or 16mm film or aperture cards.

Storage and Preservation

Low temperatures and low relative humidity promote chemical stability. Microfilms should be stored at temperatures less than 21° Celsius (70° Fahrenheit) with relative humidity less than 60 per cent and good air circulation to inhibit fungus or mold germination.

The ANSI/NAPM IT9.11 standard specifies the following combinations of temperature and relative humidity for extend-term storage of black and white microfilms of all types: 21°C (70°F) with RH of 20-30 per cent; 15°C (60°F) with RH of 20-40 per cent; and 10°C (50°F) with RH of 20-50 per cent. For colour microfilm, the ANSI/NAPM IT9.11 standard specifies 2°C (36°F) with RH of 20-30 per cent. William Saffady recommends that colour microfilm be stored in two heat-sealed foil bags for moisture protection and to limit exposure to air.

For medium-term storage (at least ten years), ANSI/NAPM IT9.11 standard specifies that temperature should not exceed 25°C (77°F) and RH remain stable within 20-50 per cent range. Humidity variations should not exceed 10 per cent per day, and temperature change should be minimized.

Microfilm should be stored in dark enclosures to minimize damage from light. Enclosures should comply with preservation standards.

Microfilm storage areas should be located in a fire-resistant space that is kept clean and free of dust particles and other contaminants, as well as certain gases such as sulfur dioxide, hydrogen sulfide, ammonia, and ozone. All building materials and storage equipment should be noncombustible and non corrosive.

Microfilms should be regularly inspected for signs of deterioration.

Duplication

All regular microfilm copying involves contact exposure under pressure. Then the film is processed to provide a permanent image. Hand copying of single fiche or aperture cards uses exposure over a light box and individually processing of the film. Roll films are contact exposed round a glass cylinder containing a lamp. Processing may be in the same machine or separately.

Silver halide film is a slow version of camera film with a robust top coat. It is suitable for prints or for use as an intermediate from which further prints may be produced. The result is a negative copy. Preservation standards require a master negative, a duplicate negative, and a service copy (positive). Master negatives are kept in deep storage, and duplicate negatives are used to create service copies, which are the copies available to researchers. This multi-generational structure ensures the preservation of the master negative.

Diazo-sensitised film for dye coupling in ammonia gives blue or black dye positive copies. The black image film can be used for further copying.

Vesicular film is sensitised with a diazo dye, which after exposure is developed by heat. Where light has come to the film remains clear, in the areas under the dark image the diazo compound is destroyed quickly, releasing millions of minute bubbles of nitrogen into the film. This produces an image that diffuses light. It produces a good black appearance in a reader, but it cannot be used for further copying.

Format Conversion

These conversions may be applied to camera output or to release copies. Single microfiche are cut from rolls of 105mm film. A bench top device is available that enables an operator to cut exposed frames of roll film and fit these into ready made aperture cards.

Transparent jackets are made A5 size each with 6 pockets into which strips of 16mm film may be inserted, so creating microfiche. Equipment allows an operator to insert strips from a roll of film. This is particularly useful as frames may be added to a fiche at any time. The pockets are made using a thin film so that duplicates may be made from the assembled fiche.

Digital Conversion

Another type of conversion is microform to digital. This is done using an optical scanner that projects the film onto a CCD array and captures it in a raw digital format. Since the different types of microform are dissimilar in shape and size, the scanners are usually able to handle only one type. However, there are some that have the possibility of swapping modules for the different microform types. Software (normally on the scanner itself) is then used to convert the raw capture into a standard image format for archival.

The physical condition of microfilm greatly impacts the quality of the digitized copy. Microfilm with a cellulose acetate base (popular through the 1970s) is frequently subject to vinegar syndrome, redox blemishes, and tears, and even preservation standard silver halide film on a polyester base can be subject to silvering and degradation of the emulsion—all issues which affect the quality of the scanned image.

Digitizing microfilm can be inexpensive when automated scanners are employed. The Utah Digital Newspapers Programme has found that, with automated equipment, scanning can be performed at $0.15 per page.

For the resulting files to be useful, they must be organized in some way. This can be accomplished in a variety of different ways, dependent on the source media and the desired usage. In this regard, aperture cards with Hollerith information are probably the easiest since image data can be extracted from the card itself if the scanner supports it. Some types of microfilm will contain a counter next to the images; these can be referenced to an already existing database. Other microfilm reels will have a 'blip' system: small marks next to the images of varying lengths used to indicate document hierarchy (longest: root, long: branch, short: leaf). If the scanner is able to capture and process these then the image files can be arranged in the same manner. Optical character recognition is also frequently employed to provide automated full-text searchable files. Common issues that affect the accuracy of OCR applied to scanned images of microfilm include unusual fonts, faded printing, shaded backgrounds, fragmented letters, skewed text, curved lines and bleed through on the originals. For film types with no distinguishing marks, or when OCR is impossible (handwriting, layout issues, degraded text), the data must be entered in manually—a very time consuming process.

COPYRIGHT

Copyright is a right given by the law to creators of literary, dramatic, musical and artistic works and producers of cinematograph films and sound recordings. In fact, it is a bundle of rights including, inter alia, rights of reproduction, communication to the public, adaptation and translation of the work. There could be slight variations in the composition of the rights depending on the work.

Copyright ensures certain minimum safeguards of the rights of authors over their creations, thereby protecting and rewarding creativity. Creativity being the keystone of progress, no civilized society can afford to ignore the basic requirement of encouraging the same. Economic and social development of a society is dependent on creativity. The protection provided by copyright to the efforts of writers, artists, designers, dramatists, musicians, architects and producers of sound recordings, cinematograph films and computer software, creates an atmosphere conducive to creativity, which induces them to create more and motivates others to create.

Copyright is a legal concept, enacted by governments, giving the creator of an original work of authorship exclusive rights to it, usually for a limited time, after which the work enters the public domain. Generally, it is "the right to copy," but usually provides the author with other rights as well, such as the right to be credited for the work, to determine who may adapt the work to other forms, which may perform the work, which may financially benefit from it, and other, related rights. It is an intellectual property form (like the patent, the trademark, and the trade secret) applicable to any expressible form of an idea or information that is substantive and discrete.

Copyright was initially conceived as a way for governments in Europe to restrict printing; the contemporary intent of copyright is to promote the creation of new works by giving authors control of and profit from them.

Copyright has been internationally standardized, lasting between fifty to a hundred years from the author's death, or a finite period for anonymous or corporate authorship; some jurisdictions have required formalities to establishing copyright, most recognize copyright in any completed work, without formal registration. Generally, copyright is enforced as a civil matter, though some jurisdictions do apply criminal sanctions.

Indian copyright law is governed by the Copyright Act, 1957. The Copyright Act was based on the Copyright Act of 1911, framed by the British during the Colonial rule and also borrowed extensively from the 1956 Copyright Act of the United Kingdom.

The Act, with five amendments, in 1983, 1984, 1992, 1999 and a substantial one in 1994, adheres to the treaties of the Berne Convention, the Universal Copyright Convention, the Rome Convention and the Agreement on Trade-Related Aspects of Intellectual Property Rights (TRIPS) agreement. [1]

- Literary, dramatic, musical and artistic works (other than photographs)—Sixty years from the beginning of the calendar year following the year in which the author dies. Please note that this will usually be more than sixty years as the time frame starts subsequent to the author's death.
- Anonymous/Pseudonymous/Posthumous works, Photographs, Movies, Sound recordings,—Sixty years from the beginning of the year following the year in which it was published.
- Section 32 states that anyone can apply to the copyright board for a license to translate work seven years after first publication. Royalties will need to be paid to the copyright owner and the royalty is determined by the Copyright

Board and not the author. There are several conditions that have to be met before this applies and there are automatic termination clauses, so please read the full-text carefully.

Subject to certain conditions, a fair deal for research, study, criticism, review and news reporting, as well as use of works in library and schools and in the legislatures, is permitted without specific permission of the copyright owners. In order to protect the interests of users, some exemptions have been prescribed in respect of specific uses of works enjoying copyright. Some of the exemptions are the uses of the work

- for the purpose of research or private study,
- for criticism or review,
- for reporting current events,
- in connection with judicial proceeding,
- performance by an amateur club or society if the performance is given to a non-paying audience, and
- The making of sound recordings of literary, dramatic or musical works under certain conditions.

Scope of Protection in the Copyright Act, 1957

The Copyright Act, 1957 protects original literary, dramatic, musical and artistic works and cinematograph films and sound recordings from unauthorized uses. Unlike the case with patents, copyright protects the expressions and not the ideas. There is no copyright in an idea.

Copyright and Titles and Names

Copyright does not ordinarily protect titles by themselves or names, short word combinations, slogans, short phrases, methods, plots or factual information. Copyright does not protect ideas or concepts. To get the protection of copyright a work must be original.

Right of Reproduction

The right of reproduction commonly means that no person shall make one or more copies of a work or of a substantial part of it in any material form including sound and film recording without the permission of the copyright owner. The most common kind of reproduction is printing an edition of a work. Reproduction occurs in storing of a work in the computer memory.

18

Instructional Television

The Satellite Instructional Television Experiment

The Satellite Instructional Television Experiment or SITE was an experimental satellite communications project launched in India in 1975, designed jointly by NASA and the Indian Space Research Organization (ISRO). The project made available informational television programmes to rural India. The main objectives of the experiment were to educate the poor people of India on various issues via satellite broadcasting, and also to help India gain technical experience in the field of satellite communications.

The experiment ran for one year from 1 August 1975 to 31 July 1976, covering more than 2500 villages in six Indian states. The television programmes were produced by All India Radio and broadcast by NASA's ATS-6 satellite stationed above India for the duration of the project. The project was supported by various international agencies such as the UNDP, UNESCO, UNICEF and ITU. The experiment was successful, as it played a major role in helping develop India's own satellite programme, INSAT. The project showed that India could use advanced technology to fulfill the socio-economic needs of the country. SITE was followed by similar experiments in various countries, which showed the important role satellite TV could play in providing education.

Background

As part of its Applications Technology Satellites programme in the 1960s, NASA sought to field test the direct broadcast of television programmes to terrestrial receivers via satellite and short listed India, Brazil and the People's Republic of China as potential sites to stage the test. The country which would receive these broadcasts would have to be large enough and also close to the equator for testing a direct-broadcast satellite. While the communist regime of China was not recognised at the time by the U.S., Brazil was also ruled out as its population was concentrated in the cities, affecting the outreach of the broadcast across the country. As a consequence, India emerged as the only suitable candidate; however, its strained relationship with the U.S. prevented the U.S. Government from directly asking for its assistance, preferring India to make the first request for assistance for its own nascent space programme.

At the same time, India was trying to launch its national space programme under the leadership of Vikram Sarabhai. India was interested in the role of satellites for the purpose of communication and asked UNESCO to undertake a feasibility study for a project in that field. Between 18 November 1967 and 8 December 1967, UNESCO sent an expert mission to India to prepare a report on a pilot project in the use of satellite communication. The expert panel concluded that such a project would be feasible. Following the report, a study team of three engineers from India visited USA and France in June 1967, and came to the conclusion that India could meet the technical requirements for the project. Following this, the Indian Government set up the National Satellite Communications Group (NASCOM) in 1968 to look into the possible uses of a synchronous communications satellite for India. This group consisted of representatives from various Cabinet Ministries, ISRO and All India Radio (AIR). The group recommended that India should use the ATS-6 satellite – a second generation satellite developed by NASA – for an experiment in educational television.

Arnold Frutkin, then NASA's Director of International Programmes, arranged to have the Vikram Sarabhai approach NASA for help. Sarabhai saw this as a great opportunity for India to expand its space programme and to train Indian Scientists and Engineers. Consequently, the Indian Department of Atomic Energy and NASA signed an agreement regarding SITE in 1969. The experiment was launched on 1 August 1975.

Objectives

As per the Memorandum of Understanding signed between the two countries, the objectives of the project were divided into two parts – general objectives and specific objectives. The general objectives of the project were to:

- Gain experience in the development, testing and management of a satellite-based instructional television system particularly in rural areas and to determine optimal system parameters;
- Demonstrate the potential value of satellite technology in the rapid development of effective mass communications in developing countries;
- Demonstrate the potential value of satellite broadcast TV in the practical instruction of village inhabitants; and
- Stimulate national development in India, with important managerial, economic, technological and social implications.

The primary general objectives from an Indian perspective were to educate the populace about issues related to family planning, agricultural practices and national integration. The secondary objectives were to impart general school and adult education, train teachers, and improve other occupational skills and to improve general health and hygiene through the medium of satellite broadcasts. Besides these social objectives, India also wanted to gain experience in all the technical aspects of the system, including broadcast and reception facilities and TV programme material.

The primary US objective was to test the design and functioning of an efficient, medium-power, wide bandspace-borne FM transmitter, operating in the 800–900 MHz band and gain experience on the utilisation of this space application.

A joint ISRO-NASA working group was established even before the Memorandum of Understanding was signed. This working group studied the possibility of using a communications satellite for TV broadcast in India. After the MoU was signed, many review meetings were held between NASA and ISRO scientists. Indian scientists visited NASA to study front-end converters and earth station operations. On India's request, the INTELSAT organisation agreed to provide free satellite time for pre-SITE testing.

The United Nations Development Programme (UNDP) provided assistance for setting up the Experimental Satellite Communications Earth Station (ESCES) at Ahmedabad and nominated the International Telecommunications Union (ITU) as the executing agency for this project. The UNDP provided a TV studio at Ahmedabad and a TV transmitter at Pij in Kheda district. It also gave assistance for setting up a TV Training Institute to train many of the programme production staff who would join All India Radio to work on SITE. UNESCO was the executing agency for this project. UNICEF contributed to SITE by sponsoring 21 film modules produced by Shyam Benegal, a noted Indian film-maker. This resulted in a lot of interaction between film-makers and folk-artists. Shyam Benegal went on to include many of these artists in his children's feature film Charandas Chor (1975).

Technical Details

ATS-F coverage of India at 860 MHz. The production of the television programmes was decentralised, with three Base Production Centers located at Delhi, Cuttack and Hyderabad, and an ISRO studio located in Mumbai. Each of the centers had a production studio, three IVC tape recorders, two 16mm projectors, a slide Projector in Tele cine and audio equipment like tape desks and turn tables. Each centre also had 2–3 full fledged synchronised sound camera units, an editing table (Delhi had two) and a film processing plant. There was also a sound dubbing studio equipped with a pilot tone recording plant and an audio mixing console.

The television programmes prepared by the Indian Government at the four studios were transmitted at 6 GHz to ATS 6 from one of two ground stations located in Delhi and Ahmedabad. These signals were then re-transmitted at 860 MHz by the satellite, which were directly received in 2000 villages by community television receivers with 3 m parabolic antennas. Regular television stations also received the signals and broadcast them to another 3000 villages in the standard VHF television band. Each television signal had two audio channels to carry audio in two major languages of each cluster. This setup was called the Direct Reception System (DRS). Apart from the direct broadcasts, the earth station at Ahmedabad was micro-wave linked to the TV transmitter built in the village of Pij. The Delhi studio was linked to the terrestrial TV transmitters of AIR. A receive-only station was built in Amritsar and linked to the local TV transmitter.

The DRS undertook terrestrial broadcasting for large cities and direct broadcasting to SITE television sets for remote villages. However, it did not provide for small towns where the TV set density was higher than in the villages while not as much as in a city. The concept of a low-power limited rebroadcast (LRB) TV transmitter system was evolved to overcome such situations. The LRB consisted of a simple receiver system having a 4.5 m chicken-mesh parabolic antenna with a low-noise block converter that served as the front-end for a low-power TV transmitter at the same location. Two suitable locations, Sambalpur in Orissa (75 villages) and Muzaffarpur in Bihar (110 villages), were tentatively identified for implementing LRB transmitter systems. This experiment was expected to provide useful data on the trade-off between DRS and LRB. However, due to financial constraints, these two LRBs had to be shelved, and instead an LRB was set up at SHAR, Sriharikota.

Village Selection

As the broadcasting time was limited, it was decided that the direct reception receivers would only be installed in 2400 villages in six regions spread across the country. Technical and social criteria were used to select suitable areas to conduct this experiment. A computer programme was specially designed at ISRO to help make this selection. As one of the aims of the experiment was to study the potential of TV as a medium of development, the villages were chosen specifically for their backwardness. According to the 1971 census of India, the states having the most number of backward districts in the country were Orissa, Bihar, Andhra Pradesh, Uttar Pradesh, Rajasthan, Madhya Pradesh, West Bengal and Karnataka. Uttar Pradesh and West Bengal were eventually left out, as they were slated to get terrestrial television by the time SITE would end. SITE was launched in twenty districts spread across the other six states. Each of the states thus selected was called a "cluster." In each cluster, 3–4 districts, each containing around 1000 villages, were identified. Finally, around 400 villages were chosen in each cluster. Close to 80 per cent villages selected for SITE did not have electricity in the buildings where the SITE TV sets would be installed. A special project called Operation Electricity was launched to urgently electrify the villages before the start of SITE. 150 villages would have television sets running on solar cells and batteries. These sets were specially designed by Indian engineers with help from NASA.

Clusters Selected for SITE

Cluster	*District*	*Maintenance Centers*
Andhra Pradesh	Hyderabad	Hyderabad
	Kurnool	Nandyal
	Medak	Sangareddy
	Mahbubnagar	Nagarkurnool
Karnataka	Gulbarga	Gulbarga, Bagalkot
	Raichur	Raichur
	Bijapur	Bijapur
Bihar	Muzaffarpur	Muzaffarpur
	Champaran	Motihari
	Saharsa	Saharsa
	Darbhanga	Darbhanga, Samastipur
Madhya Pradesh	Raipur	Raipur, Mahasamund
	Bilaspur*	Bilaspur

Contd...

Cluster	*District*	*Maintenance Centers*
	Durg*	Rajnandgaon
Orissa	Sambalpur	Sambalpur
	Dhenkanal	Dhenkanal, Angul
	Baudh Khandmals	Baudh
Rajasthan	Jaipur	Jaipur, Chomu
	Kota	Kota
	Sawai Madhopur	Gangapur

* These districts are now located in the state of Chhattisgarh.

Programming

All India Radio had the main responsibility for programme generation and the programmes were made in consultation with the government. Special committees on education, agriculture, health and family planning identified their own programme priorities and conveyed it to AIR.

Two types of programmes were prepared for broadcasting: Educational Television (ETV) and Instructional Television (ITV). ETV programmes were meant for school children and focused on interesting and creative educational programmes. These programmes were broadcast for 1.5 hours during school hours. During holidays, this time was used to broadcast Teacher Training Programmes designed to train almost 100,000 primary school teachers during the duration of the SITE. The ITV programmes were meant for adult audiences, mainly to those who were illiterate. They were broadcast for 2.5 hours during the evenings. The programmes covered health, hygiene, family planning, nutrition, improved practices in agriculture and events of national importance. Thus, the programmes were beamed for four hours daily in two transmissions. The targeted audience was categorised into four linguistic groups—Hindi, Oriya, Telugu and Kannada—and programmes were produced according to the language spoken in the cluster.

Due to linguistic and cultural differences, it was agreed that all core programmes would be cluster-specific, and would be in the primary language of the region. A brief commentary giving the gist of the programme would be available on the second audio channel, to keep up the interest of the audience in other language regions. All clusters would also receive 30 minutes of common programmes, including news, which would be broadcast only in Hindi.

Evaluation

The social research and evaluation of SITE was done by ISRO's special SITE Research and Evaluation Cell (REC). The REC consisted of around 100 persons who were located in each of the SITE clusters, at the SITE studio in Bombay, and at the headquarters of the REC in Ahmedabad. The research design was finalized by the SITE Social Science Research Co-ordination Committee under the Chairmanship of Dr. M.S. Gore, Director of the Tata Institute of Social Sciences in Bombay. Impact on primary school children was studied under a joint project involving ISRO and the

National Council of Educational Research and Training (NCERT). The overall evaluation design was divided into three stages. The first stage, the formative or input research, was a detailed study of the potential audience. The second stage, process evaluation, was the evaluation carried out during the life-time of SITE. This evaluation provided information about the reaction of the villagers to different programmes. The third stage, the summative evaluation, involved a number of different studies to measure the impact of SITE. These included the Impact Survey (Adults) to measure the impact on adults, SITE Impact Survey Children (SIS-C) to measure the impact on school children, and the qualitative anthropology study to measure, at a macro-level, the change brought by TV in rural society.

Besides the social evaluation, a technical evaluation was also carried out to help India develop future systems. All major sub-systems of the earth station were tested and evaluated before SITE was launched. This was done firstly using a spacecraft simulator from NASA, then using the Indian Ocean INTELSAT satellite and finally using the ATS-6 satellite. All the components of the Direct Reception System were also thoroughly tested. The TV set was tested by the British Aircraft Corporation. The 3-meter antenna was tested thoroughly before deciding on the final design. Data on failure rates was collected and analysis of the first 1800 failures was carried out to help design future DRS systems.

Impact

As decided in the original agreement, the SITE programme ended in July, 1976 and NASA shifted its ATS satellite away from India, despite demands from Indian villagers, journalists and others such as noted writer Arthur C. Clarke (who was presented with a SITE television set in Sri Lanka) for NASA to continue the experiment.

The SITE transmissions had a very significant impact in the Indian villages. For the entire year, thousands of villagers gathered around the TV set and watched the shows. Studies were conducted on the social impact of the experiment and on viewer ship trends. It was found that general interest and viewer ship were highest in the first few months of the programme (200 to 600 people per TV set) and then declined gradually (60 to 80 people per TV set). This decline was due to several factors, including faults developing in the television equipment, failure in electricity supply, and hardware defects, as also the villagers' pre-occupation with domestic or agricultural work. Impact on the rural population was highest in the fields of agriculture and family planning. Nearly 52 per cent of viewers reported themselves amenable to applying the new knowledge gained by them.

Similar experiments were conducted in the Appalachian region, Rocky Mountains, Alaska, Canada, China and Latin America in the mid-seventies and early eighties. These experiments demonstrated that satellite TV could play a very important role in providing education.

Before SITE, the focus was on the use of terrestrial transmission for television signals. But SITE showed that India could make use of advanced technology to fulfill the socio-economic needs of the country. This led to an increased focus on satellite broadcasting in India. ISRO began preparations for a country-wide satellite system.

After conducting several technical experiments, the Indian National Satellite System was launched by ISRO in 1982. The Indian space programme remained committed to the goal of using satellites for educational purposes. In September 2004, India launched EDUSAT, which was the first satellite in the world built exclusively to serve the educational sector. EDUSAT is used to meet the demand for an interactive satellite-based distance education system for India.

Indian National Satellite System (INSAT)

Indian National Satellite System (INSAT) is a series of multipurpose Geo-Stationary satellites launched by ISRO to satisfy the telecommunications, broadcasting, meteorology, search and rescue needs of India. Commissioned in 1983, INSAT is the largest domestic communication system in the Asia-Pacific Region. Active satellites of this series include INSAT-2E, INSAT-3A, INSAT-3B, INSAT-3C, INSAT-3E, KALPANA-1 (METSAT), GSAT-2, EDUSAT (GSAT-3) and INSAT-4A. INSAT satellites provide transponders (about 150) in various bands (C, S, Extended C and Ku) to serve the television and communication needs of India. Some of the satellites also have the Very High Resolution Radiometer (VHRR), CCD cameras for metrological imaging. The satellites also incorporate transponder(s) for receiving distress alert signals for search and rescue missions in the South Asian and Indian Ocean Region, as ISRO is a member of the Cospas-Sarsat programme.

INSAT System

The Indian National Satellite (INSAT) system was commissioned with the launch of INSAT-1B in August 1983 (INSAT-1A, the first satellite was launched in April 1982 but could not fulfill the mission). INSAT system ushered in a revolution in India's television and radio broadcasting, telecommunications and meteorological sectors. It enabled the rapid expansion of TV and modern telecommunication facilities to even the remote areas and off-shore islands. Today, INSAT has become the largest domestic communication satellite system in the Asia-Pacific region with ten satellites in service—INSAT-2E, INSAT-3A, INSAT-3B, INSAT-3C, INSAT-3E, KALPANA-1, GSAT-2, EDUSAT, INSAT-4A and INSAT-4B. Together, the system provides 199 transponders in C, Extended C and Ku bands for a variety of communication services. Some of the INSATs also carry instruments for meteorological observation and data relay for providing meteorological services. KALPANA-1 is an exclusive meteorological satellite. The satellites are monitored and controlled by Master Control Facilities that exist in Hassan and Bhopal.

EDUSAT

EDUSAT or GSAT-3 was launched in September 2004 by the Indian Space Research Organisation. EDUSAT is the first Indian satellite built exclusively to serve the educational sector. It is mainly intended to meet the demand for an interactive satellite-based distance education system for the country.

EDUSAT carries five K_u band transponders providing spot beams, one K_u band transponder providing a national beam and six extended C band transponders providing national coverage beams.

INSAT Satellites

Sl. No.	*Satellite*	*Launch Date*	*Mission Status*
1.	INSAT-1A	10 April 1982	Deactivated on 6 September 1982
2.	INSAT-1B	30 August 1983	Completed mission life
3.	INSAT-1C	22 July 1988	Abandoned in November 1989
4.	INSAT-1D	12 June 1990	Completed mission life
5.	INSAT-2A	10 July 1992	India's First Indegenious communication Satellite. Completed mission life
6.	INSAT-2B	23 July 1993	Completed mission life
7.	INSAT-2C	7 December 1997	Completed mission life
8.	INSAT-2D	4 June 1997	Became inoperable on 4 October 1997
9.	INSAT-2DT	In-orbit procurement	Completed mission life
10.	INSAT-2E	3 April 1999	In service
11.	INSAT-3A	10 April 2003	In service
12.	INSAT-3B	22 May 2000	In service
13.	INSAT-3C	24 January 2002	In service
14.	KALPANA-1	12 September 2002	In service
15.	GSAT-2	8 May 2003	In service
16.	INSAT-3E	28 September 2003	In service
17.	EDUSAT	20 September 2004	In service
18.	INSAT-4A	22 December 2005	In service
19.	INSAT-4C	10 July 2006	Not placed in orbit due to launch failure of GSLV-F02
20.	INSAT-4B	12 March 2007	In service
21.	INSAT-4CR	2 September 2007	In geo-synchronous orbit.

September 20, 2004, India's Geosynchronous Satellite Launch Vehicle, GSLV successfully launched EDUSAT the country's first thematic satellite dedicated exclusively for educational services, into a Geosynchronous Transfer Orbit (GTO) from Satish Dhawan Space Centre SHAR (SDSC SHAR), Sriharikota. It was the first operational flight of GSLV (GSLV-F01) and the third in the GSLV series. EDUSAT is now orbiting the Earth in GTO with a perigee (nearest point to Earth) of 180 km and an apogee (farthest point to Earth) of 35,985 km with an orbital inclination of 19.2 deg with respect to the equator. The orbital period now is 10.5 hours.

The 414 tonne, 49 m tall GSLV, carrying the 1950 kg EDUSAT, lifted off from Sriharikota at 4:01 pm. About seventeen minutes after lift off, EDUSAT was successfully placed in GTO. At 4.8 seconds before the countdown reached zero, the four liquid propellant strap-on stages, each carrying 40 tonne of hypergolic liquid propellants (UH25 and N2O4), were ignited. At count zero and after confirming the normal performance of all the four strap-on motors, the mammoth 138 tonne solid propellant first stage core motor was ignited and GSLV blazed into the sky. The major phases of the flight included the first stage burn-out at 104 seconds, the strap on burn-out at 150 seconds, ignition of the second stage at 150 seconds, heat shield separation at an altitude of 115 km and 227 seconds into the flight, second stage burn-out at 288 seconds, ignition of the 12.5 tonne cryogenic stage at 304 seconds and its shut down at 999 seconds after attaining the required velocity of 10.2 km per second.

EDUSAT was put into orbit at 1014 seconds about 5000 km away from Sriharikota. The separated cryogenic stage was subsequently reoriented and passivated. Soon after its injection into to GTO, the two solar arrays of EDUSAT were automatically deployed. The deployment of the arrays as well as the general health of the satellite were monitored by the ground station of the ISRO Telemetry, Tracking and Command network (ISTRAC) located in the Indonesian island of Biak. The Master Control Facility (MCF) at Hassan in Karnataka has since taken control of EDUSAT for all its post launch operations. Ground stations at Lake Cowichan (Canada), Fucino (Italy) and Beijing (China) are supporting MCF in monitoring the health of the satellite and its orbit raising operations.

Its designated orbital slot is 74 degree East longitude in the GSO. There, it will be co-located with KALPANA-1 and INSAT-3C. EDUSAT was developed by ISRO Satellite Centre, Bangalore. The payloads were developed by Space Applications Centre, Ahmedabad. Master Control Facility at Hassan is responsible for all post launch operations of the satellite.

Satellite Based Education in India

A major initiative towards providing satellite based tele-education facilities to Engineering colleges in the country was launched today (January 1, 2008) jointly by Indian Space Research Organisation (ISRO) in association with Indian Institute of Technology (IIT), Bombay. This EDUSAT network provides satellite-based tele-education facilities to students and teachers of the engineering colleges across the country.

Edusat in Kerala

The Government of Kerala is implementing the scheme named ViCTERS (Virtual Classroom Technology on EDUSAT for Rural Schools) using the broad band facilities offered by EDUSAT. The EDUSAT services in schools are implemented as part of a broader initiative which started in the year 2002-03 for ushering in technology aided education in schools—the IT @ School Project. The State has prescribed Information Technology as a compulsory subject in all its 2750 high schools (Standard 8 to 10) in the State, Lakswadeep and Gulf Countries. IT has also been made a compulsory paper (Both Theory and Practicals) in the SSLC Examination since last year. The uniqueness of the project is that the ordinary school teachers are teaching the subject—both in class rooms and Computer labs. The objective is to empower them to use modern technology for curricular transactions in class through constant use of computers and other IT related equipments.

The project is implemented in a decentralised manner wherein the schools are directed to set up computer lab on their own seeking assistance of the development funds of MP/MLAs, plan funds of Local Self Government (recently Kerala bagged the award for the best implementation of Panchayati Raj System), PTA funds, donations from expatriates, old students and philanthropists. Almost all the 54000 high school teachers have been trained and every school has a School IT Coordinator, who champions the implementation of the project on a voluntary basis, in addition to their regular job as a teacher handling his/her own subject. In the recent survey, it was found out that 52 per cent of the high school teachers teach IT in schools. Kerala high schools have over 35000 computers (numbers varying from 5 to 65) now, through this model of decentralised implementation, while it was only less than 2000 computers in the year 2002.

The first phase, i.e., building the infrastructure and expertise in schools, is over and when the state was moving towards implementing IT enabled education, the real objective of IT @ School Project, the State could roll out EDUSAT services, thanks to the timely help of ISRO. The State has set up the first Interactive Broadband network on EDUSAT for school education in India, the ViCTERS -Virtual Classroom Technology on EDUSAT for Rural Schools. The network was launched by none other than H.E. the President of India, Dr. A.P.J. Abdul Kalam on 28th July 2005 at Thiruvananthapuram. So far 35 SITs have been setup in DIETs, BRCs of SSA and in some schools in all the districts of the State. 21 SITs have also been set up in Government owned Engineering Colleges.

Five Months of Operation of Interactive Channel

The IT @ School Project in association with another Government institution, Centre for Development of Imaging Technology (C-DIT) has set up a full fledged studio. The State uplinking station has also been set up there. During these five months, it has been demonstrated, how SITs could be effectively used for the training of schoolteachers, departmental conferences and other programmes, which requires interaction with participants/field staff. The most important use of this network has been in the teacher empowerment. The ViCTERS enabled the schoolteachers of Kerala to obtain first hand information on the grading methodology, problems and issues confronted while implementing the system, from the expert faculty of SCERT. It may be noted that before ViCTERS they never obtained any such opportunity as the teachers training programme in Kerala, like else where, is a staggered process, starting with SCERT faculty training a State Resource Group (SRG) and then SRG training DRG and so on.

The new EDUSAT system greatly reduced the communication losses. Training programmes are regularly being conducted by all the directorates of general education department. The Kerala State Literary Mission Authority has started regular SSLC equivalency programme for neo-literates on all Sundays. The system is also effectively being used by Directorates of Public Instruction, Higher Secondary Education, Vocational Higher Secondary Education, Sarva Siksha Abhyan, and Literacy Mission for regular interaction with their sub-offices. The departmental conferences of Directorate of Public Instruction are a typical case. Earlier, usually the Deputy Directors of Education were called for departmental meetings at a central location. The DPI never got the opportunity to interact and explain the different schemes implemented by the directorate to the other key officers of the office of the DDE, namely,

Administrative Assistant, Section Superintendents etc. EDUSAT now provides such an opportunity for the DPI to directly interact with them and get the feed back of almost all the suboffice staff. This methodology is being used by other departments for conduct of periodic performance review of sub-offices. The advantages are vivid.

Future Plans on Interactive Channel

It is planned to have one interactive channel for the school sector and one for the higher education sector. Thus the existing 35 SITs set up under general education could be shared between the DPI, DHSE, DVHSE and SSA, all supported by SCERT. Institutions like Kerala State Literacy Mission, State Open School and Continuing Education could also use the interactive net work on Saturdays, Sundays and other holidays. It is also planned to conduct regular courses–short term and long term-for students appearing for competitive examinations like Civil Services, IIT-JEE, CAT, TOEFL, Entrance Examinations etc.

The State is planning to set up smaller networks covering various institutions. Supply orders for 39 Government owned Arts and Science Colleges are to be released soon. The State has also plans to set up SITs in B.Ed Collages, TTIs, and Nursing Colleges etc. Under SSA, it is planned to provide SITs to all BRCs. MGLCs in remote areas, forests and like would get the benefit of Interactive terminals. The SITs of 9 Lakswadeep Islands may be hooked up the Kerala NOCC. The higher education sector, which is planning to operate the second Interactive channel, is in the process of setting up a studio separately. The uplinking is envisaged through the existing NOCC, connected through leased lines.

Non-Interactive Channel

ISRO has promised to supply the equipments for upgrading the existing hub for the non-interactive channel. The programmes aired through this channel are to be received though ROTs, which is nothing but an ordinary Direct-To-Home (DTH). The Government has already formulated a three stage plan to provide EDUSAT programmes to all its 13000 schools–Government and aided-within the next two years.

The three stage action plan is as follows:

Stages/Period Targets/Objectives

I. January-February 2006

- To upgrade the hub for the second channel.
- To make available infrastructure in all the Government high schools.
- To telecast programme for SSLC students before March 2006.

II. March-May 2006

- To ensure that infrastructure is provided to aided high schools as well.
- To roll out the programme in higher secondary schools.
- To telecast programme for school vacation period.
- To develop programmes for the next academic year.
- To set up a second studio in SCERT buildings.

III. From June 2006 Onwards

- To address the vast content requirement for airing programmes on 24 hour basis as any other channel.
- To roll out the programmes to Lower and Upper Primary schools.

The Conference on Edusat

The pivotal role of education as an instrument of social change by altering the human perspective and transforming the traditional mindset of society is well recognised. The universalisation of education has become the top priority, especially for the developing countries. But the extension of quality education to remote and rural regions becomes a Herculean task for a large country like India with multi-lingual and multi-cultural population separated by vast geographical distances, and, in many instances, inaccessible terrain. Since independence, India has seen substantial increase in the number of educational institutions at primary, secondary and higher levels as well as the student enrolment. But the lack of adequate rural educational infrastructure and non-availability of good teachers in sufficient numbers adversely affect the efforts made in education.

Satellites can establish the connectivity between urban educational institutions with adequate infrastructure imparting quality education and the large number of rural and semi-urban educational institutions that lack the necessary infrastructure. Besides supporting formal education, a satellite system can facilitate the dissemination of knowledge to the rural and remote population about important aspects like health, hygiene and personality development and allow professionals to update their knowledge base as well. Thus, inspite of limited trained and skilled teachers, the aspirations of the growing student population at all levels can be met through the concept of tele-education. The concept of beaming educational programmes through satellites was effectively demonstrated for the first time in India in 1975-76 through the Satellite Instructional Television Experiment (SITE) conducted using the American Application Technology Satellite (ATS-6). During this unique experiment, which is hailed as the largest sociological experiment conducted anywhere in the world, programmes pertaining to health, hygiene and family planning were telecast directly to about 2,400 Indian villages spread over six states. Later, with the commissioning of INSAT system in 1983, a variety of educational programmes is being telecast. In the 90s, Jhabua Developmental Communications Project (JDCP) and Training and Developmental Communication Channel (TDCC) further demonstrated the efficacy of tele-education.With the success of the INSAT based educational services, a need was felt to launch a satellite dedicated for educational service and ISRO conceived the EDUSAT Project in October 2002.

While ISRO will provide the space segment for EDUSAT System and demonstrate the efficacy of the satellite system for interactive distance education, content generation is the responsibility of the user agencies. The quantity and quality of the content would ultimately decide the success of EDUSAT System. This involves an enormous effort by the user agencies. To help in this, ISRO, in cooperation with the user agencies, has already organised five conferences at regional level and one at the national level to create awareness about the EDUSAT and its capabilities.

The Conference on EDUSAT at Bangalore is yet another effort by ISRO to increase the awareness on EDUSAT capabilities among the institutions of learning and elicit the views of experts in implementing the EDUSAT system. The Bangalore Conference will have nine parallel sessions to discuss topics on Distance Education, Medical Education, Technical Education, Agricultural Education, Higher Education, Teachers' Training, Industry-Academia Interaction, Education Administration and EDUSAT Management. Recommendations arising from these parallel sessions will be discussed in the valedictory session. The Conference is expected to result in drawing a road map for the effective utilisation of EDUSAT system.

CIET Modal for all School Educational Broadcast

Educational Broadcast Policy

MHRD has formed a committee with the Additional Secretary as the Chairman and the Chiefs of all concerned educational institutions as members including CIET; it gives policy directives: distribution of time slots among them, quality, etc. (CIET has been made the nodal institution to select, coordinate and telecast all educational programmes at school level).

Standing Committee for Programme Co-Ordination (SCOPCO)

Chairman-JEA; co conveners-JD-CIET and Director, MHRD.SCOPCO convened meetings at two SIETs allotted telecast time slots to SIET-Patna, adopted uniform magazine format, laid norms for quality of programmes, initiated IT in all SIETs, etc.

History

Central Institute of Educational Technology (CIET) is a constituent unit of the National Council of Educational Research and Training (NCERT), an autonomous organisation under the Ministry of Human Resources Development, Government of India. Established in 1984 with the merger of the Centre of Educational Technology and Department of Teaching Aids, its chief aim is to promote Educational Technology especially mass media singly or in combinations (multimedia packages) to extend educational opportunities and improve quality of educational processes at the school level.

As a premier institute of Educational Technology at the apex level, major functions of the CIET are to:

- Design, develop, try out and disseminate alternative learning systems to achieve the national goal of universalisation of primary education and
- To address various educational problems at micro, and macro levels. The broad areas of activities of the CIET are as given below:
- To design and produce media software materials viz., television/radio (for both broadcast as well as non-broadcast use) film, graphics and other programmes for strengthening the transaction of curricular and co-curricular activities at the school level.
- To create competencies in development and use of educational software materials mentioned above through training in areas such as script development, media production, media communication, media research, technical operations, setting up studios, repair and maintenance of equipment.

- To train the faculty of Institutes of Advanced Study in Education/Colleges of Teacher Education and District Institutes of Education and Training in the use of Educational Technology in their teacher education programmes.
- To undertake research evaluation and monitoring of the systems, programmes and materials with a view to improving the materials and increasing their effectiveness.
- To document and disseminate information, materials and media programmes for better utilisation and to function as a clearinghouse/agency in the field of Educational Technology.
- To advise and coordinate the academic and technical programmes and activities of the SIET set up by the MHRD in six states of India.

Audio, Video Production

- 45 Audio-Radio programmes 'Umang'.
- 108 ETV programmes 'Tarang'(10-11 a.m.: 5 days a week; 15mts. TT prog. each day).
- 10 scripts on Astronomy to Inter University Centre for Astronomy and Astrophysics.
- 6 video spots (Pollution).
- Animation spots.
- Numerous continuities for capsuling in Magazine format (16 capsules/week).
- Kathak as a component of Art education through ETV—by Uma Sharma.

The launching of an exclusive Educational Channel for reaching the unreached has come through today. So far CIET of the NCERT has been feeding a time slot of 1-hour during weekdays for the children at the primary and secondary levels and 15-minutes daily for teacher education. These are being telecast on DD-I (National). Doordarshan sometimes stopped telecasting school educational programmes in favour of other entertainment programmes. We have been always pursuing Doordarshan not to drop school ETV programmes to accommodate other programmes. A dedicated Educational Channel has the potential to continuously develop viewer ship; TV has since long been identified as an agent of change in education and development. Production of school level ETV programmes in all subjects in the school curriculum with appropriate application of instructional design and with proper mix of content, entertainment and enrichment is a challenge, particularly in view of huge population of around 20 cores in formal and non-formal sectors in the age group of 6-18.

Apart from the programmes already available in CIET-SIETs circuit, new programmes are to be developed on the lines of the new curriculum, which is under preparation. Together with this, there are many areas, which in this new millennium the children should learn. They should be exposed to the rich cultural heritage of this country, its glorious past, its contribution to art-philosophy-literature-science, sacrifice of freedom fighters etc. Besides there are many new areas in education like consumer education, adolescent education, Aids education, Standards education etc. NCERT likes to utilise this channel also for popularising vocational education, which badly needs the support of regular telecast, as the schools in the rural areas do not get qualified teachers and equipment.

The present slot of 15-minutes for teacher education (5.45 a.m. to 6.00 a.m. daily) on DD-I, though grossly inadequate, is already very popular in rural areas. The Educational Channel has the potential to showcase innovations of outstanding teachers so that others are encouraged. The spotlight will be however on 'Teleconferencing' almost every week so that lessons for hundreds of teachers will be transacted online in an interactive mode.

The test transmission during 5.00 to 7.00 p.m. from EMPC-IGNOU has already started. CIET's ETV programmes for one week have already been sent to IGNOU in advance. In the final phase of transmission, which we understand will start from mid February 2000 for 10-16 hours daily; CIET's focus will be on some hard spots in the secondary curriculum. One such area is Mathematics, which is not taught properly in rural areas due to lack of resources. Considering proportion of students in the school to those in higher and professional education, CIET's programmes will perhaps constitute 30 per cent of total telecast time on the Educational Channel. The timings of these ETV programmes for the school children and teachers will have to be scheduled as per the need of the viewers. For this, a need assessment survey is already being conducted.

Educational Broadcasting in India

At the time of its independence from Britain in 1947, India was a country of great paradoxes. A country of extremes, with great poverty and deprivation, led by an educated and enlightened elite that recognized that public intervention would be critical to the development of this subcontinent sized nation. It became clear those centuries of industrial development had to be telescoped into a few decades and therefore, while there was need for policy, action on the ground was equally important. India, therefore, has witnessed the growth of educational broadcasting, both as forethought and as a consequence of policy.

If we look at the Plan documents and at the decisions taken by the government in the implementation of technology for education, we would find a vibrant, avant-garde thinking when it came to applying science for the education of people. Here we define education broadly as a component of development, going beyond the formal confines of schools and colleges and concerned with the improvement in the quality of life.

The First Five Year Plan of India, drafted within a few years of the country's independence from the British, drew attention to the expected role of communication in the process of development when it stated:

"A widespread understanding of the Plan is an essential stage in its fulfillment. All available methods of communication have to be developed and the people approached through the written and spoken word no less than through radio, film, song, and drama."

If this policy statement is coupled with the Indian constitutional provision where education is the concern of both the national and State Governments, the ideological basis for educational policy is laid. Multiple levels of policy formulation and implementation of education characterise Indian education, yet at all levels, there is an acceptance of the proactive role of government in the use of all media for education and development. The policy for this medium has not changed since and most of the pioneering experiments conducted in this country are testimonial to the national policy of utilising technology for the purpose of education.

The Landmarks

India's experimentation with the use of mass media for development began early in the 1950s. The Indian broadcaster has, since its inception, been an active partner in educational broadcasting, and both the broadcasting organisations (Akashvani or All India Radio; and Doordarshan or Indian television) and other governmental agencies have been involved in the production of educational programmes.

Doordarshan's was started as an educational experiment in 1959. The aim was to provide information to viewers with the purpose of influencing attitudes. The first educational broadcasting, done terrestrially, was with higher secondary schools in Delhi with subjects such as Physics, Chemistry, Hindi, Current Affairs, and Geography covered.

The Satellite Instructional Television Experiment (SITE) in 1975, as it came to be known, has remained to this day as the major watershed in technology applications in education and development. A quantum leap from zero to satellite communications, SITE was the first and largest experiment in human communication.

Lessons from the SITE and other such experiments underscored the critical importance of a multi-pronged approach the application of technology in education. The building up of technological infrastructure had to be backed up by developments on the ground. Specifically, this meant the building up of institutional infrastructures; capacity building; inter institutional collaboration; attention to the educational and development dimension and the importance of social research.

There was no looking back for Indian educators, broadcasters, and technocrats after the SITE experiment. The setting up of massive communication infrastructure began with the launching of India's own satellite INSAT IB in 1982. It is to the credit of the Indian educators that since 1984, educational telecasts have not only been sustained without a break, but have also grown to the extent that India has its own dedicated channels for educational broadcasting in all sectors.

Tele School

Tele school was the project for school children. A Central Institute for Educational Technology (CIET) formed the hub of production activity for school telecasts with six State Institutes for Educational Technology (SIETs) producing programmes in the regional languages. These were telecast on the national and regional networks of Doordarshan.

Countrywide Classroom

Countrywide classroom, for college students on the national public broadcaster was partnered by the University Grants Commission, university based educational media centers and a UGC established autonomous interuniversity centre, the Consortium for Educational Communication (CEC) for capsuling and forwarding to Doordarshan for transmission.

The Single Mode Open Universities

The single mode open universities are also engaged in the production and telecast of educational programmes. The Indira Gandhi National Open University (IGNOU) has been broadcasting since the late 1980s, while the B.R. Ambedkar Open University, Hyderabad has been sustaining a radio programme since its inception and a regular telecast of educational content since 1999.

Gyan Darshan

The success of educational broadcasting prompted a demand for an exclusive channel for education and the third milestone in educational broadcasting. Gyan darshan was born on January 26, 2000. Today, it is a bouquet of six channels. In essence, it is a cooperative venture with the Indira Gandhi National Open University as a nodal agency for coordinating the activities and up-linking the educational content. The programme mix is a blend of core curriculum based programmes in the areas of primary, secondary, higher, open and distance education, extension, technical and vocational education along with general mosaic programmes in areas of health, hygiene, arts, culture, environment, conservation, science popularization, etc.

In addition, there are state wide initiatives such as the SAPNET in Andhra Pradesh and the University of Goa.

EDUSAT

The fourth major landmark in India's educational broadcasting has been the development and the imminent launch of EDUSAT, a satellite exclusively dedicated to educational and development programming. Proposed under EDUSAT is the deployment of a satellite on the Ku band, and small size, low cost ground hardware. There will be 70 transmission channels available in five spot beams covering the country. The satellite promises high bandwidth two-way interactivity, multimedia multicasting, with a constant rate throughput and adopts an open standard approach for ease of expansion.

In Summary, the scenario in the use of satellites in India reflects a system that has

- An exclusive satellite for education with a capacity of 70 dedicated channels.
- Educational broadcasts on the national public broadcaster.
- Four national and one regional 24 hour dedicated satellite to cable educational television channels.
- A 24 hour TDCC channel available for use in teleconference support for.
- education.
- A huge volume of educational video content available for all sectors with the various agencies involved in educational broadcasting.
- An unknown but large number of programmes available with Doordarshan, and other government agencies on educational and development themes on a variety of topics and in all Indian languages.

Policy and Ownership

In the early years, there were few or no guidelines, no production capacities or skills in the media centers limited and little or no capacity building. There was little or no quality assurance. Production centers were left to grow as the local host institution or provincial government envisaged. As the system evolved and grew, realization dawned and policy guidelines, a credo or mission statement, memoranda of understanding and definition of each partner's responsibilities; shared funding, delegation of powers; content and technical quality norms, staff service conditions, etc. were developed. Funding allocation was also streamlined. But by then, it was a question of solving real field problems and of adjustment and compromise between existing and conflicting practices rather than designing policy and ownership patterns as part of system design.

Today, government responsibility remains that of policy definition and the provision of financial resources. Funding and policy is transmitted through independent agencies such as the Central Institute of Educational Technology (CIET) for school education the University Grants Commission and the Consortium for Educational Communication (CEC) for higher education which guide countrywide functioning of their systems respectively. Production of content is the responsibility of the various media centers established throughout the country in different educational and development institutions. For instance, State Institutes for Educational Technology are responsible for developing producing content for the school sector, agricultural extension institutions are responsible for agricultural content; health institutions produce health content in coordination with the local and regional Doordarshan stations.

Gyan Darshan has been established as a channel owned by Doordarshan; guided by the Ministry of Human Resource Development, and operated as a facility hosted by IGNOU, in cooperation with several ministries and autonomous organizations engaged in the use of educational broadcasting, each of whom funds content development from their own resources and contributes content for telecast on the national system.

National and regional advisory and steering committees comprising of stakeholders in the system meet regularly to decide policy and implementation issues. Decisions of these committees are approved by the funding agencies.

On the ground, while there seems to be shared vision among all stakeholders engaged in educational broadcasting, and the system appears to be functioning, there are differing perceptions on the ownership of educational broadcasting in India. The consequence of such differing perceptions on ownership is skirmishes and turf fights that adversely affect all aspects of governance and management.

Governance and Management

For the record, Indian educational broadcasting is a partnership and governance and management is based on memoranda of understanding signed by the different participating institutions. Yet, because each participating institutions is itself an autonomous body created either by legislation or statute, governance and management is affected, on a daily basis, by the differing perceptions of ownership described earlier. Further, because there are different governance and management practices in each institution, day-to-day system management varies substantially both in style and quality.

Funding and Infrastructure

By its very nature, public domain educational broadcasting is a non-commercial activity, and generally does not attract advertising revenues. Funding overshadows all other issues. Cost is the biggest barrier to the use of educational broadcasting. Funding for educational broadcasting remains a contentious issue, an overpowering factor determining the success of educational broadcasting. Fortunately for Indian educational broadcasters, the space segment is free, thus substantially reducing costs. Partnering institutions absorb invisible costs, while direct costs are provided for funding agencies, and out of an institution's own budget allocations reducing the financial burden on any one institution.

Content Matters

Since the primary purpose of educational broadcasting is to disseminate particular contents in the form of educational packages, the single most important element in the entire process is the content of the programmes or package of programmes. In conditions such as in India with diverse linguistic, cultural, and geographic realities, content has to reflect regional and even sub-regional groups to be effective. The decentralized nature of content production in India enables diversity of content.

The Challenge

India's educational problems are not because of the absence of strategic long or short term planning; but with the translation of planning to implementation. Most developmental projects in India can be accused of this weakness, where the problem is often well defined by policy makers, missions or projects drawn up to address these problems, funds identified, and set aside; and organisations created up to deal with the issue. Implementation gets tied up in knots of administrative politics, bureaucracy, secure government jobs, unionisation and other social issues so that both the goals, targets, time frames for implementation are lost in the process.

Yet, despite all the struggles and problems that beset educational broadcasting in India, one has to applaud the innovative and fresh approaches taken in India to manipulate the latest technological options to address educational needs. The Indian educational broadcasting system has both the awe and the envy of many in the world. The Indian educational broadcasting system has benefited from visionary leadership and ground level commitment by institutions and individuals. However, sustainability over a long time also requires that systems reinvent themselves to changing times, needs, and technologies and it is at this critical junction that the system finds itself. Which is why, one has to recognize that there has to be a paradigm shift in educational broadcasting if India is to retain its cutting edge ability to use the latest technologies on a grand scale to meet its monumental educational needs.

Educational Television in India

The Indian Beginning Television first came to India [named as 'Doordarshan' (DD)] on September 15, 1959 as the National Television Network of India. The first telecast started on September 15, 1959 in New Delhi. After a gap of about 13 years, second television station was established in Bombay in 1972 and by 1975 there were five more television stations at Shrinagar (Kashmir), Amritsar (Punjab), Calcutta, Madras and Lucknow. For many years the transmission was mainly in black & white. Television industry got the necessary boost in the eighties when Doordarshan introduced colour TV during the 1982 Asian Games.

The second phase of growth was witnessed in the early nineties and during the Gulf War, that foreign channel like CNN, Star TV and domestic channels such as Zee TV and Sun TV started broadcast of satellite signal. This changed the scenario and the people got the opportunity to watch regional, national and international programmes. Starting with 41 sets in 1962 and one channel (Audience Research unit, 1991) at present TV in India covers more than 70 million homes giving a viewing population more than 400 million individuals through more than 100 channels. Easy accessibility of relevant technology, variety of programmes and increased hour of transmission are main reasons for rapid expansion of TV system in India.

Major educational projects in India, since the inception of TV network, television has been perceived as an efficient force of education and development. With its large audience it has attracted educators as being an efficient tool for imparting education to primary, secondary and university level students. Some of the major educational television projects are discussed as hereunder:

Secondary School Television Project (1961)

This project was designed for the secondary school students of Delhi. With an aim to improve the standard of teaching in view of shortage of laboratories, space, equipment and dearth of qualified teachers in Delhi this project started on experimental basis in October 1961 for teaching of Physics, Chemistry, English and Hindi for students of Class XI. The lectures were syllabus-based and were telecasted in school hours as a part and parcel of school activities. According to Paul (1968) 'by and large, the television schools did somewhat better in the test then did the non-television schools.'

Delhi Agriculture Television (DATV) Project (Krishi Darshan) (1966)

The project named Krishi Darshan was initiated on January 26, 1966 for communicating agricultural information to the farmers on experimental basis for the 80 selected villages of Union Territory of Delhi through Community viewing of television and further discussions among themselves. Experiment was successful and that there was substantial gain in the information regarding agricultural practices. (IGNOU, 2000).

Satellite Instructional Television Experiment (SITE) (1975)

This project, one of the largest techno-social experiments in human communication, was commissioned for the villagers and their Primary School going children of selected 2330 villages in six states of India. It started on August 1, 1975 for a period of one year in six states Rajasthan, Karnataka, Orissa, Bihar, Andhra Pradesh and Madhya Pradesh. The main objectives of this experiment were to study the process of existing rural communications, the role of television as new medium of education, and the process of change brought about by the community television in the rural structure with following two type of telecast:

- Developmental education programmes in the area of agriculture and allied subjects, health, family planning and social education, which were telecast in the evening for community viewing.
- The school programmes of 22½ minutes duration each in Hindi, Kannada, Oriya and Telugu were telecast on each school day for rural primary school children of 5-12 years age group to make the children realize the importance of science in their day to day life.

SITE experiment showed that the new technology made it possible to reach number of people in the remotest areas. The role of television was appreciated and it was accepted in rural primary schools as an educational force (IGNOU, 2000).

Post-SITE Project (1977)

The target group for this post SITE project was the villagers of Rajasthan. This was a SITE continuity project and was initiated in March 1977 when a terrestrial transmitter was commissioned at Jaipur. The main objectives of SITE continuity project were to:

- Familiarize the rural masses with the improved and scientific know how about farming, the use of fertilizers and the maintenance of health and hygiene;
- Bring about national and emotional integration; and
- Make rural children aware of the importance of education and healthy environment.

This project was also successful.

Indian National Satellite Project (INSAT) (1982)

The prime objective of the INSAT project was aimed at making the rural masses aware of the latest developments in the areas of agricultural productivity, health and hygiene. It was initially targeted at villagers and their school going Children of selected villages in Orissa, Andhra Pradesh, Bihar, Gujarat, Maharashtra and Uttar Pradesh. As a part of INSAT of Education project, ETV broadcasts were inaugurated and continued through terrestrial transmission from 15 August 1982 in Orissa and Andhra Pradesh. Later, other states namely Bihar, Gujarat, Maharashtra and Uttar Pradesh were covered under INSAT service using INSAT-1B in June 1983. In each state, a cluster of 3-4 districts were selected on the basis of backwardness of the area, availability of suitable developmental infrastructure and utilization of existing production facilities.

Besides developmental programmes for community viewing, educational programmes (ETV) for two different age groups of school children (5-8 years and 9-11 years) are telecast daily. A capsule of 45 minutes duration consisting of two separate programmes—one for the lower age group and the other for the upper age group—were telecast regularly. Each programme runs for a duration of 20 minutes with five minutes change over time from one age group to the other. As of today, these ETV programmes are offered in five languages—Oriya, Telugu, Marathi, Gujarati and Hindi—for a large population of primary school children. Programmes telecast in Hindi are being received in all Hindi-speaking states in the northern belt (IGNOU, 2000).

UGC-Higher Education Television Project (HETV) (1984)

University students were the beneficiaries of this project. The University Grants Commission in collaboration with INSAT started educational television project, popularly known as 'Country wide Classroom' on August 15, 1984 with the aim to update, upgrade and enrich the quality of education while extending their reach. Under this programme, a one-hour programme in English on a variety of subjects is presented with the objective of general enrichment for undergraduates, educated public and the teachers as well. An inter-university Consortium for Education Communication (CEC) along with a chain of about 20 audio-visual media Mass Communication Research Centers was set up by the UGC at different institutions in the country, to ascertain high quality of programming for this project. Besides producing programmes at these centers, some programmes are imported from other countries, and are edited to suit the requirements of the Indian students. This project is very popular among students, teachers and other learners.

IGNOU-Doordarshan Telecast (1991)

The IGNOU-Doordarshan telecast programmes, designed mainly for Distance learners started in May 1991. Initially they were telecast on Monday, Wednesday and Friday from 6.30 to 7.00 A.M through the national network of Doordarshan with an aim to provide tele-counselling to students of open universities in remote areas. Owing to the encouraging response from viewers, the frequency of this project was increased to five days a week. This programme is very popular.

Gyan-Darshan Educational Channel (2000)

Ministry of Human Resource Development, Information and Broadcasting, the Prasar Bharti and IGNOU launched Gyan Darshan (GD) jointly on 26th January 2000 as the exclusive Educational TV Channel of India. IGNOU was given the responsibility to be the nodal agency for unlinking/transmission. It started out as a two-hour daily test transmission channel for students of open and conventional Universities. This duration was increased in February to nine hours a day. The time slot transmission was further increased due to good response up to 16-hours by 1st June and by 1st November it turned out to be 19-hours channel. Within one year of its launching, 26th January 2001, it became non-stop daily 24 hours transmission channel for educational programmes. "The programming constitutes 23 hrs of indigenous programmes sourced from partner institutions and one hour of foreign programmes. Transmission of 12 hrs each for curriculum based and enrichment programmes is being made. The programmes of IGNOU CIET-NCERT including NOS are telecast for four hours each, IIT programmes for three hours, CEC-UGC programmes for two and a half hours and one hour each for TTTI and Adult Education." (IGNOU Profile-2002). The signals for Gyan Darshan transmission are up linked from the Earth Station (augmented as one plus one system for redundancy) set up at IGNOU HQs New Delhi, and down linked all over the country through INSAT 3C on C Band Transponder. Although Gyan Darshan has made its presence felt in all Open Universities and most of the prominent conventional Universities/Schools, it still has the potential to reach to the door steps of learners through cable TV network. At present Gyan Darshan through the cable transmission covers about 90 per cent in Kerala, most parts of Tamil Nadu, a few pockets in the North East, Nashik, Ahmedabad and Pune. AsiaNet has been providing it free of cost in Kerala. Efforts are being made to make Gyan Darshan available through terrestrial transmission.

Other Avatars of Educational Television

Television may be used along with other media in distance education for interaction and to support learning materials, depending on the educational system and desired outcomes. Below are some of the possible types of technology integration:

Open Telecast

In Open Telecast, television is the only instrument for learning, and student learning is not monitored. Such Open Telecast has been found most suitable for presentation of abstract mathematical concepts (Ahrens *et al.*, 1975); construction of physical models to represent abstract ideas (Bates, 1975); Natural Sciences; Laboratory based practical demonstrations in the area of science including medical and engineering where experimentation design is complex, costly and some times in accessible; Arts and culture music and drama; Space Sciences; and Community education such as public awareness on developmental issues including public health.

Telecast with Print Support

Television along with the print support may be an appropriate combination to reinforce the concepts dealt in a course-book (Berrigan, 1976 and Kern, 1976). Here printed word may be adopted for Telecast for effective viewing, listening and study skills. It also allows review of material and limits need for distracting and note taking. It enriches and extends course curriculum.

Telecast with print and feedback here the students may submit their assignments to their learning centers for necessary evaluation and feedback, after learning through television supported by print. Learners may also interact with resource person through mail or telephone after viewing the transmission. Teleconferencing has perhaps emerged from this type of interaction. Such a system could also be used to provide learner's feedback to Course developers and resource persons on the effectiveness of lesson.

Group Telecasts

Learner groups may participate in pre and post lesson academic activities and have discussions among themselves. Counselors explain the difficult concepts and encourage learners to participate, which acts as reinforcement to their learning. This stimulates group and cooperative learning. Such experiments have been successful in many countries including India.

Edutainment

Though not as formal learning system, entertainment events provide incidental learning opportunities. Popular formats include the quiz show, soap opera, or dial-in advice shows where topics of general interest like health, sciences, commerce etc. can be taken up.

Tele Text

Tele text is another form of communication system wherein text and graphics are transmitted as digitized signals through air broadcasting or cable channel for display on television set. Here the television functions like a computer terminal for retrieval of textual information and graphics from remote database. In this system, the information is stored in centralized database, sequenced and indexed in the form of pages of text or graphics. The signal can also be transmitted over one-way cable, air via radio vertical blanking interval besides unused TV transmission lines (Johnstone and Carlson, 1998). The digitalized text messages or pages of information are continuously broadcasted in cycle. A viewer can access to all these messages on a given channel in cycle or through control unit.

Development of Tele text was developed in the early 1970s by engineers at the British Broadcasting Company (BBC) and ITC (then known as IBA), the regulating body of commercial networks in the United Kingdom. Although in 1974 general specification regarding teletext was published in UK, but is was year 1976 when first teletext service was put into practice for general public use. While teletext was being developed in England, France was proposing its own system, known as Antiope. This system, first used in 1977, was designed to transmit data over telephone lines, but failed to make use of many of the characteristics of the television signal, however, their another teletext service, Mintel was much successful. During late seventies a Canadian teletext service Telidon was developed, tested, and designed to produce very high-quality graphics. But this facility needed a complex decoder to be put to use, which was not commonly available to the consumer market at that time.

By 1984, as a result of continued development, the teletext system evolved into what is now known as World System Teletext (WST). More than 30 countries now use an enhanced version of WST worldwide, utilizing decoders installed in television receivers, which add little, if anything, to the cost of the sets. The service is available in five levels, with each level showing an increasing array of enhancements and graphics sophistication. The higher levels require more complex decoding devices with progressively larger memories capable of storing great numbers of teletext pages; thus, receivers capable of decoding levels three, four and five may cost somewhat more than their less-sophisticated counterparts. (NCAM, 2002).

Teletext in India The teletext service in India, popularly known as 'INTEXT' (Indian teletext), was started by the Doordarshan Delhi on November 14, 1985. Similar to other teletext system, in INTEXT also the data are organized into pages in the form of text and graphic symbols. The information is pooled and transmitted on a few predetermined lines in vertical 'blanking' interval of television signals. The information is in the form of magazines, each of which contains about 100 pages with details of contents of the magazine appearing on the first page, like news items, sport events, financial trends, timings of arrival and departure of important trains, weather forecast, city engagements, AIR and TV programmes to be telecast, etc. Though, teletext has the potential for delivering educational instructions, no such experiments have been reported in India.

Applications of Teletext

- Teletext uses the television for information display, which is almost universally present in homes or community centers. Thus it has the potential to become mass media for imparting education to students in general and deaf and hard-of-hearing viewers in particular.
- Teletext provides the educational content in a very concise and effective manner and thus makes learning appealing, interesting and less burdensome. Further, the facility of quick updation keeps its viewers informed of the recent happenings. It can be a very good media for career counseling along with providing information about courses-in-demand, hot careers, job opportunities, etc.
- Its use in the area of education, agriculture, weather forecasting, farm management, libraries, and industries etc. would provide effective management of services.

Television in education has undergone many incarnations. It has been used extensively in conventional and distance education formats. The developed countries are taking full advantage of television in education. This has greater scope in developing countries also. The above discussed projects on the use of television in education underline its role and significance for achieving the goals set for education for all.

Closed Circuit Television (CCTV)

Any application of television that does not involve broadcasting for public viewing; the programmes can be seen only on specified receivers connected to the television camera by circuits, which include microwave relays and coaxial cables.

Television transmitted to a particular audience at specific locations via coaxial cables, telephone wires, fiber-optic strands, microwave radio systems, or communications satellites, as compared to open-circuit (broadcast) television intended for the general public. Closed-circuit television applications include information display, remote monitoring, instruction, cable television programming, and teleconferences and special events.

Many types of closed-circuit television systems produce pictures intended for distant viewing. These images may include those taken from a space probe passing close to a distant planet, or pictures of blast furnaces or other industrial operations that could be hazardous to human observers. The low cost of modern video equipment makes practical the use of small cameras to observe sleeping children at home and to enjoy video images of people far away while chatting with them on the Internet.

Many universities and school systems employ television for teaching. Classrooms may be equipped with closed-circuit television cameras, recorders, and receivers. Lesson material is often presented via video tape recordings, CD-ROMs, or DVD recordings. In other cases, classroom receivers are supplied with signals from specially reserved broadcast channels, cable television channels, or satellite channels. Audio circuits installed at viewing locations sometimes allow two-way conversations between lecturer and students.

The standardized television broadcast system used at present in the United States, Canada, Mexico, Japan, and some other countries was devised in the 1950s by the National Television Systems Committee (NTSC). Closed-Circuit Television systems are not required to use NTSC signals, but many do, mainly for economic reasons. If the transmission path to the viewer is of low quality, however, the signal can be modified to meet more closely the characteristics of the transmission system. For example, channel bandwidth can be reduced without loss of image resolution if the user accepts a rate lower than the normal 30 frames per second in the representation of image motion. This is called slow-scan closed-circuit television.

Other applications require high image resolution, great sensitivity to light, and the ability to respond to infrared or ultraviolet light, or very rugged system components. Closed-Circuit Television requirements for high-resolution display can be satisfied by increasing the number of image scanning lines and the overall video channel bandwidth. Industrial standards exist for high-resolution closed-circuit systems.

The digital revolution has affected the design of all kinds of television equipment. Video signals can be converted into digital form and processed by specialized computers, called digital signal processors. In closed-circuit television applications, digital processing can make transmission via the Internet practical and can also provide image enhancement. The advanced television systems now entering service make use of the advantages of digital signal processing to provide high-quality images to the home, to the classroom, and to industrial locations.

Television programming transmitted by cable to specific receivers intended for a select audience. Political groups or candidates will often take advantage of a closed-circuit television system and plan fund-raising events around programmes to be shown only to invited guests. Also, live sporting events, such as boxing matches-particularly title bouts-will frequently be televised only on closed-circuit television and shown in specific locations. Tickets are sold to prospective viewers, who will be able to see the event on a television monitor at the location. Some large companies now conduct business meetings on closed-circuit television.

Closed-Circuit Television (CCTV) involves the use of video cameras to produce images for display on a limited number of screens connected directly to a non-broadcast transmission system (e.g., a network of cables). Commercial Cable TV is, technically, an example of CCTV, but the term "closed-circuit TV" is generally reserved for systems serving a small number of screens that are monitored for security purposes. CCTV is a ubiquitous feature of institutional security systems. It is employed by prisons, banks, urban police forces, airports, military organizations, utilities, large corporations, various other organizations, and wealthy individuals. Some specific applications of CCTV are:

- X-ray baggage-inspection devices at airports.
- Remote viewing of dangerous industrial processes, rocket liftoffs, and other operations.
- Perimeter security around power plants, military installations, warehouses, police stations, and other defended facilities.

- Intrusion or theft monitoring of secure spaces, whether indoors (halls, lobbies, specific doors and rooms, etc.) or outdoors (parking lots, automatic teller machines, loading docks, etc.).
- Monitoring of vehicular traffic for traffic-control purposes or detection of illegal activity (speeding, smuggling, etc.).
- Identity-checking of persons desiring entry into a building.
- Computerized recognition of individual faces, with possible identification of "wanted" persons.

Two of the most important CCTV applications are discussed in more detail below.

Perimeter Security

Prior to CCTV, in order to secure the perimeter of an area, it was necessary to post guards in such a way that their lines of sight covered the entire circumference of the area. With CCTV, it is possible to reduce the number of personnel needed to secure a perimeter by placing TV cameras at strategic points and transmitting the resulting images to a control room where a few guards can monitor many screens. Ideally, these observers will note any suspicious event on their screens and alert a response team. CCTV has thus for decades been a component of the typical Perimeter Intrusion Detection System (PIDS), which combines CCTV with devices designed to detect intrusion by other means (ultrasonic movement detectors, window alarm-contacts, etc.).

CCTV technology, however, has not proved as effective in PIDS applications as was once hoped. As vigilance studies by psychologists confirm, guards who spend hours "screen gazing" at static scenes (> 20 minutes, in tests) tend to become bored and less efficient, and are then likely to miss low-frequency events, such as a figure running up to and climbing over a fence. In the words of Geoff Thiel, a British CCTV-security expert, "Contrary to popular belief, impressive control rooms with large banks of monitors generally do not provide an effective "real time" surveillance service. The vast majority of installed CCTV cameras remain unwatched and incidents are not likely to be detected while they are occurring."

Starting in the 1980s, designers sought to combat the bored-guard effect by using automatic Video Motion Detectors (VMDs). These devices are designed to automatically detect scene action by comparing successive image-frames for changes. When change is detected that exceeds a predetermined threshold, an alarm is sounded. A guard then judges whether the alarm is false or valid.

VMDs, however, have not turned out to be a security panacea. There are too many sources of image change, especially in outdoor scenes, for a simple circuit to distinguish meaningful intrusions from nuisance alarms: shifting shadows, wind-shaken foliage, birds, rodents, blowing trash or leaves, camera movement, camera auto-iris adjustments, and the like. Faced with frequent false VMD alarms, guards tend to ignore the system altogether. VMD use is therefore restricted to artificially-lighted indoor spaces or to expensive systems that employ computer processing to reduce the false-alarm rate.

In the 1990s and beyond, artificial intelligence techniques—in particular, expert systems—have been combined with VMD to increase the effectiveness of CCTV. An expert system applies higher-level processing to information extracted from the pixels of the raw CCTV image in order to identify and track objects, usually including human intruders. Such systems are a definite improvement over simplistic VMD, and have proven their potential to ignore waving tree-limbs and rabbits hopping over lawns. However, progress remains slow, as in all artificial-intelligence efforts to navigate uncontrolled, complex, real-world situations. A large number of explicit classification rules, for example, must be generated to enable a programme to "understand" a given scene—and a scene may change its appearance radically depending on weather (e.g., fog, snowfall, rain), time of day, number and type of cars in the parking lot, and numerous similar factors. It is, therefore, difficult to make a PIDS expert system expert enough to be authentically useful. PIDS designers continue to emphasize that there is no near prospect of intelligent CCTV systems outperforming human guards, with all their weaknesses.

Public-Surveillance CCTV

Surveillance by police of sidewalks, train stations, courtyards, parking lots, and other public spaces has proliferated rapidly throughout Europe and the United States during the last decade, propelled largely by the increased availability of inexpensive electronics. Many major cities, including Copenhagen, London, New York, and Washington, D.C., now possess public-surveillance CCTV systems, most often operated by police departments. In some cases, images from these systems are being processed using facial recognition systems (also termed biometric systems, from the Greek for "life measurement"). Facial recognition systems are software algorithms that seek to extract telltale facial features from video images and match faces in photographs to those in a database. Public-surveillance systems are thus advertised as serving two basic purposes, deterrence of crime in watched areas and identification of wanted persons.

Such systems have been criticized on several grounds. In Britain, where public-surveillance CCTV has been in use since the 1980s, studies have cast doubt on whether CCTV has any tendency to reduce crime through deterrence. Crime sometimes decreases in monitored areas, but many criminologists argue that this is because criminals simply move their activities elsewhere. Further, facial-recognition software has an extremely low success rate. Several systems, including ones deployed by the city of Tampa, Florida and by the U.S. Immigration and Naturalization Service, have been abandoned within months of deployment due to their zero or near-zero success rates. Police databases have also occasionally been used by individuals with access for illegal purposes (e.g., stalking exspouses, blackmailing), and public-surveillance CCTV systems, like any powerful surveillance tool, are vulnerable to such abuse. Further, system operators, who are usually male, sometimes use CCTV systems to voyeuristically observe women; a British study found that 1 in 10 women were targeted for voyeurism by the operators of one public-surveillance system. Studies of operators of public-surveillance systems have also shown instances of selectively monitoring dark-skinned persons. Further, powerful surveillance tools may offer a tempting aid to repression of groups such as political protestors. Many aspects of public-space behaviours that are quite legal are nevertheless confidential or at least personal by nature—courtship behaviours, travel patterns, buying habits, lawyer/ client consultations, reading choices, smoking, and more. Many persons dislike the idea of such behaviours being recorded by government officials as a matter of course.

There is also widespread willingness in some countries, however, to give up a large measure of privacy in the quest for security from terrorism. A survey conducted by Business Week in November, 2001 found that 63 per cent of U.S. adults favoured increasing use of public-surveillance CCTV and that 86 per cent favoured the use of facial-recognition software to scan for terrorists in public places (as was done with taped images of over 100,000 attendees at the 2001 Super bowl). CCTV, enhanced by computer processing, will probably play a growing role in both its traditional security applications and in public life in years to come.

19

Information Technology in India

The world is in the midst of a historical transformation at the turn of the millennium. Like all major transformations in history, it is multidimensional: technological, economic, social, cultural, political, and geopolitical. There is a raging debate in the world on the mixed record of the information technology revolution, and of globalization—especially when we consider their social dimensions on a planetary scale. As is always the case with a fundamental debate, it is most often framed ideologically and cast in simplistic terms. For the prophets of technology, for the true believers in the magic of the market, everything will be just fine, as long as ingenuity and competition are set free.

All we need are a few regulatory fixes, to prevent corruption and to remove bureaucratic impediments in the path of our flight to hyper-modernity. For those around the world who are not ecstatic about surfing on the Internet, but who are affected by layoffs, lack of basic social services, crime, poverty and disruption of their lives, globalization is nothing more than a warmed up version of traditional capitalist ideology. In their view, information technology is a tool for renewed exploitation, destruction of jobs, environmental degradation and the invasion of privacy.

Of course, the real issues are not in-between, but elsewhere. Social development today is determined by the ability to establish a synergistic interaction between technological innovation and human values, leading to a new set of organizations and institutions that create positive feedback loops between productivity, flexibility, solidarity, safety, participation and accountability, in a new model of development that could be socially and environmentally sustainable.

It is easy to agree on these goals, but difficult to develop the policies and strategies that could lead to them. Some of the disagreement comes, certainly, from conflicting interests, values and priorities. But a considerable source of current disarray in social and economic policies stems from the lack of a common understanding of the processes of transformation under way, of their origins and their implications. This chapter aims to clarify the meaning of this transformation, particularly by focusing on the processes that are usually considered to be its triggers: the information technology revolution and the process of globalization.

As we shall see, in fact, these two processes interact with others, in a very complex set of actions and reactions. But they offer a fruitful entry point to discuss the connection between the new socio-economic system and the generation of inequality and social exclusion on an unprecedented, planetary scale.

Thus, after having characterized technological innovation, organizational change and globalization, I will analyse the various dimensions of inequality and social exclusion, showing the depth of our social crisis, and I will provide some hypotheses on the reasons for its accentuation in the last decade. I will conclude by proposing a redefinition of the field of social development, appropriate to tackle the issues that condition our capacity to live together in the new context of the "information age." In proceeding along the lines of this argument, I have in mind a variety of data, from reliable sources, that make somewhat plausible the analysis presented here. However, since I have just published a book that brings together many of these data, I take the liberty of referring the reader to it, in order to concentrate here on the schematic presentation (and expanded elaboration) of my argument without repeating the presentation of data sources.

The New Socio-Economic System

Information Technology, Networking, Globalization

In the last quarter of this century, a new form of socio-economic organization has emerged. After the collapse of statism, in the Soviet Union and throughout the world, it is certainly a capitalist system. Indeed, for the first time in history the entire planet is capitalist, since even the few remaining command economies are surviving or developing through their linkages to global, capitalist markets. Yet this is a brand of capitalism that is at the same time very old and fundamentally new. It is old because it appeals to relentless competition in the pursuit of profit, and individual satisfaction (deferred or immediate) is its driving engine. But it is fundamentally new because it is tooled by new information and communication technologies that are at the roots of new productivity sources, of new organizational forms, and of the formation of a global economy. Let us briefly examine the profile of this new world we are living in, which in fact is shared by all countries despite the diversity of their cultures and institutions.

Information and Communication Technology as a Strategic Tool

Information technology is not the cause of the changes we are living through. But without new information and communication technologies none of what is changing our lives would be possible. In the 1990s the entire planet is organized around telecommunicated networks of computers at the heart of information systems and communication processes. The entire realm of human activity depends on the power of information, in a sequence of technological innovation that accelerates its pace by month. Genetic engineering, benefiting from this wealth of information processing capacity, is progressing by leaps and bounds, and is enabling us, for the first time, to unveil the secrets of living matter and to manipulate life, with extraordinary potential consequences.

Software development is making possible user-friendly computing, so that millions of children, when provided with adequate education, can progress in their knowledge, and in their ability to create wealth and enjoy it wisely, much faster than any previous generation. Internet—today used by about 100 million people, and doubling this/number every year—is a channel of universal communication where interests and values of all sorts coexist, in a creative cacophony. Certainly, the diffusion of information and communication technology is extremely uneven. Most of Africa is being left in a technological apartheid, and the same could be said of many other regions of the world. The situation is difficult to remedy when one third of the world's population still has to survive on the equivalent of one dollar per day.

Technology per se does not solve social problems. But the availability and use of information and communication technologies are a pre-requisite for economic and social development in our world. They are the functional equivalent of electricity in the industrial era. Econometric studies show the close statistical relationship between diffusion of information technology, productivity and competitiveness for countries, regions, industries and firms (Dosi *et al.*, 1988). They also show that an adequate level of education in general and of technical education in particular, is essential for the design and productive use of new technologies (Foray and Freeman, 1992). But neither the sheer number of scientists and engineers nor the acquisition of advanced technology can be a factor of development by itself (neither was enough for the Soviet Union—see Castells and Kiselyova, 1995), without an appropriate organizational environment.

IT in India

Information technology essentially refers to the digital processing, storage and communication of information of all kinds.[1] Therefore, IT can potentially be used in every sector of the economy. The true impact of IT on growth and productivity continues to be a matter of debate, even in the United States, which have been the leader and largest adopter of IT. However, there is no doubt that the IT sector has been a dynamic one in many developed countries, and India has stood out as a developing country where IT, in the guise of software exports, has grown dramatically, despite the country's relatively low level of income and development. An example of IT's broader impact comes from the case of so-called IT-enabled services, a broad category covering many different kinds of data processing and voice interactions that use some IT infrastructure as inputs, but do not necessarily involve the production of IT outputs. India's figures for the size of the IT sector typically include such services.

National Informatics Centre

National Informatics Centre of the Department of Information Technology under Ministry of Communications and Information Technology, Government of India is a premier Information Technology Organization in India which is committed to providing state-of-the-art, solutions for the IT needs of the Government of India, State Governments and UTs at all levels.

NIC is providing network backbone and e-Governance support to Central Government, State Governments, UT Administrations, Districts and other Government bodies. It offers a wide range of ICT services including Nationwide Communication Network for decentralised planning, improvement in Government Services and wider transparency of National and Local Governments.

NIC assists in implementing Information Technology Projects, in close collaboration with Central and State Governments, in the areas of

- Centrally Sponsored Schemes and Central Sector Schemes,
- State Sector and State Sponsored Projects, and
- District Administration Sponsored Projects.

NIC endeavours to ensure that the latest technology in all areas of IT is available to its users.

Background

Computers were used on a large scale for the first time during the World War II for military data processing. Its non-military uses gained momentum in the post-war period. India was one of the first countries of the world to utilise the capability of computers in Education, R & D, Planning and National Development. The developments during '50s and '60s in terms of computer resources chronicled here would testify to this trend.

Arrival of Computers in India

1950	First Analog Computer at the Indian Statistical Institute (ISI), Kolkata.
1954	First Digital Computer—HEC-2M developed by A.D. Booth at Birbeek College, London for ISI.
1955	HEC-2M operational at ISI in August.
1958	URAL from the Soviet Union through the United Nation's Technical Assistance for ISI.
1961	First Commercial Computer installed by ESSO Standard Eastern Inc., Bombay (Mumbai).
1962-1964	14 computers in R & D organisation.
1963	IBM 1620 at IIT, Kanpur.
1964	IBM 1401 by IBM for ISI to supplant the above two.
1965	CDC 3600 acquired by TIFR, Mumbai.
1965-1966	30 Commercial Installations.
1966	IBM 7044 at IIT, Kanpur.
1967	10 Honeywell Computers at Department of Statistics, Cabinet Secretariat.
1968	IBM 1401 at IIT, Kanpur.
1969	IBM computer at Planning Commission under a grant of Ford Foundation.

Government of India Initiatives

- After the war with China in 1962, the Government of India realised the importance and felt the need of a strong indigenous electronics base for security and national development and accordingly set up the Electronics Committee (also known as the Bhabha Committee) under the Chairmanship of the renowned nuclear scientist Dr. Homi J. Bhabha. The Committee in its report in 1966 focused on computers as tools "to the development of a new outlook and a new scientific culture" and suggested the establishment of a National Computer Centre and five regional centers.

- The Electronics Committee convened a National Conference on Electronics in 1968 wherein Dr. Vikram Sarabhai, the then Chairman of the Committee, suggested the formation of National Informatics Organisation towards fulfilling the goal of a self-reliant electronics industry.
- Recognising the need for rapid progress in this regard, the Government of India set up a separate Department of Electronics (DOE) with effect from 26th June 1970 with Professor M.G.K. Menon as the Secretary of the Department. The department functioned directly under Prime Minister as a scientific department.
- The Government constituted the Electronics Commission in February 1971 under the Chairmanship of Professor M.G.K. Menon.
- For policy formulation and implementation through meaningful, effective and in-depth studies in the field of electronics including computer industry, an Information, Planning and Analysis Group (IPAG) of the Electronics Commission was constituted in October 1971 with Dr. N. Seshagiri as its Director.
- The Headquarters of the Department of Electronics were at Delhi and those of the Electronics Commission at Mumbai (then Bombay). The IPAG as part of the Electronics Commission was centered at Mumbai.

Objective

The long-term objective of the National Informatics Centre, as approved by the Planning Commission, Ministry of Finance and the Electronics Commission, is 'to establish the feasibility of a system for the provision of detailed information to government ministries and agencies to assist them in making decisions relating to the country's economic and social development planning and programme implementation.' (Annual Report of the Department of Electronics, Government of India, 1977-'78, p. 172.) NIC was set up with the objective to promote economic, social, scientific and technological activities, and also for macro-economic adjustment programme of the Government, through the applications of IT.

The organizational set up of NIC encompasses its Headquarters at New Delhi, State Units in all the 28 State Capitals and 7 Union Territory Headquarters and District Centers in almost all the Districts of India. The Organization employs a large pool of efficient technical manpower.

NIC Headquarters is based in New Delhi. At NIC Headquarters, a large number of Application Divisions exist which provide total Informatics Support to the Ministries and Departments of the Central Government. NIC computer cells are located in almost all the Ministry Bhawans of the Central Government and Apex Offices including the Prime Minister's Office, the Rashtrapati Bhawan and the Parliament House. Apart from this, NIC has various Resource Divisions at the Headquarters which specialize into different areas of IT and facilitate the Application Divisions as well as other NIC Centers in providing state-of-the-art services to the Government.

National Informatics Centre is the nodal Information Technology Organization for informatics development and networking in Government and Government related Organizations.

NICNET facility has been established in all Central Government Departments, 35 States/UTs and over 600 District centers to facilitate informatics development for decision support and information exchange. A high speed NICNET National Info-Highway, an incremental overlay over the existing network had been setup with SCPC, TDMA VSATs, DVB Broadband VSAT Technology and Wireless MAN to take advantage of Internet Technology in India. SATCOM Division has nearly 3000 VSATs connecting all the Districts/States/UTs of India and providing VSAT connectivity to many Government sponsored project like:

- Community Information Centers (CICs) in the Seven North Eastern States, Sikkim and Jammu & Kashmir.
- Department of Agriculture and Cooperation (DACNET) to facilitate "Agriculture-on-Line."
- GRAMSAT—Block level connectivity in Orissa.
- Chhattisgarh e-Panchayat—Connecting 146 Janpad Panchayats and 16 Zila Panchayats.
- Chhattisgarh e-Kosh—Connecting District Treasuries and Sub Treasuries of Chhattisgarh and many more.

NIC has established Informatics Technology (IT) Units in the ministries and departments of the Government of India. A number of IT units comprise an Informatics Division. The division is responsible for interacting with the users, studying their information requirements and arranging for the necessary hardware and software for the MIS support within the ministry/department. While the IT units interact with the end-users and ensure the smooth operation of the equipment and application software, as well as connectivity to NICNET; the division also catalyses projects which can integrate information from the field offices for timely and effective decision making. The latter are implemented by NIC on turnkey basis. These commercial projects are executed by NIC at no profit (cost plus), providing enormous savings to the user departments compared to what would be charged by the commercial software consultants.

Information Systems in Major Sectors

Some of the important Management Information Systems (MIS) implemented in major sectors are:

- Agriculture
- Administration
- Energy
- Finance and Commerce
- Industry and Transport

- Social Sector
- Apex Organisations
- Contracted Projects
- Budget
- Passport
- Patent Information Services
- Biomedical Information Services
- Teletext Application System
- Networks: Closed User Groups over NICNET
- Bibliographic Information Services
- Computer Aided Paperless Examination System (CAPES).

ICT and Education

The emergence and convergence of various ICTs such as radios, televisions, computers, the Internet, telephones, cell phones, videos, multimedia, CD-ROMs, software and hardware provide unique opportunities for promoting primary and secondary education, on a mass scale, in developing nations. There is a general consensus among practitioners and academics that in diverse socio-economic and cultural contexts ICTs can be successfully employed to reach out to a greater number of students and help in promoting learning and knowledge, along with exposing students to the technical skills required for many occupations. Additionally ICTs also serve as useful tools for training teachers, and in aiding them to teach course curriculums to students.

In India, since independence in 1947, various ICTs have been employed to promote primary and secondary education however there have been enormous geographic and demographic disparities in their use. Some states in the country currently have an enabling environment in place that allows for a greater use of ICTs for education, while other states lack such an environment making the use of ICTs for this purpose very sporadic.

National Policies on Education

The National Policy on Education (NPE) released in 1986, which has since been updated with amendments, is the comprehensive policy framework for the development of education in India. The original policy did not specifically mention the use of ICTs for promoting primary and secondary education, but the 1992 Programme of Action (POA) on NPE stressed the need to improve the access to computers in schools. Further, the Working group on Elementary and Adult Education for the 10th Five Year Plan (2002-07) recommended that initially one or two schools in every cluster (a small administrative unit within a block consisting of 12 to 18 villages located at a distance of 7-8 km from each other) in the country should have facilities for computer based learning, which can be used by children in adjoining schools. The Department of Education also released a draft scheme of information and communication technologies in schools in 2004, which called for providing computer-aided education to secondary and higher secondary government schools in partnership with State Governments and the establishment of schools that are technology demonstrators. Both the working group and the draft scheme called for collaborations with the private sector and IT institutes to achieve their stated goals.

Information Technology Act

The Information Technology Act 2000 emphasized technical higher education, which would help students gain employment in the IT industry; and the Science and Technology Policy 2001 called for the teaching of science at school and college levels. However none of these policies specifically mentioned the use of ICTs for primary or secondary education. Nonetheless, the National Task Force on Information Technology and Software Development (IT Task Force) constituted in July 1998 made specific recommendations stating that computers and the Internet should be made accessible to schools, polytechnics, colleges, and public hospitals in the country by 2003. The Ministry of Information Technology further advocated the recommendations of the Working Group of IT for Masses, which called for 10 PCs in each school, local language software capabilities, Internet connectivity in every school, and the inclusion of the private sector in this massive effort.

Information and Broadcasting

India has a rich history of using the medium of radio via the channels of All India Radio (AIR), and television through the national TV network Doordarshan, to broadcast educational content for all grades and levels. The government has also proposed a new FM radio policy, which calls for building hundreds of stations across the country. There is no indication as to what effect this might have on radio broadcasts of educational programmes for primary and secondary education, but the emphasis to cover more of the country's regions under a radio network will undoubtedly create more access to, and opportunities for, educational programming.

Telecommunications

The National Telecom Policy 1999 aimed to provide a balance between the provision of universal service and high end services to meet the country's social and economic needs; however it did not specifically mention the primary and secondary education sectors. The policy had very lofty targets most of which have not been achieved, but by aiming to expand the telecom infrastructure in the country the policy did potentially facilitate the use of ICTs for education. Moreover, the Department of Telecommunications Perspective Plan for 1997-2007 and the Broadband Policy 2004 did accentuate the importance of new technologies in education. Policies are roadmaps and vision documents of what governments aim to achieve in diverse sectors. A common theme in the national policies and directives enumerated above was an emphasis on the use of ICTs for primary and secondary education, even though none of the policies pertained specifically to this field. The promotion of the concept of PPPs, whereby the private sector would be invited and encouraged to partner with the government to play a greater role in providing educational services was also asserted. The National Government also embraced various recommendations that called for attaining specific ICTs related targets for schools, however most of these targets have not been realized in the time frames that were proposed.

National Programmes

Radio was the first ICT to be used for education in India and the nationally sponsored scheme on educational technology provided some radio-cum-cassette players and televisions to a limited number of elementary schools in the country. National level evaluation studies have indicated that the majority of the television sets and radio-cum-cassette players are in working condition though not necessarily in use.

Sarva Shiksha Abhiyan (SSA)

SSA is the Government of India's flagship programme for the achievement of Universalization of Elementary Education (UEE), as mandated by 86th amendment to the Constitution of India making free and compulsory education to the children of 6-14 years age a fundamental right. SSA is being implemented in partnership with State Governments to cover the entire country. The programme also has an innovative activities component for girls' education, early childhood care and education, interventions for children belonging to schedule castes and tribes, and community computer education especially for students at the upper primary school level.

SSA allocates funds to each district in the country for these innovative activities. Specifically for the computer education component SSA aims to create computer awareness and literacy among children and teachers at the elementary stage; to make teaching and learning effective and interesting through computer aided learning; to empower teachers; to generate supplementary material in digitalized and other forms; and to improve the quality of education, enrolment and retention.

Gyan Darshan

Doordarshan's educational channel Gyan Darshan was launched on January 26, 2000 in a partnership with the Ministry of Human Resource Development (HRD) and the National Government affiliated Indira Gandhi National Open University (IGNOU). This channel provides a blend of core curriculum based programmes in the areas of primary, secondary, higher, distance, technical and vocational education. Gyan Darshan 1 is the main channel and includes the countrywide classroom programmes. Gyan Darshan 2 and the Training and Development Communication Channel (TDCC) are one-way video and two-way audio satellite-based interactive systems for distance education. Gyan Darshan 3 is dedicated to technical education.

Gyan Vani

In November 2001 an FM Radio channel, called Gyan Vani, operating through FM stations from various parts of the country was initiated. With 10 FM stations on air in the first half of 2003, the network is slated to expand to a total of 40 stations. Gyan Vani stations operate as media cooperatives, with day-to-day programmes contributed by various Ministries, educational institutions and NGOs. The channel serves as a medium for niche listeners and for addressing local educational, developmental and socio-cultural requirements. The programmes are broadcast in English, Hindi and regional languages.

EDUSAT

EDUSAT, the first Indian satellite designed and developed exclusively for serving the educational sector was launched by the Indian Space Research Organization (ISRO) on 20th September 2004. This system is primarily meant for school and college level education, but it will also support non-formal education. However many implementers from NGOs and academics in the field claim that it is very premature to conclude what benefits EDUSAT can bring to the primary and secondary education sectors.

Teacher Training Programmes

The Government of India has funded a distance education programme to deliver training packages to teachers under the Special Orientation Programme for Primary School Teachers. Further, the National Council for Teachers Education (NCTE) has made technological literacy a compulsory component of secondary teacher education. IGNOU also provides teacher-training courses over radio and TV in select states. The Government of India has initiated various ICTs based programmes for promoting primary and secondary education, nationwide, and continues to explore future opportunities in this regard. Yet the majority of officials interviewed for this study were of the opinion that there was only sporadic use of national radio and television based programmes in the primary and secondary schools in Chhattisgarh, Jharkhand and Karnataka.

Therefore the impact of these National Programmes on the primary and secondary education sectors in these states is quite nebulous. A major exception is the work done by the government-affiliated agencies in Chhattisgarh, Jharkhand and Karnataka who are responsible for furthering SSA's mandates in their respective states. These agencies in turn initiate and fully or partly fund some ICTs based projects. Further as the SSA starting from 2004-05 has started allocating Rupees (Rs.) 5 million yearly to each district in the country for innovative activities, including computer education, there is an increased optimism that more ICTs based programmes and projects will be implemented in the future. The Government of India has and continues to promote the use of ICTs in primary and secondary education by releasing policies and initiating programmes. However the stark reality is that each state in the country is ultimately responsible for addressing its education sector. Thus the onus falls on individual states in the country to create an enabling environment to promote the use of ICTs for primary and secondary education.

ICT and Teacher Education

Information and Communication Technologies (ICTs) have the potential to enhance access, quality, and effectiveness in education in general and to enable the development of more and better teachers in Africa in particular. As computer hardware becomes available to an increasing number of schools, more attention needs to be given to the capacity building of the key transformers in this process, namely, teachers.

The objective of this chapter is to share some of the lessons learned in a project aimed at the training of teacher educators in the integration of ICTs in the classroom.

Based on this reflection, areas of attention in the promotion of the appropriate use of ICTs by teachers are identified.

ICTs are one of the major contemporary factors shaping the global economy and producing rapid changes in society. They have fundamentally changed the way people learn, communicate, and do business. They can transform the nature of education—where and how learning takes place and the roles of students and teachers in the learning process.

Education in the East African region faces a number of problems. These problems include the shortage of qualified teachers, very large student populations, high dropout rates of students and teachers, and weak curricula. All of these negative aspects result in poor delivery of education. The devastating effects of the HIV/AIDS pandemic worsen the education crisis, increasing poverty, a brain drain in the teaching community, budgetary constraints, poor communication, and inadequate infrastructure.

While societies in the region undergo rapid changes as a result of increased access to information, the majority of the school-going youth continue to undergo traditional rote learning. Very little is done to take advantage of the wealth of information available on the Internet. Whereas the processing of information to build knowledge is one of the essential literacy skills vital for the workforce in the 21st century, it is often overlooked in current educational practices.

In order to function in the new world economy, students and their teachers have to learn to navigate large amounts of information, to analyse and make decisions, and to master new knowledge and to accomplish complex tasks collaboratively. Overloaded with information, one key outcome of any learning experience should be for learners to critically challenge the material collected in order to decide whether it can be considered useful input in any educational activity. This is the basis for the construction of knowledge. The use of ICTs as part of the learning process can be subdivided into three different forms: as object, aspect, or medium (Plomp, ten Brummelhuis, and Pelgrum, 1997).

- As object, one refers to learning about ICTs as specific courses such as computer education. Learners familiarise themselves with hardware and software including packages such as Microsoft Word, Microsoft Excel, and others. The aim is computer literacy.
- As aspect, one refers to applications of ICTs in education similar to what obtains in industry. The use of ICTs in education, such as in computer-aided design and computer-aided manufacturing, are examples.
- ICTs are considered as a medium whenever they are used to support teaching and learning.

Technology is not new to education. However, contemporary computer technologies, such as the Internet, allow new types of teaching and learning experiences to flourish. Many new technologies are interactive, making it easier to create environments in which students can learn by doing, receive feedback, and continually refine their understanding and build new knowledge. Access to the Internet gives unprecedented opportunities in terms of the availability of research material and information in general. This availability of research material and information happens to both inspire and threaten teachers.

The computer equipment in the few fortunate schools that have them tends to be underused and lacks appropriate education content. Commonly, the computer equipment is used as objects in computer lessons. A few other subject teachers undertake courses in software packages but are unable to integrate or meaningfully insert this knowledge in their daily teaching work. A worrying tendency is that boys are the targets rather than girls when investments in ICT hardware and training are made (Kinyanjui, 2002). If not taken seriously, this will increase gender disparities in education in the sub-region.

In the education sector, curriculum review efforts are geared towards modernisation, including the incorporation of important ICT components. However, even the reviewed curricula tend to treat ICT as a subject rather than as an application tool that can be used in all other subjects, in teaching and learning. Very recent discourse indicates that future curriculum reviews may consider a fully-fledged ICT mainstreaming process.

Teacher education institutions and programmes have the critical role to provide the necessary leadership in adapting pre-service and in-service teacher education to deal with the current demands of society and economy. They need to model the new pedagogies and tools for learning with the aim of enhancing the teaching-learning process. Moreover, teacher education institutions and programmes must also give guidance in determining how the new technologies can best be used in the context of the culture, needs, and economic conditions of their country. The case study reported below has tried to do just that.

Educational systems around the world are under increasing pressure to use the new Information and Communication Technologies (ICTs) to teach students the knowledge and skills they need in the 21st century. The 1998 UNESCO World Education Report, teachers and teaching in a changing world, describes the radical implications the new information and communication technologies have for conventional teaching and learning. It predicts the transformation of the teaching-learning process and the way teachers and learners gain access to knowledge and information.

To effectively harness the power of the new Information and Communication Technologies (ICTs) to improve learning, the following essential conditions must be met:

- Students and teachers must have sufficient access to digital technologies and the Internet in their classrooms, schools, and teacher education institutions.
- High quality, meaningful, and culturally responsive digital content must be available for teachers and learners.
- Teachers must have the knowledge and skills to use the new digital tools and resources to help all students achieve high academic standards.
- Teacher education institutions are faced with the challenge of preparing a new generation of teachers to effectively use the new learning tools in their teaching practices. For many teacher education programmes, this daunting task requires the acquisition of new resources, expertise and careful planning.

In approaching this task it is helpful to understand:

- The impact of technology on global society and the implications for education.
- The extensive knowledge that has been generated about how people learn and what this means for creating more effective and engaging student- centered learning environments.
- The stages of teacher development and the levels of adoption of ICTs by teachers.
- The critical importance of context, culture, leadership and vision, lifelong learning, and the change process in planning for the integration of technology into teacher education.
- The ICT competencies required of teachers related to content, pedagogy, technical issues, social issues, collaboration, and networking.
- The importance of developing standards to guide implementation of ICTs in teacher education.
- The importance of developing standards to guide implementation of ICTs in teacher education.
- The essential conditions for successful integration of ICTs into teacher education.
- Important strategies to consider in planning for the infusion of ICTs in teacher education and managing the change process.

A number of competencies and skills are required of a 21st century learners, including digital-age literacy. A 21st century student needs to be aware of various tools for digital communication and be able to use them. Recognizing this, the concept of digital-age literacy was taken into consideration when developing the Information and Communication Technologies (ICT) curriculum.

Conventionally, teachers are trained to use a teacher-centered approach, however, in developing the new curriculum for teacher training institutions in Bhutan there was a conscious shift towards approaches that lead to constructivist and independent learning. This shift was made in recognition of the fact that through the use of computers and the Internet new forms of learning can take place, including problem-based learning, project-based learning, and authentic learning using real-life scenarios.

The use of computer technology in education can be classified into three categories.

- Computers can be considered as an "*object*" which students learn about (hardware and software).
- Computer technologies can be an "*aspect,*" which means using them as tools in subjects, such as computer-aided design courses, or as general tools in educational settings, such as the use of graphic design software to create web pages for a school.
- Computer technologies are a "*medium*" for instruction. In this category, computer technologies can be used for teaching and learning.

UNESCO is giving a high priority to the use of ICT for more equitable and pluralistic development in education, aiming to: expand the knowledge base about the issues,

The broad questions on which UNESCO focuses are:

- How can one use ICT to accelerate progress towards education for all and throughout life?
- How can ICT bring about a better balance between equity and excellence in education?
- How can ICT help reconcile universality and local specificity of knowledge? and
- How can education prepare individuals and society to benefit from ICT that increasingly permeate all realms of life?

Several points must be borne in mind as one pursues these questions. First, ICT are only a part of a continuum of technologies, starting with chalk and books, all of which can support and enrich learning. Second, ICT, as any tools, must be considered as such, and used and adapted to serve educational goals. Third, many ethical and legal issues intervene in the widespread use of ICT in education, such as ownership of knowledge, the increasing exchange of education as a commodity, and globalization of education in relation to cultural diversity.

- ICTs have become a driving force of educational reform and they are an integrated part of national educational policies and plans.
- The introduction of ICTs in schools has brought about a more positive attitude to school among learners.
- Online classrooms tend to be more successful if ICT is combined with appropriate pedagogy. The interactive feature of learning resources enable learner to become increasingly engaged in the construction of content and thus contribute to a more authentic learning situation.
- ICTs open a whole world of lifelong upgrading through distance education, asynchronous learning and training on demand. (Distance education is now being delivered in two different ways, namely: Synchronous mode: participants are using ICTs to communicate.
- Asynchronous mode: participants are learning/communicating independently).
- ICTs altering the functions of libraries and are intrinsically change the roles of libraries.
- ICTs help to break the professional isolation from which t/many teachers suffer. With ICT they can easily connect with other professionals, colleagues, and mentors, with universities and centers of expertise and with sources of teaching materials.
- ICTs are used at all stages of Problem Based Learning process to add value to student learning in ways that are not possible in a non-digital environment.
- The term ICT embraces a range of technologies broadly concerned with information and communication. The popular idea of ICT hardware in the classroom or computer suite includes one or more multimedia desktop computers or laptops and a combination of the following; digital camera, printer, scanner, CD writer, data projectors, interactive white board, robot and in science classrooms, data loggers and perhaps digital microscope.

- ICT can support both the investigative (skills and attitudes) and more knowledge based aspects (concepts).
- ICT use can greatly enhance the opportunities for children to engage in effective communication at several levels.
- ICT can improve training by providing access to better educational resources; breaking the traditional isolation of teachers; and enabling individualized training opportunities.
- E-learning provides a way for teachers to gain new knowledge and skills.
- The ease of access of information source develops the research spirit.
- Broader co-operation among individual within and beyond school is enabled through technologies.
- The availability of simulation, virtual-manipulation, graphic representation and rapid merging of data contributes to linkage in knowledge and leads to more integrated and g\better assimilated learning.
- Teacher gain information on new instructional resources and availability of support for their use much more readily with ICT.
- Teacher co-operation with others both within and beyond the school when planning activities.
- The orientation of planning is more towards students performing real works in co-operation with other students.
- Relationship between teachers and students more interactive and guiding rather than transferring information from teacher to student.
- A different vision of teaching and learning; learning seen more as continuous research than body of facts.
- Empowering learners to engage in meaningful challenging and enlightening tasks is the aim of all educators and ICT has a powerful role to play in this in every school, classrooms and beyond.
- The anytime anywhere access to information sources enables students to engage directly with expert sources when they are needed and the sight, sound, touch experience becomes a powerful motivation in learning.
- Today's classrooms need Internet access for research-distributed multimedia, curriculum on-line, access to digital libraries, distance education courses and remote collaboration tools.
- Information on demand for students also includes video, live-video broadcast, desktop video conferencing and 3D modeling.

National Policy on ICT in Education

The progress of our nation depends on the system of education that exists in our country. The aim of education is to mould the future of our nation by moulding young Indians with a balanced and well-rounded education. Over the past few years globalization, rapid technological developments and information explosion is compelling changes in the purpose and nature of education. Education in India is characterized by issues related to access, equity and quality. If India today aspires to emerge as a front-runner among the knowledge based societies, the usage of ICT in providing education of desirable quality can hardly be over emphasized.

While many states have their own ICT policy, it has been felt that a coherent and enabling policy for ICT at the national level would have tremendous benefits for the synergetic growth of our country. The National Policy would need to consist of objectives, guidelines, and practices and must clearly articulate the role of ICT in school education. The most appropriate process would be a consultative one with all the stakeholders—educationists, ICT specialists, policymakers, and communities.

While creating this policy, we need to keep in mind the context of the emerging globalised economy, and position it at the frontier of this transition. This position chapter has been divided into two sections. Section A deals with the Planning Context and Section B deals with the nuts and bolts of the Policy of ICT in Education. Some issues that need to be considered while we are planning the policy for ICT in Educationare:

Globalization

While recognizing the phenomenon of globalization, The National Curriculum—Framework for School Education—2006 speaks of the emergence of learning societies due to the multiplication of sources of information and communication, transformation of the nature of work requiring flexibility, necessity of team work and use of technologies. Integration of technology would have several other implications. This in turn would make demands on educational planners. Media production, interactive video and multimedia computer software shall have to be perceived as an integral component of the curriculum development processes, rather than external to it.

Technological Advancements

Unimaginable changes are happening every single day in the realms of technology. These advancements have been brought about due to:

- Massive installation of undersea fiber-optic cable and bandwidth that have made it possible to globally transmit and store huge amounts of data for almost nothing.
- Second, the diffusion of PC's around the world.
- Third, the convergence of a variety of software applications—from e-mail, to Google, to Microsoft Office, to specially designed outsourcing programmes—that when combined with all those PC's and Bandwidth, make it possible to create immense technological advancements.

Changing Pedagogical Paradigms of the 21st Century

Today's education faces irrelevance unless we bridge the gap between how students live and how they learn. Students will spend their lives in a multitasking, multifaceted, technology-driven vibrant world and they must be equipped to handle the challenges of the 21st century effectively. It is obvious that the old pedagogical framework of de contextualized instructional practices and fixed curriculum is clearly inappropriate. With information having increasingly short shelf life, education must empower learners to learn for themselves, and to continue to do so incessantly. It is important to understand the key learning skills of the future-Interpersonal Skills, Information Skills, Technology Skills, Basic Skills, and Thinking Skills and Learnability.

National Curriculum Framework

The NCF clearly focuses on the child as an active learner. It takes into account the importance of children's experiences, their voices and their participation. The NCF talks of the need for adults to change their perception of children as passive receivers of knowledge and those children can be an active participants in the construction of knowledge. The school should recognize the innate ability of each child to construct his/her own knowledge, and the fact that every child comes to school with a fund of pre-knowledge. The NCF recommends significant changes in Language, Maths, Natural Sciences, and Social Sciences with an overall view to reduce stress, make education more relevant and meaningful. NCF states: "Integration of Information and Communication Technologies (ICT) into schooling needs serious consideration. Teachers, educators, curriculum developers, evaluators and others will have to redefine their roles to tackle ICT rich environment and harness its full potential for the benefit of learners."

Quality of Education

Planning for ICT Policy must definitely keep in mind the quality aspect of education. It is crucial to analyse what "quality" in education means, how it can be assessed and how it can be measured. Research conducted around the world reveals that using standardized quality standards enable schools to move towards organizational excellence. Quality bench marks in the areas of Visionary Leadership, Strategic Planning, Student and Stakeholder Focus, Workforce Engagement, Process Management, and diverse Results have now been accepted. The Criteria are designed to help organizations use an integrated approach that results in delivery of ever-improving value to students and stakeholders, contributing to education quality, organizational stability and personal learning.

Current Challenges for ICT Deployment in Education

- *Professional Challenges:* One of the challenges that face us in this scenario of a paradigm shift from teaching to learning is the professional competence of the teacher. Traditionally teachers have been visualized as repositories of knowledge which they transmitted to the students. Today technology has changed this completely. Yet teachers are not euphoric about the technology revolution. They doubt the potential of technology in meeting instructional goals and they continue to be tied to the 'direct instruction' model.
- *Infrastructure Challenges:* Investment in infrastructure is one of the major challenges in education today. We need to address the following issues when investment matters are raised:
  - Is the technology investment essential to support instructional and educational goals?
  - How do we address the issues of equity? Are all the stakeholders' needs for technology supported without bias to the rural/urban learner the economically deprived learner the differently abled learner?
  - Investment in technology has emerged as a major priority for political

leadership. Along with this policy reforms and educational reform is a precondition for major investment in education.

- *Challenges of Appropriate Content:* There is a need to develop appropriate content which will support learning, teaching and administration local and relevant/ appropriate education content, keeping in mind language, culture etc.
- *Challenges of Appropriate Approaches:* Any ICT policy needs to adopt a systematic and holistic approach in which the following are addressed:
  - Curriculum
  - Assessment
  - Instruction
  - Integration of ICT into the school curriculum
  - Designing a flexible curriculum model which would embrace inter-disciplinary and cross-disciplinary thinking
- *Challenges of Monitoring of Quality of Learning*
  - Challenges due to lack of benchmarks in technology usage: Quality bench marks need to be developed:

    for technology products used in education
    for usage of software and hardware in schools
    for capacity building programmes
    for learning outcomes

An Overview of the Policy Framework as Envisaged

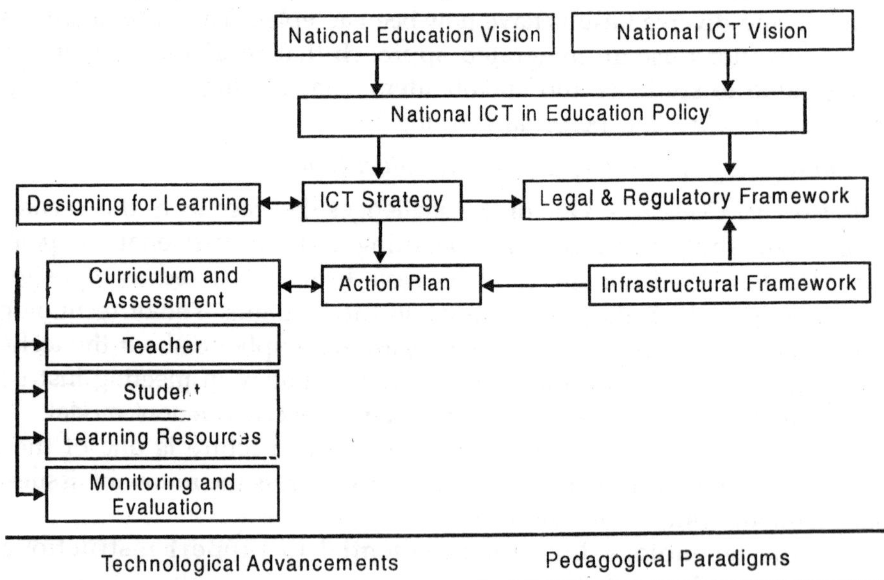

Underlying Philosophy

The ICT in Education Policy is a blueprint for the integration of Information Technology (IT) in education as a strategy to equip our children to meet the challenges of the 21st century. The ICT in Education Policy must:

- continually anticipate the future needs of society, and work towards fulfilling those needs
- develop appropriate ICT skills required for the future based on 21st century skills
- address the issues of:
  - Relevance
  - Effectiveness
  - Efficiency
  - Access
  - Equity

Goals of the ICT Policy Need to be Made in the Areas of

Overall Policy

Policy and Organisational Framework: ICT policy must aim at policy and organisation issues in the education and training community aiming at:

- Educational improvement
- Educational innovation
- Equity
- Educational research
- Resource allocation including funding policies
- Strategic planning for ICT: Strategic plans relating to the use of ICT in education and training
- Educational co-operation between different ministries of Central Government and between centre and state.

People

- *Specialists:* Provision of an adequate supply of people with specialised ICT skills who are required to provide front end and backend support
- *Professionals:* Development of ICT skills for educators and educational leaders/ managers
- *Educational Indicators:* Development of ICT skills accreditation and performance measures.

Equity

- Educational opportunities in order to address equity issues and reduction of inequities in ICT skill levels between rural and urban population, people from all races, economic backgrounds and gender. Access to remote learners who are otherwise deprived of quality teachers.
- Special educational needs, increasingly wide solutions for individuals.

  Infrastructure: ICT policy must addressing infrastructure development, including hardware, communications, and technical support and emerging technologies.

  Content, Applications and Services: ICT policy should aim at development of multiple models of delivering offline and online content and services for the education and training community.

  Regulatory Framework: ICT policy must put into place regulatory issues in the education and training community:

- Educational legislation which supports the effective use of ICT in education and training.
- General legislation from external bodies which impacts on the effective use of ICT in education and training.

Operational Dimensions of ICT Policy

Operational dimensions of any policy enable vision to be translated into reality.

Curriculum, Pedagogy and Content Development

We have to prepare for a future in which information will be increasingly accessible and the renewal of knowledge in many fields increasingly rapid. The school curriculum will have to evolve a better balance between the learning of factual knowledge and the mastering of concepts and processes. Learning would shift from information receiving towards an emphasis on finding relevant information, learning to apply information to solve problems and communicating ideas effectively.

Integrating Technology into the Curriculum and Assessment

- ICT should be integrated into the schools to meet the curricula goals.
- Effective integration of ICT in schools must consider integration issues into both the curriculum and assessment.
- When ICT is introduced into the assessment process, there is a need to reconsider the assessment approaches. There may be a greater role for formative assessment when ICT is integrated into the assessment process.
- Shift in Pedagogy, redesign of curriculum and assessment, and greater school autonomy.
- In order to optimize the potential of ICT, there should be a change in pedagogies, redesign of the curriculum and assessment, and more autonomy for schools. When ICT enters the school environment, everything in the environment has to change to take up the opportunities and address the limitations of ICT.
- The shift in pedagogical approaches should be consistent with the goals and underlying principles of the education system.

Content Development that Supports the Curriculum

- Local development of ICT-based resources is crucial to support the curriculum. It increases the relevance and enhances the authenticity of the resources for the students and teachers.
- In order to develop high quality ICT-based resources, the MHRD should attract well-established education software developers to work with pedagogues. This will also promote the transfer of skills and technologies.
- The ICT-based resources should be customizable so that they will meet the needs of the teachers and students based on their context.

Professional Development (Pre-Service and In-Service)

Teacher training is a key element to education reform; particularly training that focuses on classroom practices and engages teachers in a community of professional practice and development.

Policy in Teacher Training on ICT

- The ICT professional development programme for teachers must plan for the continuous training of teachers—from pre-service teacher education to induction to in-service professional development.
- Train the trainer and fan model could be adopted for the training.
- The ICT professional development programme should focus on both pedagogical and technological aspects of ICT integration.
- Faculty professional development in the teacher education institution is crucial to the success of the pre-service education programme in ICT. There is first a need to re-examine the existing training model with regard to objectives, methods, costs, and effectiveness.

Need for ICT Competencies and Standards before Training

- The application of ICT competency standards allows teachers and students to seamlessly integrate learning materials from a wide range of sources.
- The ICT competency standards should avoid software or product specific skills. Instead, the standards should focus on generic skills of particular applications.

Content Focus of Capacity Building for Pre-Service Teachers

- The ICT professional development programme of teachers should be planned based on the vision of the ICT Policy of the government.
- The foundation course on ICT integration in the pre-service education programme should focus on applying ICT skills to achieve pedagogical objectives, rather than teaching ICT skills in isolation. That is, ICT skills should be learnt within the context of classroom objectives and activities.
- The pre-service teacher education institution should collaborate with private or public ICT training agencies to equip trainee teachers with the basic ICT skills. These agencies are specialists in ICT training and may be more competent and effective in the training. The teacher education institution can work closely with these agencies to develop the curriculum of the workshops, and leave the training to the latter.
- Technology Infrastructure and Connectivity.
- Operational policies must include a provision and budget allocation for technical resources that are needed to accomplish the nation's strategic goals.
- This is typically a policy emphasis in the early stages of a country's use of ICT in education.
- Such plans often include the amounts and type of computer and multimedia hardware that will be purchased but they may also refer to resources related to television and radio, especially in developing countries.
- Increasingly, the Internet and local networking resources are also included, along with a budget for educational software.
- Technical support–Another important operational component is ongoing technical assistance, which teachers need not only in early phases of ICT use

but as hardware and networking technologies become more sophisticated and educational applications become more complex.

Key Implementation Points

The ICT policies in education should be an integral part of the overall ICT plan for the country. The MHRD must work closely with other Government Organizations, especially the MOICT. The ICT policies in education should refine, integrate and expand the scope of the pilot initiatives. For Example:

- Development of a Practical Action Plan for Transforming ICT for Education Policy into Action.
- Creating a Legal and Regulatory Framework for the Use of ICT in Education.
- Obtaining Support of Policy Makers and Other Stakeholders of the Various Departments of the Ministry.
- Management and Financing (national and school levels) ICT in Schools – Policy, Visions and Strategies.
- Supporting School Policies that facilitate uptake of ICT in Schools (School Leadership).
- Parents and Community Involvement.

20

Educational Video Production

Develop the Concept

First, determine the issues you are trying to help teachers address. In other words, what do teachers need? What images do they need to see to bring about changes in their teaching practices or their understanding? What is the guiding principle for the project? For example, in order to illustrate math standards with classroom video, you would need to examine the underlying spirit of the standards and the relationship between content (what is taught) and process (how it is taught).

Research your topic: Know the players; identify the issues, policies, and controversies; and locate the major resources and projects that already exist in this area. You may also want to review the National Staff Development Council (NSDC) teacher professional development standards.

Ask key questions, such as the following:

- Where will the videos be used—for example, on the Web, in teacher professional development workshops, for pre-service teacher education?
- Who is the audience? Be very specific about grade level and level of teacher expertise.
- What is the purpose of the videos? Is it to support curriculum, motivate teachers, encourage reflection on practice, launch professional conversations, and provide teachers with content knowledge? How will teachers use the videos to build on prior knowledge? (Constructivism).
- How will the videos fit in with the on-air broadcast?
- How will the videos fit in with other elements of your educational outreach programme, such as your Website, print materials, or online course?
- What is your budget?
- Do you need to create a schedule that corresponds to the broadcast? To when content is taught? To when school is in session?

Once you have decided that classroom video materials will be part of your educational outreach programme, your first step is to develop the concept for those videos. The process is very similar to the methods you're familiar with for producing any video project. The following questions can help you develop the concept for your classroom videos:

- Where will the videos be used? For example, on the Web, in classrooms with students, for teacher professional development?
- Who is the audience? If students, be very specific about grade level.
- What is the purpose of the videos? Is it to support curriculum, motivate students, provide narrative context for deeper pedagogical content, and provide teachers with content knowledge?
- How will the videos fit in with other elements of your educational outreach programme, such as your Website, print materials, or online courses?
- How will the classroom videos align with the on-air broadcast? Do you need to create a schedule that corresponds to the broadcast?
- What budget do you have available? Based on your classroom video budget, how many minutes can you afford to produce? Can you afford new shooting? Do you have enough money to cover re-clearing rights for third-party materials?

Answers to these questions will inform many aspects of your videos, including length, amount of animation, graphics, use of experts, narration, etc. They will also dictate your production timeline and the size of your production team. Note that the content will need to correlate to national content standards and, where possible, to state standards as well.

In reversioning the broadcast series Building Big, for example, the videos had to be ready six weeks prior to broadcast in order to be packaged for distribution when the broadcast programmes were released. Therefore, the production timeline was compressed.

Design the Project

To determine the project's scope, consider the following questions:

- Is the goal to capture a lot of classroom examples or dig deeply into a few examples? What are the important elements?
- How do students grapple with content, work with each other, and interact with the teacher and the materials?
- How does the lesson develop?
- Is dual-language learning an issue?
- What kinds of rubrics are used?
- How is learning assessed?
- What is the culture of the school community? How do you capture it?

Answers to these questions will help you determine the length of your videos, amount of animation, graphics, and use of experts, narration, and the number of visits you will make to a site. Then, with the project scope in mind, you can create your budget and timeline.

Background Information

Think about whether your guide is for the teacher or the student (as a reproducible), and write accordingly. Include background information only if it's really going to be useful to your audience. Through an evaluation of one such guide, the editors discovered that the 300-500 words of basic background were not enough to adequately explain the subject.

Viewing Strategies

Include suggestions for how to break up your programme's viewing, since most films are too long for typical class periods. Describe opening and closing shots of each segment, estimated time, and provide a brief description of content covered.

Lesson Objectives

Articulating the objectives of a lesson will help both your writer and advisors ensure that all the elements are on track. It will also help teachers decide whether a lesson fits into their curriculum. Include estimated time for the lesson, if possible.

Pre-viewing Discussion and/or Activities

Pre-viewing activities for students prepares them to get the most out of classroom viewing. This can ensure that students have enough background information to understand what they're going to watch. You might ask students to predict, hypothesize, and articulate their pre-viewing opinions. Or you can assign roles for viewing (i.e., one group keeps track of one theme or collects a particular type of information; another focuses on another aspect of the programme).

Post-viewing Discussion and/or Activities

These should tie into pre-viewing activities and then build further. Activities should work for a variety of learning styles and model different teaching and learning approaches, such as cooperative learning or the Five E's. Some teachers will want a completely outlined activity, while others just need a germ of an idea. It's most efficient to provide three to five strong, well-articulated activities or discussion questions.

Standards

Articulating the national and/or local educational standards your activities align with can help teachers justify using your materials and decide how best to incorporate them in the classroom.

Resources

Consider including separate resource and reading lists for teachers and students, if appropriate. These can support educators teaching and students doing activities related to your topic.

Educational outreach toolkits include everything your partners or stations need to know to do educational outreach for your project. These toolkits might include any or all of the following, depending upon your subject and budget:

- Notebook with information about the project, sample press releases, ideas for events and activities, information about partners, logos and graphics, legal and funding information, etc.
- CD-ROM with graphics, photography, sample video, a PowerPoint presentation teachers can use for their own presentations, templates for local funding proposals, press releases, etc.

Print materials, such as teacher's guides, postcards, posters, videos, your trade book, as well as inexpensive giveaways—anything that would help partners or stations implement educational outreach for your project locally.

Assemble the Team

At this stage, you're ready to assemble the project team. As with any production team, you should look for people who can work well together, complement each other's strengths, and have the requisite skills to carry out their jobs. When choosing staff, make sure to people who are sensitive to the issues of working in schools.

This is also the stage at which to recruit advisors, develop their contracts, and hold an advisory board meeting. The board should include a cross section of content experts and practitioners. Clearly define their roles and responsibilities, especially how they can best work with the production team throughout the project. Create written expectations about the review process, such as timelines for reviewing, specific kinds of questions that will be asked, and examples of helpful vs. not helpful comments.

Another aspect of this stage is to provide staff development opportunities for the staff to get steeped in the content. You may want to schedule "content school" led by an expert and/or practitioner for the project staff.

Pre-Production

At this stage you might want to assemble a "kitchen cabinet" of advisors, a mix of classroom practitioners and content experts who can help to refine the concept and suggest key elements to include.

Also during pre-production, assemble the production team. The size of the team will depend upon the scope of the video effort. For example, in the case of Building Big, there were two teams consisting of a producer, an associate producer, and an occasional production assistant.

Refine your production timeline so it correlates with a review process. Review stages should include treatment, rough cut, and fine cut. Intra-organizational staff as well as advisors should be built into the review loops. If required, include funders in the review loop as well.

Carefully review availability of rights for underlying broadcast material. Remember, clearing the broadcast programme for audiovisual use does not necessarily include versioning rights. You should also be aware of WGA and DGA requirements.

At this stage, consult regularly with other members of the educational outreach team for compatibility and integration, including course developers, teacher's guide writers, Website producers, and even graphic designers.

During pre-production, develop criteria for selecting a classroom or field locations to use when you capture the lesson for videotape. Revisit your earlier question: What are you trying to capture? Then develop a process for gathering data from sites. Plan to collect data on many more sites than you will actually videotape.

Also, develop a protocol for how you will approach and communicate with the school representatives, such as the superintendent's office, the principal, teachers, and parents.

Next, survey the sites, and review survey tapes with advisors against their list of site selection criteria.

Once the sites are selected, work closely with the teachers to identify what they are already doing, their strengths, and the needs of your project. Select the dates, times, and goals of your visits for videotaping. All along, remember to get clearances—from parents, teachers, the school district office, etc. In preparation for the shoot days, talk with each teacher to clarify what she will be teaching and how she expects the lesson to progress. Knowing this information will allow you to keep interruptions to a minimum.

Coordinate with others working on the educational outreach components of your project, such as Website or print producers, to determine the artifacts they will need. For example, they may want materials such as student work, teacher-developed materials, textbooks, posters, or assessment instruments, to incorporate into their educational outreach components.

Develop the Treatment

This is the stage in which the project concepts become concrete. Stories, images, and on-camera experts are all built into the treatment development stage.

Research is going full tilt as you look for background information, links to educational standards, on-camera talent, and stock footage. But the paramount focus of this phase is to create the narrative scaffolding on which the final videos will be built. Be prepared for dead ends, story lines that need to be adjusted, and gaps in the visual material you will have.

In terms of style and format, it is important at this stage to be acutely aware of the needs of your audience and the level of prior knowledge they may or may not bring to the material. Remember, these videos are for students, not for a general audience. You may need to take into account grade-level considerations, such as reading and comprehension level. The Building Big broadcast series, for example, presented the controversy around the Citicorp Building in New York, while the reversioned student videos emphasized the engineering solutions that were put into place to correct the building flaws at Citicorp.

This is also the stage when you determine what, if any, new production you will be doing. There is often a need for this. For the Building Big student videos, new interviews were shot with younger experts and experts of colour, and children were interviewed for their perceptions about how skyscrapers are built. Hands-on activities were modeled by parents and children in a second set of Building Big student videos, which, when distributed with the broadcast version, were a valuable extra feature in the home video market.

Production

Once your advisors have signed off on the treatment, you are ready to begin production. This is really no different from the video production with which you are already well acquainted. However, if you expect to stream these videos on the Web, consult a Web producer on the particulars of producing video for the Web. You should also identify your graphic needs and meet with your designer so the graphics will be ready when you need them for post-production.

Idiosyncratic to producing reversioned classroom videos is the interview process. You will want interviewees who can speak succinctly and at a level appropriate to your audience. They may have to carry difficult pedagogical content, so the questions you ask, in some cases, may need to be very direct and almost didactic. For example, in Building Big, an engineer was asked to provide an analogy to describe the foundation of a skyscraper and its structure. He did so by describing the building's foundation as the feet and the structure as the body. Special footage was shot to enhance that description.

At this stage you will also identify your graphic needs. Meet early on with your designer so the graphics are ready when you need them for post-production.

Once you have the treatment (lesson plan) signed off by your advisors, you are ready to begin production. This is really no different from any video production, except that school is in session while you are shooting, so keep the following tips in mind:

- Try to be unobtrusive by setting up before classes start.
- Identify and use a staging area away from classrooms and busy hallways.
- Avoid hallways when classes are changing.
- Try to negotiate the shooting day with the school schedule.
- Schools might also present particular logistical considerations, such as limited power supply, lack of elevators, limited parking, etc.

The general process is really no different from the video production with which you are already well acquainted. But if you expect to stream these videos on the Web, consult a Web producer on the particulars of video production for the Web. You should also identify your graphic needs and meet with your designer so the graphics will be ready when you need them for post-production.

Determine the supporting voices you will need, such as teachers, students, or expert reflections or commentary. You will want interviewees who can speak succinctly and at a level appropriate to your audience. They may have to carry difficult pedagogical content, so the questions you ask, in some cases, may need to be very direct and almost didactic. It is very important for the teacher to define his/her goals.

One final note about the production stage: If you bring an advisor with you to the taping, it is important to clearly define his/her role ahead of time. The onsite advisor should be someone who can easily relate to teachers. Build time into the shoot schedule for advisor input.

Post-Production

Post-production, like production, is no different for reversioned classroom video programmes than for original broadcast programmes. It is always helpful to do a paper cut, assemble materials into a rough cut, and have the rough cut reviewed by advisors. Ask advisors to respond to the tape in writing. They should view the rough cut for clarity, educational rigor, accuracy, and usefulness to the target audience. They may not always agree. Part of your job is to balance advisor responses.

At this stage, be aware that you will have to completely rewrite narration that accompanies whatever material you have taken from the broadcast. The broadcast will have been cut for a different rhythm and, more importantly, for a different audience.

At this stage you will also identify your narrator; choose someone with a tone appropriate for the target audience. Again, as with other productions, you will be building narrative sequences based on the underlying broadcast material, stock footage, stills, and graphics, where needed.

As a final check, advisors should review the fine cut, prior to narration record, music, online, and mix. This review should aim narrower than their previous reviews, as it is meant to catch any last-minute glitches.

Post-production, like production, is no different for teacher professional development videos than for other programmes. It is always helpful to do a paper cut, assemble materials into a rough cut, and have the rough cut reviewed by advisors. Ask advisors to respond to the tape in writing. They should view the rough cut for clarity, educational rigor, accuracy, and usefulness to the target audience. They may not always agree. Part of your job is to balance advisor responses. You may also want to convene a series of focus groups to review the videos.

At this stage, answers to the following kinds of questions will help you further refine your videos:

- Do you need narration?
- How much background information (context) on the school, students, and teacher(s) do you need to provide your audience?
- How much do you let the viewer observe vs. how much do you tell the viewer?
- If you hire a narrator, what is the appropriate tone?
- What are the technical considerations? For example, if you are using an Avid system, how much of the footage do you digitize?
- What resources did the teacher use that you will need to clear?
- What will your video open be?
- Will you have theme music?

As a final check, advisors should review the fine cut prior to narration record, music, online, and mix. This review is meant to catch any last-minute glitches. Finalize your packaging elements, as you would with any other production.

Distribution

Distribution varies from project to project and organization to organization. Be aware of all the materials that comprise promotion and outreach for the broadcast and educational outreach. Provide written descriptions for promotional use to distributors and publicity personnel. Make sure that you provide an adequate inventory of tapes for screenings and promotion. Help the distribution effort by suggesting national organizations, conferences, and publications that may be interested in the videos. Professional organizations like the National Staff Development Council (NSDC) and National Science Teachers Association (NSTA), National Council of Teachers of Math (NCTM), and National Council for the Social Studies are often looking for content to distribute.

Storyboard

Storyboard are graphic organizers such as a series of illustrations or images displayed in sequence for the purpose of previsualizing a motion graphic or interactive media sequence, including website interactivity. The storyboarding process, in the form it is known today, was developed at the Walt Disney Studio during the early 1930s, after several years of similar processes being in use at Walt Disney and other animation studios.

One advantage of using storyboards is that it allows (in film and business) the user to experiment with changes in the storyline to evoke stronger reaction or interest. Flashbacks, for instance, are often the result of sorting storyboards out of chronological order to help build suspense and interest.

The process of visual thinking and planning allows a group of people to brainstorm together, placing their ideas on storyboards and then arranging the storyboards on the wall. This fosters more ideas and generates consensus inside the group.

Shooting Script

A shooting script is the version of a screenplay used during the production of a Shooting scripts are distinct from spec scripts in that they make use of scene motion picture numbers (along with certain other formatting conventions described below), and they follow a well defined set of procedures specifying how script revisions should be implemented and circulated.

Camera Angle and Shots

Television is made up of hundreds and thousands of pictures, called shots, each of which must be carefully planned. To make television programmes more interesting, various types of shots are used.

Camera Distance

There are three main shots describing how near or far the camera is from the subject. A close-up shows only one part of the subject, usually in great detail. Close-ups would include shots of a person's face, or the paws of a dog walking down a path, of a hand on a doorbell, or of a tree branch. A picture showing half of the subject, such as a character from the waist up or the back end of a car, is a medium shot, while a long shot shows the whole subject: a person from head to foot or the entire car. Any of these shots can show one subject or more at the same time.

These three shots are used for specific reasons. An establishing shot at the beginning of a scene tells viewers where they are; for example, a long shot of a car driving up to a hotel or a close-up of a restaurant signs. To show the effect of one person's words or actions on the other people in the scene, a reaction shot is used.

In general, television is a close-up medium: things look better in close-up because the screen is small. However, mixing the shots provides variety and gives information needed to keep the story moving.

Camera Angle

The angle from which a shot is taken is another way to give variety as well as information. A high-angle shot positions the camera above eye-level, looking down on the subject, which consequently appears insignificant, weak, helpless, or small according to how extreme the angle is. At eye-level, the impression is neutral. A low-angle shot has the camera looking up at the subject, which then appears important, powerful, or domineering, again depending on how exaggerated the angle is. Usually the camera looks at the subject, but occasionally the camera shows what the subject is seeing. There is a reverse-angle shot.

Camera Moves

Another way to give television programmes variety is for the camera to move. When the camera changes its position by moving left or right, this is called tracking or trucking. Changing the camera's position by moving it forward or backward is known as dollying. When the camera stays in the same position but turns left or right, this is panning, and when it turns up or down, this is known as tilting. Even when the camera is stationary and not turning it can appear to move closer to or further from its subject; by using a special ring or lever on the lens, the camera person can zoom in or out.

Although these moves are useful, they should not be overused or they will lose their effect. In fact, any camera movement must be planned and rehearsed so that it will be smooth and in tune with the action.

Camera Shots

A camera shot is the amount of space that is seen in one shot or frame. Camera shots are used to demonstrate different aspects of a film's setting, characters and themes. As a result, camera shots are very important in shaping meaning in a film. Reviewing the examples on the right hand side of this page should make the different camera shots clearer.

An **extreme long shot** (animation on right) contains a large amount of landscape. It is often used at the beginning of a scene or a film to establish general location (setting). This is also known as an establishing shot.

A **long shot** (animation on right) contains landscape but gives the viewer a more specific idea of setting. A long shot may show the viewers the building where the action will take place.

A **full shot** (animation on right) contains a complete view of the characters. From this shot, viewers can take in the costumes of characters and may also help to demonstrate the relationships between characters. For more information on costumes and acting refer to Chapter 4.

A **mid shot** (animation on right) contains the characters or a character from the waist up. From this shot, viewers can see the characters' faces more clearly as well as their interaction with other characters. This is also known as a social shot

A **close-up** (animation on right) contains just one character's face. This enables viewers to understand the actor's emotions and also allows them to feel empathy for the character. This is also known as a personal shot.

An **extreme close-up** (animation on right) contains one part of a character's face or other object. This technique is quite common in horror films, particularly the example above. This type of shot creates an intense mood and provides interaction between the audience and the viewer.

When analysing a film you should always think about the different camera shots and why they are being used. The next time that you are at the cinema or watching television see what camera shots are being used.

Important

These camera shots are used in all forms of visual texts including postcards, posters and print advertisements.

It is important that you do not confuse camera angles and camera shots. Camera shots are used to demonstrate different aspects of setting, themes and characters. Camera angles are used to position the viewer so that they can understand the relationships between the characters. These are very important for shaping meaning in film as well as in other visual texts.

The following examples will help you to understand the differences between the different camera angles

A bird's eye angle (animation on right) is an angle that looks directly down upon a scene. This angle is often used as an establishing angle, along with an extreme long shot, to establish setting.

A high angle (animation on right) is a camera angle that looks down upon a subject. A character shot with a high angle will look vulnerable or small. These angles are often used to demonstrate to the audience a perspective of a particular character. The example above demonstrates to us the perspective or point of view of a vampire. As a viewer we can understand that the vampire feels powerful.

An eye-level angle (animation on right) puts the audience on an equal footing with the characters. This is the most commonly used angle in most films as it allows the viewers to feel comfortable with the characters.

A low angle (animation on right) is a camera angle that looks up at a character. This is the opposite of a high angle and makes a character look more powerful. This can make the audience feel vulnerable and small by looking up at the character. This can help the responder feel empathy if they are viewing the frame from another character's point of view. As with camera shots, you will be able to see many examples of camera angles in any film or visual text that you view. The next time that you watch television or see a film, take note of the camera angles and think of how they affect your perception (idea) of different characters.

Another camera angle that you might come across is a Dutch angle. A Dutch angle (animation on right) is used to demonstrate the confusion of a character. The example above should disorientate you.

Camera Movement

Composers of films also use camera movement to shape meaning. The following are some examples of common camera movements and how they can be used to shape meaning in films.

A crane shot (animation on right) is often used by composers of films to signify the end of a film or scene. The effect is achieved by the camera being put on a crane that can move upwards.

A tracking shot and a dolly shot (animation on right) have the same effect. A tracking shot moves on tracks and a dolly shot is mounted on a trolley to achieve the effect in the example above. This camera movement is used in a number of ways but is most commonly used to explore a room such as a restaurant. By using a tracking shot or a dolly shot the composer of a film gives the viewer a detailed tour of a situation. It can also be used to follow a character.

Panning (animation on right) is used to give the viewer a panoramic view of a set or setting. This can be used to establish a scene.

Others

An Evangelion shot (animation on right) is derived from the popular anime series 'Neon Genesis Evangelion'. This camera movement begins as an extreme close-up and zooms out abruptly, creating a blurring effect to emphasise the speed and size of the object

Lighting

Lighting is a very important aspect for shaping meaning in films. What kind of atmosphere is created in a room lit by candles? Have you ever heard of mood lighting? A room that is brightly lit by neon lights might seem to be sterile or a shadowy room might be eerie or scary. The lighting technicians in a film crew have the task of creating lighting to suit the mood and atmosphere of each scene in a film.

Consider the animations Lighting example one, Lighting example two, Lighting example three and think about what type of atmosphere is created in each.

For each example, do you think the lighting suits the characters in the frames? For instance, in Example Three the two people are very happy and the scene is lit brightly. What would be the effect on the atmosphere if the lighting were dark and shadowy, similar to Example Two?

Remember that lighting is used in still image visual texts as well as in films.

Cinematography

Cinematography is the combination of the techniques described in this chapter. This includes camera shots, camera angles, camera movement and lighting. Use the term cinematography to group all of these together, for example, 'The cinematography in that film was exceptional.

Mise en scene refers to all the objects and characters in a particular frame. More specifically, it refers to the composition of the frame. When you use the term mise en scene, you are discussing where the composer or director has placed all the elements of the scene within the frame.

WRITING A SCRIPT

Having selected a topic, considered your audience and formulated your objectives, you are ready to begin writing your script. There are three basic types:

Full Script—every word and shot are scripted with cues to shot changes or transitions.

Semi-Script—typically used in education where shots are planned but only in cues to next shot or transition are scripted.

Shot or Run Sheet—lists the basic shots with much determined during the shooting.

Bottom Line—the more organized at the front end, the easier to edit and complete the production with less likelihood for forgetting something during the production.

The Scripting Process

- Select an introductory statement that explains to your audience what your programme is about.
- State your objectives, e.g., "This programme will enable you to, Cite the indications and contra-indications for......, List and describe steps in the procedure for........., etc.
- Introduce the content for objective 1 and discuss it. After covering the information, you may want to summarize what you've said or elicit a response from your audience by asking a question. For example: "We have discussed the 4 types of teeth found in the mouth of an adult male, name them (or show an example and ask, name this tooth). Follow this question with the correct answer. It is best to engage the audience on a regular basis to maintain their attention. It is also better to use questions intermittently rather than present a long list of questions at the end of the programme.
- Introduce the information for objective 2 and discuss it. Again, after covering the material, you may wish to summarize or ask a question. In cases where the material for a specific objective is relatively brief—you may want to wait until you have covered several objectives before summarizing your material—and ask one question or more combining the information. For example, in step 2 with a patient having this condition (show example) what would be the instrument of choice for attending to this condition. This is assuming students know the indications and contra-indications for the procedure, the steps in the procedure and the instruments and what particular instrument is appropriate for this condition. Again, follow the question(s) with the correct response.
- Continue this procedure for each objective.
- Having covered all the objectives, you may want to:
  - provide a concluding statement about your topic in general; or
  - ask several questions over all the material covered;
  - restate the objectives, e.g. having completed this presentation, can you, Cite the indications and contra-indications for this procedure; List and describe the steps in the procedure, etc.

Check List

- What are you trying to teach? It may need to be divided up, e.g. handout for definitions of terms used in the procedure; a list of the armamentarium used during the procedure. The video is then used to demonstrate the procedure or technique without extending the length of the presentation trying to incorporate all the information into a single format.
- Consider your audience - what do they KNOW about what you're teaching and what do the NEED to know. For example does the audience know the names of the instruments being used, the names of the teeth being treated or have they already learned this information. If so, you don't need to emphasize this information during your video presentation.

- Formulate objectives using behavioural terms, e.g. cite rationale for procedure, list and describe steps, demonstrate technique. Behavioural terms are used because they are behaviours that can be evaluated. Ambiguous terms should be avoided, e.g. understand, get a feeling for, appreciate, because these terms are difficult to observe and evaluate. Objectives create the basis for assessing student performance. It is suggested that you integrate questions based on your objectives into your presentation to keep the student engaged. Check the following for more information.
- Follow steps above for getting started with your script.
- Consider titles, graphics and photos you may want to use to emphasize points during your presentation. These will need to be reviewed to make sure they are "visuals" (easy to read or view) rather than "visibles" that may be seen but are difficult to read or interpret. Consider copyright when using visuals obtained from another source. For a Crash Course in Copyright check this link.
- Consider location—video needs proper lighting and space to accommodate equipment. This should be checked before your "shoot."
- Consider what you will need to do your video, patient, student, assistant, materials, instruments, retractors mouth mirrors etc. and have them ready to go.
- Schedule—is scheduling of space for video necessary? Is there enough time to complete the production? Will a patient be needed and need to be scheduled or will you use another faculty member or student?
- Do you have a signed permission to videotape or photograph the patient and to use these for educational purposes? This is usually a part of the information collected at the time patients are screened...but is worth checking.
- Narration—will you be doing narration at the same time or have someone else do it as you do the procedure or technique? Will you do the narration at a later time? If at a later time...you will need enough video during the taping to cover what will be said. If your segment is 5 seconds long and your description is longer...this makes things difficult. You can lengthen a segment with the use of graphics or photos, but it is better to shoot additional footage, just in case.
- It is difficult to do "real time" narration, as you are trying to execute a procedure and talk meaningfully about it at the same time. You can try this and later decide to do a "voice over." Narrating as you do the procedure (whether used for the final or not) helps you pace your presentation and gives you adequate footage if you do "voice over."
- Avoid "white" if possible, e.g., gloves, bib, models, surface for the demonstration. If possible use blue or other muted colours. White has a tendency to cause the camera to "stop down" when it comes into the scene...as we generally use the "automatic gain control" to keep the image exposure balanced.
- Editing using new technology has become so much easier...yet it still takes time. The process is speeded up by good planning.

Core and Optional Modules

Script Writing (Optional)

Suggested Time: 10 hours

Level: Intermediate and Advanced

Module Overview

In these module students will be introduced to the challenges of script writing for audio, video, or multimedia. Although the module length does not allow for extensive study, it will give interested students an opportunity to learn the basics of structure and formatting. Students with a keen interest in script writing should take Creative Writing 20 and arrange with their teacher to write a script as one of their projects.

Storyboarding is one way of organizing and planning a production. Storyboarding focuses the students' attention on the progression of visual elements. The script is a much more detailed planning device that combines visual and text elements (for video production) or sound effects and text (for audio production). Because it will not be possible to explore all forms of script writing in this module, most activities focus on dramatic writing. Learning about the elements of dramatic writing will help the student who wishes to produce:

- a radio drama
- a video drama
- a structured documentary with text bridges and/or dramatization
- a public service video with dramatic segments (e.g., SADD video)
- Dramatic video or audio segments for multimedia production.

Equipment/supplies: access to word processing equipment, books on script writing.

Foundational Objectives

To gain a rudimentary knowledge of the craft of writing scripts for audio, video, or multimedia production.

Common Essential Learning Foundational Objectives

- To use language for differing audiences and purposes that is relevant to the students and to Communication Production Technology.
- To promote both intuitive, imaginative thought and the ability to evaluate ideas, processes, experiences, and objects in meaningful contexts.

Learning Objectives	*Notes*
To appreciate the importance of a good script in achieving a high quality product. To compare and evaluate what is being viewed.	Contact Saskatchewan and Canadian organizations to find out the names of recent films/videos that have won awards for their scripts (e.g., contact Saskatchewan Film pool Co-operative, Video Verity, Yorktown Short Film and Video Festival, National Film Board). Check with your school board to see if it has purchased a license for public performance with a film/video distributor or collective.

Contd...

Learning Objectives	*Notes*
	Preview all films/videos you propose to show students. All of the above organizations should be able to tell you how the films/videos can be accessed for educational purposes. View one or more of the short films or videos that have won script awards. Discuss why the students think the film/video won the award for its script. How would a good script have affected the finished product? List the students' ideas about characteristics of a good script.
To gain knowledge of the elements of dramatic script writing. To critique films, videos, or radio dramas.	As most (although not all) students who wish to work from a script will be producing some form of dramatic script, this section of the module explores the elements or components of dramatic script writing. There are many good books on the subject. Refer to the bibliographies for this course and secondary level English Language Arts and Arts Education. The Creative Writing 20 curriculum guide has much information on the elements of story writing, which can be adapted to suit the purposes of video or audio stories. Topics commonly discussed include: ■ setting ■ character ■ plot (cause and effect) ■ dialogue ■ atmosphere ■ theme ■ genre. The student writer will need to decide: ■ Where is the story set? ■ How will the setting affect the characters? ■ Who is the story about? ■ What happens? What incident causes something to happen? What are the consequences? ■ What parts of the story can be shown visually? ■ What will the role of dialogue be? ■ What atmosphere will be established? How? ■ What is the story's theme? ■ Will the story be any particular genre (mystery, thriller, romance, etc.)? View or listen to a dramatic film, video, or radio drama. Discuss the above elements. Answer the above questions.
To learn that plot involves characters, their actions, and consequences of their actions.	Referring to the same film, video, or radio drama, focus on the characters and the plot, and determine how the two are connected. Have the students look for actions of the characters in response to an incident or starting point, and then examine how the characters' actions lead to other

Contd...

Learning Objectives	*Notes*
	complications in the plot. Plot is composed of characters, actions, and consequences.
To begin developing the plot for their own script. To organize information.	Have students begin work on their own script by writing down their Story idea in a few sentences. Have them draw a concept map or web of how the story might develop. Have them consider all of the components listed above. Have them think about ways their plot could develop.
To learn the meaning of text and sub-text in dialogue. To apply conclusions and generalizations to new situations.	Study a page or two of dialogue from a published screen-play. Discuss the concepts of text and sub-text. Explain that dramatic dialogue is seldom about what it appears to be about on the surface. Have students write a page of dialogue between two characters in their story idea, following these guidelines: ■ Their dialogue should have text and sub-text. For example, two teenagers might be talking about the basketball game (text) when they are really checking each other out (sub-text). In a mystery, a private investigator might be asking someone about the basketball game when he's really trying to find out if his suspect has an alibi. ■ Their dialogue should have a purpose connected to moving their story forward. No dialogue should use camera or audio time without doing duty for the story. ■ In the case of video, their dialogue should not do a job that can be done visually. A character does not need to say, "I see a car coming." The camera can show that. In the case of radio drama, the dialogue should not do a job that a simple sound effect can do. A character does not need to say, "I hear thunder."
To explore the concept of structure in script writing. To discover relationships and patterns.	In this module, students will have time for only a brief introduction to structure, a full understanding of which would take many hours of study and practical experience. Most commercially successful movies with which students are familiar follow a three-act structure. Although some independent filmmakers use less traditional structures, it is probably a good idea for students to begin with three-act structure, even for a very short video or audio story. Three act structure can be explained as follows: Act 1. The first act is short and shows the audience the situation in which the story begins. Marcia happily delivers papers in her suburban neighbourhood every morning at 6 AM. One of her customers is a nice elderly man who is always up when she delivers his paper. At the end of the first act, something happens that throws the situation into

Contd...

Learning Objectives	*Notes*
	chaos and forces the character(s) to make a decision. Marcia sees a UFO, which quickly disappears. A reporter careens around the corner and tells Marcia the elderly man reported seeing a UFO and asks Marcia if she's seen it. Marcia is afraid of being laughed at and tells the reporter that she didn't see anything. End of Act 1. Act 2. The second act is the main part of the story and follows the consequences and complications of the character's decision. The elderly man who says he saw a UFO becomes a laughing stock. Marcia feels sorry for him and sends an anonymous letter to the paper saying she also saw a UFO. The paper traces the letter to Marcia's house. She admits to seeing the UFO, but now no one will believe her and she gets accused of writing a hoax letter. Marcia doesn't know what to do. Both she and the elderly man are now being laughed at. Marcia starts carrying a camera so she can take a picture if she sees the UFO again. At the end of Act 2, something happens that sends the story to a rapid conclusion. This is called the climax. Marcia is out delivering papers. The moon is still visible. She sees the UFO again. The man is there too. They take a picture. They now have their proof. They talk about how beautiful and mysterious it is, and how lucky they are to have seen it. The man says, "I never should have told anyone." They see the reporter coming. The UFO zooms off. They look at each other. The reporter asks them if they saw anything. Marcia hides her camera. They both say they've only seen the moon and they've decided that's what they saw the first time. Act 3. The third act moves quickly to a conclusion, based on the actions at the end of Act 2. The reporter leaves. The story cuts to Marcia placing her photograph in an envelope and delivering it to the man, along with his paper. End of Act 3. For homework, have students watch a movie, television drama, situation comedy, or cartoon that they like. Can they identify three acts?
To develop a story treatment using a three-act structure.	Have the students develop their story ideas in paragraph form using a three-act structure. This is called the treatment.
To learn about the components of a "shooting script." To critique texts.	Video scripts are taken to the "shooting script" stage. In practice, this is not always done by the writer, but sometimes by the director who wants to make his/her own decisions about shots and camera angles. Who prepares the shooting script depends on the relationship between the writer and director. Radio dramas are usually taken to the final stage by the writer, in consultation with the producer/director. The final script includes cues for sound and music.

Contd...

Learning Objectives	*Notes*
	Have students examine a shooting script so that they can see the kinds of decisions that can be made prior to the actual shooting of the drama. The care taken at this stage can save those hours of time later; in production, time is money.
To examine acceptable formats for scripts based on common industry practice. To summarize information in a variety of ways.	Have small groups of students research formats for different types of scripts. Include dramatic scripts, radio dramas, nonlinear multimedia scripts, documentaries, etc. (Stories Made for Radio, Coteau Books, Regina, contains several produced radio drama scripts.) Have the groups present to the rest of the class. Compile a reference binder of format examples to which student can refer when they are writing and formatting their own scripts.
To write a short script for audio, video, or multimedia. To use writing to record their ideas.	Have students develop a short script. It would be especially useful for students to develop the script for one of their production projects (10, 20, or 30 level).

21

Information Technology Changes and Challenges

The Nature of Technology

- It can be exhilarating and terrifying.
- In general, the public supports technology—in spite of disasters (nuclear reactors, the Challenger).
- In general, most of us are poorly informed about how technology actually works.
- All technologies have some basic features in common.

Defining Technology

- "Technology" is a fairly new word—coined by Jacob Bigelow (Harvard, 1820's).
- Technology—techno (Greek) art, craft, or skill and logos: knowledge.
- Teks (Indo-euro) weave or fabricate.
- Technologies are developed to help us do something we otherwise couldn't do.
- Our ability to create technology sets us apart from other animals.
- A system based on the application of knowledge, manifested in physical objects and organization forms, for the attainment of specific goals.

Features

- Reliance on technology is as old as the human race.
- Technology is a Cultural Element.
- It shapes us and at the same time is shaped by us: Socio-Cultural Change.
- Tools and techniques have indisputably assisted the physical survival of the human race.
- But technology has not spontaneously appeared. Certain elements have made technology possible.
- Organization—development of technology requires a group effort.
- One individual may be able to learn all the parts of a technology but one can not do every task required to make a technology work.
- It's a System—technology has to be supported by other components.
- History of technology full of examples of inventions looking for problems to solve.

- New technology often creates its own needs.
- Goals achieved through technology don't always have to be "practical" ones.
- New technologies often developed as a symbol of prestige.
- "The development of technology is an inherently dynamic and cumulative process.
- Leaving aside social concerns, technological change is usually one of continuous improvement of existing technologies.
- We can always make things better and faster.
- This dynamic, progressive element of technology makes it a unique human endeavour.
- Technology represents humankind's dream of continual progress.
- Some countries may be advanced technologically, but not in other human endeavours such as equal distribution of goods and services and social justice.
  - Nazi Germany—developed the Mercedes but murdered millions of Jews and others
  - Primitive societies—advanced artistry and social relationships, but little technology as we think of it
- Thus, the notion of "progress" is complex and can only be understood in the context of a given set of cultural beliefs and values.

Technology as a Metaphor

- Technology—metaphor of our human notion of continual progress.
- Technology has also shaped the way we think about our world and ourselves.
- A method of controlling a system by reinserting into it the results of its past performance.
- It is a regulation device, that when used will help an unbalanced system gain its equilibrium.

Technology and Rationality

- Technology has given us the belief that progress is a natural part of life.
- Underlying this belief is a rational approach.
- A Technologically progressive society is one in which problems are observed in systematic way and, more importantly, that solutions to problems are possible.
- Rational modes of thought do not confer moral superiority.
- Rationality requires objectivity—coolness and detachment.
- This can make for Technology that is not compatible with social beliefs and values.
- Modern technology is accessible in some form to the entire population.
- Our lack of understanding can render us powerless over it.
- Who control and understands Technology is of key importance—This influences what Technology is or is not made available to us.

The Differential Effects of Technological Change

- There are both negative and positive aspects to technology.

- Technology – greatest single source of economic growth (technology of production).

Technology Myths

- Technology can function without altering existing social arrangements.
- Technological solutions better than (less painful) social or political solutions.

"Technological change can be a subversive process that results in the modification or destruction of established social roles, relationships and values."

- Some change is small
- Some change is massive
- Economy distinctly affected by Technological change:
  1. Typesetting vs. Computers
  2. Internet Phone vs. Telephone

Effects of Technological Change

- Greatest Technology was Stone Axe.
- Stone axe – simple axe but involved many materials.
- Axe tied to gender identity – only men possessed axe.
- Introduction of steel axe by missionaries- men, women and children got axes.
- Men lost distinct identity, culture began to disintegrate.
- Small town supported by single industry: steam locomotives.
- Onset of diesel-electric locomotive.
- Once thriving community vanished within a few years.

Scientific Knowledge and Technological Advance

- Technology more than "applied science."
- Technology often emerged without scientific knowledge.
- Scientific advance sometimes depends on prior Technological advances.

The Historical Separation of Science and Technology

- Most Technologies have been developed with little scientific input.
- Greece-many Technological achievements made without out science, yet Scientific legacy more significant than Technological legacy.
- Rome-similar lack of connectivity, however Rome's greatest advances were in the area of technology with little scientific development.

Modern Relationship Between Technology and Science

- Effect of pure science on development of major weapon systems.
- Pure science had very little impact on technological development.
- Scientific knowledge after 1945, not before that time, which was arguably, critical to success of technology.

How Technology Differs from Science

- The two are very different in their basic nature.
- Science-knowledge for its own sake.
- Technology-a means to an end.

- Obviously, motives come into play, and make it difficult to cleanly categorize the two.
- Scientists-motives seen as pure, "for science sake," not influenced by politics, economy, society:
  - Works with more freedom; can abandon one theory when another appears more promising.
  - The notion that scientific progress leads to material progress has conferred more respectability on scientists than on technicians.
- Technicians-work is more structured:
  - Due to demand of product, technician cannot abandon projects as easily as scientist.
  - Under more time pressures.
- Technology still relevant even if we don't know how it works.
- Iron produced for decades before it was known what actually occurred inside furnace.
- Scientific knowledge may be a by-product of technological achievements
- Development of steam injector led to abandonment of a scientific theory of nature of heat.
- Technological developments often reach a plateau due to a lack of scientific knowledge.
- When Science and Technology have gone their separate ways, as has been the case for most of human history, they develop more slowly that when they interact with each other, as they have done to an increasing degree during the twentieth century.

Indirect Effects of Technology on Scientific Advance

- Technology supplies devices and instruments for scientific inquiry: Telescopes and galvanometers.
- Much Scientific research has been funded in the hopes that it will "pay off" one day.
- This pay off can only take place with the help of technology.
- Science succeeds over rival ways of knowing—poetry, religion, art, philosophy, and the occult- not by its ability to illuminate, not even by its ability to organize knowledge, but by its ability to produce solid results.

The Commonalities of Science and Technology

- Both based on the gathering of knowledge.
- Both advance through cumulative development.
- Both share rational thought processes—though neither is totally rational in their scope: Values, interpretation, and serendipity central to both endeavours.
- Mathematics central to both.
- Both share sense of optimism and progress

The Translation of Science into Technology

- A great deal of scientific information is translated into technology through the education of engineers.

- Science can stifle Technology because of its rigidity and movement toward a single answer (rather than several possibilities).

Printing

Of all technologies, perhaps none have had the greatest impact as printing. The development of a written language is one of the hallmarks of civilization. Spoken language characteristic of all societies, yet not all have written language. Many cultures that have written language have only developed this recently often because of the influence of other societies (missionaries, etc.)

- A written language is an essential technology.
- Keeping accounts.
- Recording history.
- Transmission of ideas and culture.

The Printing Revolution

Effects of written language were minimal when only a few people understood it. Before written language, humans developed astonishing memories to record events.

- Introduction of printing with moveable type—originated in the Orient
- 4th Cent. A.D.—Chinese copying stone inscriptions with paper rubbings
- 7th Cent. A.D.—Chinese used carved wood blocks
- Printing moved much slower through Europe
- 1400—Italy—playing cards and pictures of saints made from wooden blocks
- Johann Gutenberg—developed workable system of printing with separate pieces of type
- Printing books required more advanced technology than just printing a single page
- More advanced inks and binding methods emerged
- Books printed from moveable type were harbingers to the age of mass production.

Printing and the Expansion of Knowledge

- Printing, in particular, books, did much to transform European society
- Allowed for the transmission of ideas
- Allowed for more accurate map making and navigation
- Allowed for the advance of science—data could be recorded more accurately literacy spread.

Printing, Literacy, and Social Change

Books still very expensive and somewhat rare A more literate society could begin to ponder new ideas, especially those relating to social change. The relationship between printing and social change is reciprocal one does not cause the other, but rather, both influence the other.

Psychological Effects of Printing

Printed books fundamentally altered societies not solely from the ideas transmitted, but the medium itself altered the way we look at the world. Reading requires us to think in a sequential manner, just as a sentence is read from left to right.

Technological Change

Technological change is a term that is distinguished from technological development, yet can refer to several different yet compatible concepts.

Sociology

Underpinning the idea of technological change as a social process is general agreement on the importance of social context and communication. According to this technological change is seen as a social process involving adopters and others who are profoundly affected by cultural setting, political institutions and marketing strategies.

Elements of Diffusion

Emphasis has been on four key elements of the technological change process:

- an innovative technology
- communicated through certain channels
- to members of a social system
- who adopt it over a period of time?

Innovation

There are five main attributes of innovative technologies which influence acceptance. These are relative advantage, compatibility, complexity, trialability, and observability. Relative advantage may be economic or non-economic, and is the degree to which an innovation is seen as superior to prior innovations fulfilling the same needs. It is positively related to acceptance (i.e., the higher the relative advantage, the higher the adoption level, and vice versa). Compatibility is the degree to which an innovation appears consistent with existing values, past experiences, habits and needs to the potential adopter; a low level of compatibility will slow acceptance. Complexity is the degree to which an innovation appears difficult to understand and use; the more complex an innovation, the slower its acceptance. Trialability is the perceived degree to which an innovation may be tried on a limited basis, and is positively related to acceptance. Trialability can accelerate acceptance because small-scale testing reduces risk. Observability is the perceived degree to which results of innovating are visible to others and is positively related to acceptance.

Communication Channels

Communication channels are the means by which a source conveys a message to a receiver. Information may be exchanged through two fundamentally different, yet complementary, channels of communication. Awareness is more often obtained through the mass media, while uncertainty reduction that leads to acceptance mostly results from face-to-face communication.

Social System

The social system provides a medium through which and boundaries within which, innovation is adopted. The structure of the social system affects technological change in several ways. Social norms, opinion leaders, change agents, and the consequences of innovations are all involved. Also involved are cultural setting, nature of political institutions, laws, policies and administrative structures.

Time

Time enters into the acceptance process in several ways. The time dimension relates to the innovativeness of an individual or other adopter, which is the relative earliness or lateness with which an innovation is adopted.

Factors

The term mythologised of technology refers to how technology start and elites who invented the new technology. By focusing on its process, it is proved MacKenzie and Wajcman's argument of "social determination of technology," (Green, 2001, pp. 1-20) which means it is social that realizing technology change, and sustained it. There are four factors motivate technology innovation, which involve intellectual agenda, economic, politics, and existing infracture (Green, 2001, pp. 1-20).

Elites

It is elites who have intellectual agenda (Green, 2001, pp. 1-20) make technology change possible. However, it can not split their knowledge. Knowledge is not neutral, as it is "Socially bound knowledge" (Green, 2001, pp. 1-20).The elites can create new technology as they are able to access knowledge physically and they can afford it. Both procedures underpin knowledge privilege within social context. Moreover, to prevail the new technology in social, it acquires the avant-guards who obtain knowledge as well, which makes them able to manipulate new technology. As knowledge which plays a role of force in technology is only granted to a limit population in technology experiment period, it proves technology is not neutral.

Corporation

Corporations which are driven by economic value benefit technology and are benefited as well. In order to continue elites' experimentation, financial support is necessary, and in most case it is from corporation funding. On the other hand, corporation would like to invest the invention as the potential huge commercial benefits from it. In this case, it implies that social determines technology as technology advance can not separate from economic support and it brings economic value as well.

Government

To supply a steady environment for technology advance, the bureaucracy plays an essential role. It exerts its power and publishes laws to guarantee that investment can process properly, such as copyright. Without the safe social circumstance, the elites methodology will be stolen by the others (Green, 2001, pp. 1-20), which prevents the invention processing properly in such chaos.

Globalization as Macro-Social Context

Globalization trend is realized by technology advanced and motivates it as well. In another word, the global social change is increasingly both a cause and effect of technological enhance (Green, 2001, pp. 1-20). Merchants appeal high technology, such as electronic business to run over-sea business; it not only benefits them enlarging their markets, but also make them finish business trading quicker. On the other hand, utilizing high technology realizes global social change, and makes communication access more conveniently. There is another way of how existing in frustration implements technology advance. Public policy can stimulate technology development (Danna, 2007). For instance, feminists invented satellite to provoke masculinity domination social pattern, and by which they established their roles as early communication adopters (Danna, 2007, pp. 87-110). Before feminism movement, women are looked down on, so they provoke unequal social pattern by their contribution.

Economics

Technological change is a term that is used in economics to describe a change in the set of feasible production possibilities. Neutral technological change refers to the behaviour of technological change in models. A technological innovation is Hicks neutral (following John Hicks (1932)) if the ratio of capital's marginal product to labour's marginal product is unchanged for a given capital to labour ratio. A technological innovation is Harrod neutral (following Hicks) if the technology is labour-augmenting (i.e. helps labour); it is Solow neutral if the technology is capital-augmenting (i.e. helps capital).

Information society is a society in which the creation, distribution, diffusion, uses, and manipulation of information is a significant economic, political, and cultural activity. The knowledge economy is its economic counterpart whereby wealth is created through the economic exploitation of understanding.

Specific to this kind of society is the central position information technology has for production, economy, and society at large. Information society is seen as the successor to industrial society. Closely related concepts are the post-industrial society (Daniel Bell), Post-Modernism, Post-Modern Society, Knowledge Society, Telemetric Society, Information Revolution, and Network Society (Manuel Castells).

Development of the Information Society Model

One of the first people to develop the concept of the information society was the economist Fritz Machlup. In 1933 Machlup began studying the effect of patents on research. His work culminated in the breakthrough study "The production and distribution of knowledge in the United States" in 1962. This book was widely regarded and was eventually translated into Russian and Japanese. The Japanese have also studied the information society Johoka Shakai (Umesao), which means the highest stage of societal evolution seen in analogy to biological evolution. This concept was discussed already in the 1950s and 1960s.

Definition

There are various concepts in scientific literature that have been used for discussing information society. This section introduces some of them. Concepts such as knowledge/information economy, post-industrial society, post-modern society, information society, network society, informational capitalism, network capitalism, etc. show that it is an important sociological question in which society we live and which role technologies and information play in contemporary society. Both aspects are central issues of information society and information revolution theory.

Fritz Machlup (1962) introduced the concept of the knowledge industry. He distinguished five sectors of the knowledge sector: education, research and development, mass media, information technologies, information services.

Peter Drucker has argued that there is a transition from an economy based on material goods to one based on knowledge. Marc Porat distinguishes a primary (information goods and services that are directly used in the production, distribution or processing of information) and a secondary sector (information services produced for internal consumption by government and non-information firms) of the information economy.

Jean-François Lyotard has argued that "knowledge has become the principle force of production over the last few decades." Knowledge would be transformed into a commodity. Lyotard says that post industrial society makes knowledge accessible to the layman because knowledge and information technologies would diffuse into society and break up Grand Narratives of centralized structures and groups. Lyotard denotes these changing circumstances as postmodern condition or postmodern society.

Similarly to Bell Peter Otto and Philipp Sonntag (1985) say that an information society is a society where the majority of employees work in information jobs, i.e. they have to deal more with information, signals, symbols, and images than with energy and matter. Radovan Richta (1977) argues that society has been transformed into a scientific civilization based on services, education, and creative activities. This transformation would be the result of a scientific-technological transformation based on technological progress and the increasing importance of computer technology. Science and technology would become immediate forces of production.

Nico Stehr (1994, 2002) says that in the knowledge society a majority of jobs involves working with knowledge. "Contemporary society may be described as a knowledge society based on the extensive penetration of all its spheres of life and institutions by scientific and technological knowledge" (Stehr 2002). For Stehr knowledge is a capacity for social action. Science would become an immediate productive force, knowledge would no longer be primarily embodied in machines, but already appropriated nature that represents knowledge would be rearranged according to certain designs and programmes. For Stehr the economy of a knowledge society is largely driven not by material inputs, but by symbolic or knowledge-based inputs, there would be a large number of professions that involve working with knowledge, and a declining number of jobs that demand low cognitive skills as well as in manufacturing (Stehr 2002).

Also Alvin Toffler argues that knowledge is the central resource in the economy of the information society: "In a Third Wave economy, the central resource—a single word broadly encompassing data, information, images, symbols, culture, ideology, and values—is actionable knowledge" (Dyson/Gilder/Keyworth/Toffler 1994).

In recent years the concept of the network society has gained importance in information society theory. For Manuel Castells network logic is besides information, pervasiveness, flexibility, and convergence a central feature of the information technology paradigm. "One of the key features of informational society is the networking logic of its basic structure, which explains the use of the concept of 'network society'" (Castells 2000).

The major critique of concepts such as information society, knowledge society, network society, postmodern society, postindustrial society, etc. that has mainly been voiced by critical scholars is that they create the impression that we have entered a completely new type of society. "If there is just more information then it is hard to understand why anyone should suggest that we have before us something radically new" (Webster 2002). These critics argue that contemporary society first of all is still a capitalist society oriented towards accumulating economic, political, and cultural capital. They acknowledge that information society theories stress some important new qualities of society (notably globalization and informatization), but charge that they fail to show that these are attributes of overall capitalist structures. Critics such as Webster insist on the continuities that characterise change. In this way Webster distinguishes between different epochs of capitalism: laissez-faire capitalism of the 19th century, corporate capitalism in the 20th century, and informational capitalism for the 21st century (Webster 2006).

For describing contemporary society based on dialectic of the old and the new, continuity and discontinuity, other critical scholars have suggested several terms like:

- Transnational network capitalism, transnational informational capitalism
- Digital capitalism
- Virtual capitalism
- High-tech capitalism or informatic capitalism
- Other scholars prefer to speak of information capitalism

Overall, neo-Marxist accounts of the information society have in common that they stress that knowledge, information technologies, and computer networks have played a role in the restructuration and globalization of capitalism and the emergence of a flexible regime of accumulation (David Harvey 1989). They warn that new technologies are embedded into societal antagonisms that cause structural unemployment, rising poverty, social exclusion, the deregulation of the welfare state and of labour rights, the lowering of wages, warfare, etc.

Concepts such as knowledge society, information society, network society, informational capitalism, postindustrial society, transnational network capitalism, postmodern society, etc. show that there is a vivid discussion in contemporary sociology on the character of contemporary society and the role that technologies, information, communication, and co-operation play in it. Information society theory discusses the role of information and information technology in society, the question which key concepts shall be used for characterizing contemporary society, and how to define such concepts. It has become a specific branch of contemporary sociology.

There is currently no universally accepted concept of what exactly can be termed information society and what shall rather not so be termed. Most theoreticians agree that see a transformation which started somewhere between the 1970s and today and is changing the way societies work fundamentally. Information technology is not only Internet, and there are discussions how big the influence of specific media or specific modes of production really is.

Another problem with the idea of the information society is that there is no easily agreed upon definition of the term, which can not only include art, texts, blueprints and scientific theories, but also lies, football results, trivia, random letters, mistakes and so on. Information is not necessarily productive or useful. It can even be harmful.

Considering that metaphors and technologies of information move forward in a reciprocal relationship, we can describe some societies (especially the Japanese society) as an information society because we think of it as such.

Second and Third Nature

As mentioned earlier an information society is the means of getting information from one place to another (Wark, 1997) as technology has become more advanced over time so too has the way we have adapted in sharing this information with each other.

Second nature refers a group of experiences that get made over by culture (Wark, 1997). They then get remade into something else that can then take on a new meaning. As a society we transform this process so it becomes something natural to us, i.e. second nature. So, by following a particular pattern created by culture we are able to recognise how we use and move information in different ways. From sharing information via different time zones (such as talking online) to information ending up in a different location (sending a letter overseas) this has all become a habitual process that we as a society take for granted (Wark, 1997).

However, through the process of sharing information vectors have enabled us to spread information even further. Through the use of these vectors information is able to move and then separate from the initial things that enabled them to move (Wark, 1997). From here, something called third nature has developed. An extension of second nature, third nature is in control of second nature. It expands on what second nature is limited by. It has the ability to mould information in new and different ways. So, third nature is able to 'speed up, proliferate, divide, mutate, and beam in on us from else where (Wark, 1997). It aims to create a balance between the boundaries of space and time (see second nature). This can be seen through the telegraph, it was the first successful technology that could send and receive information faster than a human being could move an object (Wark, 1997). As a result different vectors of people have the ability to not only shape culture but create new possibilities that will ultimately shape society.

Therefore, through the use of second nature and third nature society is able to use and explore new vectors of possibility where information can be moulded to create new forms of interaction (Wark, 1997).

Related Terms

A number of terms in current use emphasize related but different aspects of the emerging global economic order. The Information Society intends to be the most encompassing in that an economy is a subset of a society. The Information Age is somewhat limiting, in that it refers to a 30-year period between the widespread use of computers and the knowledge economy, rather than an emerging economic order.

The knowledge era is about the nature of the content, not the socio-economic processes by which it will be traded. The computer revolution and knowledge revolution refer to specific revolutionary transitions, rather than the end state towards which we are evolving. The Information Revolution relates with the well known terms agricultural revolution and industrial revolution.

The information economy and the knowledge economy emphasize the content or intellectual property that is being traded through an information market or knowledge market, respectively. Electronic commerce and electronic business emphasize the nature of transactions and running a business, respectively, using the Internet and World-Wide Web. The digital economy focuses on trading bits in cyberspace rather than atoms in physical space. The network economy stresses that businesses will work collectively in webs or as part of business ecosystems rather than as stand-alone units. Social networking refers to the process of collaboration on massive, global scales. The Internet Economy focuses on the nature of markets that are enabled by the Internet. Knowledge services and knowledge value put content into an economic context. Knowledge services integrate Knowledge management, within a Knowledge organization, that trades in a Knowledge market.

Although seemingly synonymous, each term conveys more than nuances or slightly different views of the same thing. Each term represents one attribute of the likely nature of economic activity in the emerging post-industrial society. Alternatively, the new economic order will incorporate all of the above plus other attributes that have not yet fully emerged.

Intellectual Property Considerations

One of the central paradoxes of the information society is that it makes information easily reproducible, leading to a variety of freedom/control problems relating to intellectual property. Essentially, business and capital, whose place becomes that of producing and selling information and knowledge, seems to require control over this new resource so that it can effectively be managed and sold as the basis of the information economy. However, such control can prove to be both technically and socially problematic. Technically because copy protection is often easily circumvented and socially rejected because the users and citizens of the information society can prove to be unwilling to accept such absolute commodification of the facts and information that compose their environment.

Responses to this concern range from the Digital Millennium Copyright Act in the United States (and similar legislation elsewhere) which make copy protection (see DRM) circumvention illegal, to the free software, open source and copy left movements, which seek to encourage and disseminate the "freedom" of various information products (traditionally both as in "gratis" or free of cost, and liberty, as in freedom to use, explore and share).

APPENDIX

Glossary of ICT Terminology

A

Absolute Link: A term used by Web authors. In an HTML document a Relative Link indicates the location of a file relative to the document, whereas an *absolute link* specifies the full URL.

Access: The name of a Database programme forming part of the Microsoft Office suite of programmes.

Accessibility: The fundamental issue regarding *accessibility* is that everyone should have access to the services provided by ICT, e.g. computer programmes, E-mail and the World Wide Web, regardless of any visual, auditory, or other physical impairment they might have. Assistive Technology may be employed to increase access to such services, e.g. Text To Speech (TTS) screen readers, screen magnifiers, speech recognition systems, hearing assistance devices, etc. Designers of computer programmes and websites need to take account of accessibility when choosing colours, fonts and font sizes, etc.

Address Book: Usually supplied as part of your E-mail software. An *address book* in this sense is used to keep a record of all the e-mail addresses of people whom you may wish to contact by e-mail.

ADSL: Abbreviation for Asymmetric Digital Subscriber Line. A high-speed digital telephone connection that operates over an existing copper telephone line, allowing the same line to be used for voice calls. ADSL lines offer transmission speeds of at least 512Kbps, but nowadays usually in the range 1 Mbps to 8 Mbps, and are used mainly for Internet access. The term *asymmetric* is used because the data flows more quickly from the telephone exchange to the user than from the user to the exchange—because most Web users, for example, are more interested in receiving data quickly from websites rather than transmitting it. The term *symmetric* is used for connections where the data flows at the same speed in both directions, which is essential for accessing websites where there is a high degree of interactivity. See Broadband, ISDN, Kbps, Leased Line, Mbps.

Analogue: The basic meaning of analogue is "something that corresponds to something else." For example, in the context of equipment used for recording and playing back sound, analogue refers to the way in which the sound is recorded and reproduced. If you look closely at the groove of a 33 rpm vinyl gramophone record you will see that it is essentially a continuous wave, an undulating series of "hills." These "hills" correspond to the nature and volume of the sound that has been recorded. As the stylus of the record player moves along the wave it produces vibrations that are amplified and converted into sound. A parallel can be drawn with radio transmissions, where the sound signals are transmitted in the form of invisible waves. Early mobile phones worked in a similar way. Older tape recorders and videocassette recorders are based on the same principle, except that the signals representing the sound and moving images are imprinted onto a plastic tape coated with a magnetic powder. All analogue recordings suffer from background noise, and the quality of reproduction gradually degrades as the record or tape wears out. If the recording is copied, the copy will not be as good as the original, regardless of the quality of the equipment used to copy it. See the contrasting term Digital.

Anchor: A term used in connection with HTML, the coding system used for creating Web pages. An anchor is the target of a Hyperlink, i.e. a point in a Web document to which you jump when you click on a hyperlink.

Animation: The display of a sequence of images in a computer programme or on a Web page to give the impression of movement.

Anonymous FTP: An *anonymous FTP* is a convention whereby users are not required to identify themselves with an account number, user name or password when they access a website from which they wish to download publicly available programmes or files. Users may, however, be required to enter their e-mail address before accessing certain websites. The vast majority of publicly available Freeware and Shareware archives on the Web permit anonymous FTP. See FTP.

Application: A computer programme or a suite of computer programmes that performs a particular function for the user, such as a word-processor, e.g. *Microsoft Word,* or a range of functions, such as *Microsoft Windows* or *Microsoft Office.* See Computer Programme, Operating System, Windows, and Word-processor.

Artificial Intelligence (AI): The ability of a computer to mimic human attributes in finding a solution to a problem. *Artificial Intelligence* techniques are applied in various ways in computer applications in the language world, e.g. in Machine Translation (MT) programmes and in grammar and style checkers.

Attachment: A term used in connection with E-mail. An attachment can be a File of almost any kind—a document file, an image file, a sound file or a video clip—that you can add, i.e. *attach,* to an e-mail.

Audio Conferencing: A computer-based communications system that allows a group of computer users at different locations to conduct a "virtual conference" in which the participants can hear one another as if they were in the same room participating in a real conference. Unlike Video-conferencing, audio conferencing systems do not allow the participants to see one another.

Automatic Speech Recognition (ASR): A branch of Human Language Technologies devoted to the automatic processing of human speech. See Speech Recognition.

B

Backup or Back Up: Used as a verb, *to back up* means to copy a File or Folder from your computer to another Storage Medium, e.g. a CD-ROM, as a precaution in case your Hard Drive fails or is infected by a Virus. A *backup,* used as a noun or a *backup copy* describes a copy that you have made in this way. It is essential to back up new files and folders at regular intervals.

Bandwidth: The amount of data that can be sent from one computer to another through a particular connection in a certain amount of time, e.g. via a computer to the Internet and vice versa. The more bandwidth available, the faster you are able to access information. Bandwidth is usually measured in *kilobits per second* (Kbps) or *megabits per second* (Mbps). See ADSL, Broadband, Kilobit, Megabit, Narrowband.

Binary: A number system using base 2 instead of the usual (human) base 10, which is normally referred to as the decimal system. Computers use base 2 because they can only recognise two values, 1 or 0. This is simulated electronically by using a device, such as a switch, which is either on (1) or off (0). All numbers are represented by combinations of ones and zeroes, thus the number 9 is represented as 1001, the right-most column being the units column and the other columns, moving from right to left, being 2, 4, 8.

Binary File: Strictly speaking all computer files are Binary, consisting of a string of ones and zeroes, but the term *binary file* is often used to differentiate programme files and data files from *text files*, which contain only unformatted printable ASCII characters. See ASCII, Text File.

BIOS: Acronym for Basic Input/Output System. This is a built-in ROM Chip on the Motherboard containing essential programmes to manage the computer's input and output, which are loaded into memory during the boot process.

Bit: Contraction of *binary digit*. A bit is the smallest measurement unit of computer memory or data transmission speed, e.g. via a Modem. See the entry on Measurement Units.

Bitmap: A computer graphic or image composed of thousands of individual dots or *pixels*, each pixel being stored as a number. The image is displayed by specifying the colour of each pixel. Bit-mapped graphics can be imported into other applications, e.g. a word-processor, but they cannot be edited within these applications. When bit-mapped graphics are resized they usually suffer a loss of sharpness, whereas *vector graphics* can be resized without such loss.

Blackboard: A commercial Virtual Learning Environment (VLE) package, i.e. a software package that integrates online communications software with content software enabling teachers to create courses that are delivered partially or entirely via the Web. Courses using *Blackboard* might be mainly text-based, but can be enhanced with images, audio and video.

Blog: Contraction of the term Weblog. A *blog* is essentially a website that contains discrete pieces of information posted by different users. Contributors usually enter new items of information via a simple form, following the introduction of each new theme by a person who initiates the blog, and then submitted to the site, where an administrator may filter them before being posted. A blog can contain news items, short essays, annotated links, documents, graphics, and multimedia. These posts are usually in reverse chronological order and often take the form of a journal or diary. A blog is normally accessible to any Internet user, but closed blogs may also be created, e.g. to document the thoughts and experiences of a group of students or to provide a means of communication between teachers and students following a particular course. The word *blog* is also used as a verb and Blogger is used as a noun to describe someone who blogs (see next entry). A blog is usually distinguished from an Internet Discussion List (also known as a Forum), but the latter can function in a similar way insofar as it typically allows any user to post messages to it that can be viewed via the Web.

Blogger: Normally used to refer to someone who *blogs*, i.e. who regularly writes *blogs*. Also used to describe a service that provides Web-based tools used by individuals to create a Blog or Weblog.

Bluetooth: *Bluetooth* is a technical industry standard for radio technology, which facilitates the transmission of signals over short distances (up to around 10 metres) between telephones, computers and other devices without the use of wires. For example, a Bluetooth-enabled mobile phone can communicate with a desktop computer for the purpose of synchronising data, such as an appointments diary.

BMP: Abbreviation for Bitmap, a file format for storing images. This is the standard format used, for example, by *Windows Paint*. BMP image files occupy quite a lot of space compared to other formats.

Bookmark: A *bookmark* is a facility within a Browser that enables you to keep a record of Web pages that you have visited and may wish to visit again. Bookmarks are stored in a subdirectory of the Windows directory on your computer. In *Internet Explorer* bookmarks are known as Favorites (sic—spelt the American way), which is also the name of the subdirectory in which they are stored. Bookmarks are also used to mark positions in a *Word* document, i.e. positions to which you can jump from other points in the document by clicking on them with the Mouse.

Boot: (verb) To start up a computer by loading the operating system into memory. The computer is regarded as *bootstrapping* itself into operation, i.e. picking itself up by its own bootstraps. The adjective *bootable* is often used to describe a floppy disk that can be used to start a computer, e.g. when the hard disk fails or becomes corrupted for some reason.

bps: Abbreviation for *bits per second*, the smallest measurement of data transmission speed, e.g. via a Modem. Computer people normally measure data transmission speeds in *Kbps*, meaning *kilobits per second*, or *Mbps*, meaning *megabits per second*. If you have a 56Kbps modem (which is slow by today's standards) it means that your modem can transmit at speeds up to 56,000 bits of information per second.

Broadband: A general term used to describe a high-speed connection to the Internet. Connection speed is usually measured in Kbps (kilobits per second) and Mbps (megabits per second). Typically, a home user will have a broadband connection using an ADSL telephone line running at 512 Kbps to 8 Mbps. Educational institutions ideally need a symmetric connection of at least 8 Mbps to ensure smooth trouble-free connections to the Internet when large numbers of students are accessing the Internet all at once.

Browser: A software package installed on the hard disk of your computer that enables you to access and to navigate the World Wide Web—to "surf the Web" in colloquial terms. *Internet Explorer* and *Netscape* are two browsers that are in widespread use.

Bulletin Board: A type of forum on the Internet or an intranet, where users can post messages by e-mail or via the World Wide Web for other users to read and respond to. Bulletin Board Systems (BBSs) have largely been replaced by other types of online systems for communal communication, such as blogs, discussion lists and forums.

Burn: When data is written to a CD, for example using a CD-Read/Write drive, a pattern of microscopic dots is etched with a laser beam in a spiralling track on the CD surface. This is a process often referred to as "burning a CD."

Bus: Not the sort you get on to go into town. This is basically a set of parallel wires for connecting the Central Processing Unit (CPU) of a computer to all other input-output devices. Data can be transmitted in two directions, from and to the CPU.

Byte: A measurement of computer memory or disk capacity. A byte comprises 8 *bits*. See entry on Measurement Units.

C

CAD/CAM: Abbreviations for Computer Aided Design/Computer Aided Manufacturing. A process of drafting, designing and manufacturing with the aid of a computer. CAD enables the user to manipulate drawings, including 3D drawings, and viewing them from a variety of angles. CAM is a general term for computer support during the manufacturing process.

Card: In computer jargon, a *card* is an electronic circuit board, usually one which can be slotted into your computer in order to fulfill a specialised function.

Cathode Ray Tube (CRT): An older type of computer Display Screen or Monitor, in which beams of high-voltage electrons are fired at a screen causing thousands of Red, Green and Blue (RGB) dots to glow in different combinations and intensities, thus producing the full-colour image displayed on the screen. Cathode Ray Tubes are also used in older domestic TV sets. Newer types of display screens are of the LCD or TFT flat panel type—like many modern TV sets. They are much lighter, use less electricity and take up less room on a desktop.

CD-ROM: Abbreviation for Compact Disk Read Only Memory. A CD-ROM is an Optical Disk on to which data has been written via a laser—a process often referred to as "burning a CD": see Burn. A CD-ROM looks much the same as an audio CD, but can contain text, sound, pictures and motion video. Once written, the data on a CD-ROM can be fixed and rendered unalterable;

hence the term *read-only* – **but** modern computers are usually equipped with a read/write CD-ROM drive that enables new material to be stored on a special kind of CD-ROM: CD-R (recordable) or CD-RW (rewriteable). It is worthwhile investing in a read/write CD-ROM drive for making backups and storing your own multimedia materials. Blank CD-Rs or CD-RWs can be bought from computer media suppliers at a relatively low cost. You can store data on CD-Rs using a read/write drive, adding to it until it is full, and then you can format the CD-ROM so that it is fixed and can be read by a standard CD-ROM drive. You can also store data on CD-RWs in the same way, but these discs can only be read by a read/write CD-ROM drive. The advantage of CD-RWs is that they can be erased and used over and over again, but now that the cost of blank CD-Rs has fallen to such a low level it is questionable how useful CD-RWs are.

Central Processing Unit (CPU): Also known as the Central Processor. In a modern computer the CPU is a single microprocessor Chip or Microchip, an integrated circuit that carries out information processing and calculations. In essence, the CPU is the computer's "brain."

Character User Interface (CUI): A *Character User Interface* describes a way in which a computer user communicates with a computer by entering commands as *text*, i.e. in order to run programmes and to carry out other operations such as copying information from one Folder to another, deleting files, etc. Contrasted with a Graphical User Interface (GUI), e.g. *Microsoft Windows*, which allows the user to carry out such operations by clicking on *icons*, opening and shutting *windows* and dragging and dropping with a *mouse*. MS DOS and Unix are examples of CUIs.

Chat Room: A *synchronous*, mainly text-based communication facility, offering a Web-based environment where people either drop into or arrange to meet and *chat* at specific times. You type in your text online; it is seen almost immediately by others online at the same time who responds online in real time. When used for language learning chat rooms can put a great deal of pressure on students by requiring them to read fairly rapidly and to write, also fairly rapidly, with little time to reflect on the quality of the language used. A degree of caution is advised when joining a chat room. Some have been used for sinister purposes.

Client: A computer that receives services from another computer. A stand-alone computer on your desk, which you use to browse the Web, is a *client*, and the computers from which World Wide Web files are downloaded to your computer are *servers*. Similarly, a computer (also known as a workstation) connected to a Local Area Network (LAN) is a *client* that can receive information from and send information to the *server* that controls the LAN.

Clipart or **Clip Art:** A collection of image files that can be embedded or inserted into Web pages, word-processed documents, *PowerPoint* presentations, etc. Some clipart images are copyright-free or in the public domain but others may be subject to a license fee if you wish to make them public, e.g. on a website.

Clipboard: A temporary storage area in a computer's memory. It may be used, for example, to store text that you are in the process of copying and pasting from one section of a word-processed document to another section in the same document or to another document. You should find a *clipboard viewer* programme on your computer, which enables you to see what is currently being temporarily stored in the clipboard.

Compiler: A programme, which converts programmes written in a high-level *programming language*, i.e. as used by professional human programmers, into Machine Code, a language that can be "understood" by a computer. A *compiler* produces a *binary executable* programme file after the programmer has completed the programming. Programme files on personal computers can be recognised by their three-letter **.exe** or **.com** Extension after their filenames, e.g. **winfile.exe**

Compression: A technique which reduces the amount of space required to store data, e.g. as used to reduce the amount of space needed to store an image, an audio recording, or a video recording.

Computer Assisted Instruction (CAI): A term used mainly in the business world. Implies a top-down, instructor-centered approach to teaching with computers and is closely associated with Programmed Learning.

Computer Based Training (CBT): A term used mainly in the business world. Implies a top-down, trainer-centered approach to teaching with computers and is closely associated with Programmed Learning.

Computer Mediated Communication (CMC): *Computer Mediated Communication* is used as a term describing the use of the Internet as a means of fostering teaching and learning, especially the use of E-mail, Conferencing and Social Networking.

Computer Programme: A set of instructions that the computer carries out in sequence to perform a given task. Programmes are written in English-like programming languages (e.g. C, Pascal), and are then converted into binary machine instructions via a compiler or an interpreter.

Concept Keyboard: An overlay or replacement for the traditional computer Keyboard. Concept keyboards are useful for small children or learners with special needs: for example, offering pictures or symbols as an alternative to the alphabetic keyboard.

Conferencing: Computer *conferencing* is a development of E-mail designed to support many-to-many communication, whereby computer users in different locations can take part in a "virtual conference." A conference usually consists of a group of participants who have a common interest in the conference subject matter. Computer conferencing software enables the organisation, storage, structuring and retrieval of messages. Messages may be organised under different topics, by author or by date of posting. Asynchronous conferencing may take place via a Blog, Discussion List.

Content and Language Integrated Learning (CLIL): A term used to describe learning a subject such as history or geography through the medium of a foreign language and thereby learning the foreign language at the same time.

Content-Free: Used to describe a computer programme, which is supplied as an "empty shell", i.e. without content such as texts, images, audio recordings, or video recordings. The user (i.e. the teacher) is expected to provide the content, and the programme then enables to content to be manipulated in various ways, for example to set up exercises and activities for different groups of learners.

Continuing Professional Development (CPD): Further study relevant to one's profession that most bodies encourage their members to undertake. This can take the form of seminars, research, training courses, etc. The materials at the ICT4LT website can serve the purposes of CPD.

Cookie: A piece of information stored on a user's computer by a Web Browser when the user visits a website for the first time. Websites use cookies to recognise users who have previously visited them. The next time that the user visits that site, the information in the cookie is sent back to the site so that the site can tailor what it presents to the user, e.g. tastes in music or shopping habits.

Copyright: New technologies have raised all kinds of new issues relating to copyright—mainly because it has become so easy to copy materials from a variety of digital sources. We have produced a Web page at the ICT4LT site entitled General guidelines on copyright.

Courseware: A set of computerised lessons, exercises, tests and reference material.

Ctrl Key: The *Ctrl keys* can be found on either side of the space bar on a computer keyboard. They are used in conjunction with other keys as "shortcuts" for operations that would normally be carried out with a Mouse, e.g. Ctrl + S will save a file that you are working on. It is also possible to programme the Ctrl keys to carry out operations that you specify yourself, e.g. for typing foreign characters.

Cursor: The pointer, which appears on screen and is controlled by a *pointing device*, such as a *mouse*. The *cursor* usually has the shape of an arrow, but can also take other shapes: e.g. an *I-beam* in a document, an hourglass whilst an operation is under way, or the graphic image of a hand over a Hyperlink.

Cyberspace: William Gibson coined this phrase in his novel *Neuromancer*, first published in 1984 - some years before the World Wide Web was invented: "Cyberspace. A consensual hallucination experienced daily by billions of legitimate operators, in every nation, by children being taught mathematical concepts... A graphic representation of data abstracted from the banks of every computer in the human system. Unthinkable complexity. Lines of light ranged in the nonspace of the mind, clusters and constellations of data. Like city lights, receding..." Today the word *cyberspace* is used to refer to the world of the Internet, more specifically the World Wide Web.

Cybersquatter: A term normally used to describe someone who registers the name of a popular Web address – usually a company name – with the intent of selling it to its rightful owner at a high price. Cybersquatters also watch out for registered domain names that become available when the owner has no further use for them, goes bankrupt, or simply forgets to pay their registration renewal fees. This can lead to perfectly harmless and legitimate sites being transmogrified overnight into sites containing offensive material. See Graham Davies's article on "Dodgy links."

D

Data: Strictly speaking the plural of "datum", but now usually considered as a collective noun in the singular, with the plural form "data items" or "items of data." Data is information in a form which can be processed by a computer. It is usually distinguished from a *computer programme*, which is a set of instructions that a computer carries out. Data can be text or sets of figures on which a computer programme operates.

Database: A structured collection of data that can be used for a variety of purposes. Databases are usually stored on a Hard Disk inside your computer, on a CD-ROM, or at a website. A database may contain data relating to staff employed by a company or to students at an educational institution. Databases can also contain bibliographies, glossaries, vocab lists, etc. In order to set up and manage a database you need a database programme such as Microsoft Access.

Data Driven Learning (DDL): An approach to language learning pioneered by Tim Johns, University of Birmingham, whereby learners of a foreign language gain insights into the language that they are learning by using concordance programmes to locate authentic examples of language in use. In DDL the learning process is no longer based solely on the teacher's initiative, his/her choice of topics and materials and the explicit teaching of rules, but on the learner's own discovery of rules, principles and patterns of usage in the foreign language. In other words, learning is driven by authentic language data.

Data Projector: A device that enables the image displayed on a computer screen to be projected onto a wall screen or Interactive Whiteboard.

DBMS: Abbreviation for Database Management System. An Application enabling the storage, modification, retrieval, and querying of data in a Database.

Default: A setting or value automatically assigned to a computer programme or device in the absence of a choice made by the user. When you use a programme for the first time, e.g. a Browser or Word-processor, all the settings will have been preset to their *default values* – many of which can be changed to settings that you prefer, e.g. the *default* font type and size. The term *default route* is used in connection with Computer Assisted Language Learning, meaning the route that the teacher believes to be optimal for the learner to follow in a computer programme or suite of programmes – but which can be overridden by the learner if s/he wishes to follow his/her own route.

Defrag: Short for *defragment.* A process run by a defragging programme (usually supplied as part of *Microsoft Windows*) whereby parts of data files scattered around different segments of a computer hard disk are gathered together into continuous file segments. This makes applications run more efficiently and also frees up disk space.

Desktop: The main workspace in Windows, an electronic *desktop* which is displayed as the opening screen when *Windows* is started. The electronic desktop is a metaphor for the top of a real desktop, where jobs to be done are laid out in different folders, symbolised by *icons*, i.e. small images. Users open and work with programmes by clicking on *icons* on the desktop, and they can also store shortcuts to documents or websites there.

Desktop Computer: A desktop computer is one that is designed to sit permanently on a desk, as opposed to a Laptop Computer that can easily be carried around.

Desktop Publishing (DTP): An Application for laying out text, graphics and pictures in order to produce a professional-looking publication. Most modern word-processors can now achieve what older DTP packages were capable of producing. Examples of DTP applications are *QuarkXpress* and *PageMaker*, which have probably become too complex and technical for the inexperienced user and are now aimed at the professional graphic designer or layout artist.

Device Driver: Software that enables a computer to communicate with a hardware device such as a Mouse, Printer or Scanner. Hardware devices must each have the proper *device driver* installed in order to enable them to run. Most hardware devices are supplied with small programmes that are installed onto your hard drive when you use them for the first time and tell the computer how to communicate with that specific device.

Dial-up Modem: An older type of Modem that connects a computer to the Internet via a standard telephone line. Typically a *dial-up modem* connects to the Internet at a very slow data transmission speed of only 56 Kbps, whereas a modern Broadband modem connects to the Internet at 512 Kbps or much higher. Because dial-up access uses normal telephone lines, the quality of the connection is often poor.

Digital: The essential meaning of this term is "based on numbers." The modern computer is a typical example of digital technology, so are Storage Media such as CD-ROMs, DVD-ROMs, audio CDs and video DVDs, on which numbers are coded as a string of tiny pits pressed into a plastic disc. When a CD audio recording or a DVD video recording is played back, using equipment incorporating a laser as a reading device, the exact numeric values are retrieved and converted into sound or images. Digital recording is relatively free from noise and interference and gives a very high quality of reproduction. Data (including audio and video) or programmes stored on CD-ROM or DVD can be read by a computer in a similar way. There are two major benefits to digital technology. Firstly, digital technology—because it is based on numbers—is more precise. Secondly, digital technology is becoming cheaper and more powerful. Digital technology is now used in radio and TV broadcasts. Digital recordings made from any source (audio-or videocassettes, television, radio, Internet, satellite TV, microphone or Camcorder) can be edited easily, then stored on a computer's Hard Disk, CD-ROM, DVD, Flash Drive, Memory Stick, etc. They can be copied without quality loss and, more significantly, can be used by more than one learner at the same time.

Digital Camera: A camera used for taking still photographs—but some digital cameras can also record short sequences of moving images. A digital camera looks much the same as an ordinary camera but stores photographs in electronic format so that they can be *uploaded* onto a computer. The more expensive digital cameras achieve better results than can be achieved by using an ordinary camera and a *scanner.*

Digital Video Disk or Digital Versatile Disk (DVD): A *Digital Video Disk* or *Digital Versatile Disk* is an Optical Disk that is capable of storing high-quality video as well as other forms of data, e.g.

programmes, text, still pictures and graphics. It is possible that DVDs will completely replace CD-ROMs in the not-too-distant future. DVDs can only be read or written to on multimedia computers equipped with a DVD drive or Combination Drive.

Directory: A location on a disk containing a group of *files* and *subdirectories* grouped together for organisational purposes. The term is used synonymously with Folder, which has become a more common term since the introduction of Windows. Subdirectories are sometimes referred to as "child directories" of the "parent directory." The topmost directory on a computer, which is the parent of all directories on the disk, is known as the *root directory* and usually has the *pathname* C:\.

Disk Drive: A device within or connected to a computer that enables data to be read from and written onto a disk. See CD-ROM, Disk, DVD, Floppy Disk, Hard Disk.

Display Screen: The screen on which output from a computer is displayed. Also referred to as a Monitor. Older computers used a Cathode Ray Tube, which is essentially the same as that used in older domestic TV sets. Newer types of display screens are of the LCD or TFT flat panel type—like many modern TV sets. They are much lighter, use less electricity and take up less room on a desktop.

Distance Learning: A form of learning that takes place where the teachers and the students are in physically separate locations. *Distance learning* can be either Asynchronous or Synchronous. Traditional distance learning includes the mailing of printed materials, correspondence between teachers and students in writing, contact by telephone, and radio and television broadcasts. More recently, distance learning has included E-learning and/or Online Learning. The British Open University (OU) is one of the oldest established distance-learning establishments to have embraced existing technologies, i.e. radio and television, when it was set up in the 1960s. The OU continues to embrace new distance learning technologies as they become more widely available.

Domain Name: A unique name that identifies a Website. A domain name can be purchased from and registered by a *domain name* registration company, e.g. our name **ict4lt.org** was purchased from *Amenworld*: http://www.amenworld.com. Such companies also provide a service that will check if a required name is available for purchase. Domain names always have two or more parts, separated by dots. The part on the left side is specific and the one the right part is more general. Our website's domain name is divided into two parts, **ict4lt** and **org**, the former part being our project name and the latter indicating what kind of body we are: **org** = "organisation." Our domain name is therefore **ict4lt.org**. Universities' domain names in the UK always end in **ac.uk** = "academic UK." UK-based companies can often be identified by **co.uk**.

Dot Matrix Printer: An older type of printer that works by firing sets of pins in different combinations at an ink ribbon located against a sheet of paper. Such printers produce text that looks "ragged." Laser printers and ink-jet printers are now much more common.

Download: To transfer a copy of data, a computer programme, a text file, an image file, a sound file or video file from one computer to another computer. This is the main means of obtaining data and programmes from the World Wide Web.

Download Accelerator: Downloading large files from the Web can be tedious. If you connect to the Internet via a slow Dial-up Modem then you might as well make yourself a cup of coffee or take the dog for a walk while you are waiting. You may, however, find that the download process has been timed out or crashed before it has been completed. A *download accelerator* is therefore essential if you use a dial-up modem, and it can help manage and speed up the process of downloading if you have a Broadband connection to the Internet.

E

E-learning: *E-learning* (electronic learning) has become a buzzword in recent years, but it is widely misunderstood and often associated with a limited view of e-learning. Ask a dozen people what they understand by e-learning and most will probably say that it involves using a computer to access materials on the Web or to follow a distance-learning course using a Virtual Learning Environment (VLE). Here is the definition given in the UK Government's consultation document *towards a unified e-learning strategy*, July 2003:

If someone is learning in a way that uses Information and Communications Technologies (ICTs), they are using e-learning. They could be a pre-school child playing an interactive game; they could be a group of pupils collaborating on a history project with pupils in another country via the Internet; they could be geography students watching an animated diagram of a volcanic eruption their lecturer has just downloaded; they could be a nurse taking her driving theory test online with a reading aid to help her dyslexia – it all counts as e-learning.

In other words, this is a catchall definition relating to the use of ICT in teaching and learning: if you are using a computer to learn something then you are using e-learning. The whole of the ICT4LT website is, therefore, in this sense all about e-learning in the context of teaching and learning foreign languages, and this is one reason why you will not find a section headed specifically *E-learning* in the ICT4LT modules. Because of a lack of agreement on what e-learning is all about, it probably makes sense to use the term Online Learning when talking generally about distance learning on the Internet and to use CALL as a catch-all term for the use of ICT in language teaching and learning.

Electronic Whiteboard: More commonly referred to as an Interactive Whiteboard these days.

E-mail: Contraction of Electronic Mail. A system for creating, sending and receiving messages via the Internet. In order to send and receive e-mail messages you have to register with an Internet Service Provider (ISP) that provides an *e-mail service* and have *e-mail software* such as Outlook or Eudora installed on your computer. Many ISPs also offer a Web mail facility, which provides an alternative means of creating, sending and

Excel: The name of a Spreadsheet programme forming part of the *Microsoft Office* suite of programmes.

F

Feedback: Feedback is an automatic response from a computer, which may take the form of text, image, audio, video or any combination of these, to a learner's input. Input from the learner may take various forms, e.g. *(i)* clicking with the mouse to select an answer in a multiple-choice exercise, *(ii)* typing an answer at the computer keyboard, or *(iii)* speaking an answer into a microphone. Feedback in interactive language learning materials should go beyond a "boing" (wrong) or "applause" (right) or "try again" message and attempt to mimic the "live" situation when using the language results in either a response from the other person or an action showing that the language used was appropriate. Feedback is often described as *intrinsic* (implicit) or *extrinsic* (explicit).

File: A *file* in computer jargon can be used to describe many different things. It may be a Computer Programme, a document file created with a Word-processor, an image file, an audio file, a video file, etc. Think of it in the same way as you would think of a file in a filing cabinet. A file has a name that describes what it is, and the file is stored in a place where you can easily find it. Files are usually grouped together on a computer's Hard Disk in *directories* or *folders* and, as well as their names, they usually have a three-letter Extension that tell you what their function is or what they contain, e.g. **fwtt.exe** is a programme, **mystory.doc** is a *Word* document, **sally. Jpg** is a picture, and **mydog.mpg** is a video file. Files may also be stored on other Storage Media, such as CD-ROMs, DVDs and flash drives.

Firewall: A *firewall* is a software package that sits between your computer and your Internet connection, keeping an eye on the traffic going to and fro. If anything suspect appears, such as an unauthorised attempt from a remote computer to write information to your hard disk or to send information from your computer to a remote computer, it will block it and warn you. Firewalls have become essential these days due to the frequent attempts being made by *hackers* to grab confidential information from computers all around the world, e.g. your bank or credit card details, which may be stored in a file somewhere on your computer. Any computer is vulnerable while it is connected to the Internet. The writer of this paragraph speaks from personal experience: two attempts have been made by hackers to grab his Internet passwords from his computer. Both attempts were fortunately spotted by his Internet Service Provider and blocked, so no damage was done. If you access the Internet via a computer in a public or commercial organisation your ICT services department has probably installed a firewall, but if you access the Internet via a privately owned computer then you should consider installing your own firewall, e.g. *ZoneAlarm*, which is available as freeware from http://www.zonelabs.com. Alternatively, buy an add-on to an *anti-virus package* such as *McAfee VirusScan* or *Norton AntiVirus*.

Firewire: A *firewire* is in essence a facility that allows you to transfer video recordings very quickly from one device to another, e.g. from a Camcorder to a computer, using a special cable that connects to the computer's fireware socket. Many modern computers already have a firewire socket built in. If your computer does not have a firewire socket then you have to buy a firewire card and slot it in.

Firmware: Software that has been written to a ROM (Read Only Memory) chips by the manufacturers. See *ROM, Silicon Chip*.

Flash Drive: A portable Storage Device. *Flash drives* look like a small flat pen, around 5cm to 10cm long, and are easily carried in your pocket. Their storage capacity is impressive; 2GB is not unusual these days. They are used to store data that you wish to carry around, e.g. a *PowerPoint* presentation, and they can be plugged into any computer with a USB socket. Flash drives are also commonly referred to as *pen drives* or *memory sticks*.

Flash Player and **Flash Professional:** Software produced by Adobe for the development and viewing of animated and interactive sequences on the Web.

Floppy Disk: A plastic disk covered in magnetisable material, enclosed in a case, on which data is stored magnetically. A typical 3.5-inch floppy disk can store up to 1.44MB of data. Floppy disks are used for carrying small amounts of data around from one location to another, e.g. a *Word* document, but they are now being replaced by Storage Media with much bigger capacities that can contain *PowerPoint* presentations, sound files and video files.

Folder: An alternative word for a *directory* and which has become more common since the introduction of Windows. It describes a location on a disk, which contains a set of related files. A folder can be divided into sub-folders.

Font: The terms *font* (also spelt *fount*) and *typeface* are often confused or interchanged. *Font* refers to a complete collection of letters, numerals, symbols and punctuation marks that have common characteristics, including their style and size. The two commonest fonts are Times New Roman, a Serif font, which is characterised by cross-lines that finish off the stroke of each letter, and Arial, a Sans Serif font that has no cross-lines. *Typeface* is the name given to the style of a particular set of letters, numerals, symbols and punctuation marks.

Formatting: The process of preparing a writeable disk for use. Formatting creates a structure on the disk which enables it to hold data.

Forum: Often used synonymously with Discussion List. An electronic forum on the Internet or an intranet enables users to post messages by e-mail or via the Web for other users to read and respond to. See also Blog, Bulletin Board, Newsgroup, Wiki.

Fourth Generation Language (4GL): A programming language of a higher level than 3GLs such as C or Pascal—that is, the programme code is closer to English, and a 4GL function might be the equivalent of many 3GL functions. 4GLs are used for writing software for specialised tasks, such as querying databases.

Frame: An area in a Web page that scrolls independently of the rest of the Web page. A Web page can be divided into multiple frames. For example, a frame can include a navigation bar—as at the ICT4LT website—that always stays on the screen as the user moves around the other pages of the site.

Freeware: Software that can be copied and used without payment to the author(s), although there may be some restrictions on distribution.

FTP: Abbreviation for File Transfer Protocol. This is the method, i.e. a software standard, used for transferring files from one computer to another via the Internet. FTP is also used as a verb in the sense "to transfer" (a file).

G

Gigabyte: Usually abbreviated to *GB*, or *gig* in common computer parlance. A unit of measurement of computer memory or disk capacity = 1,073,741,824 bytes. See the entry on Measurement Units.

Google: A popular Search Engine. Probably the most widely used search engine on the Web. You can also use *Google* to find definitions of words. Call up *Google* at http://www.google.co.uk and in the search box: type **define:** immediately in front of the word you would like to be defined. *Google* will then locate definitions of that word on the Web, e.g. try **defining: bandwidth** or **define: ADSL**. If your term consists of two or more elements, e.g. *blended learning*, encase it in inverted commas, thus: **define:" blended learning.**

Graphical User Interface (GUI): An Interface, i.e. a software package that enables human beings to control what happens on their computers. A GUI consists of graphical elements known as *icons* and enables the user to run programmes and to carry out other operations such as copying information from one Folder to another, deleting files, etc. by clicking on these *icons*, opening and shutting *windows* and dragging and dropping with a *mouse*. *Microsoft Windows* and the much older Apple Mac interface are GUIs. Contrasted with Character User Interface (CUI), an older type of interface, which required the user to control the computer, by typing commands at the Keyboard.

H

Hardcopy or **Hard Copy:** Printed output from a computer, as opposed to output on screen.

Hard Disk: A *hard disk* is form of Storage Medium consisting of a single rigid magnetic disk or a set of such disks enclosed within a metal case, a *hard disk drive*, which is mounted internally in your computer and is used for storing the computer programmes and data that it needs in order to work. External hard disk drives can also be obtained, e.g. for additional storage capacity or backup storage. Hard disks can contain vast amounts of data, typically one or more *gigabytes*. See CD-ROM, DVD, Floppy Disk, Gigabyte, Storage Device.

Hardware: The physical elements of a computer system—the bits you can see, touch, drop, kick or fall over. Contrasted with Software.

Homepage or **Home Page:** This is the main Web page of a business, organisation or school, or of a personal website. From this page links are made to other pages on the same site and to external sites. Most people usually set up their Browser to open with this page when it starts up.

Host: Short for *host computer*. Any computer that provides services to other computers that are linked to it, via a local network or via the Internet.

Host Name or **Hostname:** A *host name* is the unique name of a computer on the Internet, which is normally written as a series of letters, for example **www.hull.ac.uk**. A *host name* is the human-friendly form of the host's numerical IP address, i.e. it's an alias for the "real" Internet address of the host computer, e.g. **150.237.176.24.**

HTML: Abbreviation for Hypertext Markup Language. The coding system used for creating pages on the World Wide Web. HTML enables the author to control how the page appears and to insert Hypertext links within one Web page or to other pages anywhere on the Web. Nowadays most Web authors and designers use an Authoring Tool such as *Front Page* or *Dreamweaver* to create World Wide Web pages. Web page files end with the Extension **.htm** or **.html**.

HTTP: Abbreviation for Hypertext Transfer Protocol. The transfer method (*protocol*) used by the World Wide Web to transmit and receive Web pages. This abbreviation normally precedes the name of a website, e.g. **http://www.ict4lt.org,** to tell your computer that this is the way in which you wish to communicate with other computers on the Internet. In practice, however, you can usually miss out the prefix **http://** as it is assumed to be the norm.

Hub: A common connection point for networked computers and other devices. Hubs are used to connect devices in a Local Area Network (LAN).

Human Language Technologies (HLT): Since January 1999 this has been the European Commission's official term for what used to be described as *Language Engineering*. The term covers a range of applications of advanced technology to human languages, e.g. Automatic Speech Recognition (ASR), Machine Translation (MT), etc.

Hyperlink: A contraction of *hypertext link*, the essence of Hypertext and the HTML language used for creating pages on the World Wide Web. In a Web document a *hyperlink* can be a sequence of letters or an image. By clicking on the area designated as a *hyperlink* by the person who created the Web page, it is possible to jump quickly to another part of the page, a different page on the same website, or to a completely different website.

Hypermedia: The extension of the *hypertext* concept to *multimedia*, describing the combination of multimedia information (text, images, audio, video, etc.) in a meaningful configuration, which is especially useful for teaching and learning.

Hypertext: A system for the non-sequential presentation of text, the fundamental concept of the World Wide Web, whereby the user can jump from one part of a text to another, from one Web page to another, or from one website to another, by clicking on highlighted (and usually underlined) *hyperlinks*. The concept of *hypertext* predates the Web by many years. Vannevar Bush is credited with inventing the concept of *hypertext* in his article "As we may think", which was written as early as 1945 and describes an imaginary machine called "Memex" – essentially a hypertext device that takes account of the way the human mind associates ideas and follows a variety of different paths rather than moving on sequentially.

I

Icon: A small symbol or picture used in a Graphical User Interface (GUI). The icons on the computer screen represent programmes or files, e.g. a picture of a painter's palette might represent a programme used for drawing and editing pictures and a picture of a book with a question mark on its cover might represent the text of a manual or a help file. In a GUI the Mouse is used to move the Cursor so that it locates over an icon. Clicking a button on the mouse then causes the programme that the icon represents to run or a file to be displayed.

Ink Jet Printer: A type of Printer that fire little jets of ink at the page in order to form the characters and graphics. One of the commonest forms of printers currently in use and capable of producing high-quality output in black and white and in full colour.

Input: Anything that goes into a computer in order to be processed and/or stored. Also used as a verb.

Input Device: Any device that is capable of inputting information into a computer system, e.g. a Keyboard, Microphone, Mouse or Scanner.

Input Validation: Many programmes contain *input validation* routines, which prevent the user doing something silly while entering data at the keyboard. A good input validation routine will ensure that the computer sifts out the important information and does any necessary conversion work, e.g. eliminating spaces or unwanted characters, or converting letters to upper or lower case.

Install: A verb used to describe the process of *installing* or *setting up* a computer programme or suite of computer programmes on the computer's hard disk for first-time use. Programmes are normally supplied on CD-ROM or DVD, but they may also be downloaded from the Web, either free of charge or on payment of a fee.

Install Programme or Installation Programme: A programme that enables the user to *install* or *set up* a programme or suite of computer programmes on the computer's hard disk for first-time use. Also known as Setup Programme.

Integrated Circuit: An electronic circuit etched onto a small piece of silicon, which has been subjected, using photo-masking processes, to controlled "doping" with certain impurities. Particular areas of the chip can then be made to act like electronic components such as diodes, capacitors and resistors.

Integrated Learning System (ILS): A computer-driven system of learning in which the content is presented in tutorial format and which monitors and records the progress of the learner.

Intel: The name of a manufacturer of *microprocessors* used in personal computers. Other companies make Intel-compatible microprocessors.

Interactive Video (IV): A system consisting of a computer connected to a 12-inch *videodisc player*, allowing the presentation of still images or video clips combined with some kind of interactivity, e.g. carrying out a set of exercises linked to the images or to the video clips. Very popular in the 1980s but now technically obsolete and replaced by integrated multimedia computers incorporating DVD or CD-ROM drives. One of the best-known educational interactive videodiscs was the *Domesday Disc*, created by the BBC in 1987 to commmemorate the 900th anniversary of the creation of the Domesday Book (1087).

Interactive Whiteboard (IWB): Often abbreviated to IWB. A touch-sensitive projection screen that allows the teacher to control a computer directly by touching the screen, i.e. the whiteboard, rather than using a Keyboard or Mouse. A Data Projector has to be connected to the teacher's computer in order to project the image onto the interactive whiteboard and special software has to be installed on the computer in order for the whiteboard to become active and sensitive to touch – which may require the use of an "electronic pen" or it may work in reaction to one's finger or hand.

Interface: An *interface* in computer jargon is a connection between two systems. It can be Hardware or Software. It may take the form of a plug, cable or socket, or all three, for example where a Printer or Scanner is connected to a computer, and then it's a hardware interface. There are also software interfaces that enable one programme to link with another, passing across data and variables. The term *interface,* also known as *user interface,* also describes the software that is used to enable human beings to communicate with a computer, for example *Microsoft Windows*, which is a Graphical User Interface (GUI) in common use on personal computers.

Internet: The *Internet,* or simply "the Net," is a computer network connecting millions of computers all over the world. It provides communications to governments, businesses, universities, schools and homes. Any modern computer can be connected to the Internet using existing communications systems. Schools and universities normally access the Internet via their own educational networks, but private individuals usually have to take out a subscription with an Internet Service Provider (ISP). Although the Internet is in fact a network of networks, it appears to users as a network of individual computers. The Internet dates back to the group of interconnected networks that evolved from the ARPANET of the late 60's and early 70's. It has grown from a handful of interconnected networks into a huge network of millions of computers. The main Internet services of interest to language teachers are E-mail and World Wide Web.

Internet Explorer: A Browser produced by the Microsoft Corporation and supplied together with the Windows operating system.

Internet Service Provider (ISP): A company that provides a subscription service to enable you to access the Internet. An ISP has a network of computers permanently linked to the Internet. When you take out a subscription with an ISP they link your computer to their network, usually via an existing telephone line, but dedicated lines are also provided by some ISPs. ISPs also give you an E-mail address and space on the World Wide Web for setting up your own website.

Interpreter: Software that converts the human-readable Source Code of a programme which has been written in a high-level programming language such as BASIC, one statement at a time, into machine instructions as the application is run. Interpreted applications need to be distributed with runtime programmes and function libraries.

Intranet: A private network inside a company or educational organisation and used over its LAN (Local Area Network). A sort of local Internet. Contrasted with Internet, which is publicly available.

IP Address: Short for Internet Protocol Address. The unique numerical address of a computer on the Internet, expressed as four sets of numbers (maximum 3 digits each) separated by dots: e.g. **150.237.176.24** for one of the computers at the University of Hull—where the ICT4LT website is located. Computers on the Internet are nearly always referred to by more memorable *domain names*, which are mapped onto their *IP addresses* by special Internet computers known as *name servers*.

iPod: The name of a portable (mobile) Media Player designed and marketed by Apple. The **iPod first** appeared in 2001. As well as being capable of storing and playing back audio recordings, newer models can also record and play back video. The iPod has become popular for storing recordings, mainly music, downloaded from the Web or transferred from audio CD to a computer and then moved across to an iPod using a software package known as **iTunes**: http://www.apple.com/itunes/.

ISDN: Abbreviation for Integrated Services Digital Network. A type of digital telephone service, used for transferring large chunks of data to and from the Internet without a Modem. Gradually falling out of use these days with the introduction of ADSL broadband services. ISDN lines normally operate at 128 Kbps, which is faster than a standard 56 Kbps Dial-up Modem but slower than an ADSL connection, which runs at a speed of at least 512 Kbps..

IT: Abbreviation for Information Technology. Essentially, technology relating to information processing, i.e. computer technology, but see also ICT, C&IT, both of which describe the converging of information technology and communications technology. The term IT is rapidly being replaced by ICT in order to reflect the important role that information technology plays in communications by e-mail, the Web, satellites and mobile phones.

J

Java: A programming language, invented by Sun Microsystems, that is specifically designed for writing programmes that can be downloaded to your computer through the Internet and immediately executed. Using small Java programmes, called *applets*, Web pages can include functions such as animations, interactive sequences, etc. You need to set up your browser to enable it to interpret and run the Java applets. Java is similar to a programming language known as C++ but it has been considerably simplified. Not to be confused with JavaScript.

JavaScript: *JavaScript* is a script language, a system of programming codes created by *Netscape*, that can be embedded into the HTML code of a Web page to add functionality, e.g. interactive sequences, questionnaires, etc. Although it shares many of the features and structures of the full Java language, JavaScript is essentially quite different and was developed independently.

Joystick: A device that looks a bit like a gear lever in a car. This is connected to a computer and is used mainly for controlling the Cursor in fast action games.

JPEG or JPG: Abbreviation for Joint Photographic Expert Group. Pronounced "Jaypeg." A file format used for storing images. The JPEG/JPG format uses a palette of millions of colours and is primarily intended for photographic images. The internal compression algorithm of the JPEG/JPG format, unlike the GIF format, actually throws out superfluous information, which is why JPEG/JPG files containing photographic images end up smaller than GIF files containing photographic images. If you store an image, say, of a flag containing just three colours in JPEG/JPG format it may end up bigger than a GIF file containing the same image, but not necessarily a lot bigger – it depends on the type and range of colours it contains. JPEG/JPG files containing photographic images are normally smaller than GIF files containing photographic images. JPEG/JPG files are commonly used for storing images on the Web.

K

Kb: Abbreviation for Kilobit.

Kbps: Abbreviation for *kilobits per second*. A unit of measurement of data transmission speed, e.g. via a Modem.

Keyboard: The keyboard of a computer is used to enter information, which the computer displays or processes. It looks much the same as a typewriter keyboard, but has a few additional keys that have special functions.

Kilobit: Usually abbreviated to *Kb*. A unit of measurement consisting of 1,024 *bits*, mainly relating to data transmission speed.

Kilobyte: Usually abbreviated to *K or KB*. A unit of measurement of computer memory or disk capacity = 1,024 *bytes*.

L

LAN: Abbreviation for Local Area Network. A Network of computers at one site that provides services to other computers connected to it. A *LAN* is usually limited to an immediate area, for example the floor of a building, a single building or a campus. The most important part of a LAN is the Server that delivers software to the computers (also known as *workstations* or *clients*) that are connected to it. The *server* is usually the most powerful computer in the network Users of computers connected to a LAN can access their own files remotely and exchange information with the server and other users connected to the network.

Language Engineering: The older term for a range of technologically advanced applications of ICT to natural (i.e. human languages), including Automatic Speech Recognition (ASR) and Machine Translation (MT). Since January 1999 the European Commission has favoured a new term, Human Language Technologies (HLT).

Laptop Computer: A *laptop computer* is a computer that is light and can easily be carried around. Contrasted with Desktop Computer.

Laser Printer: A type of Printer that works by firing a laser at a rotating drum. Laser printers produce high-quality output at a reasonable speed.

LCD: Abbreviation for Liquid Crystal Display. A technology used for producing a type of flat panel computer Display Screen, which is replacing the older type of Cathode Ray Tube display screen. A more advanced form of technology for producing flat panel display screens is known as TFT (Thin Film Transistor). LCD and TFT screens are also used in *digital cameras* and *camcorders.*

Learning Object: A self-contained piece of learning material with an associated learning objective. Essentially, a *learning object* should be capable of being reused in a variety of applications and may be described as a Reusable Learning Object (RLO). Examples include interactive sequences made up of different combinations of texts, images, audio and video clips, and self-contained exercises that might be incorporated into a website or Courseware created with the aid of an Authoring Tool, or a Virtual Learning Environment (VLE).

Learning Platform: A term used to describe the software and systems that are used to deliver E-learning. Some confusion surrounds this term: sometimes it is used synonymously with Virtual Learning Environment (VLE) and sometimes with Managed Learning Environment (MLE). Many people use it as a catchall term to describe software and systems designed to manage, deliver and provide access to E-learning materials.

Linux: A Unix-type Operating System, similar to Windows and the Apple Mac operating system. Linus Torvalds originally created Linux with the assistance of developers around the world. The Source Code for Linux is freely available to everyone.

M

Machine Assisted Translation (MAT): The use of computers to assist human beings in the process of translating natural language. MAT systems are normally used as only aids for human translators who have to intervene in the process of translation by machine, making corrections and amendments as necessary. Contrasted with Machine Translation (MT), which normally describes a fully automatic process.

Machine Code: The machine-readable form of a computer programme, produced by conversion of the human-written programme (source code) into binary code by a *compiler* or *interpreter.*

Machine Translation (MT): The use of computers to translate natural language. A related term is Machine Assisted Translation (MAT), which normally implies that the computer does part of the job and human beings correct and amend the text that it produces.

Macro: A sort of mini-programme that can be incorporated into other programmes, comprising a series of keystrokes that you may wish to use over and over again. For example, if you perform a task repeatedly in *Microsoft Word*, you can automate the task using a *macro*. A macro is a series of commands and instructions that you group together as a single command to accomplish a task automatically. Instead of manually performing a series of time-consuming, repetitive actions, you can create and run a single macro—in effect, a custom command that carries out the task for you. A macro can be saved and called up whenever you need it. A degree of caution needs to be exercised if you are given or sent a file, e.g. a *Word* DOC file, containing a macro, as macros can harbour *viruses*. Make sure you know where the file comes from.

Mainframe Computer: Loosely speaking, a very large computer which can serve many users at remote terminals.

Main Menu Bar: The *main menu bar* is normally located at the top of the screen when you are using an application such as a word-processor or Browser, consisting of a set of names of *drop-down menus* that enable a variety of different tasks to be carried out.

MAN: Abbreviation for Metropolitan Area Network. A network of computers located at different sites within a large fixed area, such as a city.

Matching: In CALL programmes, matching is the process of comparing the learner's inputs at the keyboard with what is stored in the computer.

Mbps: Abbreviation for *megabits per second.* A unit of measurement of data transmission speed, e.g. via a Modem. A typical Broadband connection to the Internet transmits data at 1 Mbps to 8 Mbps.

Media Player: Used in two main senses: (1) a programme that enables your computer to record, store and play back audio and video recordings; (2) a device such as the portable iPod *media player* that is also used to record, store and play back recordings.

Megabit: Usually abbreviated to *Mb.* 1,024 *kilobits* or 1,048,576 *bits,* a unit of measurement, usually relating to data transmission speed.

Megabyte: Usually abbreviated to *MB.* 1,024 *kilobytes* or 1,048,576 *bytes.* A unit of measurement of computer memory or disk capacity. Roughly 180,000 words of text—an average-sized novel.

Mega Hertz: Usually abbreviated to *MHz.* A unit of measurement relating to the Clock Speed of a computer or, put simply, a measurement of how fast its Central Processing Unit (CPU) runs. Typical clock speeds of modern computers range from 500MHz upwards. Faster clock speeds are normally expressed in Giga Hertz or *GHz* (= 1000MHz).

Memory: Most people use this term to refer to a computer's temporary internal main memory or RAM. Memory may also refer to ROM (Read Only Memory), which is permanent and part of a computer system as supplied by the manufacturer.

Memory Stick: A small electronic card, also known as a *memory card,* which is inserted into a Digital Camera or Camcorder for storing photographs or movie files that can then uploaded to a computer. This term is also used as an alternative to Flash Drive.

Menu: A list of options from which a computer user makes a selection in order to determine the course of events in a programme. This usually involves keying in a single letter or number, or selecting text or an Icon with a Mouse.

Menu Bar: Most computer programmes display a *menu bar* or set of menu bars at the top of the screen, from which choices can be made by the user to carry out certain operations, e.g., saving a File, printing a document, or setting up the programme in different ways.

Microchip: Also referred to as Chip or Silicon Chip. Invented in 1958 by Jack St. Clair Kilby, while he was working at Texas Instruments, Dallas, Texas: http://www.ti.com/corp/docs/kilbyctr/jackstclair.shtml. An electronic circuit etched on to a small piece of silicon, which has been subjected, using photo-masking processes, to controlled "doping" with certain impurities. Particular areas of the chip can then be made to act like electronic components such as diodes, capacitors and resistors.

Microcomputer: A generic name for a class of computers distinct from bigger mainframe computers and minicomputers. Two of the defining characteristics of a *microcomputer* are that it should be built around one Microprocessor and that it should be standalone, i.e. capable of operating independently from any other computer or computer Network to which it might be connected. Modern Desktop and Laptop computers fall into this category.

Microphone: Essential for making sound recordings in multimedia CALL programmes. Microphones used in multimedia applications are much the same as those used with standard audiocassette devices. Choosing the right kind of microphone is vital. See Condenser Microphone, Dynamic Microphone.

Microprocessor: The *microprocessor* is the Central Processing Unit (CPU) of a computer, where all the data processing and calculations are carried out. It's a single silicon chip containing millions of transistors etched on to its surface, connected to the Motherboard by an array of pins at its base.

Microsoft Office: A suite of programmes produced by Microsoft Corporation, comprising a Word-processor (*Word*), a Spreadsheet (*Excel*), a Presentation Programme (*PowerPoint*), an E-mail package (*Outlook*), a Database programme (*Access*), and a Desktop Publishing package (*Publisher*).

Millenium Bug: A flaw in computer programmes which was thought likely to cause a breakdown in computer systems worldwide following the commencement of the Year 2000—or Y2K in computer jargon. The Millenium Bug was due to year dates having been stored in older computer programmes as two digits, e.g. 89 instead of 1989. The bug is most likely to arise when one year date is compared with another, when 00 (instead of 2000) is perceived as older than 89 (instead of 1989). The Millenium Bug proved to be far less of a problem than was anticipated, but it did manifest itself in computerised stock control systems, whereby batches of canned food with sell-by dates after 2000 were accidentally scrapped before their time.

Minicomputer: Smaller than a Mainframe Computer and bigger than a Microcomputer. Small businesses often rely on minis. Minis can handle many users at once. Today's minis are much more powerful than yesterday's mainframes.

Modem: Short for modulator/demodulator. A device, which converts computer data to a signal that can be transmitted over a standard telephone line. It can also reconvert a signal coming into a computer via a telephone line so that the computer can understand it. Modems are used to connect computers with the Internet.

Modern Language Aptitude Testing (MLAT): A type of testing that aims to predict how well an individual can learn a foreign language in a given amount of time and under given conditions.

Monitor: The screen on which output from a computer is displayed. Also referred to as Display Screen.

Motherboard: The main electronic circuit board of a microcomputer, to which other circuit boards (also known as *cards*) can be connected in order to fulfill special functions, e.g. a Sound Card or Video Card. Typically, the motherboard contains the BIOS, CPU, RAM, ROM and all the controllers required to control standard peripheral devices, such as the Display Screen, Keyboard and disk drives.

Mouse: A *pointing device* that is used by moving it around on your desk and pressing (clicking) a button. Most mice have two buttons (left and right) but some have three. Apple Mac computers use a mouse with just one button. Moving the mouse causes a pointer or Cursor to move around the screen, and clicking a mouse button once or twice when the pointer is hovering over an icon or word activates a command, e.g. starts a computer programme or initiates an action inside another programme such as *Microsoft Word*. A mouse is used with computers that use a Graphical User Interface (GUI). See Pointing Device.

MP3: Abbreviation for MPEG Layer 3: see MPEG. MP3 is a file format for storing high-quality audio files that can be played back on computers and portable *media players* such as the iPod. MP3 has the advantage of taking up far less storage space than the WAV format without loss of quality. See also WMA, which is and alternative audio file format.

MP4: Abbreviation for the MPEG-4 file format. There are two basic types of MP4: **MP4 AAC (Advanced Audio Coding)** and **MP4 AVC (Advanced Video Coding)**. The MP4 AAC file format is used to store audio files in a more manageable size without affecting the quality. MP4 AAC's best-known use is as the default audio format of Apple's **iPhone, iPod** and **iTunes Media Player**. The MP4 AVC file format is used to store video files in a more manageable size without affecting the quality. It is also increasingly being used for storing video on iPods and similar portable devices.

MPEG or **MPG:** Abbreviation for Motion Picture Expert Group. Pronounced "Empeg." A standard file format for storing movies in digital format and high-quality audio files in a variation known as MP3. Video files stored MPEG format can be recognised by the Extension **.mpg** or **.mpeg.** MP3 audio files can be recognised by the Extension **.mp3**. A newer file format is MP4. MP4 files that can be recognised by the Extension **.mp4**. See ASF, AVI, MOV, RM, which are alternative video file formats. **MPG:** A contracted form of MPEG.

MS DOS: Abbreviation for Microsoft Disk Operating System. An *operating system* for the personal computer, written by Microsoft Corporation, but now superseded by *Microsoft Windows*. MS DOS is a character-based system, whereby the user has to type commands at a prompt.

Multimedia: The integration of two or more types of information (text, images, audio, video, animation, etc.) in a single application.

Multimedia Personal Computer (MPC): An enhanced Personal Computer that is able to play sound and video and allows the user to make sound and video recordings. MPCs are virtually a standard nowadays.

N

Name Server or **Name Server:** Also known in full as Domain Name Server. A special type of Internet computer which converts a website's *domain name* into a unique numerical *IP Address* that identifies the computer where the website is stored. When you try to connect to a website with a domain name such as **hull.ac.uk** (University of Hull), a request is first made to a *name server* to resolve this name into an *IP address*, which is then used to locate the computer where the website is stored and to establish a connection with it.

Narrowband: A term used to describe a slow-speed connection to the Internet, normally via a Modem and less than or equal to 64 Kbps. Contrasted with Broadband.

Natural Language Processing (NLP): A general term used to describe the use of computers to process information expressed in natural (i.e. human) languages. See Human Language Technologies.

Navigation: This describes the process of finding your way, i.e. *navigating*, around a series of menus within a computer programme or finding your way around the World Wide Web by means of a Browser.

Netscape: A popular Web Browser.

Network: A group of computers connected together, either by physical connections such as cables, or by wireless connections. The Internet is a worldwide network of computers to which virtually any computer can be connected.

Newsgroup: A type of public online *forum*, which anyone can read and contribute to. All users of a *newsgroup* can post messages, and every user can read all the messages that have been posted. Many newsgroups are distributed worldwide by the Usenet system: http://www.usenet.org.uk. Newsgroups have now been superseded to a large extent by blogs and electronic discussion lists.

Notebook Computer: A type of Laptop Computer, but even lighter and thinner—and therefore easy to carry around.

O

Offline: Not connected to a computer or network of computers. Often used in the sense of working with software stored on a stand-alone computer. For example, if you use a package such as *Microsoft Word* you are working with *offline* software, and if you use learning materials stored on CD-ROM you are also working *offline*. Constrasted with Online.

Online: Connected to a computer or network of computers, especially the World Wide Web. Often used in the sense of working with software stored at a remote location. For example, if you use learning materials stored at a website you are working *online*. Contrasted with Offline.

Online Learning: The use of the Internet to follow a course that usually results in the award of a diploma or certificate. Closely associated with the concept of E-learning, which often—but not necessarily—implies some form of *online learning*, i.e. using E-mail and the World Wide Web. E-learning, i.e. electronic learning is a broader term, embracing the use of ICT in general in teaching and learning as well as online learning.

Open and Integrated Learning System (OILS): A variant of Integrated Learning System. The word *Open* adds an extra dimension, indicating that the user can access the system freely and leave it at any time.

Operating System (OS): A suite of programmes that starts up when you switch on your computer and manages and runs all the other programmes installed on the computer. *Windows* is the *operating system* developed and produced by the Microsoft Corporation.

Optical Character Recognition (OCR): OCR software is used conjunction with a *scanner* to convert printed text into digital format. For example, a page from a printed book can be placed on the scanner and the OCR software will be used by the scanner to detect the individual words from which it is made up and then convert them into a form that can be stored on a computer, e.g. a *Word* document. A great time-saver.

Optical Disk or **Optical Disc:** The generic name for a type of computer disk, which uses a laser to read and write data.

Outlook: A popular E-mail programme, part of the *Microsoft Office* suite of programmes.

Output: Anything that comes out of a computer after being processed. Also used as a verb.

P

Package: Loosely speaking, a programme or suite of programmes such as *Microsoft Office*, but often has the sense of a set of programmes designed to be used by people who wish to use the package in different ways.

Pathname: The pathname of a File on a computer specifies exactly its position on disk, and consists of at least three parts: *(i)* drive letter, *(ii)* directory, and *(iii)* filename, e.g. **c:\windows\user.exe**. One or more subdirectories may also be included in a pathname, e.g. **c:\windows\system\user.exe**.

PDF: An abbreviation for Portable Document Format. This is a file type created by Adobe that allows fully formatted, documents to be transmitted across the Internet and viewed on any computer that has Adobe *Acrobat Reader* software—a proprietary software viewing programme available for free at the Adobe website: http://www.adobe.com/uk/. Businesses and educational institutions often use PDF-formatted files to display the original look of their brochures or for publishing a complete magazine in electronic format. Using the full Adobe *Acrobat* software package, it is possible to create a high-quality piece of artwork or a brochure, which preserves the look of the original, complete with fonts, colours, images, and formatting. Documents in PDF format can be published on the Web without having to be converted into HTML. PDF files can be distributed via *e-mail*, *CD-ROMs* and *local area networks*. They can also contain *hyperlinks*, QuickTime movies and sound clips.

Pentium: A generic name for a faster type of Personal Computer that superseded the earlier 486 range of slower computers. Essential for running modern multimedia software and accessing the Internet.

Peripheral Device: Often abbreviated to *peripheral*. Virtually any device, which can be connected to a computer. This term includes modems, printers, scanners, interactive whiteboards, etc.

Personal Computer: The generic term for IBM-compatible microcomputers. See Microcomputer, Multimedia Personal Computer.

Pixel: A contraction of *picture element*. What you see on a computer Display Screen is made up of thousands of coloured *pixels* or small dots, which can be set according to the user's choice to produce either low-resolution output, medium-resolution output or high-resolution output, the usual combinations of pixels across each line of the screen (horizontal pixels) and down each line of the screen (vertical pixels) being 640 x 480, 800 x 600, 1024 x 768, 1280 x 1024. Thus, the more pixels on the screen the higher the *resolution* (i.e. producing a finer, sharper image) and the greater the variety of colours that can be displayed.

Platform: Often used as an alternative term for a computer system, including both the hardware and the software. Essentially this term describes something that is used to build something else. The term *platform-independent*—used to describe software—means that the software can be run on any computer. The term *learning platform* refers to the technology used to provide a single online location at which course resources can be made available to learners these resources can include course materials, communications tools such as E-mail and Conferencing, and a storage area for learners' work. The term Virtual Learning Environment (VLE) may also be used synonymously with the term Learning Platform.

Plug-in: An extra piece of software that a Web Browser needs to run certain elements of a Web page. Web pages incorporating multimedia files often need to use Flash Player, QuickTime, RealPlayer or Shockwave Player as *plug-ins.* Sites that require a plug-in usually provide a link to a site from which the essential plug-in can be downloaded.

Pod Cast: A *pod cast* is a broadcast digital audio recording, usually in MP3 format, made available via the Internet in a way that allows the recording to be downloaded automatically for listening at the user's convenience. Cf. Vodcast, which is a broadcast digital video recording, usually in MPG format. So-called RSS feeds make pod casts and vodcasts different from digital audio and video recordings that have simply been made available via the Web, namely by using an RSS feed you can subscribe to or sign up for a series of pod casts or vodcasts. It's rather like the difference between popping into your local newsagent to buy an occasional copy of a magazine and taking out a subscription for a magazine that appears at regular intervals. However, the terms *pod cast* and *vodcast* are often used loosely to describe digital audio and video recordings in general. Many broadcasting stations now offer pod casts and vodcasts, e.g. the BBC: http://www.bbc.co.uk. The term *pod cast* takes its name from a combination of iPod (Apple's portable digital Media Player) and *broadcasting*, but pod casts and vodcasts do not necessarily require the use of an *iPod* or similar device. Pod casts and vodcasts can simply be downloaded to a computer and played using a standard Media Player programme.

Pop-up: A small Window that appears within a programme or over the top of a Web page to deliver additional information. Pop-ups on the Web can be annoying as they are often used for unwanted advertising material.

Portal: A Web page, website or service that acts as link or entrance to other websites on the Internet. Typically, a portal includes an annotated catalogue of websites and may also include a Search Engine, E-mail facilities, a Forum and other services. Also known as a Gateway.

PowerPoint: The name of a Presentation Programme forming part of the Microsoft Office suite of programmes.

Presentation Programme / Presentation Software: Used to describe software such as PowerPoint, part of the Microsoft Office suite of programmes. *Presentation Software* is used in conjunction with a Data Projector and a wall screen or Interactive Whiteboard in order to display a series of slides relating to a business presentation, a lesson or lecture.

Printer: More or less self-explanatory. An external device attached to a computer for device for producing printed output or Hardcopy.

Printout: Anything produced on a printer after being processed by a computer programme.

Programme: The American spelling is standard in computer jargon, enabling a useful distinction to be made in British English between a *computer programme* and a *programme* in the sense of a *programme of study*. A talk entitled "Turning programmes into programmes" (or maybe it was the other way round) was presented by a British Council officer at the annual TESOL conference in the USA in 1987 – which puzzled the American audience but made sense to the British participants.

Programmed Learning: Also referred to as *programmed instruction*. A teaching method involving a pre-constructed sequence of steps and associated feedback based to a large extent on the behaviourist ideas of B.F. Skinner. The steps in the learning process are usually self-administered and self-paced, the learner being presented with information in small manageable pieces and only progressing to the next piece of information when s/he has successfully demonstrated that the current piece of information has been understood. Early Computer Assisted Instruction (CAI) was based to a large extent on programmed learning.

Programming Language: A formal, structured, English-like language in which computer programmes are written. The instructions, known as *code*, are converted into binary machine instructions via a *compiler* or an *interpreter*. C++, Pascal, and BASIC, are examples of popular programming languages.

Protocol: In Internet terminology *protocol* usually refers to a set of rules that define an exact format for communication between systems. For example the *HTTP* protocol defines the format for communication between Web *browsers* and Web *servers*. See also Browser, FTP, HTTP, and Server.

Public Domain: Material that is copyright free, whose copyright has expired, or which cannot be copyrighted. Many people think that because something is on the Web it must be in the public domain. This is not so. A work is in the public domain only if it is explicitly stated to be so. You may be lucky to find material on the Web that is stated to be copyright-free or in the public domain, and then the terms of using it are much more liberal. Look for a clear statement saying "The materials on this website are in the public domain" or something similar. If you wish to use materials from someone else's website, check the terms of use, which you will usually find at the bottom of the Web page or via a clickable link at the bottom of the page.

Q

QuickTime: Software used for viewing movies and listening to audio recordings: **http://** www.apple.com/quicktime. **QuickTime** is often needed as a Plug-in, when you are accessing audio or video materials on the Web.

R

RAM: An acronym for Random Access Memory, referring to the dynamic memory in the silicon chips in a computer. RAM chips are the memory chips used as the temporary working area for running and developing programmes. Data in RAM can be read and written to (i.e. change) in microseconds, as opposed to the much slower data access times for disks, but RAM's contents disappear the moment the computer is switched off. The more RAM a computer has, the more flexibility the user has. RAM used to be measured in *kilobytes (KB)* but now it is usually expressed in *megabytes (MB)* and even *gigabytes (GB)*. The amount of RAM a PC has could crudely be thought of as its "mental capacity."

RGB: Abbreviation for Red Green Blue. The name given to the Additive Colour system that is used to display colours on computer screens, where red, green and blue light of varying intensities is combined to produce millions of other colours.

Resolution: A measure of the number of *pixels* or small dots displayed on a computer *display screen*, *printer* or *scanner*. One normally talks in terms of the quality of resolution, using the expression *low-resolution, medium-resolution* and *high-resolution*. The resolution of a computer *display screen* is normally expressed as two numbers representing the horizontal and vertical resolution, i.e. dots across each line of the screen and down each line of the screen: e.g. 640 x 480, 1024 x 768, etc. The resolution of a Printer is normally referred to by the number of *dots per inch (dpi)* - i.e. square inch. See Bitmap, Colour Depth, Display Screen, dpi, Pixel, Scanner.

ROM: Acronym for Read Only Memory. ROM chips in a computer contain data and programmes as supplied by the manufacturer that can be accessed but not changed, i.e. they are *read-only*. ROM is also used to describe Storage Media such as CD-ROMs and DVD-ROMs. Originally such media contained data and programmes that could not be changed or erased, and new data and programmes could not be stored on CD-ROMs or DVDs, but newer CD-ROM and DVD drives allow certain types of CDs and DVDs to be *written to* as well as *read*—so the term has become a misnomer in this respect.

Root Directory: The topmost directory in the directory hierarchy, from which all other directories are descended. On a PC's hard disk this has the pathname C:\.

Router: A hardware device that connects computers to a Network or that connects one network with another network. *Routers* are now available at low prices and can be used for connecting two or more computers together in home networks, so that data can be exchanged between the computers on the network and so that all the computers in the network can access the Internet.

RSS (Really Simple Syndication): *RSS* is a fairly recent development in Internet technology that enables users to subscribe to websites that change or add content regularly, for example news sites (such as the BBC), and sites containing *blogs* and *pod casts*. RSS makes use of software that presents new additions to a website as list of subject headings or the first line or two of a news item, with a clickable link to the full article, blog posting or pod cast. Thus, instead of the user having to browse websites for new information in which s/he is interested, an update of what is available is sent directly to the user, an *RSS feed*. An application known as an *aggregator* or *feed reader* can check RSS-enabled websites and display any updated information that it finds. A good explanation of RSS is provided at the BBC website: http://news.bbc.co.uk/1/hi/help/rss/

S

Scanner: A device used to convert hard copy, e.g. a printed page, photograph or photographic negative, into a form that can be stored on a computer.

Scroll: To move up and down or from side to side through a document or a Window to view or access all of its contents.

Search Engine: A search facility provided at a number of sites on the *World Wide Web*. Search engines enable the user to search the whole of the Web for key words and phrases and to locate related websites. This is a useful facility for locating information. Commonly used search engines are provided by Alta Vista, Ask, Google, Lycos and Yahoo.

Server: A computer, which provides services to other computers, which are known as *clients*. For example, when you click on a link in a Web page your Browser sends a request to a remote computer, known as a Web Server, which *serves* the requested page to your browser, which then displays it on your computer screen. A Local Area Network (LAN) has a *server* that delivers software to the computers (also known as workstations) that are connected to it. It is usually the most powerful computer in the network Users connected to a LAN can access their own files remotely and exchange information with the server and other users connected to the network.

Silicon Chip: An encased piece of extremely pure silicon on to which electronic circuits are etched. The circuitry of modern computers is based on silicon chips that perform a vast range of different tasks.

Simulation: A type of programme that simulates a real-life situation, allowing the user to carry out experiments which could have dangerous consequences or which are impractical in a normal learning environment. An early example of a simulation for language purposes was *Granville*, a programme dating back to the 1980s in which the learner was asked to imagine that he/she had won a holiday in Granville, France, and had to survive for a number of days on a limited budget. The borderline between simulations and *adventure games* is rather fuzzy. The latter tend to be set in fantasy worlds, whereas the former are more down-to-earth.

Social Networking: A term applied to a type of website where people can seek other people who share their interests, find out what's going on in their areas of interest, and share information one another.

Software: The opposite to Hardware. A generic term describing all kinds of computer programmes, applications and operating systems. Software is not tangible, being a set of instructions written in a Programming Language comprising a set of instructions that the computer executes.

Sound Card or **Soundcard:** A *card*, i.e. an electronic circuit board, inside a computer that controls output to speakers or headphones and sound input from a Microphone or other source. A sound card is essential for multimedia applications. Also known as Audio Card.

Source Code: The human-readable form of a *computer programme*, which is converted into binary computer instructions by a *compiler* or *interpreter*.

Speech Recognition: A branch of Human Language Technologies (HLT) devoted to developing programmes and devices that enable computers to recognise, analyse and transcribe human speech.

Spreadsheet: Essentially an accounting programme, e.g. *Excel*, which forms part of the *Microsoft Office* suite of programmes. Such programmes might, at first sight, not appear to have a great deal to offer the language teacher, but bear in mind that they can also be used for organising vocab lists and for maintaining students' marks or grades.

Spyware is a term that may be used synonymously with *adware* but it implies more sinister motives on the part of the person who has dumped it onto your computer, e.g. with a view to stealing private information such as bank account numbers, credit card numbers, passwords, etc.

Storage Device: Equipment used for accessing and recording (i.e. *storing*) computer programmes, texts, images, audio recordings and video recordings, etc. The term Storage Medium refers to the actual material used for storing such information, although a Flash Drive, for example, could be referred to both as a *storage device* and as a *storage medium*.

Synchronous: "At the same time." Often used to refer to communication in a Chat Room or via Videoconferencing, where the participants have to be present at their computers at the same time. See Asynchronous, Conferencing.

T

Tag: A term used by Web authors. In *HTML*, a *tag* is a markup, which controls how the text it defines is rendered by the browser. For example, **<a href="http://www.ict4lt.org">ICT4LT</a>** in HTML appear on screen as the hyperlink ICT4LT.

TCP/IP: Abbreviation for Transfer Control Protocol/Internet Protocol. The main data transfer protocol used on the Internet.

Telnet: A programme, which allows you to log in to a remote Host computer and carry out, the same commands as if you were using a terminal at the host site.

Text File or **Textfile:** A data file consisting entirely of printable ASCII characters, i.e. plain unformatted text. Text files often have a **.txt** Extension after the filename (e.g. **readme.txt**) and their contents can be viewed using programmes such as *Windows Notepad*. The term *text file* is also used to describe files, i.e. texts, created by authoring packages such as *Fun with Texts*, which then *manipulates* the texts into a set of activities for completion by the learner.

Text Manipulation: Text-manipulation programmes have been popular with language teachers since the early 1980s. They consist of a set of activities for the learner, typically consisting of Cloze, gap-fillers, line re-ordering, decoding and total text reconstruction: Total Cloze. In most text manipulation programmes the teacher inputs the text, and the computer then creates the activities—or most of them—automatically. **Text Maze:** See Maze.

Toolbar: A *toolbar* is a type of Menu Bar, normally located at the top of a computer screen, that contains *icons* for the most commonly-used commands in an application, e.g. in a word-processor or Browser. Typically, a toolbar appears under the Main Menu Bar, which normally consists of set of names of drop-down menus.

Touch-sensitive Screen: A Display Screen, which enables the computer to react to the touch of a finger. Useful, for example, in programmes involving maps, where the learner may be asked to touch part of the map to show where a town, river or mountain is located.

Trojan: Trojans are programmes—usually malicious—that install them or run surreptitiously on a victim's machine. They do not install or run automatically but may entice users into installing another programme. e.g. a game that actually installs a hostile piece of software and causes considerable damage to your computer. The name derives from Trojan Horse, the hollow wooden horse in which, according to legend, Greeks hid and gained entrance to Troy, later opening the gates to their army.

U

Unicode: The Unicode Worldwide Character Standard is a character coding system designed to support the interchange, processing, and display of the written texts of the diverse languages of the modern world. In addition, it supports classical and historical texts of many written languages: http://www.unicode.org.

Uninstall: A verb used to describe the process of removing an unwanted application from your computer's hard disk.

Uninstall Programme: Basically what it says: a programme for removing (*uninstalling*) an unwanted application from your computer's hard disk. Install, Installation Programme, Uninstall.

Universal Serial Bus (USB): A means of connecting peripheral devices, such as *scanners* and *printers*, via a cable with a USB connector on each end, to a computer. USB sockets, to which the cables are connected, are found on all modern computers A USB socket can also deliver power to devices that need it, so that separate power cables are not necessary.

Unix: An Operating System widely used on large computer systems in corporations and universities, on which many *Web servers* are hosted. A PC version of *Unix*, called *Linux*, is becoming increasingly popular as an alternative to *Windows*.

Upload: To transfer a copy of a computer programme, a text file, an image file, a sound file or a video file from one computer to another computer. This term can also be used to describe the process of: *(i)* transferring a photograph from a digital camera to a computer, *(ii)* transferring a sound recording from a digital sound recorder to a computer, and *(iii)* transferring a video recording from a Camcorder or Digital Camera to a computer.

URL: Abbreviation for Uniform Resource Locator. Also known as a Web Address. A URL contains the location of a resource on the Internet. A URL specifies the address of the computer where the resource is located, which may be the homepage of a website, e.g. http://www.ict4lt.org, or a sub-page, e.g. http://www.ict4lt.org/en/en_mod2-1.htm. The **http://** prefix can usually be omitted from a URL when it is entered in a Browser.

User-friendly: Mainly used to describe Software. Software that is easy to use and offers guidance if the user does silly things is described as user-friendly. This term may also be applied to certain types of Hardware.

V

Video Card or **Videocard:** An electronic circuit board inside a computer, which controls the display on the Monitor, i.e. the computer screen. Video cards are usually add-on cards inserted into expansion slots, although sometimes-video circuitry is incorporated into the Motherboard. Sometimes referred to as *graphics card.*

Videoconferencing or **Video Conferencing:** A computer-based communications system that allows a group of computer users at different locations to conduct a "virtual conference" in which the participants can see and hear one another as if they were in the same room participating in a real conference.

Videodisc or **Videodisk:** A technically obsolete Storage Medium, an Optical Disk, 12 inches in diameter, used mainly to store still images or video clips. Now replaced by CD-ROMs and DVDs.

Videodisc Player or **Videodisk Player:** Equipment used for accessing information -- usually still images or video clips—stored on videodiscs. Now technically obsolete. See Videodisc.

Virtual Learning Environment (VLE): A VLE is a Web-based package designed to help teachers create online courses, together with facilities for teacher-learner communication and peer-to-peer communication. VLEs can be used to deliver learning materials within an institution or within a local education authority. They may even address a wider constituency, and may be used on a worldwide basis. VLEs have certain advantages in terms of ease of delivery and management of learning materials. They may, however, be restrictive in that the underlying pedagogy attempts to address a very wide range of subjects, and thus does not necessarily fit in with established practice in language learning and teaching. The two most widely used VLEs in language teaching and learning are Blackboard and Moodle. Such systems are also referred to a Course Management System (CMS), **Learning Management System (LMS)** and **Learning Support System (LSS)**. Compare also Managed Learning Environment (MLE) and Learning Platform.

Virtual Reality: The simulation of an environment by presentation of 3D moving images and associated sounds, giving the user the impression of being able to move around with the simulated environment. Users wear helmets and visors that convey the images and sound and gloves that give them the experience of touching objects. The film *Lawnmower Man* (1992) focused on a character experiencing virtual reality, albeit with negative consequences.

Virtual World: A type of online three-dimensional imaginary world or game in which participants and players adopt amazing characters or *avatars* and explore the world, engaging in chat or playing complex games.

Virus: If you surf the Web, use e-mail or floppy disks sent to you by other people, you need to be protected against virus invasions. A virus is a nasty programme devised by a clever programmer, usually with malicious intent. Viruses can be highly contagious, finding their way onto your computer's hard drive without your being aware of it and causing considerable damage to the software and data stored on it. Viruses can be contracted from files attached to e-mail messages; e.g. Microsoft Word files, or direct from the Web. Be very wary of opening an e-mail attachment of unknown origin, as this is the commonest way of spreading viruses. Software used to protect your computer against the invasion of computer viruses is known as *anti-virus software.*

Visual Display Unit (VDU): A Monitor connected to larger computers. Usually referred to as VDU. Rather an old-fashioned term nowadays, Display Screen being the current favoured term.

W

WAN: Abbreviation for Wide Area Network. A network of computers located at geographically separate sites.

WAP: Abbreviation for Wireless Application Protocol. A system that enables you to browse online services, e.g. relating to information about the weather, traffic conditions, shopping, etc. via a special type of mobile phone. WAP is the mobile phone equivalent of the World Wide Web. Newer mobile phones include WAP browser software to allow users access to WAP sites.

Webcam: A camera connected to a computer and linking it to the Internet. Webcams can be set to transmit a live picture every few minutes from a location to a website, displaying a live view of a landscape, cityscape or interior of a building, or they can be used in Videoconferencing.

Webquest: A *webquest* is a task-oriented activity in which the learner draws on material from different websites—but other sources may also be consulted—in order to achieve a specific goal, e.g. researching a topic and *(i)* answering a series of questions posed by the teacher, *(ii)* creating a presentation or *(iii)* writing an essay, etc. The skills that are required in a *webquest* mainly involve reading and listening, but there may also be communicative speaking exercises.

Web Server or **Webserver:** A computer or a software package running on a computer that delivers, i.e. *serves,* Web pages to its *clients*:. Every *Web server* has an IP Address and possibly a Domain Name. For example, if you enter the URL **http://www.ict4lt.org/index.htm** in your Browser, this sends a request to the Server whose domain name is **ict4lt.org**. The server then fetches the page named **index.htm** and sends a copy of it to your browser. Any computer can be turned into a Web server by installing Web server software and connecting the machine to the Internet. By far the most popular Web server software in use worldwide is the Open Source Apache software: http://www.apache.org

Website: An area on the World Wide Web where an organisation or individual stores a collection of pages of material—**Web pages**. The pages are usually interlinked with one another and with other websites. Every website has a unique Web Address or URL. The full URL of the ICT4LT website is http://www.ict4lt.org

Wiki: A website or similar online resource which allows anyone to set up a resource in which content can be created collectively, as in a Blog, Discussion List or Forum. Its main difference is that it also allows anyone who views the *wiki* to add to or edit the existing content as if they were adding to or editing, for example, someone else's *Word* document. Wiki also refers to the software used to create such a website. Wiki derives from the Hawaiian "wiki-wiki", meaning "quick." **Wikipedia** is the best-known example of a wiki. It's a collaboratively written encyclopaedia: http://www.wikipedia.org.

Window: An area of a computer screen set aside for a special purpose. Modern computers, such as the Macintosh and most personal computers, divide the screen into discrete sections, known as *windows,* within which different pieces of software can be run at the same time—although not necessarily strictly at the same time, as normally only one window is active:

Windows: The name of a range of several different Graphical User Interface (GUI) operating systems produced by the Microsoft Corporation. *Windows 3.0* and *Windows 3.1* were the first operating systems of this type, produced by Microsoft, to appear in the early 1990s. The Apple Macintosh computer, however, had been using a GUI (which was not known as *Windows*) from the mid-1980s. *Microsoft Windows* is currently the most widely used GUI for personal computers. It exists in various versions, e.g., Windows 95, 98, XP, and ME, NT, 2000.

Windows Explorer: Microsoft's tool, provided as part of *Windows* that enables you to inspect and manage *folders* and *files* stored on your computer. *My Computer* is an alternative tool, also provided as part of *Windows*.

Wireless Mouse: A Mouse that does not require a cable connection to a computer, but which operates via infrared or radio signals.

Wizard: Software that guides the user step-by-step through a complex task, such as setting up software on a network or configuring a printer to output data in a special format, e.g. for printing labels from a database programme.

WMA: Abbreviation for Windows Media Audio. Microsoft's audio encoding format that is starting to gain popularity due to its high-quality output at lower file sizes.

Word: A popular word-processing package, produced by Microsoft.

Word-processor: Probably the most widely used computer Application. Modern word-processors allow the user to create fine-looking documents including images, tables, photographs, and even sound and video recordings if they are to be viewed on screen rather than from the printed page. In many respects they are similar to Desktop Publishing applications. Word-processors normally include a spellchecker, a grammar checker, a style checker and a thesaurus, as well as tools for writing in HTML, the coding language used for producing Web pages. Word-processors have been widely used in teaching and learning foreign languages ever since they first appeared.

Workstation: A term that is rather loosely used these days. Most people use it in the context of any computer that forms part of a Network. Formerly, this term was applied to a particular type of powerful computer used for scientific and engineering calculations, e.g. the *Sun Workstation*.

World Wide Web: Usually referred to simply as **the Web**. This is the most powerful and fastest growing Internet service. The World Wide Web was the brainchild of Tim Berners-Lee, who in 1989 invented the HTML coding language that is the basis of the Web. The Web became a public service in 1993. It is a huge collection of resources of information, including learning materials, which is accessed by means of a computer programme known as a Browser. The World Wide Web is only part of the Internet, but many people treat both terms as synonyms. .

Worm: A computer worm is a self-replicating hostiie computer programme, similar to a computer Virus. A virus attaches itself to and becomes part of another programme, but a worm is self-contained and does not need to be part of another programme to propagate itself. Worms can cause considerable damage to computers.

WORM: Acronym for Write Once Read Many. Now a rather dated term, originally applied to a type of Optical Disk on which information could be written just once and could not be amended or erased.

Y

YouTube: A website to which you can upload your own video clips and view video clips uploaded by others: http://www.youtube.com.

Z

Zip: Used as a verb to describe the process of compacting data files or programmes in order to cut down the amount of storage space they require by compressing them into one tightly-packed file and thus to make it easier for them to be transported on floppy disks or transmitted electronically to other locations, e.g. via the Internet. Proprietary programmes, such as **WinZip** or **WinRar**, can be used to zip data and files. Zipped files are recognised by the Extension **.zip** or **.rar** (for files created with WinRar) and have to be unzipped before they can be used, again using proprietary programmes.

Index